Turkey's Violent Formation

Turkey's Violent Formation

*New Social Contracts at the End
of the Ottoman Empire*

Hans-Lukas Kieser

I.B.TAURIS
LONDON • NEW YORK • OXFORD • NEW DELHI • SYDNEY

I.B. TAURIS
Bloomsbury Publishing Plc
50 Bedford Square, London, WC1B 3DP, UK
1385 Broadway, New York, NY 10018, USA
29 Earlsfort Terrace, Dublin 2, Ireland

BLOOMSBURY, I.B. TAURIS and the I.B. Tauris logo are trademarks of Bloomsbury
Publishing Plc

First published in Great Britain 2024

Cover design: Holly Capper
Cover image: Unsigned cartoon, published during the Lausanne Conference, depicts
Ankara's First Army as a war machine goddess. (Zümrüdüanka, 28 May 1923)

A catalogue record for this book is available from the British Library.

Library of Congress Cataloging-in-Publication Data

Names: Kieser, Hans-Lukas, author.
Title: Turkey's violent formation: new social contracts at the end of the Ottoman empire /
Hans-Lukas Kieser.
Other titles: New social contracts at the end of the Ottoman empire
Description: London; New York: I.B. Tauris, 2024. | Includes bibliographical
references and index.
Identifiers: LCCN 2024009034 (print) | LCCN 2024009035 (ebook) |
ISBN 9780755649556 (hb) | ISBN 9780755649549 (pb) | ISBN 9780755649570 (ebook) |
ISBN 9780755649563 (epdf)
Subjects: LCSH: Turkey–History–20th century. | Turkey–Politics and government–20th
century. | Turkey–Foreign relations–Germany. | Germany–Foreign relations–Turkey.
Classification: LCC DR576 .K54 2024 (print) | LCC DR576 (ebook) |
DDC 956.1/02–dc23/eng/20240402
LC record available at https://lccn.loc.gov/2024009034
LC ebook record available at https://lccn.loc.gov/2024009035

ISBN: HB: 978-0-7556-4955-6
PB: 978-0-7556-4954-9
ePDF: 978-0-7556-4956-3
eBook: 978-0-7556-4957-0

Typeset by Deanta Global Publishing Services, Chennai, India
Printed and bound in Great Britain

To find out more about our authors and books visit www.bloomsbury.com and sign up for
our newsletters.

Contents

List of Figures   vi
Acknowledgments   vii

Introduction   1

1   Democracy Versus Genocide?   9

Part I Reform and Massacre in an Expiring Sultanate-Caliphate

2   Fair Futures! Missionaries against "Indian Removal," "Armenian Atrocities"   27
3   Islamic Empire and the Politics of Societal Massacre   45
4   Choosing War in the Crisis of Reform: The 1914 Agreement for Anatolia
    and Germany   62

Part II Turkey's Ultranationalist Refoundation

5   Pact, Not Peace: The Lausanne Treaty's "Near East Peace"   83
6   Rıza Nur: Cofounder of the Republic, Delegate in Lausanne, Pan-Turkist   99
7   The Destruction of Dersim   107

Part III Revolution and Anti-Democracy: Biographical Approaches

8   Ziya Gökalp: Mentor of Ultranationalism, Advocate of Education   121
9   Patriot Cavid Bey: Victim of Judicial Murder in Ankara   137
10 Mahmut Bozkurt: Revolution, Racism, and the Secular Republic   152
11 Parvus in Turkey: A Merchant of Revolution and War   163

Part IV End of Empire, Time of Genocide: Turkey's and Germany's Affinity

12 Johannes Lepsius: A German Patriot and Protestant Internationalist   183
13 Ambassador Wangenheim and the CUP: Sliding into Moral Defeatism   190
14 Democrat Matthias Erzberger and Turkey   202
15 Germany and the Armenians: A Fatal Failure   211

Epilogue   228

Notes   233
Index   273

Figures

Map 1   Ottoman total war   77
Map 2   Displacement, expulsion, and genocide in Anatolia (1914–23)   78
Figure 1 Caricature "dedicated to the Lausanne Conference"   93

Acknowledgments

Most books have a history of their own. Often, their making takes much more time and patience than one first expects. This book goes back to a suggestion by Rolf Hosfeld, the founding director of the Lepsiushaus in Potsdam. When the first manuscript was ready in 2021, this institution, Rolf's loved ones, and a broad network of friends of the Lepsiushaus sadly and unexpectedly lost him. This book is dedicated to the memory of Rolf Hosfeld, writer, historian, and academic director, as well as to all those who trust in and fight for resilient democracy and peace.

Rolf had invited me to rethink and revise unpublished or hardly accessible texts of mine for a new monograph on the end of the Ottoman Empire. He believed in a coherent book that would reveal deeper connections and rarely seen correlations, and that would interest readers beyond an expert audience. Special circumstances enabled a prompt and timely completion of the first manuscript: Covid-19, Australian travel restrictions, and my university's ban on offshore work and research led to a frugal unpaid leave in Switzerland, freeing up time for preparing the manuscript. I am very thankful to Rolf Hosfeld and Roy Knocke who supported this first stage, and I am particularly grateful to copy-editor Maja Palser for her invaluable work in not only linguistically polishing that manuscript but carefully rethinking many of its passages in view of its readers. Warm thanks to Lucien Palser who translated chapters 13 and 14, which are based on earlier German versions.

I received feedback and critique on the first manuscript, which enabled me to revise and reshape it significantly while preparing for publication with I.B. Tauris, a longtime publisher of mine. Many thanks to I.B. Tauris, in particular to Senior Editor Rory Gormley, who warmly welcomed the project and helped reshape it as well as to Project Manager Mahesh Meiyazhagan and his team of copy-editors. A very special thanks goes to my dear colleague Yeşim Bayar, who carefully read the final manuscript. Her invaluable observations and suggestions helped me add the finishing touches. Finally, I also thank the Australian Research Council—I am an investigator of its Discovery Project "Aftermaths of War: Violence, Trauma, Displacement" (DP200101777) and thus have benefited from generous research support. Warm thanks to the inspiring and supportive project team: Frances Clarke, Joy Damousi, Philip Dwyer, Mark Edele, Reto Hofmann. I also thank the College of Human and Social Futures at the University of Newcastle, New South Wales, for their "research output support" for this book in 2021.

The following lines serve to show my own sources of certain chapters, including those, or certain passages, taken from earlier publications. Chapter 2 is an updated version of "Removal of American Indians, destruction of Ottoman Armenians: American missionaries and demographic engineering," *European Journal of Turkish Studies* 7-2008. Chapter 3 is an adapted version of "Religious dynamics and the politics of violence in the late Ottoman and post-Ottoman Levant," *Cambridge World*

History of Violence, vol. 4 (Cambridge: Cambridge University Press, 2020, 263–85) (© Cambridge University Press 2020, reproduced with permission of the Licensor through PLSclear). Chapter 4 is an update and synthesis of three sources: "The Ottoman road to total war," in *World War I and the End of the Ottomans. From the Balkan Wars to the Armenian Genocide* (London: Bloomsbury–I.B. Tauris, 2015), 29–53; *Talaat Pasha* (Princeton, NJ: Princeton University Press, 2018), 151–80; and my contributions to "Reform or cataclysm? The agreement of 8 February 1914 regarding the Ottoman eastern provinces," *Journal of Genocide Research* 17:3 (2015), 285–304, co-authored with Mehmet Polatel and Thomas Schmutz. Chapter 7 is a revised and adapted version of a no longer available online article titled "Dersim Massacre, 1937–1938," published with the group Mass Violence & Resistance at SciencesPo in Paris in 2011.

Chapter 8 revisits a paper that started from findings in my political biography of Talaat Pasha and led to a biographical article entitled "Europe's seminal proto-fascism? Historically approaching Ziya Gökalp, mentor of Turkish nationalism," published in *Die Welt des Islams* 61 (2021), 411–47. Chapter 9 reconsiders and summarizes observations and thoughts on Cavid, made in *Talaat Pasha* and *When Democracy Died* (Cambridge University Press, 2023). Chapter 10 is an update based on "Ethno-nationalist revolutionary and theorist of Kemalism: Dr Mahmut Esat Bozkurt," in *Turkey beyond Nationalism* (London: I.B. Tauris, 2006), 20–7, and "Mahmut Bozkurt und die 'Revolution des Rechts' in der jungen Republik Türkei," in *Revolution islamischen Rechts. Das Schweizerische ZGB in der Türkei* (Zurich: Chronos, 2008), 49–58. Chapter 11 is an updated version of "World war and world revolution. Alexander Helphand-Parvus in Germany and Turkey," *Kritika: Explorations in Russian and Eurasian History* 12-2 (2011), 387–410. Chapter 12 is a free translation and enriched update of "Nahostmillenarismus, protestantische International und Johannes Lepsius," in *Johannes Lepsius—eine deutsche Ausnahme* (Göttingen: Wallstein, 2013), 59–68; Chapter 13 an updated translation of "Botschafter Wangenheim und das jungtürkische Komitee," in *Das Deutsche Reich und der Völkermord an den Armeniern* (Göttingen: Wallstein, 2017), 131–48; and Chapter 14 an updated translation of "Matthias Erzberger und die osmanischen Armenier im Ersten Weltkrieg," in *Matthias Erzberger. Ein Demokrat in Zeiten des Hasses* (Karlsruhe: G. Braun, 2013), 103–19. Chapter 15 is an adapted updated version of "Germany and the Armenian Genocide," in *Routledge History of the Holocaust* (New York: Routledge, 2011), 30–44.

Introduction

Extreme violence or periods of coercion or repression play a part in the political formation of many countries. Few modern nation-states, however, have been founded on the perpetration and material benefits of an in-country genocide that they keep denying, as is the case with Republican Turkey. This fact of massive foundational violence against former fellow nationals during the war-torn final decade of the Ottoman Empire is therefore still an incisive challenge for Turkey's political future and its dealing with history. Many cadres involved in genocide during the Young Turk dictatorship in imperial Istanbul were again in leading positions during the formation of the Republic, "new Turkey," which was proclaimed in 1923 and henceforth centered in Ankara. While this study asks for radical interrogation and introspection, it does not perceive late Ottoman and early post-Ottoman history as a continuum of violence, and by no means understands violence as something essentially more inherent to certain humans than to others.

A Young Turk Legacy of Genocide

The Young Turk genocides have meanwhile been named and clarified, at least as far as the main events and the immediate contexts in the 1910s are concerned. Yet, a full historical understanding of Turkey's formation requires far-reaching analyses beyond genocide studies. Using various insights, case studies, and reflective essays—the result of three decades of research[1]—this book attempts to clarify the process that took place at the end of the Ottoman Empire. It elaborates on the failed quest for societal peace (*huzur* in Turkish), notwithstanding the 1923 Near East Peace of Lausanne. More of a pact than peace, the Lausanne Treaty was concluded between potentates: Ankara's victorious nationalists, who were former imperial cadres, on the one hand, and Western national empires, notably the new mandatory powers in the post–Great War Middle East—Britain and France—on the other.

In contrast to many other books on Atatürk, Kemalism, and the making of modern Turkey, this study carefully interweaves its topic with Europe's contemporary history and terminology, benefiting from the distance and hindsight of a century. Its broad context is modern global history, focusing on the cataclysmic final decade of the Ottoman Empire that concluded a century of controversial reform efforts. Its pivotal point is the Conference of Lausanne whose still-valid treaty liquidated the Ottoman Empire, thus establishing the post-Ottoman political architecture. The Near East Peace Treaty of Lausanne is a case in point.[2] Ending a decade of wars, allowing for economic recovery, and ending or containing any sort of public violence has a value of its own. Real peace, however, is concluded among partners that legitimately speak for entire societies. It includes justice and freedom, that is, equity and civil liberties. It prevents continued conflicts via compromise, allowing peace to take societal roots and last. It thus constitutes more than the absence of interstate wars or agreements on matters of interest that, however, discriminate against others.

This book does not pretend to offer a comprehensive treatment of its vast topic. Providing a multifaceted understanding by diverse approaches which may seem loosely connected at first glance, it however aims for a deeper nexus that this Introduction and Chapter 1 further elaborate on. Even if centered on the modern age, an inquiry into the end of the Ottoman world cannot make do without more far-reaching reflections. Considering the eschatological expectations of three Levant-centered monotheisms and their respective community-building "covenants," peace in the Eastern Mediterranean "Bible Lands" is an ambitious issue with exceptional historical depth. Civilizational and historical myths, as well as religion—faith, loyalty, hope, mobilizing force, and organizational unit—bleed into almost all conflicts in the modern Levant. This deserves attention throughout all chapters of this volume.

From the late Ottoman period to the twenty-first century, Turkey's best minds have grappled with how to organize their polity to ensure basic peace, and not be distracted by promises of national or imperial grandeur that so easily fuel partisan or autocratic politics. What shorthand answers to these pitfalls and challenges can a historian provide? Much is achieved by finally coming to terms with the foundational extreme violence of an era that this study calls the "construction of the Turkified Anatolian nation-state" (1913–38) and intricately linked—by agreeing and focusing on the ongoing core challenge of establishing a better future—that of democratic social contracts among all people concerned.

No doubt, despite repeated destruction, Turkey has remained a dynamic human landscape that carries plenty of unfulfilled, historically well-rooted promises. Its cultural, geographic, and geostrategic position has afforded this medium power particular importance in the history of both the Middle East and Europe. Yet, violence- and crisis-ridden, at best half-democratic—at present (early 2023) again markedly autocratic—and polarized from its birth in 1923, Republican Turkey to a large extent owes its continued existence to geostrategic benefits and the ambivalent strategic value it presents for the West. *Turkey's Violent Formation* is about a foundational era of extreme violence and about the effects of an extreme ideology that it refers to as proto-fascism, ultranationalism, and anti-democracy. It was not solid constitutional ground, but war, collective emotion, common enemies, the shared benefits of genocide, and finally, an advantageous settlement with Western powers that grounded the genesis of the polity.

In his diary, Young Turk finance minister Cavid Bey applied the terms ultranationalism (*müfrit nasyonalizm*) and chauvinism (*şovinizm*) both to his party's politics in the Ottoman capital Istanbul and to the mainstream in Ankara's subsequent National Assembly.[3] An exception within his cohort, Cavid had remained loyal—at least in the seclusion of his diary—to the constitutional ideals of the 1908 Young Turk Revolution. Cavid's party, predominant within a broader Young Turk movement and called the Committee of Union and Progress (CUP), shaped Turkey's violent transformation and launched the Kemalists, most of whom had been CUP members. Many members and sympathizers of the Young Turk current, especially those from hitherto discriminated groups, had, however, espoused a constitutional-democratic perspective. But this orientation was entirely lost both after the enthusiasm of 1908 and again in 1919 after the Great War defeat had triggered some political soul-searching.

The same has happened many more times since then, every time closing windows that had briefly reopened toward more democracy. The re-descent into anti-democracy reactivated polarizing and scapegoating patterns anchored in the formation of Republican Turkey.[4] This study takes an in-depth look at these patterns, which were inherent in Turkish nation building. Thus, in 1926, the newly established nation-state made Cavid, the constitutionalist patriot, the victim of a judicial murder by Gazi Kemal (Atatürk).[5]

Foundational "Anti-Democracy," "Ultranationalism," "Proto-Fascism"

In this book, the terms "ultranationalism" and "proto-fascism" refer to a revolutionist chauvinism that originated from the political right, but partly overlapped with contemporary left-wing radicalism as exemplified by Russian Bolsheviks after 1920. Both currents, in their desire for power, radically rejected democratic constitutionality and civic liberties. The CUP blended ideas of class struggle with an ethnoreligious onslaught against non-Muslims that had already started under its predecessor Sultan-Caliph Abdulhamid II. Established in 1913, the CUP party-state no longer counted the Ottoman Christians as co-nationals, but as aliens: as capitalist exploiters conniving with foreign forces. The CUP elite thus redefined the Ottoman nation as a community of Turkish-speaking Muslims. Imperial proto-fascism, ultranationalism, and pan-Islamism coexisted during the defining final Ottoman decade, and they need to be clearly written into an updated post–Cold War, post-nationalist, post-colonialist, and post-orientalist historiography of the formation of Republican Turkey.[6]

Research on the late Ottoman period has progressed remarkably since the end of the twentieth century, and it has clarified broader contexts ranging from political to social and religious history. Multiple newly accessible multilingual sources have made it possible to establish, revise, or adjust narratives regarding the end of the Ottoman Empire, including the particularly turbulent 1910s.[7] Most notable is the CUP, from which the Kemalists and other post-Ottoman parties in different countries emerged or by which they were profoundly shaped. Important parts of this book concentrate on agency and ideology related to these late and early post-Ottoman actors, most of them imperial Sunni state employees, who shaped Turkey's nationalist formation from the 1910s to the 1930s. For the ruling elites and their clientele, it was a successful struggle for national survival; for the victims, however, it was a dark period of persecution and genocide. Comprising pan-Turkist, Islamist, and ultranationalist phases, this foundational era was followed by a variegated, but all in all domestically peaceless (*huzursuz*), aftermath that has continued into the twenty-first century.

The transformation of the multi-ethnoreligious Ottoman Empire occurred against the background of a failed constitutional revolution and squandered reforms lasting from the mid-nineteenth century to the early 1910s. Consequently, a new type of imperial single-party regime emerged, in which a new cohort of imperial nationalists ruled the late Ottoman realm. Their most prominent figure was CUP party leader Talaat Pasha, a self-declared founder of "new Turkey" ahead of his factual successor, Atatürk.[8] He and his closest circle welcomed Europe's Great War as an opportunity for a national-revolutionary flight forward, and for ridding late Ottoman society of those it considered alien or adversary. Their wartime regime started to remake the Ottoman social fabric according to the identitarian ideal of Talaat's congenial friend, the pan-Turkist ideologue Ziya Gökalp. They thus became the *génocidaires* of more than a million fellow Christian Ottoman nationals: Armenians, Assyrians, and notably Pontic Rûm. This extreme violence—that did not entirely end with the end of the Empire—profoundly affected generations of victims and perpetrators. It has marked Turkey's political fabric as a whole. This foundational issue implies challenges to scholarly analysis and international diplomacy that have not been (fully) met even after a century. *Turkey's Violent Formation* intends to address these challenges.

The cadres of the defeated CUP wartime regime reorganized in Ankara. From there, they were not only fighting the Western Great War victors—Britain, France, and Greece—but also Kurds who desired self-determination and Anatolia's surviving Christians who sought to return, rebuild their lives, and reclaim their properties. At the Paris Peace Conference, the claims made by the non-Turkish representatives of these groups were taken into consideration. However, their cause was inauspiciously connected with the designs of Western national empires. Three years later, they were not even admitted to Lausanne's negotiation table. Why? Facts of war and violence had pulled the rug out from under the Paris-Geneva peace, that is, the Paris treaty system and its Genevan pillar, the League of Nations. From 1920, the Turkish nationalists collaborated with the Russian Bolsheviks in a convergence of violent revolutions from both the left and right. Fully operational until the Lausanne Conference, this anti-Western synergy served both sides in their rejection of the Paris-Geneva peace architecture. Moscow and Ankara divided Armenia in 1920, thus prefiguring Poland's division in 1939. They considered both Armenia and Poland as weak and contemptible creatures of the League of Nations.

The Kemalists reestablished the state from Ankara, thus safeguarding a future in power and privilege for imperial elites and their interest groups with whom they had cooperated during the 1910s. Thanks to their Bolshevik-backed military victory in the 1919–22 Anatolian wars—whose main part was the "Greco-Turkish War"—they could enforce the revision of the Sèvres Treaty in Lausanne and acquired sovereignty over the whole of Anatolia. By 1925, their new Republic was a full-fledged dictatorship, and by the 1930s a totalitarian state.[9] Revolutionary socialism on the one hand and radical ethnic nationalism on the other were widespread phenomena in wider Europe and the Far East at the end of empires. The most prominent examples of ultranationalism in Western historiography were those in interwar Italy, Germany, and Japan. Well-explored in scholarship, including for their role on the eve of the First World War,[10] nationalisms in the Balkans came close to ultranationalism. But they remained restrained after the Great War and contained until the disintegration of Yugoslavia. However, the religiously tinted (pan-)Turkish nationalism—so-called "Turkism"— which began in the 1910s, has, by and large, remained exotic to historians of Europe. The early momentum, impetus, and far-reaching impact of imperial and post-imperial Turkism deserve their full and critical integration into the history of wider Europe from the 1910s onward. This comprises their still largely overlooked impact on the German far right.[11]

The interaction with imperial Germany, Turkey's senior ally during the Great War, is of particular interest for a revised European understanding of ultranationalism and the emergence of the politics of genocide (see Part IV in this book). Both countries remained in a special, in many ways unclarified relationship. It therefore took more than a hundred years for Germany to recognize the Armenian genocide, for which it was co-responsible. It was not only imperial Germany but also the Western national empires that preferred a pact with power over democracy in the wake of the Lausanne Treaty. Any farsighted mindfulness for small peoples and minorities had a difficult stand after 1923. Misled by Western liberalism, Armenians, Assyrians, Kurds as well as neighboring Syrians, Arabs, and Persians, had to leave the Conference of Lausanne empty-handed. They all had set great hopes on the League and the Western promise to liberate and protect hitherto subordinate peoples, in particular the small ones. But in 1923, they all saw the League's project of democratic self-determination die.

Appeasement characterized the pact of interests and the framing of history at the Lausanne Conference. This stance went on with the post-1945 alliance with Ankara. Turkish crimes against humanity and human rights issues therefore remained taboo topics in Western diplomacy. The post-genocidal conditions of minorities in Turkey and the 1938 extermination of Kurdish Alevis in Dersim are among several fundamental issues that only entered Western universities after the beginning of the twenty-first century. University Kurdish Studies and professional Armenian genocide scholarship had begun a little earlier. In view of coming to terms with violent state formation and anti-democracy, this book has chosen a democratic-contractual approach to society and polity building (see Chapter 1).

The Parts and Chapters of This Book

This book comprises fifteen chapters and is divided into four thematic sections. The introductory Chapter 1 on "Democracy Versus Genocide" amounts to "prolegomena" that lay bare the study's deeper nexus, that is, the reflections underpinning the main notions and arguments. On one hand, these prolegomena focus on genocide in the twentieth century while also touching on elements of a history of violence throughout the ages; on the other hand, they emphasize democratic social contracts as grounding peace and functioning polities. From this perspective, the chapter reflects on the role of pacts and covenants in human society reaching back to ancient times; the role of scapegoats in establishing social cohesion; and the phenomenon of "communities in crime."

Part I, titled "Reform and Massacre in an Expiring Sultanate-Caliphate," starts with a comparative-contrastive case study (Chapter 2). A group of internationalist Protestant missionaries belonging to the US-American organization ABCFM[12] sided with victims of persecution related to modern nation building: Indigenous Americans forcibly removed from their lands by settlers and state officials as well as Ottoman Armenians who were under threat and eventually evicted from their home territories. In both cases, the ABCFM had to deal with crimes against humanity, which it decided to fight against, albeit with little success. Abstractly speaking, Part I investigates sociopolitical struggles between those seeking an egalitarian democratic social contract and wanting incisive reforms, and those seeking to maintain imperial hierarchies or to promote a new supremacist national identity. Although democratic in name, the latter lacked the affirmation of human equality, as demonstrated by its exclusion of non-whites, for example. Conservative imperial reactions contrasted with new late Ottoman regulations that promised equality and constitutionality. Egalitarian reforms were met with violent reactions by Ottoman Muslims who insisted on religious supremacy, not least because they were postulated by European powers that were seen as dangerous aggressors.

The number of Ottoman Christian victims of sociopolitical violence rose into the thousands, in the 1890s into the hundreds of thousands, and in the 1910s—now targeted by the state's violent demographic engineering—into the millions. The Ottoman authorities saw themselves as being on the defensive against Western interference and claims of equality by non-Muslims. Politico-religious propaganda henceforth increasingly dealt with Ottoman Christians as foreign elements in the body of the state, and thus as agents of foreign powers. Central authorities largely sided with local Sunni lords they co-opted to maintain a minimum of power in peripheral, notably oriental—Kurdish and Armenian—provinces where the state never took solid roots (Chapter 3). The reactionary groups insisted on their imperial privilege, the sharia, and the maintenance of inequality. From the early twentieth century onward, they clashed with revolutionist imperial elites—the Young Turk organizers of the 1908 Revolution—but colluded with them a few years afterward. During the 1910s, the CUP dictatorship betrayed its 1908 ideals: it violently "cleansed" and homogenized a religiously plural society by erasing the Ottoman Christian communities. The rulers and associated interest groups believed in thus strengthening the state which their future depended upon.

The constitutionalist current homed in on comprehensive social contracts that treated ethnoreligious and racial diversity according to the principle of equality, thus allowing for democratic power sharing. The other, which won the day, made short shrift of ethnoreligious complexity and political plurality. Consequently, elites adopted violence, coercion, and repression as central political means by which to establish the rule of the predominant group in whose name they spoke. Although it mainly focuses on late Ottoman Turkey, this part reflects on modern politics of violence in general and encompasses Middle Eastern as well as US-American and other historical experiences. Its particular focus is the immediate eve of the First World War, when a robust international reform plan offered one last chance for a modern plural Anatolia, which was ultimately squandered (Chapter 4).

Part II, titled "Turkey's Ultranationalist Refoundation," and Part III, "Revolution and Anti-Democracy: Biographical Approaches," deal with the foundation of the nation-state, that is, the period starting with CUP single-party rule in 1913 and ending with sole ruler Atatürk's death in 1938. They explore the attempted rebuilding, on radical Turkish-nationalist bases, first of the empire, and after the Great War defeat, of a territorially downsized state. They specifically focus on the methods applied to save central state power and the continued dominance of Sunni elites close to the CUP. This fight for preserved power includes the 1914 flight forward into war; genocidal demographic engineering; and the production of ultranationalist political and historical thought.

Part II starts with Chapter 5 on the Conference and Treaty of Lausanne, followed by Chapter 6 on Rıza Nur, the vice-chief of Ankara's delegation in Lausanne. Nur was a cofounder of Ankara's 1920 National Assembly Government, a prolific ultranationalist author, and one of the main sources for pan-Turkism and Lausanne Treaty revisionism in the decades that followed the Lausanne Conference. He eventually fell out with Atatürk's circle, partly due to his opposition against the abolition of the caliphate. As a pan-Turkist in the vein of Ziya Gökalp, Nur pursued the Eurasianist ideal of a great, strong, and culturally self-confident Islamic Turkey in equidistance from other powers. This is a stance also largely adopted by the currently ruling circle in Ankara, who rehabilitated Nur.

Chapter 7 delves into the darkest episode of Atatürk's era, the 1937–8 campaign in the mountainous province of Dersim, whose name was then Turkified as "Tunceli." Labeled a mission of Kemalist civilization, the campaign amounted to a genocide of—according to conservative estimates—about 15,000 civilian victims by the Turkish army. The victims were Kurdish Alevis and a few Armenian genocide survivors who had found refuge in Dersim during the First World War. This chapter also touches on the ideological corollary of the Republican genocide in Dersim, namely an official Turkish History Thesis promoted nationally and internationally by President Atatürk and his close entourage. It claimed Turkish indigenousness in Anatolia and spread— and still spreads among nationalists—the vision of prehistoric high civilization by Turks—"proto-Turks," "Turanians"—in Asia and Europe. Pan-Turkish in a historical sense and thus in full accordance with Nur's vision, this highly speculative and ultranationalist, but never revoked thesis (mis)used prehistorical discoveries and state-sponsored large-scale craniometry. In this same spirit, Ankara incorporated the Syrian province of Alexandretta in 1938. Atatürk spoke of supposedly Hittite origins of Antioch, renamed the city Hatay (place of Hittites), and falsely claimed that the Hittites were of Turkish origin.

Part III, "Revolution and Anti-Democracy: Biographical Approaches," analyzes *Turkey's violent formation*, using political and intellectual biographies as a starting point, thus broadening the approach already introduced in Chapter 6. Chapter 8 focuses on Ziya Gökalp, the main mentor of Turkish nationalism and close political friend of Talaat Pasha. Like most CUP cadres after the Great War defeat, Gökalp sought the proximity of ex-CUP general Gazi Kemal Pasha (Atatürk). He wrote pro-nationalist articles and relocated to Ankara. Cavid Bey, by contrast, feared Gazi Kemal's growing autocracy and rejected xenophobic Turkism (Chapter 9). Chapter 10 paints a portrait of Mahmud Esat Bozkurt, a signature "revolutionary from the right" and an unrelenting sympathizer of Mussolini and Hitler. Despite his violent racism against Kurds and Jews, his thought displays some interesting paradoxes as well as a consciousness of democratic deficit. Almost immediately upon earning his doctoral degree from the University of Fribourg in Switzerland, he was appointed minister of economy, and later minister of justice, in Ankara. In 1926, he introduced the Swiss Civil Code, thus abrogating the sharia (Islamic law) in core aspects of life such as family, marriage, and inheritance.

Chapter 11 examines the role of Helphand Parvus, a Russian-Jewish-German socialist revolutionary who moved between left and right revolutionism. Living in Istanbul from 1910 to 1915, he got close to the CUP leaders and German diplomatic circles, enriching himself as a merchant of war goods in the process. A former leader of Russia's 1905 revolution alongside Leo Trotzki, he became an articulate partisan in world revolution by way of the Great War and the German-Turkish war alliance. Upon his return to Germany in 1915, Parvus remained close to the decision-makers in Berlin as an active pro-war socialist.

Part IV, titled "End of Empire, Time of Genocide: Turkey's and Germany's Affinity," deepens the focus on Germany and its strained but intimate interactions with the late Ottoman Empire, specifically with Turkey under Talaat and Enver Pasha. It, too, adopts biographical approaches in order to examine what was, on many levels, a problematic liaison. In Chapter 12, the pastor, author, and humanitarian activist Johannes Lepsius is portrayed as a German patriot of the aspiring Wilhelmine Empire who was nevertheless active in internationalist networks. These included interconfessional circles and, most notably, American missions in the Levant, where he lived for several years. This wide and conflictual horizon made him an outstanding witness to his strained and turbulent time and to, in particular, the Armenian genocide. Besides Lepsius, the special Turkish-German relationship involved personalities as varied as the above-mentioned Parvus; Ambassador Hans von Wangenheim who served in the Ottoman capital from 1912 until he died, a broken man, in 1915 (Chapter 13); and Matthias Erzberger, a member of the Reichstag temporarily on a mission in Turkey in early 1916. Erzberger headed Berlin's democratic current from 1917 onward. It was only then that he realized the magnitude of the Armenian genocide, its impact on Germany, and the necessity of univocal democratic rejection of exterminatory social Darwinist politics. Four years later, he was killed by right-wing activists while serving as a minister in the Weimar Republic (Chapter 14). During the Great War, imperial Germany and imperial Turkey were bound together by war constraints, propaganda, and the denial of the Armenian genocide. On many levels, this fatal bond impacted both countries for decades. A painful and shameful story, the Armenian genocide and Germany's role in it are the topics of the last chapter of this book (Chapter 15). The epilogue reemphasizes the main findings of the study, reflecting on the consequences to be drawn.

The chapters in this book can be read separately, as they do not follow a tight chronology and narrative line. A few minor repetitions are deliberate, and the index may help readers in case of unknown names and notions. Also, readers may skip Chapter 1 and study these "prolegomena" at a later stage.[13]

1

Democracy Versus Genocide?

These short "prolegomena" introduce *Turkey's Violent Formation* with an inquiry from historical and theological perspectives. As a preliminary chapter, they connect the modern terms "genocide" and "democracy," reflecting on the contrastive relationship of these notions, one constructive, the other destructive. The capacity or incapacity to deal with otherness, plurality, and failures is a core criterion for the strength and quality of a democratic social contract.

This book attempts to combine the analysis of destruction and dysfunction with the question of construction, that is, cooperative life, the warranty of individual rights, and the commitment to the common good and truthful history. As humans, we must deal with an ongoing gap between the human readiness to commit crimes on a large scale and human faith in, and capacity for, human dignity and self-esteem. Analysis, narration, and the benefit of hindsight shall here contribute to the bridging of abysses through historical understanding. Clarifying the dark side of late Ottoman and early post-Ottoman Turkey, this historical study takes up the challenge: How can we arrive at new social contracts in a modern human geography marked by repeated, insufficiently addressed extreme violence?

What makes genocide a crime *by intention* as defined in the United Nations (UN) Convention on the Prevention and Punishment of the Crime of Genocide is a purposeful ideology that underpins the criminal act: constructing a new state or power organization by destroying others, that is, by murderously excluding them from a new social contract in the making. Constitutive of a fundamental wrong, it inaugurates a new, crime-based, scapegoating social cohesion. *Turkey's Violent Formation* calls this kind of social contract antidemocratic because, in this case, the destruction of others, enrichment at their cost, greed for unshared power, and a fundamental lack of universal references take center stage. Haunted by this deficit, anti-democracies are inherently restless and expansionist. They depend on myths of grandeur, enemy images, and the denial of crimes. While anti-democracy lacks active and pluralist grassroots consent, the long-term vitality of a functioning democratic polity is fueled both by active participation on all levels of society and by shared universal references.

A Question of Social Contract

Murder is at the core of violence and crime. The murder of a people—the deliberate large-scale destruction of an ethnoreligious group—takes center stage in the concept of genocide as defined in the UN Convention on the Prevention and Punishment of the Crime of Genocide.[1]

In December 1948, a quarter of a century after the Lausanne Conference, international diplomacy insisted again and even more clearly on principles that had been lost in Lausanne. However, it did so primarily with a view to post–Second World War Europe and not out of particular concern for the Middle East, where the Lausanne Treaty and its social Darwinist spirit continued to apply. The recovered principles are set out in the UN Declaration of Human Rights and the UN Convention on the Prevention and Punishment of the Crime of Genocide. Three years earlier, in 1945, Article 1 of the UN Charter had once again formulated the fundamental right to self-determination, also of small peoples, that had been sacrificed at Lausanne's negotiating table.

The problem of political violence must be traced back to its core, that is, to the question of how to successfully build a human polity and how to deal with the issue of "insiders" and "outsiders." The positive emphases here are on modern societies and polities whose common will to live is based less on national or imperial myths than on a recognized common good and mutual recognition as equal humans. "Good" comprises immediate self-preserving interests of survival, welfare, law, and order, as well as the self-interested commitment to fundamental law, human equality, and the preservation of the habitat of humankind. In the terminology used here, political violence (in a broad sense) is a matter of social contracts that encompass states, communal life, regional autonomies, international structures, and globally acting companies. The capacity to minimize violence, repression, and exploitation indicates the democratic quality of the social contract. However, this quality does not dispense with the capability to defend against antidemocratic aggression.

This is not the place for an elaborate political philosophy (for which this author does not feel qualified), but this chapter serves to make transparent the explicit and implicit arguments in this book. *Génocidaires* emerge among particularly radical leaders of polity, nation, or empire (re)building. For the sake of their project, they purposefully destroy other human groups or nations that they consider enemies or bothersome outsiders in a common habitat. "Otherizing" humans and using scapegoats, they reject equality- and human rights-based polities. They thus also block their own path toward becoming a democracy. In compensation, as it were, they pretend to engineer something more grandiose, just, or "natural": new great nations, societies, empires. They use religion or quasi-religious ideologies (of race, society, or history) to underpin the grandeur, legitimacy, and historical necessity of their project.

In twentieth-century revolutions from the right and the left—notably those by Turkists, Nazis, and Bolsheviks—we find blatant examples of genocidal violence in the name of a nation, race, empire, or new society. While cases of "anti-democracy-cum-genocide" perpetrated by these self-declared revolutionaries are particularly evident during the period of the two World Wars, we can pinpoint many more that took place before and after. The World Wars induced, in the words of the contemporaries Max J. Metzger and Kurt Tucholsky, a marked "moratorium on the Sermon on the Mount" in which not only "Old Testament patterns" of expulsion and extermination became prevalent throughout modern Europe, but even basic laws, including the Mosaic Law itself, lost their meaning as protectors of human dignity, however minimal.[2]

What is democracy? Codified in a nondiscriminatory constitution, a democratic social contract defines the political and legal system. We might call a democracy "full-fledged" if it implements a functioning free and general electoral system; institutional balances in favor of minorities or weaker parts of society; social solidarity and security; civil liberties and universal human rights that prevent alienation (in the Marxist and the general sense); and elements of popular decision-making ("direct democracy" versus elitism and clientelism). A full-fledged democracy—a mature social practice of liberty and human dignity—is a utopia that comes to full fruition only if it finds strength by interconnecting with and being scrutinized by other democracies or a democratic federation of nations. An important consequence of law-based democracy is that if required, constitutional law tops popular national sovereignty and the will of majorities.

Far from grandiose rhetoric or the idea of a grand nation or empire, democracies depend on a combination of the pragmatic pursuit of self-preserving common interests and internalized sublime references, codified in constitutions. Democracy stands for individual liberties, the will and freedom to soul-search and seek the truth, and the participation and responsibility of all members of the law-based polity. This is how, in a nutshell, "democracy in its full sense" is understood in this book. Throughout all ideological rivalry of the modern era, "democracy" has remained a key notion of any constructive polity building. For this reason, it figures among the most claimed and abused terms.

Any rights, and any programs of crime prevention, are quixotic without vital social contracts established in the interest of defending one's own rights and those of others. The imperative of genocide prevention, as inscribed in the 1948 UN Convention,[3] has largely remained wishful thinking. It ranked and continues to rank far behind interest politics. This is exemplified in the cases of Indonesia, Biafra, Cambodia, Rwanda, and— once again since the exterminatory campaigns against Iraqi Kurds in the late 1980s— the Middle East. Scholars, while investing a great deal of analytical effort into dissecting the phenomena, risk merely remaining voyeurs of destruction or, worse, becoming merchants of past evil. The history of violence as well as the politics of commemoration need to protect themselves from being captured by the logic, dynamic, and spectacle of violence. The honest affirmation of positive references is therefore just as necessary as the attention to past dysfunction.

As long as the common good is not clarified and established as the guideline for analysis and assessment, the abysses of evil will remain subject to partisan manipulation, downplaying, and exploitation in public history. Most notorious, in this respect, is the decades-old doublespeak on genocide, informed by the official denial or non-recognition of the Armenian genocide by Turkey's allies. It took decades until both the US Senate and House of Representatives remorsefully acknowledged, in late

2019, that they had left the extermination of the Ottoman Armenians unrecognized for reasons of diplomatic expediency.[4] The argument, therefore, does not concern a quixotic vision of non-violence, but a basic understanding of polities and societies that are enabled—and indeed have throughout long periods of human history succeeded— in minimizing violence, maximizing cooperation, and abiding by universal norms and historical truths as much as possible.

Although the struggle might last generations, democracies form vital communities that possess the capacity to revise inherent wrongs such as the exclusion of whole groups from equal participation in political and social life. In the case of a deficient social contract with inbuilt mass crimes (see below), the shared but denied—or justified—crime is a strong element of both national cohesion and long-term conflict. Examples of such crimes against humanity are genocide, slavery, land-grab-based settler colonialism, and murderous plundering within the context of revolutionary class struggles. "Crime against humanity" is a much broader notion than "genocide." This crime violates the belief in humankind as one "nation" held together by a utopian universal social contract and common fundamental law, and within a common home: the earth and the universe.

The already existing concept of crimes against humanity was developed further by the lawyer Hersch Lauterpacht, paralleling and yet also contrasting the work of Raphael Lemkin, who, like himself, came from early twentieth-century Eastern European Galicia. He did this alongside his scholarship on human rights, thus emphasizing irreducible individual rights. Lauterpacht fundamentally rejected the vision of states as "primitive tribes," as they might be regarded in their exercise of "barbaric" collective extermination. Lemkin, in contrast, fully focused on the horror of such extermination—without dissecting and analyzing it through the primary prism of violated collective *and* individual human rights.[5] It was upon Lemkin's insistence that "genocide" was finally codified in the 1948 UN Convention. The notion of crimes against humanity is closely related to the conceptualization and development of the notion of common humanity and the terminology surrounding human rights. "Crimes against humanity" were first codified in the 1945 Nuremberg Charter. Today, they are primarily defined by the 1998 Rome Statute of the International Criminal Court. They comprise murder and other crimes "when committed as part of a widespread or systematic attack directed against any civilian population, with knowledge of the attack" (Article 7 of the Rome Statute).[6]

This book classifies "genocide" as a subcategory of the universal notion of "crimes against humanity." This umbrella term dates back to the eighteenth century and new notions of human equality and dignity brought about by "the Enlightenment." The latter, in particular, contributed to the development and reconceptualization of premodern covenants as democratic social contracts. In contemporary French terminology, "crimes against humanity" were referred to as *"lèse-humanité"* and were thus universal. They constituted a crime against the *citoyenneté universelle*— an imagined cosmopolitan community—and therefore a crime that surpassed *lèse- nation*—a crime against the nation. The universal notion of *lèse-humanité* redefined the great premodern crime, or *crimen magnum*, of *lèse-majesté*—a crime against a divine right-based monarchy.[7]

Modern thought overcame premodern categorization and stretched beyond royal, imperial, or national interests. It upheld the positive counterpart to *lèse-humanité*, the new supreme notion of humanity's "common good" (*bien commun*). But just as the Mosaic Covenant confronts us with commands to commit genocide (see below), "Enlightenment" thinking involved the use of "emancipated" reason and rationality to facilitate mass murderous hubris. Sociologists have honed in on the menace of mass-killing "gardener states," while for theologians the industrial killing of fellow humans epitomized the abandonment of humankind's relationship with God, in whose image every individual had been created and was thus valued.[8]

The Turkish Case

Lemkin's concept and his intellectual biography, including his autobiographical notes and his main publication on Nazi war rule, leave little doubt that at the core of his definition lies what others before him had called "murder of a nation" (Arnold Toynbee), "Völkermord" (Johannes Lepsius), or "eradication of the Armenian race from the Turkish Empire" (Ambassador Hans von Wangenheim). These three men wrote as contemporary observers of the extermination of the Armenians under the Young Turks (CUP).[9]

The main person behind the politics of genocide in the 1910s was Talaat Pasha, whose assassination and trial triggered Lemkin's coining of the term.[10] His and his party-state's approach served to make Asia Minor—by way of "gardening" or demographic engineering—an exclusively Turkish-Muslim "national home" (Türk Yurdu), and as such the center of a renewed Ottoman Empire. The genocide perpetrated by the Young Turks is a case in point: in the early 1910s, among the political frustration and looming cataclysm of the late Ottoman period, efforts toward egalitarian social contracts were abandoned—although they had explicitly been aimed at in the 1908 constitutional revolution and former reform edicts (see Chapter 4). Instead, conditioned by a prevailing imperial bias, the new vision of not only a restorationist but also a modernist and expansionist Turkish-Islamic national empire took center stage, before being reduced to its Islamic-nationalist contents in Anatolia after defeat in the Great War.

In this book, the generic term "imperial bias" refers to the understanding and projection of power as top-down—imperial, subordinating, and exploitative—as opposed to egalitarian, democratic, inclusive, law based, and well institutionalized (i.e., not centered around a charismatic leader). As Ronald G. Suny observed, it was the deep-seated structure (and bias) of imperial rule in late Ottoman Turkey that allowed for the shift from everyday top-down order and oppression to pogrom, massacre, and genocide to proceed with comparatively few obstacles.[11] Nevertheless, in order to fully achieve their goal, the rulers in Istanbul required fitting new ideologies, opting for war and supremacist pan-Islamic pan-Turkism from 1913 onward. In 1915, the genocide thus went hand in hand not only with perilous defeats and imperial security concerns during the first year of the First World War; it also required the new and dominant ideology of Islamic Turkification and of Turkish-Muslim greatness that sought expansion toward "Turan" (the "Turks' eternal, infinite motherland," vaguely centered in Central Asia). Mehmed Talaat's confidant Ziya Gökalp was the main prophet of Turkification and Turanism (Islamic pan-Turkism, see Chapters 6 and 8).

A Young Turk ideologue and the spiritual father of Turkish nationalism, Gökalp rejected a negotiated social contract by arguing that given, "natural" corporatist bonds dispensed with the need for democratic consent. Defeat in 1918 forced the predominant elites, including Gökalp, to get by without imperial chimeras. He and his cohort had to accept the Kemalist abandonment of empire, but they did not revise the corporatist definition of nation. Gökalp, a proto-fascist ideologue, thus inspired a leader-led, culturally unified modern polity that was primarily based on one predominant ethnoreligious identity, and therefore on assimilation or exclusion. The CUP's explosive mix of pan-Islamism/pan-Turkism had determined imperial Turkey's turn toward genocide during the Great War. Although the Young Turks lost their gamble in that imperial war, they succeeded in cleansing Asia Minor in ethnoreligious terms to make it an exclusively Turkish-Islamic entity. The early Kemalists defended these results in their Anatolian wars ("War of Liberation"), and the Lausanne Treaty endorsed this outcome.

Retrospectively, in a utopian long term, the Young Turk cohort—which included the early Kemalists, most of them former CUP members—would have done much better to focus from the start on the common constitutional construction of Asia Minor, the core land of what was in the 1910s still an imperial state. Obvious as it may be in hindsight, such wisdom was missed, and the mass killing of fellow citizens was never atoned for afterward. Instead, it remained inscribed in the foundation of post-Ottoman Turkey, and Kemalism remained defined by Gökalp's corporatist understanding of the nation.[12] All this made for a state within which, for a century to come, democratic rule of law became almost impossible. Without a true social contract, Turkey would remain a country of domestic crises, coups, violence, and systemic repression. As Chapter 5 details, at the Conference of Lausanne, Ankara achieved full sovereignty in Anatolia according to its "National Pact" (Misaki-i Millî) that rejected any claims by non-Turkish natives regarding self-determination, former dispossession, and crimes against humanity. The Lausanne Treaty was not a consent-based post–Great War fundament for Anatolian Turkey and the Middle East, but a pact between ex-CUP cadres and Western national empires.

As Ergun Özbudun, one of Turkey's most prominent contemporary constitutional lawyers, recently stated, "The persistence and deepening of social and political cleavages [. . .] has resulted in direct or indirect military and judicial interventions— that is profound constitutional crises or disjunctures—without ever being rehearsed in the context of constitution-drafting. This has been because there has not been a fully representative and inclusive constitution-drafting process in Turkish republican history."[13] The notorious and hitherto unbridged split between secularism and religion in Republican Turkey is rooted in the 1910s, the nation-state's first foundational decade. During this time, dictatorial CUP rule destroyed the seeds of consensual constitution-making by resorting to jihad, *ummah*, and the othering of non-Muslims. These were Islam-related patterns and concepts put into the service of imperial ultranationalism. Assertive Kemalist secularism struggled, but never succeeded, to fully overcome the Islamist roots of Turkish nation building (see also Chapters 6, 7, and 9).

Both prominent genocides in the first half of the twentieth century—that of the Armenians in the First World War and that of the Jews in the Second World War—largely obeyed religious categorization, both on a mental and an operational level. The Ottoman Interior Ministry segregated and "removed" the Armenians based on the records of the church administrations which determined their belonging to any given *millet* (organized religious community): Armenian Gregorian, Catholic, or Protestant. Wherever the central administration was able to implement this in the provinces, its scheme also comprised Armenians who had recently converted to Islam. This same method was later also implemented by the Nazis, who determined Jewish identity based not on non-existing biological testing, but on the registered confessional belonging dating back to the grandparents of targeted individuals. They were interested in religious registration insofar as, to them, it was indicative of a largely fictitious national-racial status. Religious observance was not an issue in either case; "otherness" and otherizing according to new national boundaries, however, were. In both cases, the perpetrators made organizational use of the victimized group's religious leaders in order to help identify and round up members of their community.

Just as the genocide, expulsion, and flight of Armenians and other Christian groups had led to the demographic de-Christianization of Asia Minor between 1913 and 1923, the Shoah (Jewish catastrophe in Europe, 1933–45, including the genocide/"Holocaust," 1941–5) drastically reduced the Jewish presence in Europe. Religious categorization determined the process of de-Christianization from the genocide to the so-called population exchange agreed upon in Lausanne. During this process, Asia Minor lost about four million Ottoman Christians. The religious split also informed the Anatolian wars (1919–23), when Ottoman Muslims led by ex-Young Turk officers under Gazi Kemal (Atatürk) defeated the Armenians, Alevi Kurds, and Greeks, including Rûm or Romaioi (Greek-Orthodox Christians indigenous to Anatolia).

The ensuing Lausanne Treaty was the final pillar of the post–First World War treaty system. Its compulsory resettlement of "Greeks" (Rûm) and "Turks" (Muslims in Greece) was based exclusively upon religious affiliation.[14] Turkish-speaking Christian natives of Anatolia had to leave what had, for millennia, been their home, just as Greek-speaking Muslims had to leave Northern Greece. Ankara pushed—more categorically than anyone else at Lausanne's negotiating table—for a comprehensive implementation of the compulsory transfer of Ottoman Christians. They were to be disposed of and the few small remaining groups to be made totally "incapable of doing harm" (Ankara's delegation chief Ismet Inönü).[15] Western diplomacy's tacit endorsement of genocidal demographic engineering and victorious ultranationalism during negotiations in Lausanne is the most influential political link between Young Turk and Nazi rule, between the Armenian genocide and the Holocaust.

Thus, old religious categorizations went hand in hand with entrenched divisions, fueling modern notions of exclusion and myths of pure, vital nations. Instead of being overcome, premodern socio-religious boundaries in anti-liberal currents—such as Turkism, Italian Fascism, and German National Socialism—contributed to organizing politically convenient hatred, even if the political language of the ruling elite did so (more or less) without premodern religious rhetoric. Instead, a social Darwinist, racialist, and nationalist supremacist vocabulary prevailed among them.

Potentially genocidal ideology exalts a majority and states the impossibility of egalitarian coexistence with targeted groups. It rarely postulates the explicit necessity of their extermination. Misleading terminology such as "relocation," "deportation," "resettlement," and so on, makes the proof of exterminatory intent notoriously difficult. A large amount of evidence, particularly regarding factual policy on the ground, has, in retrospect, allowed for solid conclusions concerning intent to be drawn. In addition, exterminatory intent has, at times, explicitly been mentioned by modern perpetrators. Heinrich Himmler's infamous Posen Speeches are a case in point, though not entirely exceptional as far as genocidal explicitness is concerned.[16] Ancient examples of boasting about destroying enemy cities and mass killing entire populations abound.[17]

A Path Forward toward Covenant-Based Peace and Law-Based Polities?

An overall historical picture of democracy versus genocide must not be simplistic. A critical approach to violence and anti-democracy requires historical precision. General dichotomies or a pretended detection of perpetual, quasi-natural cycles of violence—as by social Darwinism—do not help.

Despite the present state of the world and the horrors of modern history, *Turkey's Violent Formation* highlights dialectical historical progress toward more democracy, individual dignity, and a problematization of scapegoating and collective violence. "Dialectical process" means that progress has hitherto met with disturbing re- or counteraction, with which history nevertheless did not end. Humans have had to reckon—and they have reckoned—with the "dark sides" of their progress. Regress and applied hubris have time and again been recognized by contemporary or posthumous generations. The main universal-human orientation has thus never been entirely lost out of sight. It comprises the dignity/sanctity of individual human life and extends to a sense of responsibility for life and life's habitat in general.

The commandment to respect the rights of others and the belief in the inviolability of life, human dignity, and certain truths are more than just "soft values." They are deeply inscribed in texts that history has bequeathed to us from the best minds of mankind. Whether we refer to them as fundamental, natural, or divine laws or as human rights, the orientation toward—rudimentary—universal norms has existed for thousands of years and has left deep traces in written history. They have challenged polities and encouraged humans to become effective and responsible members of a greater whole. Religion—especially revelation-based monotheism—has carried the message of human equality in a universal perspective throughout the ages. Its "greater whole" is ultimately humankind, called upon to live and develop its potential on earth and in the universe. Some may argue that modern human rights and genuine social contracts—as opposed to scapegoat-based pacts or deals—hail from the Abrahamic belief in a covenant between humans and one good, true, and universal god, a god of humans made equal in his/her image. Others may place more emphasis on the debate-

and dialogue-based urban democracy of ancient Greece or may refer to other ancient experiences, achievements, or experiments.

About four millennia ago, according to a singular passage in Genesis (14:18-20), Abraham, the "father of monotheistic faith," encountered Melchizedek, the enigmatic priest-king of (Jeru-)Salem.[18] This happened at a decisive moment in Abraham's life as told in Genesis: just after a victorious raid to rescue relatives from rapacious enemies; and just before God made his covenant with Abraham saying that he would be blessed with land (in Palestine) and progeny (worldwide). As it is told, the encounter with Melchizedek appears unconstrained, almost fortuitous, by no means forced or provoked. However, it proved a revealing, "apocalyptic," and future-oriented, though not yet explicitly eschatological moment: Abraham gave Melchizedek "one-tenth of everything," thus bestowing his belonging and acclaim to the leader of Salem while refusing any material gains from his raid. King Melchizedek brought bread and wine, rather than royal riches or insignia, to the encounter. Abraham (at that moment still named Abram) possessed slaves, as was common among wealthy men in the patriarchal slaveholder societies of his time. Nevertheless, there must have been a great deal of trust between him and his slaves, as they accompanied him on the raid as armed men. In Genesis, Salem appears as a microcosmic model polity of humble humans living by, as is written, "the highest God." Thus, Abraham's special blessing is, right from the start of the Abrahamitic "history of salvation," tied to a strong, albeit vague idea of a municipal polity, as Salem presented it in a nutshell: a peaceful city, the center of a functioning just society and polity where there is public trust.

Political self-organization from an—albeit rudimentary—universal and egalitarian perspective appears to have started in geographically limited communities eager to transcend constellations of domination, submission, exploitation, and imperial hierarchy. Ancient Israel under Mosaic Law, including the Decalogue, is another, perhaps the best-documented, example of this early road toward a society based on universal law; and despite heavy ruptures and changes, this road was never entirely discontinued. Ancient Israel had initially done without kingship—an institution that got along badly with the covenant's claim to human equality and humility.[19]

The Decalogue's "Love your neighbor as yourself" and the related ancient "Golden Rule" enshrine the inviolable human dignity of others and oneself. The prophets in the Hebrew Bible invoked a covenant, or God-given social contract, among the tribes of Israel. However, they considered it a covenant to be opened to "the peoples" (humankind). They were voices of a critical spirit, perceiving the gap between promised potential and the social-political realities in which they lived. While the covenant lacked civic liberties and many other aspects of modern democracy and addressed only Jews, in prophetic perspective, it was based on the belief in human equality and comprised a global promise and mission. Jewish monotheism vacillated between universalism and exclusivism.

As God is invoked and enters the equation, theology factors heavily in the archaeology of human rights and the crimes of humankind. From ancient to modern times, the group-defining boundaries of the social contract or covenant have posed the basic question: Who is included, and who is excluded? The Hebrew Bible also contains what a prominent Holocaust scholar has called "genocide commands"[20] against those considered enemies or dangerous outsiders to the community and its new project. This reflects the calls to exterminate Canaanites during the ancient Israelite conquest of the land of Canaan. Although the exterminatory command three millennia or so ago mirrored realities of war, destruction, otherization, and existential communal self-assertion—of which much can be poignantly read in *The Iliad*—their radical formulation in the name of a universal god requires further thought.

Certain parts of the Hebrew Bible ("Ancient Testament"), traditionally called the Books of Moses, Joshua, and Samuel, contain passages that define and order the complete extermination of other tribes and peoples: "Now go and attack Amalek, and utterly destroy all that they have; do not spare them but kill both man and woman, child and infant, ox and sheep, camel, and donkey," said Prophet Samuel to King Saul (1 Sam. 15:3, *The New Oxford Bible*, 2001). The outright genocide commands in those texts of Numbers 31, Deuteronomy 20, Joshua 6, and 1 Samuel 15, to be enacted by the old Israelites during their protracted conquest of the land of Canaan (later called Palestine by the Romans), were supposed to save nascent Israel from detrimental native aliens. Canaanites and Amalekites were not only considered a security threat but also seen as impure outsiders who threatened to spoil the virtuousness of the chosen people's project from within. Whether contemporary or retrospective, factual or textual, or all these combined: the commands for extermination in the Ancient Testament reveal difficult truths about humans struggling to organize themselves into a better, more just polity.

Although demanded as an act of "obedience to the voice of Yahweh," such total extermination resembled a "whole offering" sacrificed to a bloodthirsty ancient Mesopotamian deity like the god Asshur.[21] Although two distinct phenomena, genocide and human sacrifices in the ancient world need to be considered together. Ancient Greek literature describes such sacrifices as cruel and horrifying.[22] The inhibition to sacrifice individuals due to empathy and a notion of dignity and sanctity of human life must not be entirely separated from the reluctance to exterminate others collectively. Both ancient Israel and Greece rejected human sacrifices, which nevertheless still took place in extraordinary situations. If they happened, they were— at least rhetorically, according to existing sources—linked to an explicit wish to please God or a deity.[23] There is an analogy to the allegedly divine commands and higher duty of extermination to which pious humans had to obey. In any case, killing was the crudest, most fear-inspiring demonstration of power over others, and neither ancient Greeks nor Israelites escaped the cycles of violence thus in motion.

Therefore, the tension between a collective departure toward more humane universal horizons on one hand and categorical commands to commit mass murder for the sake of the new project on the other is inscribed in passages of the Hebrew Bible. Israel's new project in the ancient world seemed to necessitate total otherization; a deathly exclusion from their own future; a stirring up of hatred carried to the extreme but understood as imperative to self-preservation. Thus, inscribed in the project of ancient Israel is a paradoxical nexus between genocide and a new social contract for the sake of common humanity, albeit still codified within tribal boundaries. The early, paradoxical link between biblical utopia and extreme violence has often appeared as a scandal and a stumbling block, as indeed it is—notwithstanding comparable contemporary accounts of the destruction of whole communities.

However, the paradox must be understood within the wider context of dialectical progress that comprises the later "scandal of the cross," which it has theologically struggled with ever since. In his "mimetic theory," the anthropologist René Girard insists on the polity-founding role of common violence, especially of scapegoating, and on Jesus's role in the Gospels in unmasking scapegoat mechanisms of human self-organization. Ancient foundational myths about exclusion and victimization end with the justification and embrace of, or at least resignation to, the viewpoint of a perpetrating majority. The Gospel narrative, in contrast, clearly exposes the crucifixion of an innocent individual whose side it persistently takes. In contrast to typical self-righteous success narratives, it insists on the "loser's" (i.e., Jesus's) ultimate validity and truth ("justification"). The crucified individual—"son of humankind"—finally accepts his fate willingly, thus revealing and establishing a higher truth. The Gospel narrative fundamentally opposes contemporary and posterior national opinion leaders. Vis-à-vis undecided imperial Roman overlords of its time, the Jewish politico-religious establishment in Jerusalem had framed the execution as just and necessary, and the victim entirely deserving of his fate. Rabbinic Judaism perpetuated this understanding.

According to mimetic theory, scapegoats and bloody sacrifices were and continue to be inherent elements of "archaic" polities worldwide. These require, mystify, and control the killing of the scapegoat in order to domesticate "original," "essential," and "foundational violence" as well as to reinforce compulsory solidarity, collective discipline, and belief in the group's unique identity. Denial of wrongdoing or making it an act of salvation is not only intrinsic to maintaining the group's identity but also to the construction of historical narratives and national norms regarding concepts of right or wrong.[24] In contrast to archaic yet persistent conditions of scapegoating, democracies strive to fight off the entrenched rationale of othering and to liberate societies from archaic routines. The supporters of French Jewish Captain Alfred Dreyfus at the end of the nineteenth century wanted, like Dreyfus himself, to believe in an age of emancipation, independent justice, and secular, meritocratic Republican citizenship in France. Their belief only partly came into being. Biblical prophecy—in the Torah as well as the Gospels—prefigured the belief in a "free society," and ultimately in liberated humankind on earth, held together by a law-based covenant without any birth- or race-related privileges.

The Gospel narrative fundamentally questions the former paths of community and polity building in the name of God or gods. In the long aftermath of the much-pondered "scandal of the cross" (Paul in Corinthians), any use and justification of scapegoats for the sake of community or nation building was metaphysically condemned as reactionary and criminal. Although scapegoating persecution did by no means end, it has since then been exposed and recognized as "shameful," and no longer by any means acceptable as a sacred duty.[25] Theologically speaking, with Paul, the scandal of the cross put an end to the pre-Jesus era of bloody sacrifices and thus to a blood-based understanding of purification and community foundation—especially in the name of a universal god or principle. The untiring detection and rejection of scapegoating is an indicator of democratic maturity, that is, of a social contract with effective universal references. For a theologian like Karl Barth—the pre-eminent academic voice against Nazism in interwar Europe—every other human being, every neighbor, is a reminder of God, that is, of the fundamentally transcendent other.[26]

Violent Anti-Democracy

What distinguishes democracy from anti-democracy and all forms of religious or secular totalitarianism is the capacity to constructively deal with otherness. In glorifying strength and success, fascism nurtures an exterminatory contempt for small nations and for weaker "others" in society—minorities, scapegoats, nonconformists, or "invalids."

The scandal of the cross, together with the Sermon on the Mount, unmistakably revoked former genocide commands and related attitudes; they forbade the killing and robbing of human scapegoats for the purpose of community building and preservation. Nevertheless, the logic of the genocide commands remained efficacious in Christian traditions. This was not only the case during the anti-Jewish pogrom and the colonialist massacres of indigenous populations. Hutu Christians referred to biblical genocide commands during the 1995 Rwandan genocide against (mostly Tutsi) Christians.[27] These facts call for clarification in order to contextualize the ancient commandments and to appreciate their Gospel- and human rights-based revocation. The same is true for passages in the Koran and Hadiths that call for violence and extermination.[28] Religious respect for holy scripture will otherwise remain open to abuse and haunted by the spell of allegedly godly mass killing.

The "Islamic State" (IS) of the 2010s provides the most recent and graphic example of a group that committed genocide by making direct references to the holy scriptures of a monotheistic tradition. It sought to revive the premodern leader-centered "social contract" between the Muslim faithful and their caliph by modern means, albeit without the traditional respect for the basic rights of the subordinate yet legally protected Christian and Jewish *dhimmis*.[29] By perpetrating systematic scapegoating, murder, rape, and plunder, the IS perverted Islam in its primal sense of "submission to God," but believed it could create bonds of a new caliphal community by extremely violent means. IS ideologists picked relevant passages in the Quran and the Hadiths in order to justify a genocide against the Yazidis that included systematic massacres, plunder, slavery, and the transfer of children.[30] The 1988 "Covenant of the Islamic Resistance Movement" of Hamas envisages a future for the Jews between extermination and total subordination to Islamic rule,[31] whereas the Israeli far right flirts from time to time with applying the old genocide commands against the Palestinians referred to as "Amalekites." Such references have multiplied after the jihadist Hamas massacre of October 7, 2023.[32]

Although centrally organized, the genocide against the Armenians in Eastern Anatolia and Northern Syria in 1915–16 was largely carried out as a "domestic jihad" against Ottoman Christian scapegoats. Their extermination or expulsion was believed to save and renew society by purifying it from alien and treacherous elements. Turkey's staunchest nationalists—and there are many—still venerate, to this day, Talaat Pasha, the main architect of the Armenian genocide and direct predecessor of Atatürk, praising him as a great patriot and loving father of the nation. For them, a *génocidaire* statesman like him acted rightly, audaciously, and effectively. Shedding the blood of scapegoats and dispossessing them (i.e., Anatolian Christians), he liberated and enriched the nation. Even more thoroughly tied by religion and race, the Turkish-Muslim nation was thus renewed and rebuilt. In a similar vein to the Young Turks before him, and IS in later years, "secular" Baath party leader Saddam Hussein, president of Iraq from 1979 to 2003, made ample use of Quranic references in his genocidal Anfal campaign against Iraqi Kurds in the 1980s.[33]

While Islam impacted modern genocide rhetorically, doctrinally, and operationally, it was Christian anti-Judaic traditions that informed antisemitism, the matrix of the Shoah. However, they scarcely directed action. (Neither could the lynching of African Americans, endemic in and constitutional to segments of American society, use direct references to the Gospels.) During the Holocaust, action was informed by the modern language of the Nazis' antisemitism in which German racism took center stage. The Nazis' Hitler-centered racist and *völkisch* messianism rejected human rights- and law-based checks and balances *a priori*. Although it had a rational administration, it was archaic tribal-racial solidarity cloaked in the modern language of social Darwinism that determined the social pact in "New Germany" that made the Jews its main scapegoats. Shared by many millions, Hitler's egomaniac pursuit of German grandeur rejected any subordination to universal humanity. It made the exclusion of the Jews operational based on religious community records.

The Nazis' exterminatory demographic engineering did not start with Jews and Slavs but with mentally ill Germans and handicapped German children who were all considered obstacles to optimal performance capacity in social Darwinist terms. According to the UN Convention, the Nazi euthanasia program did not constitute genocide. Evidently, however, it was by no means a less vicious crime.[34] This proves the limits of the term "genocide," and it confirms that historians do well by conceptualizing genocides within the terminology of crimes against humanity, and political violence in relation to polity building and social contracts.[35]

In contrast to the eminent Catholic anthropologist Girard, who remained taciturn on the modern challenges of polity building (and even pilloried the idea of social contracts), this study understands democratic social contracts as the historically informed response to the challenge of nation building and minimizing violence.[36] Being rooted both in local practices and universal references enables democratic polities to dismantle ideologies and make the application of human rights and human duties viable. However, most modern social contracts—codified constitutions of existing nation-states—comprise elements from both sides: democracy and anti-democracy. Antidemocratic social contracts require the exclusion, robbery, and murder of stigmatized others in order to constitute and reproduce themselves, that is, the predominance of autocratically and discriminatorily ruled majority groups. In other words, these contracts constitute pacts and deals between potentates and interest groups who victimize others and make use of scapegoat logic. Put pointedly, anti-democratic contracts amount to "communions in crime." They constitute regimes that require systemic victimization and rejection of universal norms.

History displays many gray zones. Most modern states are a mix of both: more or less serious assertions of basic rights go hand in hand with national histories that include whitewashed collective crimes. From a democratic perspective, social contracts are deficient in that they include systematic plunder, exclusion, and scapegoat logic, while still being grounded on a strong and efficacious affirmation and codification of human rights. The US Constitution is one such example. Elements in social contracts that result from, and are related to, extreme violence are rarely mentioned outright in constitutions. They resurge in public history and reveal themselves in a polity's national foundation, its political patterns, and politico-historical culture. Some relevant markers are visible on the surface of constitutions—such as that of "Eternal Nation," "Sublime Indivisible State," "Immortal Leader," or "Incomparable Hero" in the current Turkish constitution's preamble. In this case, they reveal the country's unitary, leader-centered nationalism.[37]

While polities based on genocide rarely thrive in the long term, those starting with a strong constitutional commitment to human rights, even if it is tarnished by the ongoing perpetration of crimes against humanity, might be able to overcome their shortcomings. US history, for example, is shaped, to this day, by foundational tensions between human rights and crimes against humanity. The US Founding Fathers' emphatic recognition of basic rights and universal equality coincided with their continuation of slavery and the perpetuation of crimes, including systematic dispossession, against the indigenous population (see Chapter 2). This initial exclusion, exploitation, killing, and expropriation served the dominant group's pursuit of happiness and the creation of a democracy for their own people.[38]

Nevertheless, the dialectics of right and wrong fueled powerful progress and soul-searching, including the eventual abolition of slavery and the implementation of equal civil rights. Its deeply polarized political and social landscape, however, indicates that the United States is far from having achieved a fully functioning social contract, and therefore far from having overcome the deficit of its birth. Nonetheless, it has continued to demonstrate the power of democracy. Its best minds of change and progress have not ceased to insist on democracy, that is, on a fundamentally egalitarian polity of humans created equal in the image of God. This is especially true of African American voices that cling to the promises of democracy against an all too understandable, but too determinist, "Afro-pessimism."[39]

When the League of Nations' Project Died: The Near East Peace of Lausanne

A hundred years ago, after the Great War, the Covenant of the League of Nations signified the first serious, if failed—or merely "experimental"[40]—attempt to globally promote democratic social contracts. Democratizing, human rights-based nation-states should be globally bound by the League's 1919 supra-covenant. This experiment coincides with the end of premodern empires in wider Europe and an emerging global competition between a liberal US-American and a Russian-led communist projection of the future. However, the insertion of the League's new internationalism into treaties concluded according to the traditional logic of victorious national-imperial European powers (Britain, France, Italy), as was the case in Paris, proved unfortunate. Anti-democratic detractors took this as a *carte blanche* for antidemocratic revolutionary violence against the Paris-Geneva peace.

Geneva's League of Nations, a crucial corollary of the Paris system after the Great War, constituted a significant attempt at establishing a post-imperial international peace based on a global social contract that encompassed polities, economies, labor, and health.[41] The Paris treaty system was initially intended to rest on the League of Nations. The League, in turn, would have to check, balance, develop, and, where necessary, revise the victor-dominated decisions made in Paris, including the treaties themselves. For its mentors, founders, and most committed insiders, the League rested on a democratic credo—in President Wilson's famous words: "No peace can last, or ought to last, which does not recognize and accept the principle that governments derive all their just powers from the consent of the governed." This attempt at a safe peace based on a global covenant, democratizing states, and self-determined small nations failed. This failure coincided with the liquidation of the Ottoman Empire at the Conference of Lausanne and the abandonment of Ottoman Turkey's small nations.[42] In contrast to all other treaties of the Paris treaty system, the League's Covenant no longer headed the Lausanne Treaty.

People from various strands of society, from American Iroquois and Eastern European "Yiddishland" to Armenia, Kurdistan, and China, had set great hopes on the burgeoning League. Among its strongest proponents at the end of the Ottoman Empire were the internationalist sons and daughters—teachers, doctors, professors— of American missionaries whose parents had first set foot in the Levant during the early nineteenth century, founding new institutions there and propagating the utopia of democratic futures, having felt disillusioned by their home country under President Andrew Jackson (see Chapter 2). For them, modern democratic thought relied on appreciating humans, including American "Indians" and Africans, as equals in the image of one good universal god—also politically and legally.[43]

It will be difficult to project real peace without a covenant that follows the example of what the League of Nations initially intended. But political imagination must stretch beyond Western racial civilization and beyond identification with the Anglo-Saxon empire, as was the case after the Great War.[44] Real peace depends on functioning democratic contracts underpinned by human rights and duties. Turkey, whose birth was internationally certified by the Lausanne Treaty, mostly proceeded without the supposedly soft values of justice, freedom, democracy, and historical truth. In Lausanne in 1923, these values were subordinated to the supreme good of national sovereignty and the need for a deal with the Western national empires, which were neighboring mandate holders. Although a noted diplomatic achievement, the settlement at Lausanne perpetuated the lack of democracy. It lacked the main ingredients for a peace that would both contain or minimize future violence and come to terms with the genocide and crimes against humanity of the pre-Lausanne era.

Allied to the Bolsheviks during the Anatolian wars, Ankara pioneered its own political path after the Great War. As was the case with Bolshevism, it resulted in a dictatorship, albeit hailing from a revolution from the right; that is, an ultranationalist fight in the name of Islam and Turkishness that had started with the Young Turk regime in the early 1910s. The Kemalists, the heirs of the Young Turks, managed, in Lausanne, to reach a compromise with the liberal-capitalist West, which was the main pillar of the Paris-Geneva peace. Successfully obstructing minority rights and, without civic liberties, domestically fascist, it could henceforth—in contrast to the Soviet Union—participate in the capitalist world, take loans, cooperate in international institutions, and count on perpetuated appeasement.

Part I

Reform and Massacre in an Expiring Sultanate-Caliphate

Turkey's Violent Formation, and in particular Part I of the book, is steeped in a dialectic of religiously and ideologically tinged sociopolitical struggles that oppose democratic-minded people to their adversaries, that is, those seeking social equality and democratic social contracts, and those wanting to maintain imperial hierarchies or to promote a new supremacist national identity. Both antidemocratic impulses come together in the case of nominally democratic Western national empires in areas unchecked, or insufficiently bridled, by the elementary human right of equality. Although there exist many gray areas, this ideal-typical contrast helps to clarify complex situations and long-term developments.

In Ottoman Turkey of the nineteenth century, imperial Sunni attitudes reacted against new late Ottoman currents and regulations that promised constitutional equality. Egalitarian reforms thus were met with violent reactions by Ottoman Muslims, notably in peripheral provinces. The number of Ottoman Christian victims of sociopolitical violence rose into the thousands, in the 1890s into the hundreds of thousands, and in the 1910s—now targeted by the violent demographic engineering of an ultranationalist imperial state—into the millions. Ottoman state representatives as well as provincial and urban Sunni leaders saw themselves on the defensive against Western interference and the claims of equality by non-Muslims supported by the West.

Fair Futures! Missionaries against "Indian Removal," "Armenian Atrocities"

If we abstract from the human aspect, the exclusion of the Armenians from the body of their [Turkish] state was no less a constraining necessity than [. . .] was the extermination of the Indians for the new state of the white people in America.
Dagobert von Mikusch, *Gasi Mustafa Kemal zwischen Europa und Asien*[1]

Hundreds of men lie dying, dead; Brothers of ours, though their skins are red; Men we promised to teach and feed. O, dastard nation, dastard deed!
Walter N. Wyeth, *Poor Lo! Early Indian Missions*[2]

This chapter describes and compares two distinct instances of the removal of peoples from their native lands. The removals in question were organized at different times by two great powers, one rising and one crumbling. The removals were different in quantity and quality, but both were claimed to be unavoidable for the purposes of state building. The American Board of Commissioners for Foreign Missions (ABCFM) was a privileged witness and an outspoken critic of both: the removal of the indigenous Americans (American "Indians") from Georgia and Carolina in the 1830s and the removal of the Armenians from Asia Minor during the First World War. This exterminatory removal comprised nearly all Ottoman Armenians and paved the way for an exclusively Turkish nation-state. In both cases, the ABCFM defended an integrative, non-exclusive vision of the societies concerned. In the midst of turmoil, it displayed great courage and tenacity against local and national strongmen who promoted the removals.

Introduction

The state-organized removal of entire groups from their territories in the nineteenth and twentieth centuries followed a rationale of nation building and social engineering. It was deemed necessary for the building of modern, strong, and homogeneous states that were thus made fit for survival in a globalizing world. Considered detrimental and non-assimilable to the new nation in the making, the targeted groups were "otherized," marginalized, and removed. Removal led to traumatic, often deadly consequences. Watchful contemporaries who held alternative sociopolitical visions opposed such removals as criminal. Referring to law, truth, humanity, and the Gospel, they challenged both the permissibility and the long-term wisdom of such policies. Before being removed, the targeted groups were classified and registered, mostly according to ethnoreligious criteria, on the basis of existing data or new census lists. The removal of indigenous tribes in the United States did not involve mass death to the same degree as Turkey's late Ottoman genocide of its Armenian nationals. Nevertheless, this chapter argues that modern nation building succumbed to the dark sides of demographic engineering not only in Turkey but also—paradigmatically, though perhaps less strikingly—in the United States.

The ABCFM was an interdenominational organization backed by Protestant churches in New England and other parts of the United States. It reached a large Protestant public in America and in Europe through its publications and was part of what we might call a "Protestant International" (distinct from and in competition with the Socialist International) of the nineteenth century. The ABCFM made its main investment in the "Bible Lands" of the late Ottoman world, thus giving its own Gospel-inspired answer to Western diplomacy's notorious and intriguing "Oriental Question." This issue referred to the puzzlingly uncertain future of the late Ottoman world. The Protestant International fostered faith in historical progress and the coming of the "millennium"—the reign of God and Jesus on Earth. For them, however, Jesus's second coming depended as much on human agency as it did on apocalyptic turns. This Christian internationalism rested upon transnational reformed, mostly Calvinist, networks. In contrast to Lutheranism, it projected global futures—the coming "kingdom," or rather republic, of Jesus on Earth—in democratic and federalist terms.[3]

This chapter also reflects on the role of witnesses. It ponders the value of stances at odds with what rulers, the elite, and most people accepted as compelling rationales of historical progress—even if later generations were to condemn them. On a general level, the nineteenth and twentieth centuries saw a clash of projects influenced by two contrasting political visions: the appreciation, exploration, and empowerment of ethnoreligious diversity on one hand, and the state-engineered discrimination and social Darwinist exclusion of groups based on ethnoreligious, class, and other distinctions on the other. As part of a common global future in modern polities, it was necessary for legal equality to prevail. In the Ottoman Empire, the modern project of such plurality-cum-equality found its entrance during the Ottoman Reform Age (Tanzimat). However, the engineers of the Tanzimat were no less influenced by the French concept of a unitary, more or less homogeneous centralist nation-state. In this vein, they—and others—promoted, empowered, and exalted the features of one majority group at the expense of others. Wherever this happened, it was an almost impossible challenge to expose such rationales from within Darwinist state foundations and to argue successfully against them.

The American "Indian Removal"

In 1838–9, large parts of the Cherokee nation were forcibly relocated from their homes in northern Georgia and South Carolina, some of them in manacles. Around 4,000 out of the approximately 16,000 victims died during the enforced 116-day journey that took them over a distance of about 1,000 kilometers to "unorganized territory" west of the Missouri, now Oklahoma. This was the so-called "Trail of Tears," the deadliest of several enforced expulsions of indigenous peoples from Florida, Georgia, Alabama, South Carolina, and Mississippi in the 1830s. In total, they involved about 100,000 individuals, many thousands of whom died. Many more could not cope with the trauma, descending into a lifetime of misery and alcoholism that carried through into subsequent generations. "Heart-sick and weary, they never became reconciled to their lot," Rev. Walter N. Wyeth wrote in 1896.[4] In modern legal retrospect, this destructive displacement of civilians constituted no less than a crime against humanity.

Theoretically, at least, a voluntary removal with due compensations would not have infringed human rights. However, the Indian Removal Act of May 28, 1830, was a departure from the policy of respecting the established rights of the indigenous population. It authorized the government to grant tribes western prairie land in exchange for their territories, especially in the southeast. Thus, a group of Cherokees had already voluntarily left their land in 1835-7.[5] However, this act allowed for negotiation and voluntary relocation only, not for coercion and violence, as happened in 1838-9. American "Indians" were not recognized as US citizens until the 1920s. Meanwhile, in the 1910s, the Armenians were excluded as citizens from their own state's redefinition of nationality, before being removed and killed. There were no negotiations regarding territorial exchange or the destination of displaced people with representatives of the Armenian community in or before 1915. The Young Turk regime decreed a number of protective yet deceptive regulations. These potentially protective measures were in no way complied with.[6]

Former general Andrew Jackson, the seventh US President (1828-36), implemented the removal of indigenous tribes as a top priority of his presidency. Jackson is regarded as the man who, as part of his strong, popular, and populist presidency, established modern mass democracy; he left a "vigorous and well-organized Democratic Party as a legacy."[7] Sadly and ironically, Jackson's egalitarian mass democracy bore few ties to constitutional human rights; rather, it was something akin to Carl Schmitt's radical idea of a homogenized mass democracy, which he developed a hundred years later (see Chapter 5 and Epilogue). It obeyed the vision of a modern American republic that concentrated power and riches in the hands of white men. Thus, it clashed with both the anti-removal and the anti-slavery movements of the time. "Most new voters in the South and the West wanted Indian removal. Most new voters in the South wanted slavery."[8]

A demagogue as well as a democrat, Jackson was the model of an American nationalist. He had experienced the American Revolution and was celebrated as a military hero who had crushed the tribe of the Creeks in 1813-14. He perceived the indigenous people as erratic and inferior to the white settlers. For him, they were a threat to the national integrity of the fledgling United States, especially as many tribes had believed that Great Britain was more likely to respect their property. They thus had been, in his opinion, on the wrong side during the American Revolution and its wars and could not be trusted again. Indian attacks, or retaliations, had been a cruel reality for settlers before and after those wars. Settler militias acted brutally and rapaciously in return, and Governors had only partial control of them. They ultimately proved a major instrument in hastening the removals.[9] In comparison, the Young Turk rulers of the 1910s also did not enjoy full control over regional strongmen. However, they feared the Armenians as educationally superior rivals, not as "savages." In contrast to armed Indian resistance, Armenian defense was weak because Armenians did not generally bear arms.

The Trail of Tears, however, did not involve what were deemed to be "savages" but, significantly, one of the so-called "Five Civilized Tribes." The Cherokee had in many respects adapted their way of life to that of the white man, occasionally even to the point of keeping slaves. They utilized European know-how, were successful farmers, formed a tribal government modeled on the US government, and very quickly became literate, developing an alphabet for their own Iroquoian language in 1821.[10] Three factors proved to be relevant in the displacement of the Cherokee: their regional autonomy, their wealth in terms of cultivable land and gold, and their success in finding their own, semi-autonomous path in modern America. Jackson's Indianophobia and his fear that the Southern states would secede if he opposed them concurred with the expansive greed of white Georgia and the pressure of its settlers in the 1820s and 1830s: the whites wanted to be in control of all of Georgia. They suspected the Cherokee of being a fifth column against their regional designs and the missionaries to the Cherokee of being agents of the North.[11] In Turkey, analogous elements, albeit on a much larger scale (greed, fear, the pressure of Muslim migrants, exclusive Turkish-Muslim claims to Anatolia, "treacherous" Armenian foreign relations) spoke against the Armenians during the Great War.

In general, people (historians included) tend to bow to the weight of past realities and do not fundamentally question the making of realities and alleged constraints. President Jackson feared that "independent, sovereign Indian nations would prove easy prey for manipulation by hostile powers." Whether delusional or not, removal was, in his view, "the only way to safeguard the Constitution of the United States and the nation's survival." US historian Sean Wilentz calls Jackson's removal policy insidious and ruinous for the Indians, but "neither genocidal nor far-fetched." Historian Harold Bradley considers the fact that Jackson failed to comply with the Supreme Court's decision to implement federal authority in Georgia in favor of the Cherokees, an "indelible stain" on his record. The Supreme Court had ruled against Georgia on this issue, but Jackson sympathized with Georgia's local government and, after years of anti-Indian harassment, enforced the Indian Removal Act of 1830.[12]

In December 1828, just after Andrew Jackson's election, the state of Georgia had extended its jurisdiction to Cherokee land, on which gold had been discovered. This land, which belonged to the tribe according to a treaty, was now mapped out for distribution to white citizens of Georgia. Among other discriminations, the new Georgian jurisdiction prohibited the Cherokee from being "a witness or party in any suit where a white man should be defendant" and any contract between a white man and a tribal member without the testimony of two white witnesses. The purpose was to "render life in their own land intolerable to the Cherokee" and plunder them, as the anthropologist James Mooney (1861–1921) stated. In the years just before the final Trail of Tears, bands "of armed men invaded the Cherokee country, forcibly seizing horses and cattle, taking possession of houses from which they had ejected the occupants, and assaulting the owners who dared make resistance."[13] In the years before the Armenian genocide, the question of Armenian agrarian property, robbed by Kurds, was a core issue of Ottoman interior politics and of the international "Armenian Question." Depending upon the cooperation of regional lords and tribal chiefs, the ruling Young Turks were unable, and eventually unwilling, to resolve this conflict according to a fair rule of law.

Alongside acts of individual and collective indigenous resistance, a major obstacle to removal, both on a local and a national level, was the ABCFM. This first US overseas mission had begun its work among the Cherokee in 1816, six years after its foundation in Boston in 1810, and three years before it sent its first missionaries to the Ottoman Empire. The historian Clifton J. Phillips called that mission a "brilliant, but practically unknown, chapter in the history of the American frontier."[14] Largely identifying with the oppressed, the American Indian mission of the early ABCFM founded churches and schools "in the wilderness," thus reinforcing those territories as part of Cherokee property. "Will any bring it to the bar of God, when these wretched Indians point to us, as the cause of their ruin," Levi Parsons wrote in his diary when he was still a student at Andover/Harvard. "Reason, religion forbids."[15] Parsons was to be the first American missionary to the Ottoman Empire in 1819. When the Cherokee negotiated a new treaty "giving up a part of their ancestral domains" in 1818, the ABCFM secretary "hurried to Washington and helped insure the inclusion of a clause granting the Indians perpetual rights to their remaining tracts in the South."[16]

American settler communities largely branded indigenous peoples as "other." In the eyes of missionaries, however, they were above all fellow humans. An initial ABCFM policy for assimilation focused on teaching English, which the missionaries initially thought would aid the survival of the Cherokee. Soon, however, they adopted a more integrative approach, promoting the vernacular and launching a bilingual Cherokee-English newspaper. Indeed, they attempted to bring to the Cherokee the best of what they believed to know and to possess. The Cherokee were to become shareholders of a common good, in a holistic sense; to be equals both according to the principles of human equality and as fellow believers in the Gospel. As far as the ABCFM was concerned, racial and cultural differences could never serve as a motive for discrimination, and neither, of course, could envy of material possessions. Moreover, the Cherokees' visible "progress in civilization" and acquisition of wealth spoke against all those who despised indigenous peoples as evolutionary inferior. Contrary to the prejudices of many Yankees, the ABCFM defended marriages between whites and indigenous Americans in the 1820s. Thus, in the context of its time, this mission bravely passed the test when it came to the promotion of anti-racist ideals.

This "exam," however, was easy compared to what Jeremiah Evarts, the leading ABCFM secretary in 1821–31, considered to be the decisive test for the entire bourgeoning US society: to resist the sin of forcible Indian removal. To him, this amounted to a struggle "for the soul of America," that is, for what he patriotically believed to be the "manifest ethics" of the American project. After 1828, Evarts and the missionaries on the ground, supported by sympathetic publishers as well as a number of politicians in Washington, led an extensive fight against the Jackson administration's removal policy. Under the pseudonym of William Penn, Evarts wrote a series of articles that were printed by several papers and cited in Congressional debates.[17] Despite these efforts, Congress passed Jackson's bill in May 1830. Evarts continued the fight, writing in one of his last essays of November 1830:

> The people of the United States are bound to regard the Cherokees and other Indians, as men; as human beings, entitled to receive the same treatment as Englishmen, Frenchmen, or ourselves, would be entitled in the same circumstances. Here is the only weak place in their cause. They are not treated as men; and if they are finally ejected from their patrimonial inheritance by arbitrary and unrighteous power, the people of the United States will be impeached. [18]

However, it was not the Gospel, the common good, and equal human rights that prevailed, but the rule of force. Evarts died, exhausted, in May 1831.[19]

At a meeting between representatives of the Cherokee and the ABCFM at the end of 1830, resolutions against the removal were adopted. ABCFM missionaries Samuel Worcester and Elizur Bitler were imprisoned for staying on Cherokee territory without the permission of Georgia authorities. Their appeal to the Supreme Court was supported by the ABCFM and its sympathizers in Washington. On March 3, 1832, Chief Justice John Marshall declared the Cherokee Nation to be a distinct community outside the jurisdiction of the State of Georgia and cleared the prisoners of all charges.[20] In contrast, the Armenians were both citizens of the Ottoman state and members of a distinct community, or *millet* (see below); although autonomous in certain regards, their *millet* was within the territory and the main jurisdiction of the state.

As soon as they understood that Jackson favored Georgia and wanted to pursue the removal despite the rulings of the Supreme Court, the missionaries realized that their cause was lost—at least on the terms they had fought for until then. Removal now seemed to be unavoidable. Recognizing this reality, the missionaries refrained from backing those Cherokees who had opted for armed resistance; it was members of this group that killed the representatives of a minority faction that had finally signed the pro-removal New Echota Treaty of 1835.[21] The majority of the Cherokees, however, remained in passive resistance.

"The soldiers came and took us from home," a Cherokee woman stated, recalling the eve of the Trail of Tears in autumn 1837:

> they first surrounded our house and they took the mare while we were at work in the fields and they drove us out of doors and did not permit us to take anything with us not even a second change of clothes, only the clothes we had on, and they shut the doors after they turned us out. They would not permit any of us to enter the house to get any clothing but drove us off to a fort that was built at New Echota. They kept us in the fort about three days and then marched us to Ross's Landing.[22]

The main agent of the relocation was the army. The victims had been defined by the first major census of Cherokees living in North Carolina, Georgia, Alabama, and Tennessee.

Compiled by the Federal government in 1835, it listed the name of the head of each family.[23] Total destruction, as in the case of the Armenians, did not occur. "However tragic the removal of the southern tribes was, the tribes moved west under treaties that recognized them lands in the West," historian Francis P. Prucha concludes.[24] A number of white Georgians became nostalgic, albeit without fundamental self-interrogation. "The little cabins and wigwams of the Indians," a white planter wrote in 1840, "which are scattered about among the mountains and on the water courses from which they were driven and also the graves of their friends from which they were so unwilling to be removed makes one melancholy to look at, but still it was no doubt for all the best."[25]

During the Trail of Tears, the missionaries accompanied the deportees, rebuilding missionary stations in the West.[26] However, the deportation had broken the enthusiasm for a creative Cherokee renaissance in their homeland, and the ABCFM's fervor for the Indians subsided. Moreover, the political commitment against removal had not pleased all supporters of the ABCFM. Many of them preferred missionary news from overseas that reassured rather than troubled those at home. After the Indian Removal, the ABCFM concentrated more than ever on its more promising overseas missions, in particular on those in the Ottoman "Bible Lands."

The Destruction of the Ottoman Armenians

The main facts, contexts, and results of the destruction of the Armenians in Asia Minor during the First World War have become common scholarly knowledge since the end of the twentieth century.[27] I will therefore limit my following observations to points relevant to the comparative perspective of this chapter and to some lesser-known aspects of the question.

The hierarchical difference between Muslims and non-Muslims was an established social fact of the Ottoman system, as was the distinction between Armenians, Rûm, and Jews according to their religious affiliations. These distinctions constituted the *Pax Ottomanica* that warranted coexistence within a hierarchical, inegalitarian imperial plurality. The religiously defined system of *millets*, that is, autonomous communities,[28] was thoroughly reformed after the Ottoman Reform Edict (*Hatt-ı Hümayun*) of 1856. The Tanzimat (1839–76) introduced Western norms into reforming institutions, seeking a modernized, centralized Ottoman polity that included semi-autonomous ethnoreligious communities. Among these recognized communities of Christians and Jews, the Armenians were the most dynamically developing group. They experienced an educational boom and a cultural "national renaissance" in the nineteenth century and rapidly implemented a democratizing *millet* reform in accordance with the *Hatt-ı Hümayun*. Most Ottoman Armenians were members of the traditional *Ermeni Gregoryen milleti* (or *millet-i Ermeniyan*). The new small *Protestant milleti*, established in 1847 under the lead of the ABCFM, was also mostly Armenian. Overall, the pioneering institutions of the ABCFM in Ottoman Anatolia had a large Armenian clientele.

Armenian men and women played a prominent role in late Ottoman literature, theater, journalism, medicine, science, law, and commerce. In contrast to the

Orthodox Ottomans (Rûm) and the Christians of the Balkans, where nationalists sought independence from the Ottoman Empire, Armenians were called *millet-i sadike*, the "loyal nation." They were eager to take on functions within the state of the Tanzimat, imbibing ideas of a reformed, ethnically diverse and politically pluralist Ottoman state under the rule of modern law. In that sense, they shared the ABCFM's ideal of egalitarian politics emancipated from the hierarchies of the preceding centuries. The American polity hoped for by the early ABCFM would have implemented indigenous rights and citizenship in a similar way; thus, the United States would have become a society whose claim to equality and pluralism did not limit itself to white men. Unsurprisingly, the ABCFM strongly identified with the reforms of the Tanzimat and supported its Ottomanist vision. However, it focused much more on legal and social progress than the statesmen themselves, who were most concerned with restoring power. Nevertheless, "Ottomanism"—the concept of a common modern patriotism—was "perhaps the Tanzimat's most significant contribution to the empire."[29]

The ABCFM took the equality of Muslims and non-Muslims proclaimed by the Tanzimat, and later by the Young Turk Revolution of 1908, seriously. However, by empowering the Oriental Christians, the Tanzimat and the ABCFM contributed to imperial Muslim resentment, particularly in Eastern Asia Minor. Against this background and the territorial losses in the Balkans, Sultan Abdülhamid II (r. 1876–1909) established his modernizing yet anti-egalitarian policy of Islamic unity. By the same token, this policy reacted against the 1878 Congress of Berlin that detached most of the Balkans from Istanbul's direct rule and internationalized the—then so-called—Armenian Question. American missionaries saw the problem of the Armenians in eastern Asia Minor (Anatolia) not as "one of autonomy nor of any change of laws, but merely one of the enforcement of law."[30] They did not promote Armenian autonomy or independence and took a clear stance against the revolutionary violence that newly founded Armenian organizations adopted when the promises of reforms in Eastern Anatolia failed to be implemented. The 1878 Berlin Treaty had promised such reforms in order to warrant the security of life, property, and dignity of a threatened Armenian population in that region (Art. 61). Missionaries agreed that if the Ottoman government was chronically "unable or unwilling to guarantee these loyal subjects such basal rights, then they must appeal to Europe to take measures to enforce the provisions of the Berlin treaty relating to security and order in these provinces."[31] According to the assessment made by the ABCFM representatives, the state withheld rightful protection of a group which it structurally discriminated against; above all, it yielded to the will of eastern Anatolian regional lords, great Muslim landowners, and tribal leaders. This mirrors the terms upon which the ABCFM had protested the US government's unwillingness to impose federal law upon Georgia, its settlers, and militias.

Statistical struggles over the number of Armenians in eastern Anatolia had begun after the Congress of Berlin. Creeping unofficial removal (coerced migration) of Armenians during the period of Sultan Abdülhamid II was accompanied by the Kurdification of certain regions and the resettlement of Muslim migrants from the Balkans and the Caucasus. ABCFM sources mention over-taxation and direct threats as reasons for Armenian emigration.[32] Removal of Armenians in favor of Muslim settlers corresponded with the policy of the palace. The most direct demographic impact was made by large-scale pogroms in autumn 1895. In the 1890s and early 1900s, the ABCFM compiled comprehensive documentation of this and other instances of anti-Armenian mass violence and dispossession. Its press contributed significantly to international publicity and to a humanitarian movement in support of the victims.[33]

Resolving the "agrarian question," the question of lost or stolen Armenian land, was one of the main issues concerning Ottoman politics after 1908, both nationally and internationally. From its formation in 1907, the alliance between the CUP—the main party of the Young Turks—and the Armenian Dashnaktsutiun (Armenian Revolutionary Federation) was based on the agreement that the stolen land would be restored, and safety of life and property established.[34] However, after initial serious efforts by both CUP and Armenian representatives, the matter dragged on. In late 1912, Armenian representatives finally turned to European diplomacy. Cooperation between Russia and Germany led to a substantial reform plan that the Ottoman government signed in February 1914. For many international observers, including the ABCFM, a thoroughly revised first Russian draft of these reforms constituted a compromise which would bring more security and democracy to eastern Anatolia (see Chapter 4).

Since the Berlin Congress, the Armenian Question and Armenian Reforms had been discussed both by the Ottoman state and internationally, but never in terms of a possible removal. The projected modern reforms for a multiethnic eastern Asia Minor (art. 61 of the Berlin Treaty and in particular the Reform Agreement of 1914) aimed first of all to guarantee the safety, and secondly, the equality of the Armenians living there among a Muslim majority. Nevertheless, the reform discussion had a demographic bias from the onset. As early as 1879, Captain Claytons, one of the British officers dispatched to eastern Anatolia after the Congress of Berlin, had considered the possibility of making clearer ethnoreligious demarcations in Anatolia by allocating the eastern regions to the Armenians, for example, and the rest of the country to the Turks.[35] The Ottoman state of the Tanzimat reforms had not succeeded in improving the general safety in the Kurdish-Armenian eastern provinces. Equality of Muslims and non-Muslims in terms of law, taxes and legal practice, as outlined in the 1856 Reform Edict, was only partially implemented, if at all; traditional structures of social life were dismantled.[36] Two serious attempts at concrete reforms according to art. 61 of the Berlin Treaty were finally signed by the Ottoman government in 1895 and 1914. However, destruction caused by massive societal and state-controlled violence followed in both cases.

This is analogous to President Jackson's implementation of the Indian Removal despite the contrary decision of the Supreme Court in favor of Indian rights shortly beforehand. Once the American state had decided on removal and had legislated accordingly, the ABCFM continued for a while to denounce this policy as illegitimate and in breach of a treaty and of fundamental rights. The Ottoman Deportation Act of May 1915 (a provisional law as the Parliament in Istanbul was closed) made the removal official. In contrast to the Indian Removal, however, the Deportation Act disguised its target, range, methods, and destination. It stemmed from a new, precarious, and dictatorial party regime, established by coup in 1913, that sought national-imperial salvation by war, including war against parts of its own population. After a short period of Ottomanism, or common constitutional patriotism in the aftermath of the Young Turk Revolution of 1908, the CUP thus embarked on a revolutionist right-wing policy. This was based on the vision that Anatolia had to be made the national home of the Muslim Turks. Consequently, the CUP scrapped the principles of the Tanzimat and went on to comprehensively destroy the Armenian presence in Asia Minor.

The CUP's new exclusionary approach to Asia Minor used the demographic classification of the millet system. Related data could be found in the millet administrations. The centralizing state, however, sought also to collect its own data and ethnographic insights into what was a highly diverse Anatolian society. From 1913, the CUP party-state was intent on social and demographic engineering; this required an understanding of populations outside the traditional Ottoman categories, including groups outside the *millet*, such as Alevis and Kurds. Before and during the First World War, members of the CUP, therefore, conducted relevant studies while the regime was implementing ethnic cleansing and genocide that sought to Turkify-Islamify Anatolia. The minister of the interior, Talaat, led the demographic remodeling of Anatolia by telegraph from Istanbul.[37] In the first half of 1914, using its armed Special Organization, the CUP organized boycott and terror campaigns against Greek-Orthodox Rûm in Eastern Thrace and the Aegean littoral, during which about 200,000 people were deported to Greece. Expulsion was determined by *millet* membership, in other words, by religion. The Armenian genocide of 1915 primarily concerned the members of the Armenian-Orthodox community (*Ermeni Gregoryen millet*). However, based on ethnoreligious as well as racial logics, it also included recent converts as well as the much smaller numbers of Armenians in the *Protestant milleti* and *Katolik millet*. Due to foreign pressure, exceptions were, however, more frequent in these cases. As was the case for the Jews under Nazi rule, the final decision was not based on any ethnic, or biological, or racial factors, but on former religious registration (in this case going back to the grandparents' generation).

In late 1912, the CUP branded the Armenian appeal to European diplomats an act of high treason. It also resented the Dashnaktsutiun's predictable refusal to join the Special Organization in a (suicidal) guerrilla war against the Russians in the Caucasus in August 1914. When general mobilization began in early August 1914, one ABCFM member observed a government blindly leading its country toward a catastrophe: "Poor Turkey, poor Turkey, going it blindly, with a man at the head of the army, whose name is LIGHT [Enver], but he has certainly turned on the dark slide on his lantern, and is rushing headlong, pell-mell over the precipice, to sure destruction, was there ever such blindness?"[38] CUP officers began to speak openly of the need to destroy the Armenian community although most Ottoman Armenian men served loyally in the army. Enver Pasha's disastrous defeat at Sarıkamış at the end of 1914 and his brother-in-law Cevdet's subsequent unsuccessful campaign in northern Persia led to high levels of casualties, epidemics, and a brutal war on the Eastern Front. Several thousand young Armenians fled to Russian Armenia, most of them becoming volunteers in the Russian army. In the spring of 1915, Ottoman propaganda spread the idea of a general Armenian rebellion that internal military documents do not confirm.

The first Ottoman victory at the Dardanelles on March 18, 1915, saved the Young Turk leaders from depression after these initial defeats. A few months earlier, euphoria had spread among the party-state's elites after a secret alliance with allegedly invincible Germany was concluded on August 2, 1914. The first victory in March 1915 further strengthened the Young Turk leaders' resolve, and fostered, according to the Austrian military attaché Joseph Pomiankowski, a "brutal chauvinism" against the Armenians and Christians in general.[39]

Heading the Special Organization which had lost its main raison d'être after the complete failure of the pan-Turkist "Turan" campaign, Dr. Bahaeddin Şakir returned from Erzurum to the capital for decisive meetings of the CUP Central Committee. On April 24, 1915, security forces began to arrest, torture and murder the Armenian elites in Istanbul, followed by the whole of Anatolia. On the same date, a telegram sent by the minister of the interior, Talaat, to the military governor of Syria, Cemal Pasha, announced that henceforth, Armenians should be deported not to Konya, as had been the case with the Armenians from Zeytun, but to Northern Syria. Using a much more veiled language that did not directly mention the Armenians, a provisional law published on June 1 permitted both the use of force against the population and mass deportations, if "national defense" was at stake. The main removal and deportation of the Armenians from Eastern and Western Anatolia and the province of Edirne toward the Syrian deserts was implemented from June to October 1915. By then, Şakir's Special Organization had found a new, genocidal, raison d'être.[40]

In eastern Anatolia, men and youngsters were mostly massacred on the spot; those in the army were separated into labor battalions and killed. Women and children endured starvation, mass rape and enslavement during the deportation marches. Deportations from the west included men, and the victims were transported partly by train. Several hundred thousand destitute deportees arrived in Syria in summer and autumn of 1915. Ali Fuad, the governor of Deir ez-Zor who attempted to help settle the deportees, was replaced in July 1916 by the hard line Salih Zeki. In contrast to those enduring the Trail of Tears, the Armenian deportees were not resettled as had been promised by the authorities, but isolated in concentration camps and starved to death or massacred. With the exception of approximately 150,000 saved by Cemal Pasha and resettled in Southern Syria after formal conversion to Islam, those who had survived until then in the camps were also massacred.

Widely varying numbers have been proposed, but the most reliable estimate is that more than half of the nearly two million Ottoman Armenians living in the Ottoman Empire in 1914 were killed between 1915 and 1916. International holocaust and genocide scholars from Raphael Lemkin to Yehuda Bauer have called this destruction a defining genocide of the twentieth century.

The ABCFM as a Witness, a Humanitarian, and a Missionary of Evangelical Modernity

Although the ABCFM was antagonistic toward the leaders of the United States in the 1830s, this did not result in its members breaking with the system or with their home country. Many ABCFM members did, however, leave their country—sometimes for three generations—yet continuously kept in touch with parts of the society left behind. The missionaries' encounters with CUP officials in 1915, in contrast, were strained confrontations between opposing systems of reference and cohorts. Elderly Christian missionaries were faced with radical young men of action with openly anti-Christian sentiments.

In 1914, the young CUP leaders of the Ottoman Empire were committed to a total war as allies of Imperial Germany; they believed they were fighting for their political (imperial) survival. In stark contrast, the United States of the 1830s was in control of its progressing Western frontier and by no means threatened in its existence. The destruction of the Armenians was determined within a conspiratorial single-party regime, not a formal democracy as was the case in the United States. The ABCFM members were witnesses to this in both the 1830s and in 1915. In the latter case, however, they were no longer able to identify with—and struggle within—the existing system as they had done under the Tanzimat. After 1908, the ABCFM had renewed its hope in playing a leading role as a force of social progress in a prospering young Turkey. After the CUP's *coup d'état* in January 1913, however, it lost almost all its hope in the government.[41] It no longer believed in any existing rule of law in the Ottoman state. There was therefore no longer a place for public lobbying in the Ottoman capital; no chance of hindering the scheme, as the ABCFM had optimistically attempted (though ultimately failed to achieve) in Washington eighty-five years earlier.

The Americans observed the CUP's rule in action, both in the capital and in the provinces. The observation was particularly detailed in Mamuretülaziz, where it led to the compilation of many detailed reports, including that of a list of fifty-two local perpetrators of the genocide.[42] Henry Riggs, a teacher at the ABCFM's Euphrates Colleges, observed the transit camps of the deportees through a telescope during the summer of 1915; "for most of the women and children," he wrote, "was reserved the long and lingering suffering that massacre seemed to them a merciful fate—suffering such as was foreseen and planned by the perpetrators of this horror. I speak guardedly and state as a fact this horrid indictment of the Young Turks by whom the crime was committed."[43] Another witness was Floyd Smith, a doctor who had been stationed with the ABCFM in Diyarbekir since 1913. Until Dr. Mehmed Reşid's governorship, which began in March 1915, Dr. Smith had enjoyed good relations with the government and Reşid's predecessor, Hamid Kapancızâde.[44]

This changed with the arrival of Reşid and his extremely violent methods:

> By getting a large force of police and gendarmes the new vali [Reşid] succeeded in apprehending the larger part of these men [deserters]. He soon started the imprisonment of prominent Armenians using as justification the false statement that they were sheltering deserters. [. . .] Most people had weapons in their houses in remembrance of the event [pogroms] of twenty years ago, but I feel positive that there was no idea of a general uprising. About the first of April a proclamation was posted demanding arms. Men were imprisoned right and left and tortured to make them confess the presence and place of concealments of arms. Some went mad under the torture.[45]

One such confession concerned an Armenian close to the ABCFM, who was forced to sign an absurd document stating that the organization was preparing an insurrection in Diyarbekir and that Smith, its agent, was an Armenian. The ABCFM's property in the city was seized by the government and Smith deported before the final drama—the straightforward murder of the Christian population, Armenians and Assyrians without removal toward Syria—ensued.

The very rapid deterioration of relations between local functionaries and the ABCFM—which had been present in the eastern provinces, including the province of Diyarbekir for three generations—was a strong indicator of the gravity of the situation. It revealed the new spirit of social Darwinist engineering that Governor Reşid, a former military doctor and CUP emissary, had brought with him to the eastern provinces in 1915. In applying regulations on so-called "abandoned property," Dr. Reşid founded a commission for the administration of the deportees' assets. However, as was the case in other places as well, the commission ignored the goal to protect the property of the deported as declared by regulations, transferring it instead to the state and the Muslim population.[46] Thanks to its experience and its broad network of institutions throughout Asia Minor, the ABCFM understood the comprehensive nature of the party-state's anti-Armenian policy early on. In many places, missionaries were present during the first phase of the Armenian genocide, that is, the massacres and removals in Asia Minor in 1915. This was much less the case during the second phase in 1916, when most of the survivors of the removal were starved to death in Syrian camps, and those remaining were massacred. William Peet, the ABCFM treasurer and informal head of the "Bible House" in Istanbul, was one of the best-informed contemporaries. He stood in close contact not only with the ABCFM and European missionaries in the provinces, but also with members of both the German and the US embassies.[47]

As well as bearing witness to the unfolding events, missionaries on the ground were able to provide both provisional material aid and words of consolation; in some places, such as Mamuretülaziz and Urfa, they helped a number of individuals escape.[48] On July 14, 1915, Peet cabled to Boston that there were many urgent calls, but that the ABCFM relief funds were exhausted. This led to the establishment of a largely ABCFM-based humanitarian organization called Near Eastern Relief (NER) two months later. The NER supported efforts of "humanitarian resistance" in Syria, an underground network initiated by Armenians in Aleppo.[49] In 1916–17, it was led by the Swiss missionary teacher Beatrice Rohner. Support for her also came from the ABCFM, the German *Hilfsbund für christliches Liebeswerk im Orient*, German and American diplomats, as well as Swiss connections in Aleppo and Basel. Protected in part by Cemal Pasha, Rohner built legal orphanages with local Armenians and communicated covertly with the deportees in the camps. She was the only missionary who was able to write an extensive witness account of the second phase of the genocide.[50] Both in 1915 and 1838–9, ABCFM missionaries accompanied victims on their sad journey, although in the case of the Armenians, Mary Graffam was the only missionary who was allowed to do so, and even then only for a period of a few days.[51] Beatrice Rohner followed the deportees separately to Aleppo.

Both in the 1830s and in the 1910s, the ABCFM informed the wider public, lobbied for the victims, and organized humanitarian help using its networks and knowledge. At times, for example during the Balkan Wars in 1912–13, it also lobbied for Muslim victims, though it was in that case unable to rely on a broader public in the West. The NER, too, supported needy Muslims. As an institution that strove for an "evangelical modernity"—a synthesis of Enlightenment, Bible, and Evangelism—the ABCFM generally had a complex relationship to rulers, especially to its own US government. Despite frictions, it enjoyed substantial diplomatic support for its educational, evangelical and humanitarian endeavors in Ottoman Turkey overall. Whether there was friction or collaboration depended on protagonists, periods and places. James Barton, secretary of the ABCFM in the early twentieth century, for example, was much more in line with the US government and American nationalism than Jeremiah Evarts, the leading ABCFM secretary during the struggle against the Indian Removal. Men and women on the ground tended to be more universally-minded than missionary strategists or lobbyists at home. Feelings of Anglo-Saxon superiority and American exceptionality existed among ABCFM members, in particular from the late nineteenth century onward. Nevertheless, this was held in check by a vibrant internationalism and a critical attitude toward all forms of social Darwinism.

Nationalist Modernity—Short-Circuited and Genocidal

Returning to the beginning of the chapter, as Dagobert von Mikusch wrote in the first German biography of Mustafa Kemal (Atatürk), "the exclusion of the Armenians from the body of their [Turkish] state" was for many of von Mikusch's German readers during the interwar period, "no less a constraining necessity than [. . .] was the extermination of the Indians for the new state of the white people in America."[52] This stood in sharp contrast to the views of the American missionaries. Also, many Germans admired Atatürk, the heroized Turkish general-turned-statesman. They envied the Republic of Turkey that they perceived as an emergent radical nation-state—even though they were aware of the violent population politics that had led to a Turkified Anatolia. They felt compelled to conclude that such genocidal population politics were required in order to do away with minority issues and successfully establish a strong, efficient, and healthy, if undemocratic, state.

The Paris Treaties, including Versailles and Sèvres, displayed an unfortunate mix of lofty principles, demands for minority rights, and the imperialistic goals of the victors of the World War. Thus, the idea of an egalitarian, pluralistic society lost traction. The Treaty of Lausanne unmasked this imperial bias: it constituted the choice of a strongman's pact that openly obeyed power, not rights, and thus reinforced the sovereignty of the mighty over a just peace. Germans—and many others—therefore came to believe that a homogeneous nation-state was the only viable future, and that this was incompatible with integrating howsoever defined "aliens" that would weaken its unity. Extermination was a foregone conclusion for social Darwinist minds, if an alleged alien, unassimilable people wanted to live and assert its own identity on its native soil. Leaders of the prevailing majority "rightfully" enforced their exclusive rule by force wherever they could do so.

Even after the Second World War and the Holocaust, a number of Western scholars agreed with Dagobert von Mikusch, stressing "inevitable" cultural clashes and the necessity of implementing "iron laws of modernity" in the case of both the American Indians and the Armenians. They called their fate a "tragedy," not a crime against humanity, as missionaries had done at the time. Guenter Lewy, an American political scientist, denied both the genocide perpetrated by the CUP[53] and any crime against humanity against indigenous Americans. He wrote that:

> In the end, the sad fate of America's Indians represents not a crime but a tragedy, involving an irreconcilable collision of cultures and values. Despite the efforts of well-meaning people in both camps, there existed no good solution to this clash. The Indians were not prepared to give up the nomadic life of the hunter for the sedentary life of the farmer. The new Americans, convinced of their cultural and racial superiority, were unwilling to grant the original inhabitants of the continent the vast preserve of land required by the Indians' way of life.

Such relativizing discourses claim realism and emphasize constraint. They stress arguments of security and survival. The limit of this type of lazy or cynical argument is more than reached when systematic breaches of basic law, and crimes against humanity, take place—as in the cases explored in this chapter. Can the negation of any viable existence for "the other" ever be sincerely pondered against arguments of security and efficiency? When clashes and destruction are declared unavoidable and predetermined, the argumentation exonerates perpetrators from responsibility: it becomes flawed, unethical, and, yes, intellectually lazy.

The extermination of Armenians affected all of Asia Minor and more than ten times the number of people that were impacted by the Indian Removal of the 1830s. More than half of the "removed" Armenians were killed by systematic violence and starvation. They were not resettled as the Cherokees were. Therefore, the Armenian removal was a comprehensive destruction of a targeted ethnoreligious group, a clear-cut case of genocide. By contrast, the Indian Removal was initially "only a relocation." It was nevertheless based on racism and greed. This brutal attitude toward fellow humans predictably produced massive "collateral damage" as well as destructive long-term consequences for the targeted group and its individuals. Describing all this as "necessary" for the establishment of a "state of white people" as Mikusch did, stems from a social Darwinist, narrow-minded understanding of human reality. Similar to the perpetuation of slavery, it severely damaged the constitutionality of the rapidly growing republic, and thus the young country's nascent democratic contract. The establishment of a polity based on an all-encompassing social contract was thus postponed for generations.

While the argument of civilizational backwardness could not be proffered in the case of the Armenians (they were the most eager and successful students of Western education in the Ottoman world), it was used extensively in the case of the American "Indians." Paradoxically, however, it was precisely the "Five Civilized Tribes," which had largely settled down and were economically productive, who were first affected by removal in the 1830s. Beyond all their vindicatory rhetoric, the perpetrators in both cases wanted to accumulate power and riches in their own hands and those of their clientele. They ceded to the temptation of power and greed, and therefore forcibly removed, killed and dispossessed vulnerable people. Such policies seemed to solve troublesome questions of coexistence once and for all. Those responsible were either applauded or tacitly condoned by a majority of the population. If we compare the context of a world war with that of a struggling rising settler republic, we can see that in spite of the difference in scale, handling, outcome, and subsequent historical treatment, there were similarities regarding the key elements.

Twenty years before it was implemented, the Indian Removal would have been seen as completely illegal and an improper topic for public discussion. This changed in the 1820s, when the pressure from the white settlers increased, gold was discovered, and Andrew Jackson became president. Contrary to the Indian Removal, the Armenian removal from Anatolia had never been discussed in advance, at least not publicly. Any public discussion of—or allusion to—such a huge scheme would have been inconceivable in peacetime, and impossible in the CUP's repressive party-state. It would also have been contrary to the doublespeak that the late Ottoman government was accustomed to using when facilitating mass coercion and violence. The fact that his own state infringed upon fundamental rights as part of its more or less normal operations challenged Jeremiah Evarts's faith in America's future. It led him and his missionaries to concentrate their utopian energies on the ABCFM abroad, above all upon the Ottoman "Bible lands." The Cherokee mission, and with it the vision of a modern, prosperous, self-determined future for that part of US society on its ancestral soil, had been a crucial issue. With the failure of the ABCFM's vision for the Cherokee, a particularly sensitive test of modern American millennialism (also labeled millenarism or millenarianism) had failed in the United States itself.

As a result, the ABCFM's millennialist visions for the Ottoman world became all the more important from the 1830s onward.[54] The ABCFM had abandoned the old Puritan idea that America was the "promised land" or new Kanaan from the start. As early as the 1810s, it had set its sights on the Ottoman world as the focal point of the global millennium, including the restoration of a modern Israel by way of "restoring the Jews to Palestine and to Jesus."[55] After a first pioneering yet unsuccessful phase that focused on the Jews, the Armenians became central to the ABCFM's Near Eastern mission. Compared to its Indian mission, this was much more extensive and had an internationalist scope. It included European collaborators and endeavored at times to mobilize an international public. In both cases, attempts at initiating a modern evangelical present based upon human rights failed catastrophically. Nevertheless, this challenging legacy led to a profound questioning of history and its human makers. It exposed the makers' recipes as short-sighted and short-circuited. It left posterity unreconciled with unrepaired, unrecognized historical crimes and the demographic engineering of modern states. Subsequent generations had to revisit the issues in question in order to confront the lasting damages caused by their founding fathers on the road toward national modernity. They were called to repair them, where possible.

Repairing the Future

The ABCFM archives contain accurate reports on what happened during both the Indian Removal and the destruction of the Armenians. They form a crucial archival basis for the historical reconstruction of those events and their contexts. However, after the 1830s and subsequently after the First World War, the ABCFM did not publish much and never really came to terms with the failure of its visions. It experienced painful losses in terms of friends, clients, faithful visions and property, particularly within its Turkish mission. The missionaries' silence was in part due to the limited chances of being heard in an American society that cultivated a culture of victory and success. National exceptionalism and religious triumphalism did not teach how to cope with pervasive, collective loss. For decades, the missionaries' handwritten or typed retrospectives have lingered in archives, waiting for scholars to come and deal with their burning yet almost-forgotten issues. Though belatedly, an impressive number of relevant papers from the ABCFM and other missionary archives were published at the end of the twentieth and in the early twenty-first century.

Utopian or not, biased or not, the ABCFM's voices deserve exploration not only for the richness of their eyewitness reports, but because of their alternative visions for the future. They believed in fundamental and revolutionary changes, while stubbornly opposing violence and war. Accordingly, they resisted any discourse that termed destructive policies "tragedies" and forceful removal "inevitable history." Instead, they identified them as deeds committed by humans in accordance with the interests, conceptions, and (subjective) constraints of majority leaders. ABCFM members drew the strength and motivation for their occasionally risky stance from their belief in the Gospel as well as their embrace of the Enlightenment (not in the French sense, but in a specific Anglo-American Protestant understanding that combined biblical millennialism with modern progress).

While they offered assistance and left important testimonies, they were not able to reverse the outcome of the forceful policies in question. At the post–First World War Peace Conference in Paris in 1919, area expert Clarence Ussher, a former ABCFM missionary in Van, pleaded in vain for the systematic repatriation of Armenian survivors and Kurdish refugees. He and his missionary circle tried everything in order to reestablish a functioning coexistence in the crisis-ridden regions of Eastern Asia Minor.[56] Historical failure does not, however, eliminate the chance of success for a rightful vision in the changed context of a more distant future.

No matter how far in the past, acts of forceful removal or destruction demand responsibility, response, and at least symbolic reparation, that is, a public recognition of truths. We may call this an unmissable human reality and unavoidable justice. If the indigenous Americans "are finally ejected from their patrimonial inheritance by arbitrary and unrighteous power, the people of the United States will be impeached," Evarts had written in 1830. Old truths can often only be openly affirmed much later. Although mixed with pathos and apologetic rhetoric, the official words at the 175th Anniversary of the Bureau of Indian Affairs on September 8, 2000, obey this elementary logic of recognition:

Let us begin by expressing our profound sorrow for what this agency has done in the past. [. . .] On behalf of the Bureau of Indian Affairs, I extend this formal apology to Indian people for the historical conduct of this agency. And while the BIA employees of today did not commit these wrongs, we acknowledge that the institution we serve did. We accept this inheritance, this legacy of racism and inhumanity. And by accepting this legacy, we accept also the moral responsibility of putting things right. [. . .] Never again will we be complicit in the theft of Indian property.

Kevin Gover, Assistant Secretary-Indian Affairs Department of the Interior[57]

In the same vein, a recent American textbook states that "Everyone judges the westward removal of eastern Indians as one of the great injustices in United States history." Future textbooks in Turkey will have to use even stronger terms. The Indian Removal evolved, like the genocidal Armenian removal, in a complex, but rapid manner "from an unthinkable scheme to accepted policy." Acceptance of removal and genocide is a story "of greedy men who lied so convincingly that they themselves came to believe their deceits." In spite of all this, however, there are also stories, albeit muted, of people who risked "their lives and reputations for decency and justice."[58]

Islamic Empire and the Politics
of Societal Massacre

When religion offers an incentive to commit violent acts, killing and death appear as ultimately meaningful. Violence, in these circumstances, becomes an affirmation of identity, that is, a confession of faith and belonging. When, at the same time, there exists a lack of faith in a viable political project, violence can become the ultimate act of self-affirmation through killings and, possibly, self-immolation. The "Islamic State" (IS; or Islamic State of Iraq and Syria, ISIS) is a particularly blatant twenty-first-century example of an organization that makes such connections between religion, violence, and death—in this case labeling them "jihad." Its credo can be summed up as "I kill therefore I am (neco, ergo sum), and even more so if I die."[1] The IS drew explicitly on certain Islamic as well as modern Islamist tenets, but it also emerged as a reaction to the neo-conservative US invasion of Iraq. Whether directly experienced or merely feared, Western power had, since Napoleon's invasion of Egypt, served as a pretext for intra-societal violence against indigenous non-Muslims, who were seen as agents of hostile global powers.

The war in Syria in the 2010s has been an extremely violent phenomenon. A civil war with various changing domestic fronts, it has, since its beginning in 2011, become the scene of an international struggle involving most of the main regional and global powers. Together with neighboring Iraq, Syria at war has displayed a new and deep Sunni–Shiite divide and given room to the extremist eschatological experience of a self-declared Islamic state. During the 2010s, Turkey, the West's North Atlantic Treaty Organization (NATO) partner, has turned to domestic authoritarianism under the dominant AKP party (the *Adalet ve Kalkınma Partisi* or Justice and Development Party, led by Recep Tayyip Erdoğan), and to a political Sunni Islam tinged by neo-Ottomanism. Since 2016, it has been teaching the virtues of jihad in its schools. Such neo-imperial confessionalism has determined AKP Turkey's active partisanship on the side of Islamist forces during the war.

These recent events have considerably altered not only the Levant,[2] but the rest of the world as well. Fundamental historical reconsiderations regarding these formerly Ottoman core lands are required to acknowledge the real power and significance of religion throughout their history, including the entire modern era. The modern Levant's most violent period was the final decade of the Ottoman Empire (1912–22), which included the Balkan Wars, the First World War, genocide, internationalized civil wars, and massive refugee issues, many of them consequences of deliberate ethnoreligious cleansing. Analogous violent patterns continued to haunt the region in various guises after the results of a decade of extreme violence were endorsed by the Lausanne Treaty of 1923. This treaty constituted the diplomatic foundation of a precarious reorganization of the former Ottoman world and a supposed solution to the notorious "Eastern Question" in modern European diplomacy (see Chapter 5).

This chapter concentrates on two related issues: domestic jihad in late Ottoman and post-Ottoman times, and the more general connection between public violence, religion, and eschatology. Faith-fueled public violence has been a prominent feature in the modern Levant since the eighteenth century. At this time, the Ottoman Empire was still vast, stretching from Anatolia and the Balkans to the South Caucasus, Iraq, greater Syria, the Arabian peninsula, and North Africa. In contrast to contemporary states in, or originating in, Europe, or to Russia (its most feared and most hated adversary), the Ottoman Empire lost territory and could expand neither continentally nor through colonies or frontiers. In religious, ethnic, and linguistic terms, its core lands were more diverse than those of any other contemporary empire—imbued with a unique depth of thousands of years of written history, and with a monotheist eschatology on the revelation of final futures permeating its biblical, Koranic, Hadithic—Sunni and Shiite—geography. Combined with ideologies such as Islamism and Zionism, these circumstances have made the late and post-Ottoman world a modern global hotspot of unresolved conflicts that have produced a theater of violence with global ramifications.

In line with the whole book, this chapter argues that modern coexistence among different groups is not viable without democratic social contracts. However, stark communitarian and eschatological traditions have particularly prevailed in the modern Levant, aborting any sustained efforts at establishing such contracts based on egalitarian relations. Even those states and movements that sidelined political Islam, such as Kemalism (the founding ideology of the Republic of Turkey under Mustafa Kemal Atatürk), could only do so for restricted periods of time, and without achieving societal peace. Divisive Muslim, Christian, and Jewish eschatologies provide religious visions of an ultimate future, thus adding to the sense of incommensurate existence—although the pragmatics of life call for a decent, contracted coexistence. Yet, successful pragmatics depend upon viable tenets of faith in political philosophy, theology, and eschatology.

This chapter starts with a general introduction, followed by sections on public violence and eschatology, the "Eastern Question" and its connection to violence against Ottoman Christians, and a close focus on the Levant's most violent decade— the 1910s—followed by the Kemalist era. In the early twenty-first century, the Levant, including Turkey and Israel, saw a strong resurgence of politico-religious forces, sectarian developments, and eschatological currents. Both Kemalism and Labor Zionism had only seemingly overcome the political force of traditional religion.[3]

Social Contract, Prophetic Monotheism, and Public Violence

Welcoming acts of public violence and viewing them as justifiable human behavior is not a matter of course. Human decency, shame, and empathy are key barriers.

Overcoming them requires incentives that draw on a combination of perceived danger, entrenched social conditions, and religion. Violence that is publicly committed and justified has been a frequent occurrence in the modern Levant from the late eighteenth century to the present day. Like the notorious lynching violence endemic in parts of the United States, it remained largely unpunished and repeated itself in various ways. Lynching cost the lives of thousands of African Americans in the United States from the late eighteenth century onward; domestic jihad in the Levant was even deadlier, claiming the lives of many hundreds of thousands of non-Muslim civilians.

The question here therefore concerns displays of public violence actively participated in by leaders who resort to politico-religious arguments as a means of justifying their actions. Such violence is generally tolerated by state authorities and at times state-organized. There exists a type of pact between the public, the perpetrators, and the state that incites and tacitly encourages or tolerates violence. It relies on a consensus regarding what constitutes a threat toward the state's main community; that is, the Islamic *ummah*, the seminal community of faith that, according to Koranic tradition, forms the center of any legitimately ruled polity. Thus, we are confronted not primarily with military aggression but with patterns of intra-societal or domestic violence implemented along politico-religious lines.

What are those lines, and what do they signify? Why has the Levant not been reorganized by modern social contracts to the same extent as other regions of the world, while premodern, hierarchical arrangements in the Ottoman world were comparatively effective in maintaining internal peace? Such profound historical questions can only be responded to rudimentarily here; however, my general, tentative answers are simple: the Levant is the cradle of monotheism and therefore the focus of powerful eschatological projections. These have overruled or mitigated modern constitutional precepts that, in turn, had previously delegitimized premodern agreements.

Beginning with the Ottoman Tanzimat ("rearrangement" or "reform" state) in 1839–76, the modern states in the Levant launched a series of failed attempts at establishing constitutional patriotism and civil religion by means of functioning, modern social contracts. This failure is not least due to the fact that the challenge was greater than elsewhere. The Ottoman Empire's premodern hierarchical fabric allowed non-Muslim communities a high degree of non-territorial religious and cultural autonomy. Modern egalitarian plurality was not, however, facilitated by regional differentiation. In other historically diverse and regionalized polities such as in Switzerland, for example, geography reflected and protected recognized ethnoreligious differences. The Ottoman *millet* system (concerning subordinate Christian and Jewish Ottoman communities, so-called *millet*), and the religious hierarchies of the Koran from which it was deducted, presented further obstacles in establishing equality within a socially pluralistic context. Moreover, the centralist state tradition of the late Ottoman capital, emulated by most post-Ottoman rulers, did not allow for true regionalization.

Constitutional "Ottomanism," a concept that aimed, generally speaking, to establish democratic unity among the diverse population of the empire, only enjoyed limited currency; it mainly prevailed among small parts of the late Ottoman state elites and among non-Sunni groups who, as minoritarians, had a high interest in equality and legal security. Weak constitutionalism went hand in hand with the ongoing political relevance of religious rifts and prejudices. Under these circumstances, peace did not stand a real chance.

Entrenched in divisive premodern language, eschatological expectations remained strong, even more due to the fact that the Levant represents the central stage for both biblical and Koranic eschatology. Such resilience in eschatological expectations also applies to Turkey and Israel, two post-Ottoman countries that, in Kemalism and Zionism, held seemingly strong secular ideologies. The predominance of Kemalist and Zionist secularism did not, however, last far beyond the second third of the twentieth century. It was propagated by leaders who drew on national salvation narratives and religious sources: David Ben-Gurion, the "modern father of Israel," with his Zionist reading of the Hebrew Bible on one hand, and Ziya Gökalp with his messianic interpretation of Islam and Turkish ethnohistory (the latter fully adopted by Atatürk) on the other. In the 1910s, Gökalp, the prophet of Muslim-Turkish greatness during the First World War and the pre-eminent spiritual father of Turkish nationalism, blended the force of political Islam with a new sort of ethnic ultranationalism called pan-Turkism (see Chapter 9).

Ethnoreligious social unrest stood at the center of the modern West's "Eastern Question." A major diplomatic issue that included the challenging crisis affecting the Ottoman sultan-caliph's realm, it ultimately revealed the limitations of contemporary Western methods in establishing modern polities in the Levant. From the late eighteenth century onward, leading Western statesmen and observers questioned the future of a premodern, slowly reforming Islamic realm. Contrary to the wishful diplomatic thinking that followed the Lausanne Treaty and the foundation of the Republic of Turkey in 1923, the Eastern Question was not resolved with the end of the Ottoman Empire. It had started with struggles for independence in the Balkans (moving from Serbia and Greece to Bulgaria and finally Macedonia) and culminated in the Armenian Question and the genocide of the 1910s. Neither limiting itself to Western conspiracies nor to notions of despotism and violence as a necessary means of establishing an Islamic Orient, it essentially concerned open questions regarding rules for a functioning society, both in the Levant and further afield. Although Western technical know-how was in high demand from the eighteenth century onward, the image of an often brutally expanding West did not inspire faith among the Ottomans, instead encouraging many of them to revert to their own premodern tenets and structures.

Repeated failed attempts at establishing social peace are tantamount to a matrix of violence. The apocalyptic mood conveyed by late Ottoman Islamic scholars from the eighteenth century onward ran in conjunction with invocations for an improved imperial era and for the supposed "restoration" of an ancient Sunni-Orthodox social order. The belief that the perceived domestic enemies of the endangered imperial order had to be eliminated for the salvation of a state considered symbiotic with religion (*din ü devlet*) was not only held by extremists but also by mainstream Sunni Muslims, the community closest to the Ottoman state. If the authorities did not, or could not, act in an acute crisis, religion demanded pre-emptive and punitive public violence to be exerted *intra muros* by locally organized male mosque-goers. The "infidel's" (*gavur, kafir's*) blood was declared halal, and mass murder was deemed an act of heroism and salvation. Most instances of such recurrent intra-social attacks were associated with vociferous *tekbîr/takbîr*, the invocation of God ("God is greatest"), and at times also with references to the sultan-caliph. Islamic terminology, the rejection of European modernity, and the social envy of Christian neighbors concurred in frequent social upheavals that took the form of pogroms.

Significant examples of these upheavals include the large-scale public slaughter of Armenians under Sultan Abdulhamid II, particularly in 1895, when almost 100,000 victims were killed between October and December.[4] In the late 1870s, Abdulhamid had reacted against military defeat and Europe-backed reforms that, in his eyes, weakened the state. He promoted a politics of Islamic unity—a kind of Muslim nationalism or late Ottoman Islamism—that contemporaries fittingly termed "pan-Islamism," as he himself had emphasized its global dimension. He regarded Muslim unity as the only viable and coherent force against increasing Western influences and centrifugal tendencies within the empire. If we leave aside the devastating impact of reactionary violence, it is true that non-Muslims benefited disproportionately from Western commercial, diplomatic, missionary, educative, and philanthropic penetration of the late Ottoman world. Yet this boom was not the political conspiracy that Abdulhamid's propaganda claimed it was, but rather resulted from the *zimmis*'[5] readiness and will to escape subalternity and participate in nineteenth-century globalization.

In autumn 1895, the soldiers of the garrison in Erzincan tied Korans to their standards and entered the city, demanding that the Armenians be exterminated and the sharia implemented.[6] Though Abdulhamid called for, formed, and empowered modern Islamist enthusiasms, he was not able to fully control them. Urban mob violence, organized in mosques, together with some regional gang and tribal violence directed against villages, played the main role in the 1895 massacres. Such perpetrators of unofficial domestic jihad claimed they were fighting foreign evil and were not fully controlled by the central authorities. Yet they were influenced by an empire-wide parallel structure of religious figures affiliated to the palace that Abdulhamid had established alongside the official administration. They all conjured up the specter of Western and Armenian rule over eastern Asia Minor, resulting from reforms wanted by Europe and non-Sunnis of the region. Jihad was declared by local religious leaders who claimed to do so in the name of the sultan-caliph. At times, local instigators defied the sultan, accusing him of being too pliable when confronted by foreign intrusion and unable to reassert his forefathers' exercise of power in times of Ottoman glory.[7]

Unrest against non-Muslim minorities, including Yezidis and Alevis, has remained a powerful weapon and a trademark of militant Islam in the Levant. A tradition of explicit Islamist throat-cutting of civilians who have been declared disloyal unbelievers runs from the nineteenth to the twenty-first century. As already alluded to, tens of thousands of mostly Armenian men and youngsters were killed, sometimes by their own neighbors, over the course of only a few weeks in autumn 1895. These acts of mass murder, spoliation, and rape were perpetrated by a large Sunni male population that had organized in the local mosques of towns in central and eastern Asia Minor, supported or vociferously backed by women. Tribes sometimes joined in the violence or spread it further into rural areas. Violence was declared sacred and salutary; killing and robbing became a festival, a competition even. In contrast to the genocide of 1915, however, Christians were able to save themselves by converting to Islam; during the First World War, this was only the case in particular circumstances.

Eschatology and Violence

The eschatology rooted in Ottoman history calls for an imperial, state-centered restoration and for a strong leader (*reis*) who is able to establish absolute power. This *reis* is seen to symbolize a mythical world conqueror (*sahib-kırân*) in the manner of Muhammad and the conquering sultan-caliphs. More recently, however, especially in the latter half of the twentieth century, other Muslim eschatologies have come to the forefront; influenced by the seminal Egyptian author Sayyid Qutb, and consistent with other violent eschatological traditions, they anticipate and strive for the breakdown of existing states and societies. Quoting holy scriptures and theologies or ideologies of salvation, this type of Muslim, Christian, Jewish, or secular apocalypse attempts to violently enforce the eschatological reign of God, creating a divinely ordained society, or *societas perfecta*, on Earth. Extreme violence and ruthlessness against perceived enemies serve to confirm the group's own—supposedly rightful—authority and to take a leap toward the exalted future. There is no stronger recent example of this than the actions of IS in Iraq and Syria in the 2010s, an utterly eschatological enterprise whose killings were choreographed as a service of worship in front of the local population as well as a global online audience. Though limited to a local public, analogous patterns were present during the massacres in 1895.

Since the eighteenth century, various agents have been projecting eschatology into the Levant from the West. Protestant American missionaries in particular believed in peace-centered (post-millennialist) and at times violent (pre-millennialist) visions that fueled their lasting engagement on late Ottoman territory. They linked their visions to Jesus's kingdom on Earth, and initially also to the quest for "Israel's restoration," that is, the restoration of the Jews to Palestine and therefore to Jesus. Often acting independently from home country governments, and emphatically non-violent in their actions, they were nevertheless perceived as agents of a threatening, malevolent Western Christianity. Their unanimous support for constitutionalism reinforced reactionary forces that were convinced of a general conspiracy against Islamic rule and sovereignty. There were conflicts between missionaries and oriental (Armenian, Greek, Arab, and Assyrian) Christians, most acutely in the 1830s and 1840s. They mostly involved representatives of the *millet* hierarchy who feared radical changes. However, these conflicts never escalated into general violence, and they lost their virulence toward the end of the nineteenth century.

Although they were perceived as subversive forces, missionaries and other foreigners were rarely in danger under Ottoman rule; they were supported by protective home countries that were able to pressure the Ottoman government, if required. It was a different situation for Ottoman non-Muslims, however, especially for groups such as the Armenians, Assyrians, and Yezidis, who, though in friendly contact with foreigners, were not backed by another home country. Perceived and devalued as "others" outside the *ummah* and as agents of foreign powers, while often socially envied, they became the preferred targets of public violence throughout and beyond the late Ottoman era. This violence climaxed in the cataclysmic final decade of the Ottoman Empire (1912–22). One of the main frontlines during the Ottoman First World War was the interior. Condoned by major sections of society and perceived by many perpetrators as jihad, state-led violence then resulted in the removal and extermination of the majority of Ottoman Christians. Inspired by a political messianism called Turanism (a mix of pan-Turkism and pan-Islamism), the ruling Young Turks party, known as the Committee of Union and Progress (CUP), thus brought the process of othering in the late Ottoman era to the apex of genocide.

The main instances of internal violence in late Ottoman politics paid off, in that they made the perpetrators rich in terms of goods and power, even though they remained politically insecure. This is particularly true for the massacres in 1895 and the genocide in 1915 when, besides confiscations by the state, many local Muslims enriched themselves with spoils from their Armenian neighbors. Many patterns of violence therefore appeared to be functional and invited analogous acts in the future. As a rule, it was not only central or local authorities that profited from them but also the collaborators and bystanders that stood behind the proactive perpetrators on the ground.

Many contemporaries considered the removal and murder of the Armenians in 1915–16 an unprecedented, countrywide state crime. After the Lausanne Treaty of 1923, however, the international allure and prestige of Turkey's modernist "national revolution" meant that these violent policies remained not only free of sanctions but that their appeal spread beyond the post-Ottoman world. Right-wing revisionists, especially in interwar Germany (Ottoman Turkey's ally in 1914–18), admired Turkey's diplomatic success, its radical politics, and its unashamed, transformative use of internal conflict. The victors of the First World War condoned this stance when they abandoned the elementary demands for justice and, through the Lausanne Treaty, ceded to most of Turkey's demands concerning the treatment of minorities (see Chapter 5).

Ankara's demands in Lausanne included unrestricted Turkish power over Asia Minor; a complete silence regarding the Armenian genocide with no prosecutions and reparations; and a compulsory so-called population exchange to which a disproportionately high number of non-Muslims were submitted. Lausanne thus established peace for a high price that mortgaged the future. The victors of the First World War were led to believe that their appeasing diplomacy constituted unavoidable *realpolitik*. In reality, instead of establishing a stable postwar era, this last treaty of the post–Great War Paris treaty system had the effect of corroding international politics and laying the ground for violence to come. In former parts of the Ottoman Empire, the "divide and rule" practices of the interwar period's mandatory regimes similarly failed to contribute to social contracts beyond religious and partisan bounds. As a result of the course set in Lausanne in 1923, equality, suprareligious political thought, and inclusive institutions have remained a utopian challenge. Imperial and eschatological myths relate to age-old religious discords and continue to pervade a highly fractured human geography. Here, promises of apocalyptical fulfillment and of a paradise for "martyrs" live on. While Cold War politics heavily impacted the Levant, the ideological influence of the Cold War was limited in the region.

Dying while partaking in jihad is, historically speaking, the most commonly accepted form of publicly becoming a *shahid/şehit* ("martyr") in Sunni and Shiite Islam. The condensed credo "I kill (in faith), therefore I am (a believer)—even more so, if I die" is reminiscent of propagandistic European First World War theologies that helped transform millions of humans into killers in the name of God and the nation. The management of violence and death is a powerful weapon that helps to establish authority and controls hegemonic relations along the lines of race, class, party, religion, and empire. Life thrives in societies where killing is not an (implicitly) accepted political tool—where social contracts enable common prosperity and the law is in force to diminish personal and party power that depends upon coercion and violence. If being killed while killing is believed to be endorsed by God, this opens the door for abuse of faithful people by power strategists. The common consumption and/ or perpetration of violence creates a compelling communion in crime that establishes or reestablishes the identity of the group in question—like in the case of a militant *ummah* in the 1890s, and again during the First World War.

This aspect, the affirmation of an active Sunni identity, was present in all anti-Alevi urban pogroms in Turkey in the second half of the twentieth century.[8] Recurrent anti-Alevi violence in Turkey is characterized by proud affirmations of Sunni and radical right-wing Turkish identity. Such violence is particularly serious in the case of Kurdish Alevis.[9] The heterodox group of Arab Alawis in Syria—although historically different from the Alevis and less brutally persecuted—experienced a similar history of discrimination before being positively discriminated under the French Mandate and the Baath regime. These divisions fundamentally shaped the civil war in Syria in the 2010s.

Western Aggression and Domestic Jihad

The public use and consumption of violence became utterly manifest in former core Ottoman Arab territories occupied by IS. The global scale of the spectacle, which was not only played out in front of crowds of local spectators but also on the internet, accompanied by discourses of eschatological Wahhabism, was a new phenomenon.[10] Although patterns of public violence in the same geography were present to a much greater extent during the First World War, they were never globally visible. Moreover, eschatology and holy scriptures did not serve as a public endorsement of political acts to the same degree as with twenty-first-century jihadists.

There is an interrelation between domestic jihad against Ottoman non-Muslims and the expansion of modern Europe's imperial nation-states. Imperialist Europe did little to inspire democracy and genuine interest in spreading the rule of law. Europe's Eastern Question began to emerge in the late eighteenth century; from the mid-nineteenth century onward, it centered around postulates of suprareligious constitutional rule. The inclusion of the Ottoman Empire in the "European concert" of monarchical powers in the mid-nineteenth century did not have the desired positive impact on the Ottoman world. Despite new departures and comparatively groundbreaking constitutional texts such as the Reform Edict of 1856 and the first Ottoman constitution of 1876 (revised in and after 1908), egalitarian plurality during the Tanzimat remained a utopia. Sultan Abdulhamid II's Islamist authoritarianism drew the course in the opposite direction, with the CUP deviating even further during the final decade of the Ottoman Empire.

Diversity, as well as legal and actual equality, posed a particularly difficult challenge; the Ottoman realm could not be divided into democratic homelands and imperial dominions, as was the case with the national empires of modern Europe. While their European homelands were ethnically and religiously relatively homogeneous, the legal standards of Western Europe did not count in the mixed colonies. Thus, the Levant exposed the challenges and dysfunctions of human societies on the threshold of global modernity more directly than did contemporary European states, or states originating in Europe and acting on a global scale, such as the United States, Canada, and Australia. In their periphery, the latter could more easily disguise violent anti-egalitarian patterns that violated human rights.

In many cases, modern Europe continued to follow premodern premises, such as royal rights of conquest and land grab. This led to lawless frontiers, military government, and discrimination against indigenous people overseas—a stark contrast to the modern rule of equal law in their European home countries. Lynching, as well as slavery and discriminatory post-slavery structures in US-American culture, were fundamental features of a racially biased society. In the United Kingdom, a combination of proletarian misery, the transport of convicts and children to Australia, and a pervasive, deep-seated race and class mentality contradicted modern human rights. Many of these phenomena can be subsumed under imperialism and colonialism. Colonial and settler violence took place within "democracies" that excluded entire domestic groups from equality, and thus from a core principle of democracy.

There was still, however, the experience of (relatively) democratic rule of law and freedom at home, far from colonial frontiers. This was an important distinction between the late Ottoman Empire and Western Europe, where a considerable number of Ottoman political refugees found asylum. Rule of law took basic human rights seriously in core institutions, parliamentary debates, and domestic public spaces. This positive experience served as an essential historical connection for renewal in post–World War Europe because it allowed well-known principles to be reclaimed. In the late Ottoman Empire, by contrast, this was not the case, even in its capital and the parliament. The same is true for post-Ottoman states in general. Following the footsteps of the CUP, they have largely functioned as repressive partisan regimes in which favoritism, systemic corruption, and (self-)censure rule.

The modern, post-American and post-French Revolution era coincided with an acute and permanent Ottoman crisis in which local and geostrategic dimensions were entangled as never before. New scenes of violence erupted when international stakes were invested in Cairo during the French invasion of Egypt and of parts of greater Syria at the end of the 1790s. French aggression and repression of resistance led to the rise of urban mob violence against Ottoman Christians based on being equated with a foreign power. This was locally declared a jihad and was henceforth a pattern to be repeated in other contexts. Conjuring up real or imaginary foreign threats, and without foreign intervention, ringleaders organized such domestic warfare in other Ottoman towns such as Aleppo and Diyarbekir, where Ziya Gökalp grew up, as well as in metropolises such as Istanbul, Izmir, and Beirut. Violence against Ottoman Christians was henceforth more than just a case of "collateral damage" or a facet of "normal violence" which it might already have been regarded as in late-eighteenth-century Cairo: it became built into the fabric of late Ottoman society. In March 1800, the Ottoman general Nasif Pasha called on Muslims to make jihad against Christians; the targets of these killings were the Ottoman Copts and Syriacs of Cairo, who were considered members of a global body of hostile Christianity.

Late Ottoman public violence was intimate; it often targeted neighbors and even friends who were seen to have broken a contract of submission and loyalty. When, after an 1850 anti-Christian pogrom in Aleppo, a contemporary Arab writer reported that there was no Muslim in those neighborhoods "who did not commit these atrocities; not even ten per cent out of one hundred," he may have slightly exaggerated—or he may not.[11] In many late Ottoman crises, religious categories and polarization proved strong enough to blur the lines between Ottoman and European Christians. At times, this category included groups that were considered local Christian allies, such as the Alevis or the Yezidis. Stigmatized as heretics, these groups were also targeted and more brutally excluded from interacting with the *ummah* than the Christians.

The new dimension of late Ottoman violence went against traditional codes, transcended traditional factions, and included public violations of women. The resulting misogynistic trends far exceeded premodern discrimination against women, including the tradition of *cariye* (devalued non-Muslim female slaves). Similar incidents to those that occurred in Cairo in 1800, as described above, also happened in areas far from Europe where no attacks on Ottoman territory were involved. Ottoman Christians, and, on a lesser scale, the much smaller group of Ottoman Jews, were at risk of being openly targeted by violence as soon as egalitarian reforms were broached. The reforms were fought and lobbied for by well-organized groups, most notably the Ottoman Armenians. An additional factor to religious hierarchy in society and of anti-Christian violence was social envy in response to the economic and educational successes of the *zimmi* and the desire for revenge instigated by leaders facing diplomatic pressure or military defeats against "Christian" (European) powers. Such resentment served as an argument in many pogroms. Both the anti-Armenian massacres that occurred in 1909 and 1895 and the genocide of 1915 took place following important instances of European diplomatic support for egalitarian reforms (see Chapter 4).

In the late Ottoman era, an increasing number of Western nationals had begun to live in Ottoman towns close to non-Muslim neighborhoods, establishing new networks in business, diplomacy, health, and education. As a result, Levantine Christians and Jews were not only able to advance their own personal careers but also to improve life within their communities (*millet*) in terms of education, health, and autonomous administration. Starting in 1839, the liberal reforms of the Tanzimat, most notably the 1856 Reform Edict, made these developments and, with them, a high degree of organized diversity possible. The millets, above all the Armenian Protestant and the Armenian apostolic communities, became, in a nutshell, non-territorial parliamentarian systems within the empire. Late Ottoman public violence was, within the context of these developments, generally perpetrated in defense of a premodern empire and its pre-reform hierarchical social order. Jihad against perceived domestic enemies and the looting of property were endorsed by a widespread understanding of sharia; hate speech was combined with the discourse of a sultanate-caliphate in urgent need of militant defense against traitors and "unbelievers" within the empire.

From a global perspective, late Ottoman, predominantly Sunni public violence thus constitutes a reaction to the loss of power by a dominant group that still possessed considerable regional means of force against potential domestic opponents. Mob violence utilized terror in compensation for weaknesses on other levels. Yet these forces made both regional and central rulers susceptible to blackmail by local factions. Using unauthorized violence at times, these factions not only threatened minorities but also foreign representatives, thus creating diplomatic conflicts. The authorities were responsible for law, order, and security, particularly when it came to protecting foreigners. In critical times, such as in 1895, and during the comparable, though more limited, massacres of Armenians in Adana in 1909, they concentrated on protecting foreigners while at the same time allowing local perpetrators time slots during which they were free to kill, rape, and loot the property of local Christians.

Another poignant chapter in the history of modern Middle Eastern violence involves forced conversions, including the dangerous and painful ad hoc circumcisions of men. These acts of humiliation were intended as public displays of the supposed superiority of Islam. The targets of such coerced conversions were not limited to the mostly provincial Christians, but included Alevis and Yezidis. The Yezidis were subject to a related military campaign in the 1890s. The genocide of Yezidis conducted by ISIS in 2014–17 also included forced conversions. It mirrored the Ottoman campaigns and utilized age-old stigmatizing discourse.

The people were conditioned to accept the late Ottoman massacres and the genocide of 1915—which included large-scale spoliation—via a combination of Islamist discourse, social envy, and impunity for murder and robbery. The state tolerated, promoted, and organized such violence while empowering Muslims and granting them preferential treatment. Many Ottoman Muslim refugees (*muhacir*) from the Balkans and the Caucasus were settled on the land and in houses that had belonged to Ottoman Christians. Public discourse justified such privileges as compensation for imperial losses and for a supposed supreme Muslim suffering in the modern age. These policies, along with a sense of Muslim victimhood, derived from a sweeping interpretation of the modern age: evil, anti-Muslim European designs that began in the eighteenth century had peaked during the First Balkan War, while the Western press and scholarship suppressed positive contributions to human civilization by Muslims and Turks.

The Most Violent Decade (1912–22) and Kemalism

A decisive new factor in the politics of internal conflict under the CUP in the 1910s was the interplay of domestic jihad with a new, radical Turkism that the dictatorial CUP leadership adopted on the eve of the First World War.[12] It complemented Abdulhamid's Islamism (Hamidism), generating a modern national identity based on Islam and "Turkishness." The CUP regarded Hamidism as reactionary and therefore unfit for the exercise of modern imperial power. Turkism, on the other hand, strove for Turkish salvation by embracing Turkish roots and seeking expansion into a huge Central Asian motherland it called "Turan." It promised to make Asia Minor a sovereign Turkish homeland governed and inhabited exclusively by Muslim Turks, to the exclusion of other groups rooted in the same soil. While Islamism warranted support in the provinces, Turkism provided the CUP with the backing of large parts of Istanbul's intelligentsia and with power on the streets of the capital through students and organized parts of the populace.

The main prophet of Islamist Turkism in the 1910s was Ziya Gökalp; Istanbul's predominant political leader at the time was his friend Mehmet Talaat (Pasha). After 1913, the Turkists' ideology of war and violence stood in stark contrast to the hopeful promise of democratic equality, multicultural synergy, and pragmatic collaboration that had emerged during the Ottoman spring following the Young Turk Revolution of July 1908. This vision had turned into a bloody dystopia within just a few years. Political infighting and Talaat's disillusionment with parliamentarism, coupled with continued territorial losses and hostile European diplomacy, all contributed to the CUP's embrace of war and violence. The European powers did not actively maintain Ottoman integrity despite the promises of the 1878 Berlin Treaty. Thus, the constitutional ideals of 1908 that had valued hitherto discriminated groups and made the Armenian Revolutionary Federation (the main Armenian party) their political ally were hastily abandoned by Talaat and his followers.

The dynamics of the Ottoman descent into violence began with the Balkan Wars, which in turn coincided with the reemergence of the conflict concerning the Berlin Treaty's reforms for eastern Asia Minor in 1912–14.[13] The political atmosphere made it easy for detractors to denounce internationally monitored, egalitarian reforms as anti-Ottoman, anti-Sunni conspiracies. Ottoman warfare became a factor in the cataclysm that hit wider Europe in July 1914. Culminating in the genocide of 1915–16, it ended provisionally when the post–Great War wars in Asia Minor were decided in 1922. Seen from Istanbul, the political situation had already been polarized by Italy's invasion of Ottoman Libya in the autumn of 1911, reinforcing the age-old lines of "Europe versus the Orient," and "Christians against Muslims." The First Balkan War in autumn 1912 entrenched these lines even more. Heavy losses in this war made the CUP leadership resentful against Christians in general, both at home and further afield. It is important to note, however, that Talaat's acceptance of war and domestic polarization on the eve of the First Balkan War in September and early October 1912 had been his own choice. The weak performance of the liberal-conservative cabinet in power during the war played into the hands of the future putschists.

In 1913, the CUP installed the first imperial single-party regime of the twentieth century, almost four years before the Bolsheviks. Domestically at a nadir after the temporary success of an anti-CUP coup in July 1912, they embraced the hazardous politics of war and a putsch, managing to establish their regime after their own coup in January 1913. In 1914, they set about combining the politics of imperial restoration and expansion with comprehensive demographic engineering and a right-wing revolutionary transformation of society. By establishing a Muslim war *ummah*, the CUP secured a safe support base for its radical regime. Unprecedented in Levantine history, internal violence, organized or instigated by authorities, took the lives of over a million Armenians and Assyrians in 1915–16. These events included widespread routine torture and mass killings (in contrast to 1895, the latter occurred more frequently outside of towns, albeit not exclusively), the routine rape of countless Christian women and children, the mass starvation of hundreds of thousands of deported Armenians, and the trading of children and women at slave markets in towns across Mesopotamia.

In 1922, following an extremely violent decade, Kemalism—named after the former CUP general, Mustafa Kemal Atatürk, who after 1918 had become the decisive leader—was established as the favored brand of radical Turkish nationalism. Having also shifted its focus from Talaat onto the new leader and the Ankara-based Republic, Gökalpian Turkism in turn rapidly established its dominance after 1923. It repudiated political Islam, and instead emphasized Gökalp's ethnonationalist tenets. However, Kemal's decisive War of (Turkish-Muslim) Independence in 1919–22 was fought together with Sunni Kurds in the name of Islam. Allied to the Bolsheviks, the early Kemalist movement cooperated with late Ottoman political Islam to win the war for Asia Minor, before rejecting it in favor of a radical and exclusive Turkism. The brusque rejection of political Islam won Turkey the sympathy of the West and also pleased Soviet Russia. Yet the break suppressed any serious soul-searching regarding previous instances of jihad and genocide. Decades later, this unclarified history facilitated the return of Islamism. Post-1918 attempts at making a break with extreme violence, including trials against perpetrators and a few attempts at public ostracism, failed within only two years.

Those responsible for the anti-Christian violence in the final decade of the Ottoman Empire therefore remained in power at almost all levels of the post-Ottoman administration, except at the head of the state itself. For decades, the perpetrators, their successors, and their spokesmen in the new capital Ankara continued to perpetuate the rhetoric of CUP propaganda by rationalizing the CUP's use of violence as self-defense. Even though the context had changed, late Ottoman patterns of violence and their public justification played a significant part in the formation of the Republic of Turkey. Echoes of the Armenian genocide could be felt in the military campaign of 1937–8 that killed more than 12,000 civilians in the Alevi Kurdish region of Dersim and transferred surviving children from one group to the other. In the second half of the twentieth century, acts reminiscent of the 1895–6 anti-Armenian pogroms, albeit not on the same scale, were perpetrated against Alevis on the basis of their supposed heresy and communism.

Talaat and most CUP Central Committee members understood the First World War as a jihad for the sake of establishing Turkish power.[14] In their view, the violence between 1911 and 1922 was perpetrated in defense of the Islamic empire, the state, and as a last sovereign resort for Turkish-speaking Muslims in Asia Minor. It was expansionist, combining a seemingly constitutional parliamentary rule with an aggressive party dictatorship inspired by Gökalp's pan-Turkism, built on Islam's supposed supremacy. Skeptical of Islam, Kemalism attempted to base its own authority on a pseudo-scientific "Turkish History Thesis" that claimed ethnohistorical "Turkishness" as the cradle of human language and civilization, supposedly native to Anatolia since prehistoric times. The sociopolitical conclusion was similar: Turkishness was supreme, and non-Turks, *a fortiori* non-Muslims, had no claim to and no equal rights in Anatolia.

Despite their defeat in the First World War, the main players saw the violent removal of Christians as a crucial achievement, and the Treaty of Lausanne as a diplomatic triumph, at least as far as the genocide was concerned. Against the backdrop of such "successful violence" the CUP prefigured the lasting domestic patterns and behavior of various post-Ottoman power players, namely the Kemalist single-party regime and the Arab Baath parties. Similarly, the reverse conversion of AKP luminaries in Ankara from fresh reform-oriented democrats in the 2000s to war-prone, national-Islamist authoritarians under Erdoğan in the 2010s displays a political behavior that is reminiscent of the early 1910s.

This perpetuation of patterns prevails although Kemalism abstained from imperial ambitions and repressed political Islam until the end of the 1990s. However, it did this only insofar as Islamic competition presented a threat within the politico-cultural arena, not when it underpinned common concepts of the enemy. When the superficially secular post-Ottoman regimes began to show major shortcomings in the second half of the twentieth century, Islamism developed into the hegemonic ideology of the Levant (and the Islamicate world in general). Kemalist actors reared up forcefully one last time during the military putsch of September 1980, when violence and mass imprisonments primarily targeted left-wing and Kurdish militants. This intervention did not stop the return of political Islam in Turkey. Instead, it resulted in a semi-official Turkish-Islamic synthesis, with compulsory Islamic instruction being introduced into public schools after the coup.

As a comparatively strong, messianic ideology based on both Gökalp's Turkism and the cult of Atatürk, Kemalism had inspired a state whose structure was, however, no less at risk than that of other post-Ottoman states. It, too, lacked a genuine democratic social contract, separation of powers, and nonpartisan state institutions, as its foundation was based on violence and coercion, not on consensus building across societal borders. Turkey was caught up by Islamism comparatively late, after its role as a Middle Eastern cornerstone of NATO in the Cold War had expired and a promising road to real democracy had been usurped by authoritarianism. The "religious turn"—the emergence of religion on the political stage—was a global phenomenon of the second half of the twentieth century. Besides Islam in the Middle East, we also saw the rise of the religious right in the United States and a religious shift involving an explicit eschatological reading of Zionism by Jews and Christians in post-1967 Israel. At many places, also in Turkey, this religious turn remained long hidden in the shadow of ideological Cold War conflicts.

Turkey's re-intensified interaction with the European Union—which had condemned the 1980 putsch and recognized the Armenian genocide[15]—opened new windows of opportunity and access to new instruments of conflict resolution from 2000 onward. This led to more consensual policy building that included steps toward a new constitution based on universal standards, a more open approach toward Kurds, and negotiations with Kurdish leaders. Importantly—long been denied by the Turkish state—it comprised steps toward confronting the issue of mass violence in modern

Turkish-Muslim history. These constructive developments were, however, frustrated in the context of an anti-Kurdish war policy that began in the southeast of Turkey in July 2015, continuing in northern Syria since 2016.

Facing Violence: Imperial Islam, Turkish Nationalism, Apocalypticism

Between 1914 and 1923, Asia Minor lost more than six million of its over fifteen million inhabitants. Two-thirds of them were Christians, half of whom were killed. The organizers of anti-Christian persecution gave agents of domestic jihad ample opportunity to kill, rob, and rape. Less than 800,000 of the approximately four million deaths during the Ottoman First World War were soldiers. Internal conflict, dysfunction, and violence caused far more fatalities than military combat on the frontlines. Rebellions and internal warfare during the interwar period continued to cause dozens of thousands of casualties in the former Ottoman world, many of them Kurdish civilians.

In 1923, the 1878 Berlin Treaty was replaced by the even more fundamental Lausanne Peace Treaty, which, in terms of its main tenets, is still valid today. In real terms, the post-Ottoman world has never come to a peaceful rest. After the Second World War, Israel's wars took center stage. Since the late 1970s, interstate and domestic wars such as the Iran–Iraq war, the anti-Kurdish Anfal campaign, the Lebanese civil war, the Kurdish guerrilla wars in Turkey, the 1991 Persian Gulf war, the US invasion and its long aftermath in Iraq, the civil war in Syria, and the war in Yemen have killed millions of people and forcibly removed many more. Added to this toll are tens of thousands of violent deaths in Israel–Palestine, after the suspension of the 1990s peace process. This small place on the post-Ottoman map also urgently needs an overarching democratic social contract. In contrast to the Cold War–related mass violence in Southeast Asia, unrest has increased in the Levant since the late twentieth century. In both areas, it has been openly shaped by ethnoreligious categorization. In both, jihad has played a major role.

Since 1945, there has been an incomparably higher death toll through war and violence in the post-Ottoman world than in continental Europe including war-torn former Yugoslavia, Europe's own post-Ottoman region. Unsettled issues and a lack of social contracts have kept this vast expanse of human geography in a state of violent unrest since the cataclysmic events of the 1910s. Jihad has played a crucial role in this violence—internally even more so than toward the exterior. Contrary to its promises, Kemalism failed to overcome Islamism, acting instead as an ersatz Islam and perpetuating former patterns of imperially biased, leader-centered politics that favored (in this case, urban) Turkish-speaking Sunnis.

Inspired by the social sciences, recent research on violence has emphasized social, political, economic, and spatial factors, and helped deconstruct monolithic ideas regarding societal polarization. Yet it has long failed to address significant elements. The genocide of 1915, a topic dismissed by Western academia until the end of the twentieth century, is the most striking among them, and its long-term consequences still wait to be explored. The political impact of religion is another. Twentieth-century scholarship largely failed to analyze and measure the resilience and power of prophetic religion. Historical developments in the Levant went against the grain of disciplines rooted in Western Enlightenment. Sectarian resurgence and violence since the 1960s have taken Cold War–focused Western intellectuals and strategists by surprise: most notably the civil war in Lebanon, the Islamic revolution in Iran, and later the explosion of jihadist violence in and beyond the Levant.

Internalized ethnoreligious differences and hierarchies accompany categorical eschatological expectations with claims of superiority. Social contracts resulting from a pragmatic negotiation based on democratic equality are therefore very difficult, as is manifest in Turkey, Syria, Iraq, Israel–Palestine, and the whole former Ottoman world. Myths of power, identity, and hierarchies hold sway in politico-religious discourses and practices. Research must expose them. Among the strongest imperial myths are Islamist, (pan-)Turkist, and neo-Ottomanist narratives that refer to the Ottoman sultanate-caliphate, the most durable Islamic empire in history. Among the strongest religious myths is apocalyptic Wahhabism, whose birth goes back to the eighteenth century when it reacted against an Ottoman capital that it considered to be weak, corrupt, and subject to European influences. Referring to the Koranic society of the seventh century as well as to holy scriptures, it has, in recent decades, developed a violent global apocalypticism. As a result of the 1979 Iranian Islamic revolution, Shiism also strongly displays eschatology on the surface of its political discourse. The historic-religious lines dividing Shiism from Wahhabite and neo-Ottomanist Islamisms, however, are deep and have determined antagonistic alliances on the Syrian battlefields in the 2010s.

The current Sunni and Shiite apocalypticisms cannot be understood without considering their interactions with the West. Not only do they react against American intervention and presence in the Middle East, but they are also influenced by products such as the films, books, pamphlets, and games of a late twentieth-century US "industry" of apocalypticism. This industry sold—and continues to sell—pre-millennialist representations of religious violence. Militant Islam in the spirit of ISIS claims to hasten Jesus's, that is, the messianic mahdi's second coming and his establishment of a global Muslim rule by means of war; this is a pattern of Sunni eschatology of which many Christians are not aware. According to the Koran, the Prophet Jesus never died; he survived crucifixion and, in the Islamic understanding of the revelation (apocalypse), will return to power at the end of times. Although most Christian traditions reject the idea that the "millennium" or "Kingdom of Jesus" can be forced by violence or conquest, sales-oriented premillennialist fantasies have made its arrival a spectacle of unavoidable mass killing. Shiite eschatology displays faith in its own militancy and in Jesus's coming at the side of the mahdi, the revealed "hidden imam." Though shaped by centuries of subalternity vis-à-vis Sunni predominance, Shiite mahdism rooted in Iran's Islamic Revolution marginalizes previous Sufi or liberal interpretations. In its emphasis on global Muslim superiority, it mirrors Sunni eschatology.

Considering the political weight of religious legacies, while refusing essentialism, this chapter has explored patterns of violence rooted in ethnoreligious inequality and conflicting eschatology with a particular emphasis on domestic jihad. Often controlled by or existing in tandem with state power, such patterns exist in the post-Ottoman Levant to this day. They encompass demographic engineering, genocide, exterminatory urban warfare, serial suicide attacks, pogroms, mediatized atrocities, and war in the name of nation, religion, and eschatology.

In line with the entire book, this chapter has understood the persistence of violence and brutalization of societies as consequences of the lack of effective democratic social contracts. It has dealt with failed attempts to achieve such contracts in the late Ottoman and post-Ottoman Levant. It has argued that negotiating them is nowhere more demanding than in a region where the historical claims of all revealed monotheisms meet and religious mobilization is rewarded. Given the force of diverging eschatologies in claiming supremacy for their groups and projecting the future in absolute terms, it is hard to see an end of polarization in the present Levant. But still, the elementary desire and need for a decent life beyond dogmas, myths, and maximalism has the chance to prevail in the long term.

4

Choosing War in the Crisis of Reform

The 1914 Agreement for Anatolia and Germany

On February 8, 1914, Ottoman Grand Vizier Said Halim and the Russian chargé d'affaires Konstantin Gulkevich signed a reform project for seven Ottoman eastern provinces (*Accord Russo-Turc du 8 février 1914*, henceforth Reform Agreement), which covered roughly half of Asia Minor.[1] This international Agreement differed considerably from a first Russian draft the year before. On the eve of the First World War, it constituted a fragile yet central element in securing the future of Ottoman coexistence in Asia Minor on more egalitarian, democratic, participative, and regionalist terms. Nevertheless, it remains little-known among most Great War historians in the West.

Often called the "Armenian Reforms," it was also the last seminal, more or less consensual project in European diplomacy before the latter's breakdown in the July crisis of 1914. Instead of making efforts toward establishing Ottoman coexistence, reform, and international consensus building, important Ottoman and non-Ottoman protagonists then chose the road toward cataclysm. One of the main consequences of the war in wider Europe was the formation of a Turkish nation-state in the Levant that excluded the Christians living in the territory while attempting to assimilate non-Turkish Muslims, especially Kurds, into "Turkdom." This chapter is a reminder that the agreement of 1914 briefly offered a completely different perspective. It played a crucial role on the road that, instead of leading to a peaceful democratizing evolution, ended up at a place of nationalist imperialism, total war, and, in 1915, genocide. The main postulates of the Reform Agreement—recognition of local languages, fair participation in the state, democratic regionalization, cultural and political equality—remained valid and would vigorously return in the early twenty-first century.

Reassessing the Reform Agreement of 1914

The Reform Agreement restricted the Young Turk government's sovereignty and therefore constituted a major motivating factor in its pursuit of a war that would allow its annulment, backed by an alliance with Germany. The suspension of the Agreement in August 1914, and its annulment the following winter, were major stages on the road toward the comprehensive destruction of the Armenian community, which began in April 1915. The agreement had projected an internationally monitored and comparatively democratic, regionalized future for the mainly Kurdish-Armenian Ottoman eastern provinces. This chapter reassesses the Reform Agreement in the light of recent research on the cataclysmic final Ottoman decade.

Considering this aborted Reform Agreement is crucial to understanding the road that led to total war and genocide, and hence to the factual disintegration of the Ottoman social fabric in 1915. Encompassing roughly half of Asia Minor (present-day Turkey), it would have provided the territory with a much less ethnonationalist route through the twentieth century. Its legal substance homed in on a locally adapted democratizing peace within an Ottoman framework, albeit under international supervision in that region. Though differing in content, it bore some resemblance to the special monitored status of late-Ottoman Lebanon, which, in the 1860s, had established lasting peace in the area.

In contrast to many scholarly analyses, especially those based on Kemalist historiography and Young Turk members' memoirs, this study approaches the final Ottoman decade from a non-deterministic standpoint that refuses to discount the Reform Agreement as some sort of imperialist trick. On the contrary, I see both the reform deliberations and the agreement as having opened a temporary window of opportunity for peace and coexistence. It was a compromise where no one lost out— neither any group in the eastern provinces nor the Ottoman government. By 1913–14, the main CUP rulers had, however, already largely decided upon a path informed by imperial ultranationalism. Only concerted external pressure could restrain them.

In the eastern provinces, the most pressing problems of the late Ottoman period related to the so-called "land question." Land problems had been a pivotal part of the "Armenian Question" since the second half of the nineteenth century. Solving them— various instances of land-grabbing perpetrated by regional actors, most notably Sunni Kurdish lords, against Christian peasants—presented the greatest challenge of the reform issue. It was therefore rightly referred to by some contemporary diplomats as a Kurdish-Armenian Question. The way in which it was approached varied according to different perspectives within the government: the Armenian representatives on one hand, and the Muslim leaders dominating the rural parts of the eastern provinces on the other, with the Alevis in between.

Since the Young Turk Revolution of 1908, consensual coexistence had relied upon the Turkish-Armenian accord, in particular the cooperation of the CUP and the most important Armenian party, the Armenian Revolutionary Federation (ARF, Dashnaktsutiun). In January 1913, as earlier mentioned, the CUP had taken power through a putsch, establishing a dictatorial regime and definitively putting an end to the 1908 ideal of a constitutional Turkey based on ethnoreligious coexistence. It wanted unrestricted Turkish-Muslim sovereignty, and it was for this reason that the CUP government, and Muslims in general, feared international interference; any reform issue involving international cooperation was suspected of being an imperialist ploy designed to prevent Ottoman sovereignty and divide the empire.

It is true that the proposed reforms linked local and Ottoman matters to international politics. The CUP inherited the issue from the preceding liberal-conservative government, which had ruled from July 1912 to January 1913 and whose foreign policy, led by Minister Gabriel Noradunghian, had been more open to international consensus building. In insisting on reforms in 1912–14, European diplomacy was referring to promises made in the 1878 Berlin Treaty, which had moved the—then so-called—"Armenian Question" to the center of the modern West's notorious Eastern Question. The July crisis of 1914, however, led to a general diplomatic breakdown and did away with the international preconditions for a societal peace to be secured by the Agreement.

Europe's diplomatic collapse in summer 1914 thus featured a collapse of constructive reform for Asia Minor, the broken promise of Armenian security, and, as a consequence, the deathly abandonment of the Armenians. This chapter takes a particular look at the German engagement for reform that ended abruptly in July 1914. Its final part explores the road that led from the aborted international reform project to a mission of brutal de-Christianization—first in the eastern provinces, where reforms had been planned, and subsequently in the whole of Asia Minor and Eastern Thrace. Although the CUP's rule had been increasingly dictatorial since 1913, and despite the previous rupture between the ARF and the CUP, the Ottoman Armenians had, until 1914, remained astute envoys, successfully pressing their case in Europe.

After mid-July 1914, in light of a possible large-scale war, leading CUP men pushed to ally with Germany. This shut down diplomatic processes and opened up a course of action determined by the constraints and mentality of war, with which they had been familiar since the Balkan Wars. The Ottoman Armenians, by contrast, were defenseless without international support when their own state turned against them. By the end of July, it became clear that Germany would sacrifice the Reform Agreement in favor of war and a military alliance. It thus "saved" the CUP partners from monitored international reforms and henceforth backed them in their domestic policy, or at least did not intervene.

In early 1915, half a year after embracing active participation in the World War, the most influential leaders of the party-state agreed upon a genocidal policy against the Ottoman Armenians and other Christians (Assyrians and Pontus Rûm). In this, they were passively, and in a few instances actively, supported by Germany, while international diplomacy remained paralyzed (see Chapter 15). Turkey's German ally suppressed its interest in Ottoman Christians and a reformed Ottoman coexistence in favor of what it considered military and strategic priorities: total military victory (*Endsieg*) in a global conflict to result in enhanced global German influence (*Weltgeltung*). The vision of the 1914 Reform Agreement therefore remained utopian: Europe and late Ottoman Turkey failed to meet the challenge of law-based coexistence posed by the Armenian Question.

Late Belle Époque Diplomacy: The Challenge Posed by the Armenian Question

In 1913, Germany stood at a critical threshold both with regard to the Eastern Question and to its own relationship with the late Ottoman Levant. Would the *Kaiserreich's* fresh flirtation with the CUP's dictatorship involve stronger mutual engagement and interference in Ottoman internal affairs with the aim of establishing constitutional rule? Or would the unfinished, fragile constitutional democracy of the German Empire lose its political and moral compass in the quagmire of the Eastern Question, and the Armenian issue in particular? We all know the latter happened.

Despite the European diplomatic fiasco in the Balkans in 1913, the CUP regime remained internationally weak prior to the crisis of July 1914. The international aspect of the Reform Agreement was domestically significant. If duly introduced, it would determine Turkey's domestic future, even against the CUP's will and fervent desire for unchallenged, centralized sovereignty. If Germany cooperated with internationally monitored reforms, however, the political course of the Ottoman world would be corrected and the committee dictatorship somewhat neutralized.

One attempt at such corrective measures had been made during the liberal-conservative cabinet in late 1912, when Armenian representatives had repeatedly demanded the implementation of a reform plan according to Article 61 of the Berlin Treaty. This added an international dimension to the cabinet's renewed attempts at restoring order and resolving the "land question" in the eastern provinces from October 1912 onward. When a solution had still not been found by early December, the cabinet received a warning from the Russian Foreign Minister Sergej Sazonov, again reminding it of the Berlin Treaty.[2] By December 18, 1912, it had prepared a reform plan for the provinces of Van, Bitlis, Diyarbekir, and Mamuretülaziz. One of Grand Vizier Kâmil's main ideas was to assign British inspectors as advisors during its implementation, thus countering Russian pro-Armenian pressure.[3] One of the primary governmental arguments against confronting the issues in the eastern provinces had repeatedly been the necessity to implement reforms across the whole country, not only in one part of it.

Finally seeking a breakthrough after four years of being strung along since 1908, the Armenian *millet* assembly decided on December 21, 1912, to present the reform issue to an international platform and to lobby in the European capitals.[4] The main representatives on this platform included Bogos Nubar Pasha, Ottoman deputy Krikor Zohrab, and the Catholicos of Etchmiadzin, Kevork V. The main Armenian political parties (ARF, Hunchak, and Ramgavar) joined in a common project for the first time. The aim of the Armenian initiative was to ameliorate the conditions of life on the ground. Because it introduced new standards and European monitoring, it was a potential game changer for the whole country. The radicals surrounding Minister of the Interior and party leader Talaat therefore deemed it a fundamental threat to their political goals and denounced the Armenians' appeal to foreign support as treason. For the Armenians, international assurance was essential; trusting reforms introduced by the CUP regime alone would, after all, have been irresponsible.

From the standpoint of human rights and dignity, the Armenian appeal to diplomacy came in direct response to the government's incapacity to safeguard basic, egalitarian justice and security, and a solution to the issue of stolen land. In 1914, Governor Hamid Kapancızâde—a high functionary and close collaborator of Talaat who stood on friendly terms with the British expert Robert Graves—traveled to the eastern province of Diyarbekir for the first time in his life. He described the situation as follows: "I found the place here not only an administratively neglected province, but a [whole] region that was derelict, because subordinate and peripheral. As in many of our provinces, one could scarcely ascertain that the administration of a state had reigned here for centuries." Outside of towns,

> the lack of administration and the practice of patronage left the rule to local tribes, more precisely, to gangs. Every extortioner who managed to summon forty bandits was a government. [. . .] If anybody had explained to me in advance this primitive state of affairs that I witnessed in 1914, I would not have believed him, saying that he exaggerates.

This was a devastating judgment from a loyal, capable, forthright governor. In March 1915, he was displaced for his honest assessment of the situation. In his retrospective memoirs, written before his death in 1928, Hamid went so far as to write that "nowhere and never had we become the master and protector of the country. We resided as bad tenants in the countries that we had invaded."[5]

After the Balkan Wars, mediations for sorely needed reforms in the eastern provinces continued alongside postwar negotiations. In both, Talaat played a key role. Fearing a similar scenario to that in Macedonia, which had come under international control, he was mainly concerned with the preservation and reestablishment of central state power. The Armenian concerns of survival, human dignity, and property rights also applied to other groups, particularly the Assyrian Christians and Alevis. Largely unarmed, the Armenian and urban Assyrian Christians (*Süryani*) formed a well-educated portion of the provincial population in Eastern Asia Minor.

The political and social opening in the aftermath of the 1908 revolution had not lasted—a countrywide constitutional rule had not been implemented. Thus, what had particularly for non-Sunnis been a hopeful moment ended in disappointment. In the eastern provinces, well-meaning governors such as Celâl Bey in Erzurum had been the exception, not the rule. Since 1911, state authorities and local CUP branches had been siding more and more openly with anti-constitutional landlords. Confronting tribal leaders and gangs carried the risk of upheaval and complete loss of control and was therefore avoided by Istanbul. The massacres, urban riots, and unrest that had plagued the region since the 1890s, including Adana in 1909, were still fresh in people's memories.

Reform Efforts Versus Radicalization

In light of a scheme that aimed to resettle hundreds of thousands of *muhacir* from the Balkans in Asia Minor, the newly established CUP dictatorship became prone to taking drastic measures, including massive demographic engineering. The main concerns were no longer constitutional rule and participatory politics but the countrywide instatement of a party-state, along with a unitary Turkist agenda for Anatolia.

This agenda followed a modified understanding of Turkish nationhood which basically included Muslims and excluded indigenous Christians. It thus not only undermined the constitutional equality of Ottoman citizens but made belonging to the Ottoman nation dependent on Muslim faith and, more and more, on belonging to cultural-racial "Turkdom." From this anti-Christian stance, a resentful brand of Turkish nationalism began to spread rapidly, fueled by a fervent reaction against perceived aggression and injustices by "Christian" powers. Intensified nationalist mobilization, CUP propaganda glorifying war and fueling outrage over real or invented atrocities during the Balkan War—all played determining roles in establishing an ultranationalist mentality. This mindset was averse to any internationally monitored reform.[6]

In contrast to non-Muslims, non-Turkish Muslims were deemed assimilable to the new understanding of national identity. In its more popular occurrences, this understanding corresponded to late nineteenth-century Ottoman Islamism. Anti-Christian boycotts, initiated by the CUP, proved a strong indicator of this development. After Austria-Hungary's annexation of Bosnia-Herzegovina, Bulgaria's declaration of independence, and Crete's unilateral union with Greece in autumn 1908, Muslims found themselves united in their demands for the empire's sovereignty and security. Boycotts of Austrian, Bulgarian, and Greek businesses and goods extended from Trabzon to Beirut. Large crowds, often numbering in the thousands, protested publicly, burning or tearing up Austrian-made fezzes. By 1910–11, the boycott campaign also began to target the shops of Christian and Jewish Ottoman citizens.[7] Thus, whereas the 1908 and 1909 boycotts had been exclusively directed against foreign "Christian states," those in 1913 targeted Ottoman Christians, especially the Rûm, outright. After the Balkan Wars, Ottoman Macedonia was almost entirely lost. The CUP blamed this situation on foreign interference and foreign-mandated reforms. It did not publicly question its own call to war in September 1912, the Ottoman military defeat, or the well-known, long-term deficits in Ottoman administration. Since late 1913, the CUP had viewed the Armenians and entente powers as fabricating a "new Macedonia" in Eastern Anatolia. The CUP branches in the eastern provinces absorbed this perspective into their rhetoric, connecting it with local resentments that had fed the violence during the anti-Armenian pogroms in 1895. This Hamidian legacy, along with the juxtaposition of Armenia and Macedonia, were strong factors in the dramatic growth of the CUP's anti-Armenian stance.

This development was illustrated not only by the ideological mentorship of Central Committee member Gökalp, who had been involved in the anti-Armenian current in Diyarbekir, but also by a more general Kurdish unrest. Local power holders, including Kurdish sheikhs and tribal chiefs, feared the restitution of seized Armenian land; this added further momentum to Abdurrezzak Bedirhan's attempt at a Kurdish nationalist movement in autumn 1913. Intriguingly, Abdurrezzak also profited from Russian assistance, which contributed to the CUP's fear of—and mistrust in—Russia during the reform negotiations. In losing the support of local power holders, it would also have risked losing its precarious hegemony over the eastern provinces for good.[8] Angry and vengeful mindsets in Western and Eastern Asia Minor concurred, giving rise to extreme, Islamist and Turanist (pan-Turkish) anti-Christian public hate speech. In contrast to the Islamist reaction of 1909, it now came from voices close to, or even within, the CUP (which, while in opposition to Sultan Abdulhamid's rule before 1908, was already familiar with similar refrains among some of its pamphleteers).

Under international pressure, the CUP cabinet of Grand Vizier Mahmud Şevket had continued the reform efforts undertaken by its predecessor, even if there was, as dissenting CUP Central Committee member Mustafa Hayri noted, "obstruction by a few persons in the committee."[9] He was probably referring to Gökalp, Şhakir, and Talaat, even though Talaat knew that some compliance was inescapable. In contrast to the previous year, Hayri now occupied a critical stance in relation to "the road chosen by Talaat Bey." When it came to reforms, he was ready for duty, deeming "the land question one of the country's vital questions." His colleagues, meanwhile, feared losing political prestige due to popular Islamic reactions against proposals for a commission or temporary peace tribunals. Finally, Hayri, Rahmi, and Necmettin Molla, all prominent CUP members, decided to propose to Talaat that Hayri be nominated as a minister so that he would have sufficient executive power to deal with the land question. (He was, in fact, again made a minister of foundations in late April 1913, though not responsible for the land question in the East, before becoming a *sheykhulislam* in 1914.)[10]

A secret cabinet meeting on April 15, 1913, adopted the idea of a general inspectorate for the eastern provinces. Analogous to the plan of December 18, 1912, it included the involvement of British experts, though in this case, it proposed two regions with two separate British-led inspectorates. Ultimately, the anti-Russian undercurrents of the scheme were too evident, and Britain declined to nominate any general inspectors.[11] In June, the unresolved Armenian Question and the reform issue were therefore very much on the diplomatic table once again. At the end of June, the Russian ambassador distributed a draft reform plan written by André N. Mandelstam, a lawyer and expert on international law and dragoman at the Russian embassy. Submitted to a conference of six ambassadors scheduled to begin in July, it proposed the unification of six eastern provinces under one general inspectorate governed by a European or—analogous to the special status of Lebanon—Ottoman Christian inspector.[12] In response, Talaat, once again minister of the interior, busied himself preparing an account emphasizing the governmental position on the reforms.[13]

Failing to consider that Talaat's strategic goal might be obstruction, Germany supported the Turkish side during the July 1913 conference of ambassadors in Istanbul. From early 1913 up until this point, its position had been aligned with the general European stance that real reform was needed in order to secure the Armenians' future in Turkey. Yet, as can be seen in diplomatic correspondence of the time, this was not a firm conviction. According to Finance Minister Cavid, Talaat's close collaborator, German ambassador Wangenheim, lacked any solid and sound opinion on the Armenian issue. This view was echoed by General Pomiankowski, who, too, described a wavering and thus pliable Wangenheim.[14] Even before a final agreement had been reached, the ambassador had once again naively asserted that "the present Turkish government will do all to make the new regime [of reform] succeed in Armenia."[15] On another occasion, he said that "only their conversion to Islam could provide them [the Armenians] rest and security for life and property." When it came to the Russian desire for Armenian reform, he oscillated between conviction and mistrust in its authenticity (the latter of which the committee leaders did all they could to encourage).[16] In late September, German-Russian discussions finally established a compromise between Russian and Ottoman reform drafts.

Once again, Talaat tried to play the British card against Russian influence. He generally took a hit-and-run approach, using intimidation or friendly surprise of his targets to effect immediate success. In early October 1913, he blindsided two British experts who worked in the government: "Talaat Bey, who was now the dominant personality in the Cabinet, came to see Crawford and me at the Ministry of Finance and made us the following rather startling proposal," Graves reports. Talaat again wanted Britons as general inspectors, in this case, David Crawford and Robert Graves. Again, the British government declined.[17]

Cavid himself had many informal talks with German and other diplomats on the reform issue, all of which he reported to Talaat. In turn, Talaat sent him numerous telegrams and letters, which Cavid summarized in his diary. Fully loyal to Talaat's stance on the matter, Cavid used all his persuasiveness to categorically refuse European control and draw Germany closer to Turkey. He insisted that the CUP was committed to Armenian security and "willing to realize reforms in Armenia [*sic*]." He deployed a panoply of arguments to show that Armenian propaganda was at fault, Europe was insincere, and Russia was provoking troubles in the eastern provinces. He ridiculed European humanitarian discourse. "No European control" became a mantra around which all of his rhetoric revolved. "We do not want a new Macedonia to assume shape, and we have no time for European sermons," he preached in one of his interviews with undersecretary of the German Foreign Office Arthur Zimmermann, reproaching him that "In similar cases, we saw Germany always on our side; now it proceeds together with Russia. This produces a bad impression in our country."[18]

Both Cavid and Talaat accepted foreign inspectors as long as they were chosen by the Ottoman government. Moreover, Talaat in this case had a good sense of what the other side in the negotiations wanted to hear. As of late November 1913, this meant that inspectors could be chosen from small European countries, that they would be given full authority, and that Ottoman Christians would enjoy proportional representation in provincial councils, in the police force, and in the civil service. "We must say to the powers that we will fulfill these points. This declaration from our side will be reckoned as the guarantees that the Armenians want, but it does not mean the acceptance of an obligation." The crucial point continued to be international backing and control of the reforms, that is, a guarantee of international support that contradicted the CUP's claim to entire sovereignty, thus not only hurting its pride but substantially restricting its power. Relinquishing the request for guaranteed foreign support was, however, not a realistic avenue for the Armenian side to take, even if their interlocutors resented this. Muhittin Birgen, then a twenty-eight-year-old lead writer for the CUP newspaper *Tanin*, understood himself as belonging to the CUP's left wing, which "backed minority rights and previously had had good relations" with and sympathies for the social democratic ARF. His memoirs, however, depict the affront he felt when the ARF explained that "we have no trust in you anymore. We are obliged to demand guarantees by the powers, above all, Russia."[19]

A meeting between Talaat, CUP leaders Halil (Menteşe) and Midhat (Bleda), and Ottoman-Armenian deputies Vartkes and Halajian, as well as two other Armenians at Halajian's home in late November, again focused on this point. Talaat conceded all essential objectives which, in addition to those mentioned, included new laws on the use of regional languages and the autonomy of schools.[20] At this point, a full agreement seemed possible. What was the use of beautiful promises, however, if trust was lacking and international control was refused? The left wing of the CUP undoubtedly also prioritized a unified Turkish-Muslim state and had no sincere intentions of pursuing regional Armenian or other collective rights. Informal meetings between Talaat and Armenian representatives continued until late December 1913. Confidence-building steps were still possible, and the Armenians were hopeful that they might succeed. On December 24, Zohrab met Talaat at Halil's residence with the aim of winning him over. Zohrab's willingness to compromise exceeded that of his ARF friends. Talaat, however, continued to resist the crucial points of Armenian security and opposed a future governed by a rule other than that of the dictatorial committee. By December 26, he had concluded that the government was better off negotiating with the great powers directly, without interference from Armenian compatriots.[21]

Nevertheless, after initiating another meeting with Vartkes and Zohrab on December 28, Cavid exclaimed hopefully in his diary that on the matter of the inspectors, "we will be able to agree. The same is true for the issue of guarantees!"[22] This proved presumptuous. On January 10, 1914, Zohrab wrote, "To whom could I express my pain?" He was referring to what he deemed a fundamental and fatal break with the CUP. In his view, the ARF should have followed his example of continuing to informally negotiate with "the Turks" rather than leaving everything in the hands of Russia and Germany. A significant nonpartisan figure of post-1908 constitutional Turkey, Zohrab, more than almost anyone else, had believed in a future Turkish-Armenian alignment and felt that something essential had irrevocably broken down in late 1913 and early 1914.[23]

In late 1913, Russian anger at the new German military presence in the Ottoman capital under Otto Liman von Sanders led to further delays in the finalization of the Reform Agreement. CUP leader Ismail Enver's nomination as Pasha and minister of war in early January 1914 further amplified Russian suspicion. In light of former War Minister Nâzım Pasha's assassination during the CUP coup a year earlier, Russian Foreign Minister Sazonov regarded him as an ignoble murderer.[24] Talaat had used his dominance in the cabinet to elevate Enver and to push for Ahmed İzzet Pasha's resignation. Since early July 1913, he had been planning to "make one of us minister of war." From late November onward, this plan also included appointing Cemal as minister of the navy and Cavid as minister of finances.[25]

Under decisive German mediation, a substantial—now, indeed, internationally monitored—reform plan was signed on February 8 by the grand vizier, Said Halim, and the Russian chargé d'affaires, Konstantin Gulkevich. This plan had far-reaching consequences for Talaat's administration of domestic affairs; it divided Asia Minor into seven (not six, as in the first draft) eastern provinces that were further separated into northern (Erzurum, Trabzon, Sivas) and southern parts (Van, Mamuretülaziz, Bitlis, Diyarbekir). These provinces were to be placed under the control of two European inspectors selected from neutral countries. The plan also prescribed the publication of laws and official announcements in local languages, provided for an adequate proportion of Muslims and Christians in councils and the police force, and transformed the *Hamidiye*, an irregular Kurdish cavalry, into cavalry reserves. Even if limited to Eastern Asia Minor, the plan's unmistakable political principles would impact the entire country. By February 1914, and for the first time since 1878, international diplomacy possessed the necessary instruments to make its point in Eastern Asia Minor. The reform plan would be implemented and Talaat had to acquiesce—if there was no dramatic surprise in the near future. Once the general inspectors were chosen, it was scheduled to be implemented in the summer of 1914. The selection and appointment process took the entire spring.

Amazing Success of Terror and Coercion: Rûm Removal in Spring 1914

By April 1914, fundamentally different perspectives for an Ottoman future intriguingly coexisted. In the preceding months, a refugee crisis with *muhacir* from the Balkans had revealed the misery brought on by war in many places in Western Anatolia and presented a heavy financial burden for the state. In its wake, there was clearly a peaceful path which welcomed, or at least accepted, the possibility of European-influenced reforms: Finance Minister Cavid had, since March, succeeded in his negotiations for a substantial French loan of 800 million pounds, from which the commercial milieu expected a great boost for Turkey and Europe. When he returned to Istanbul from Paris on April 14, "all important persons from the political and economic spheres waited for him at the [Sirkeci] train station. A general feeling of relief spread throughout the whole population." Louis Rambert—a Swiss insider in Istanbul's political and financial life[26]—speculated that in light of recent experiences, "nobody desired to restart war" on that day.[27]

Existing simultaneously, albeit in direct contrast to this, was a cataclysmic perspective, directly related to the previous Balkan Wars. Viewing life as a battle, it believed that war necessarily reproduced itself in the struggles for survival and power, both domestically and internationally. Social Darwinist convictions, the *Zeitgeist* in Europe's era of high imperialism, were particularly well entrenched in the CUP, which shared their expectations of cataclysmic worldwide revolutions. Since the eve of the First Balkan War, the party, under Talaat's leadership, had internalized war and warmongering. Instead of revising its affective disposition, defeat only radicalized it: their losses would have to be avenged multiplicatively. Dominated by a Turkish-Muslim definition of the Ottoman nation, the CUP was steeped in the idea that betrayal by non-Muslims had caused the late Ottoman problems and losses. The victors of the First Balkan War had applied patterns of anti-Muslim ethnic cleansing, to which the CUP reacted with similar patterns that began to take on larger dimensions. By late 1913, a comprehensive anti-Christian campaign of demographic engineering was looming on the horizon. The CUP press aggressively claimed that the suffering of the Rûm did not compare to that of the *muhacir*.[28] Victimhood became an instrument of propaganda. Negative emotions merged with ethnoreligious stigmatization quickly became the justification for substitutional revenge toward Ottoman Christians. From this initial stage, a brutal policy of ousting the Ottoman Rûm emerged.

A direct consequence of the Balkan Wars, the anti-Rûm policy was first implemented in Thrace. The area was home to a number of Ottoman Rûm who either had relatives in Greece, were Ottoman-Greek dual nationals, had sympathized with Greece during the Balkan Wars, or even participated as soldiers on the Greek side.

Summarizing Talaat's new policy as it was emerging in late 1913, Halil stated that "Talaat Bey prioritized cleansing the country from the population elements [*anâsır*] that had revealed themselves as treacherous during the Balkan War." He continued, "The proceeding was like this: Officially the governors and the other functionaries were not involved. The CUP organization would accomplish the task and terrorize the Rûm. [. . .] In consequence, nearly 100,000 Rûm fled to Greece without being hurt."[29] A second step, in spring 1914, targeted the Rûm living on the Aegean coast. Plans for further expulsions through systematized terror were made during several secret CUP meetings in Istanbul in May and June 1914. Lasting the entire night, one such decisive meeting at Talaat's residence resulted in tangible preparations for young CUP officers to lead terror squads on the ground. As CUP leader Halil writes in his memoirs, "nearly 200,000 Rûm went to Greece by June 1914," as a consequence.[30]

The expulsion of Aegean Rûm was a terrific success. It was also paradigmatic in its management of information—including public lies—and its secret amalgamation of gangs, diplomats, the army, the central government, and central as well as local branches of the CUP. Starting in early June, Talaat inspected the results of the operation in the regions of Edremit, Aydın, and finally İzmir, where he arrived before mid-June. He was satisfied that the ousting had succeeded without degenerating into great chaos and facing significant resistance. On June 18, Grand Vizier Said Halim declared that his "vigorous" minister Talaat had reestablished order; the previous violence had regrettably, but spontaneously and understandably, emerged from the embittered *muhacir*. In reality, organized squads and armed bandits had in almost all cases purposely created chaos, looted, and sometimes killed.[31] For experienced observers, the publicity was flimsy. "In reality, they oust[ed] the Greeks," Rambert noted in his diary on June 16.

When, on June 18, the cabinet invited the ambassadors to send delegates to accompany Talaat and witness his efforts at calming the population and halting emigration, Rambert simply noted, "They disguise the facts. [. . .] Nobody here [in Istanbul] talks sincerely about what happens." From June 20, Talaat began to put his plan into action in Izmir, with delegates sent by European powers in the supporting roles. He now felt self-confident enough to play games with the European diplomats. In a private conversation with Russian consul Andrew Kalmykow and Vali Rahmi, he bluntly confessed that the "Greeks [Rûm] cannot remain. They are forced to leave. They must go."[32] Looking at him, Kalmykow remembered the decisive expression in Talaat's eyes and the resolute tone of his voice. Evidently, Talaat failed to inspire confidence in the terrorized people, who continued to flee. The appeasement of European diplomats saved the government a few precious days; otherwise, war with Greece was impending. If it were to break out, the government would go so far as to also expel the Rûm from Istanbul, thus again inducing incalculable international risks, as Rambert was told. The sultan—moved and upset by the information he had received from a delegation sent by the Rûm Patriarchate—immediately summoned Talaat. According to palace secretary İhsan, an ear witness, the now cold-blooded political liar Talaat swore to the sultan by the name of God and the Prophet that all news about persecuted Rûm was malicious slander intended to destroy the ancient Ottoman state.[33]

After the expulsions in Thrace and on the Aegean coast, the rulers of the party-state became crafty in their demographic engineering, publicly glossing over facts and implementing diplomatic theatrics. The removal of the Rûm announced another, even larger repercussion than that of the Balkan Wars. According to Rambert, "The ousting of the Greeks [Rûm] exposes Greece to a much bigger danger, because the Greeks established in Asia [Minor] count several millions." This number far exceeded that of *muhacir* from the Balkans. Turkey henceforth pioneered what Rambert had already called "an enormous triage of nations," that to him "was foreseeable, because among peoples that exit a horrible war, hates and vengeances make difficult the common life on the same territory."[34] Post-1918 Europe would have to face a deterioration of coexistence that most Europeans had previously thought to be relegated to another world. Now it had taken place within the limits of modern Europe, understood as the dense interactional space of, in the terminology of this book, larger (wider, greater) Europe.

In the immediate aftermath of Talaat's anti-Rûm exploits, the unexpected assassination of Archduke Franz Ferdinand in Sarajevo on June 28, 1914, triggered the July Crisis in Europe. This saved the string-pullers in Istanbul from a possible war with Greece that could have led to a pan-European war. On June 29, 1914, Talaat was back in the capital; on June 30, he met with Vramian and Armen Garo, his former political friends in the ARF, in order to again discuss—in spite of everything that had happened—reforms and the selection of Ottoman assistants to the European inspectors. The rapid removal of more than 100,000 people had left him overconfident. "I am Bismarck," he allegedly said with a smile when Garo reproached him and his closest friends for being drunk on their recent exploits. Talaat had, in Garo's eyes, metamorphosed since the *coup d'état* in January 1913, expressing faith in a future policy of Turkification of the Kurds and alluding to the possibility of removing the Armenians from Ottoman Armenia. "As usual, Talaat was very polite and open," reads Garo's memoir of his last meeting with Talaat on June 30, 1914, continuing that "in the manner of an overconfident person who makes fun of the other, he conjured a satanic smile on his face" when fundamental disagreements emerged during the talk.[35]

On July 6, 1914, the expulsions were discussed in the Ottoman parliament, after the Rûm deputy Emmanuil Emmanuilidis had presented it with the appalling facts. Talaat continued his deception before the deputies, pretending that spontaneous popular boycotts against non-Muslim merchants had motivated many Rûm to emigrate of their own free will. He furthermore declared that the government lacked the money to build new villages for the *muhacir*, hence the need to settle them in Rûm villages. He even insisted on the fact that if he had sent them to the deserts of Syria and Iraq—as he did a year later with the Armenians—they would all have died. The misery of the *muhacir* thus served as the main justification for the removal of the Rûm.[36] Talaat's multiple denials of any wrongdoing by the central government in May and June 1914 were covered by the Ottoman press. After the discussion on July 6, it attacked Emmanuilidis in an attempt to undermine his credibility; the newspaper *Le Jeune-Turc*, in particular, excelled in doing so.[37] On July 13, Talaat assigned Mehmed Reşid as Inspector General Hoff's Ottoman assistant, with the rank of vali, in Van. There was no question that, with his virulent resentments against Ottoman Christians, Reşid would not be a constructive collaborator in the reforms for Eastern Asia Minor. A cofounder of the CUP, he had, during the Balkan Wars, become a (pan-)Turkist hard-liner and a committed enemy of the Rûm, though not yet explicitly of the Armenians.[38]

Reform-Adverse Destruction, War, and Genocide—Backed by Germany

The CUP leaders' negative attitude toward internationally monitored reorganization clashed, to a certain extent, with a newly acquired German conviction that incisive reforms were needed if a peaceful future coexistence in late Ottoman Asia Minor was to be assured. This was in line with German plans to penetrate Ottoman Turkey economically and thus increase German influence in the Levant.

However, as a result of the July 1914 crisis, German officialdom lost the cooperative spirit it had acquired during the reform negotiations with Russia. Ready to reanimate anti-Russian stereotypes, it merged them with those cultivated by late Ottoman elites and Young Turk war propagandists. German war propagandists residing in Istanbul, as well as jihad propaganda that had been in German production since October 1914, completely dismissed any solidarity with Ottoman Christians and disregarded important truths and insights that Germany had acquired during the reform negotiations.

Once the diplomatic architecture of the Belle Époque had broken down and international pressure for reform had ceased, the lukewarm reform sponsor Germany stood alone with its politically unripe ideas for Asia Minor and its peoples. It had nothing to offer in opposition to the Young Turks' readiness for revolutionary change and violent demographic engineering. On the contrary, it allied with the revolutionists at the reins of the Ottoman Empire, offering the backing they needed for radical interior change.

The spirit and the contents of the reform program were thus completely destroyed by the new situation in summer 1914, of which the ousting of the Rûm on the Aegean coast in the late spring of 1914 had been an unmistakable precursor. This first comprehensive destruction of Ottoman coexistence fueled an idea that established itself on the eve of the First World War: the transformation of Asia Minor into a *Türk Yurdu*, that is, a safe and fully sovereign haven for Anatolia's Muslims, including the *muhacir* from the Balkans and the Caucasus. Despite the removal of the Rûm, however, there was in the early summer of 1914 still hope among reform-minded people in Asia Minor—Armenians and non-Armenians alike—that the peaceful influence of a robust agreement for the eastern provinces would become manifest.

On August 6, 1914—four days after concluding the secret German-Turkish war alliance—Wangenheim accepted the abolition of the Ottoman "capitulations" (special premodern privileges for foreigners) and "a small correction of her [Turkey's] eastern border which shall place Turkey into direct contact with the Muslims of Russia."[39] He knew that this would impact upon the eastern provinces and the still-valid Reform Agreement—the only convincing and realistic life perspective for non-Sunnis, and in particular Armenians, on the ground. In the autumn of 1914, he finally realized that Caucasian and central Asian territories with Turkic-Muslim populations were being targeted by irredentist pan-Turkish CUP propaganda to the detriment of Christians. Nevertheless, Germany did not oppose the gradual Ottoman annulment of the Reform Agreement, which began with the withdrawal of the general inspectors in August 1914 and officially ended with their outright dismissal in early January 1915.[40] Ottoman Armenians were increasingly concerned about the future. While many Armenians in the Caucasus still believed that Russia would win a swift victory and redeem Ottoman Armenia by imposing not only the Reform Agreement of February 8, 1914, but the further-reaching Mandelstam draft,[41] only a few young Ottoman Armenians shared this optimism.

Only in a report to the Reichkanzler on February 2, 1915, did Wangenheim hint at the end of the agreement and the devastating effect this would have on the Armenian population.[42] At the same time, he understood and accepted that the termination of the agreement was just one of several steps taken by the CUP government to implement its absolute sovereignty. In a note to Grand Vizier Said Halim in late May 1915, Minister of the Interior Talaat made clear that he considered the question of reform a completely internal matter that had unfortunately become international. He argued that a special administration would lead to the partition of the Ottoman homeland. Therefore, the Armenian problem had to be eliminated.[43] Ambassador Wangenheim and his superiors in Berlin acquiesced. While they abandoned the Armenians and all former concerns for peaceful coexistence in Asia Minor, they did all to appease their hypersensitive ally and to maximize its military capacity for the common war effort. They disregarded the fact that Germany had taken responsibility for the reform project and the people it concerned.

The Reichskanzler also failed to react when, on April 12, an urgent report from Walter Rössler, consul in Aleppo, informed him directly that, according to the province's governor, the former Vali of Erzurum Celâl Bey, an anti-Armenian current was gaining the upper hand in the CUP government. Celâl prophetically added that this development boded ill for the whole of Turkey and asked the Reichskanzler to instruct the German ambassador to act against this current.[44] In the following crucial weeks, however, Wangenheim followed a general line of instruction that put the military alliance over all other considerations regarding the future. Approached in late May 1915 by Minister of War Enver Pasha about "relocating" Armenian families from the "reform zone" to Mesopotamia, Wangenheim simply complied.[45] When Rössler asked him, in a telegram of June 3, to intervene with Enver as the first deportees arriving in Aleppo were being sent to places where they would perish, Wangenheim responded that he had to refrain from doing anything in this matter, due to the CUP government's determination to bring its anti-Armenian campaign to completion.[46] Dropping its commitment to the agreement and complying with CUP radicals in their exterminatory removal of the Armenians, Germany lost its moral compass and political soul (see also Chapter 15).

Even if they exaggerated German responsibility, Kurdish women hit the nail on the head when they sang in the spring and summer of 1915: "German, German / Why didn't you establish lawfulness? / Your house be cursed, German!"[47] In July 1914, many

European leaders, in particular German leaders, had believed war and cataclysm to be inevitable; meanwhile, Talaat and his circle pro-actively embraced the new scope of action offered by a global war. In the Ottoman world, the main responsibility for choosing upheaval over peaceful, incisive reform lay with the CUP government and with local players, including Kurds, who had refused land restitution and monitored reform altogether. Hand in hand with CUP affiliates on the ground, regional chiefs and urban notables often took a proactive role in the genocide; this impacted considerably upon a government that considered it opportune to side with them. In 1919, Celâl Bey wrote in retrospect that what had most preoccupied his government in Erzurum had been the land question.[48] He concluded that if the central government had committed itself to correcting land-grabbing by local lords in order to help powerless people, the main cause for interreligious conflict would have been solved, and thus constitutional Turkey would have been saved.

A Rationale of Violent National-Imperial Self-Assertion

In dealing with the reform question, this chapter has discussed the non-linear road to, and the total character of, the Ottoman First World War. In early August 1914, with the German-Ottoman military alliance and the party-state's unambiguous preparation for war in the Caucasus, the idea of war and demographic engineering took on a new dimension and definitively killed the Reform Agreement.

This chapter has exposed a signature feature of the Ottoman total war: war toward the exterior in tandem with interior mass removal and genocide targeting Ottoman Christians, most notably the Armenians (see Maps 1 and 2). Removal and genocide defined the unique character of the CUP war strategy from the first months after its official entrance into the First World War in November. Driven by ideology and imperial security concerns, these extreme measures worsened the domestic situation of the empire. They destroyed the imperial social fabric, and eventually the empire itself. Eastern Asia Minor was to remain a deeply crisis-ridden region for the next hundred years.

The trajectory scrutinized in this chapter began with the Berlin Treaty, leading to the 1914 Reform Agreement, and finally, to total war. Articles 61–2 of the Berlin Treaty had demanded full religious freedom in the Ottoman Empire as well as reforms in order to secure lives, property, and dignity of the obviously threatened Armenians in the eastern provinces. The politics of Muslim unity and Sunni empowerment under Sultan Abdulhamid had obstructed the implementation of both these articles. To this end, the sultan had established new infrastructures, schools, mosques, and militarized tribal units, organized a campaign for coercive conversion of Yezidis, and permitted large-scale anti-Armenian massacres. He thus started a lasting antidemocratic polarization along religious lines. In doing so, he wanted to save the empire according to his authoritarian and anti-egalitarian understanding of sultanate-caliphate. Neither the Young Turk Revolution and its attempt at parliamentary constitutional rule nor the balanced and innovative compromise of the international February 1914 Agreement could break the polarization and the politics of violence and mass coercion largely promoted under Abdulhamid. After its parliamentarian phase, the CUP not only followed its former enemy in this respect but outdid him both qualitatively and quantitatively.

The radicalization of the CUP was both endogenous and dependent upon the political macro-context of the early 1910s. The Ottoman Empire suffered massive Ottoman losses both during the Italian invasion of Libya (September 1911–October 1912) and the First Balkan War (October 1912–May 1913). These were partly self-inflicted as, in 1912, the CUP leaders had—in temporary opposition—sought their political salvation in warmongering. In 1913, again in power, these "sons of conquerors" (*evlad-ı fatihan*)

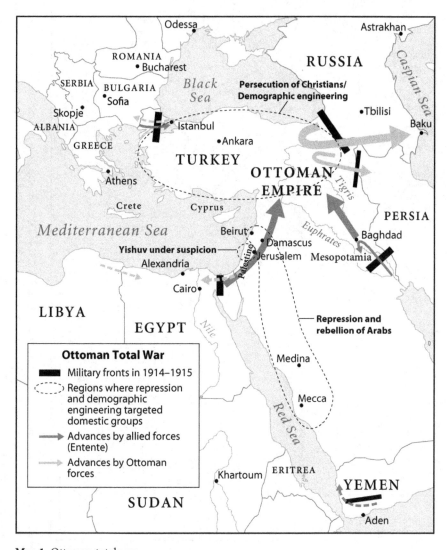

Map 1 Ottoman total war.

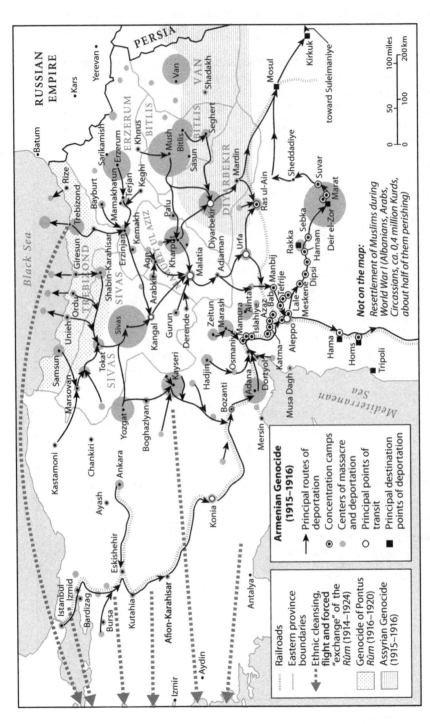

Map 2 Displacement, expulsion, and genocide in Anatolia (1914–23). This map does not include the early republican era and the Dersim genocide of 1938. In late Ottoman times, Dersim was a part (*sanjak*) of the province of Mamuretulaziz, comprising the area between Kharput and Erzincan in Northeastern Anatolia.

The following labels appear within the map:

PERSIA

RUSSIAN EMPIRE

Yerevan

Kars

Black Sea

Batum
Rize
Trebizond
Bayburt
Sarikamish
Giresun
Shabin-Karahisar
Ordu
Unieh
Marsovan
Samsun
Tokat
Sivas
Kangal
Gurun
Derende

Mamakhatun
Erzerum
Terjan
Keghi
Kemakh
Erzinjan
Arabkir
Agn
Palu
Kharput
Malatia
Diyarbekir
Adiaman
Mardin

Mush
Bitlis
Sasun
Khnus
Seghert
Van
Shadakh

ERZERUM
BITLIS
VAN
SIVAS
DIYARBEKIR
TREBIZOND
MAURET UL AZIZ

Ras ul-Ain
Sheddadiye
Suvar
Marat
Deir el-Zor
Sebka
Rakka
Hamam
Dipsi
Meskene
Lale
Tefrije
Babi
Manbij
Azaz
Urfa
Adana

Mosul
Kirkuk
toward Suleimaniye

Zeitun
Marash
Mamura
Aintab
Islahiye
Osmanije
Katma
Aleppo
Hama
Homs
Tripoli

Kastamoni
Chankiri
Ankara
Ayash
Eskishehir
Kutahia
Afion-Karahisar
Konia
Bursa
Bardizag
Izmid
Istanbul
Antalya
Aydin
Izmir
Mersin
Dortyol
Bozanti
Hadjin
Kayseri
Boghazlyan
Yozgat

Musa Dagh
Mediterranean Sea

Not on the map:
Resettlement of Muslims during World War I (Albanians, Arabs, Circassians, ca. 0.4 million Kurds, about half of them perishing)

Armenian Genocide (1915–1916)
→ Principal routes of deportation
⊙ Concentration camps
● Centers of massacre and deportation
○ Principal points of transit
■ Principal destination points of deportation

Railroads
Eastern province boundaries
Ethnic cleansing, flight and forced "exchange" of the *Rûm* (1914–1924)
Genocide of Pontus *Rûm* (1916–1920)
Assyrian Genocide (1915–1916)

100miles
200km
0 50 100
0 100 200

craved disproportionate revenge and a resettlement of *muhacir* at the cost of Ottoman Christians. This brought about the large-scale expulsion of Ottoman Greek Orthodox Christians (Rûm) in June 1914 and the determination to embrace world war in July. The CUP hawks' alleged struggle of survival amounted to an all-out war in the name of an overstretched Islamic-Turkish empire. Domestically, it targeted Christians with dispossession and genocide; to the outside, it meant imperial restoration and reexpansion, including "toward Turan," that is, the Caucasus and Central Asia. War permitted the termination of the Reform Agreement, the abrogation of the notorious "capitulations," and the escalation of demographic engineering in Anatolia.

Part II

Turkey's Ultranationalist Refoundation

Ottoman total war began with a large-scale, never-seen-before military mobilization in August 1914 and low-scale warfare in the Caucasus against imperial Russia and local Christians. It led to the declaration of jihad in mid-November and failed regular offensives at different fronts in the winter of 1914–15. The first military success on this path was the defense of the Ottoman capital at the Dardanelles, beginning in March 1915. The trajectory reached its climax during the following months when, in April, the Young Turk regime merged the war at its borders with a "war"—genocide—at home.

From the perspective and mindset of the CUP elite, it was a total and revolutionary fight for national-imperial survival and re-empowerment against exterior and domestic enemies. A fatal decision away from reforms, this path violently transformed Anatolia into a dictatorial Turkish national home (*Türk Yurdu*) at the expense of its non-Turkish indigenous population. This formative period started with CUP one-party rule in 1913 and ended with sole ruler Atatürk's death in 1938. Extreme violence marked the years 1915–22. Because unrepented and denied, or even openly embraced as a method of success, it never truly ended, as proves the genocidal assimilation of Dersim in the year of the death of the "Eternal Leader."

Part II thus explores the rebuilding, on exclusionary Turkish-nationalist bases, of a territorially downsized state, after the CUP's attempted imperial restoration and expansion had failed in the Great War. It deals with genocide, demographic engineering, and the production of ultranationalist political and historical thought; and it reveals through the prism of the Lausanne Near East Peace Conference the seminal importance of Turkey's achievements far beyond the former Ottoman realm. Lausanne endorsed the results of the previous policy in Anatolia, without clarifying the genocidal mass crimes behind them, and it sweepingly abandoned the victims and survivors of this pioneering ultranationalist policy. The success and appeasement of ultranationalism in Lausanne heavily mortgaged the future of the Middle East and of interwar Europe.

Pact, Not Peace

The Lausanne Treaty's "Near East Peace"

The Near East Peace Treaty of Lausanne definitively liquidated the Ottoman Empire.[1] Its signing on July 24, 1923, concluded a series of post–Great War treaties, including the Treaty of Paris-Sèvres that Lausanne thoroughly revised. It thus set the coordinates for the post-Ottoman future of the Middle East. Although in line with the Paris peace treaties of 1919–20, it opened up a new era of diplomacy that started by endorsing a seemingly brand-new actor: Turkey's nationalist government in Ankara, the legal successor of the Ottoman Empire whose capital had been Istanbul, and the victor of the Anatolia wars, including the Greco-Turkish war, after Ottoman defeat in 1918.

Conventional Western diplomacy and historiography have considered the Treaty of Lausanne "the most successful and durable of all the post-war settlements," and the Republic of Turkey, whose future rested upon it, "the success story of the Near East."[2] Concluded eight months after the Conference began, the Treaty of Lausanne ended a long decade of wars (1911–22) both within the late Ottoman world and between European countries and the late Ottoman Empire. It reestablished Turkish diplomatic relations with Britain, France, and other countries. The traditional diplomatic and academic mainstream typically took a positive outlook, presenting the Lausanne Treaty as the ultimate solution to modern Europe's notorious Eastern Question,[3] that is, to the question of how the future of the multireligious Ottoman world and its relation to Europe should look.

The Treaty of Lausanne stands in the diplomatic center of *Turkey's violent formation* as a restive, *huzursuz* nation-state.[4] We can only understand and assess this formation and its individual elements historically if we take the formation as a whole in its defining contexts: the end of the Ottoman Empire; a Europe-centered international system that had descended into world war; aging Western national empires eager to reap some Middle Eastern fruits of their Great War victory; and their dire need of an appeased Turkey.

Reassessing the Lausanne Conference in Its Defining Contexts

A hundred years after 1923, a historically informed retrospective therefore presents a sobering picture: aging Western imperialism conceded in Lausanne with the antidemocratic ultranationalism of the hitherto Bolshevik-backed elite in Ankara.

Almost all politicians in Ankara had been involved in the former national-imperial party-state of the Young Turks (CUP).

Appeasing Turkey and driving a wedge between it and Russia was one of the main goals of the Western powers during the Lausanne Conference. In the early 1920s, Bolsheviks and Turkish nationalists, including the latter's pan-Islamic networks, had formed an efficient "anti-imperialist International of antiliberal revolutionists."[5] Ankara successfully played the ace of a double specter: Bolshevism and political Islam.

At the Conference table, Ankara's delegation asserted principles that, for optimists, would sooner or later lead the country to a democratization from within, as long as Turkey was left fully sovereign and shielded from outside critique. With or without such—quixotic or purposive—hopes, the Lausanne Treaty manifestly endorsed ultranationalist claims to the detriment of weaker groups. It signed off on vertiginous political methods that breached customary law but seemed to promise stable international constellations. The "Peace of Lausanne" indeed provided some enduring stability in international relations.

However, when it came to human rights and democracy, it gave way to a dark era in Europe and the post-Ottoman world, from which—in contrast to Europe—Turkey and the Middle East never recovered. In the critical rationale of this book, this sobering result hails from the fact that the diplomatic constellation in Lausanne disabled any serious regard for fine-grained self-determination, rule of law, democracy, and politico-historical soul-searching.

The Lausanne Conference catalyzed the abolition of the caliphate as well as the "Kemalist Revolution," which imposed secular standards promised at the Conference. Not only for small nations like the Armenians, Kurds, and Assyrians, therefore—the Conference's main victims—but also for supporters of the caliphate and the sharia in the Islamicate world, who had venerated Gazi Kemal as a hero of jihad, the Peace of Lausanne presented a serious disenchantment. Both the abolition of the sultanate on November 1, 1922, and of the caliphate on March 3, 1924, were closely linked to the Lausanne Conference.

The long-prevailing positive outlook on the Lausanne Treaty was above all conditioned by Western authors writing within the context of the US-led post-1945 alliances that valued Turkey as its strongest Middle Eastern partner, or by sympathy with anti-colonialist and anti-imperialist Kemalist narratives. They neither seriously considered that Lausanne had endorsed—thus made diplomatically successful—demographic engineering and, implicitly, genocide, nor pondered that this legacy facilitated the coming of the Shoah. A pact among new strongmen and aging imperialists, the "Peace of Lausanne" gave a social Darwinist rationale the ultimate say. Lausanne has therefore been highlighted as a diplomatic nexus linking the Armenian genocide to the Holocaust.[6]

"By 1918, with the definitive excision of the total Christian population from Anatolia and the Straits Area, except for a small and wholly insignificant enclave in Istanbul city, the hitherto largely peaceful processes of Turkification and Moslemization [of Anatolia] had been advanced in one surge by the use of force," wrote two political scholars at Princeton University, summarizing the first, particularly violent phase of

Republican Turkey's formation. They could hardly have put their social Darwinist rationale more bluntly when they added—only a few years after the Holocaust:

> Had Turkification and Moslemization not been accelerated there by the use of force, there certainly would not today exist a Turkish Republic, a Republic owing its strength and stability in no small measure to the homogeneity of its population, a state which is now a valued associate of the United States. [. . .] this struggle for Anatolia had become a fight which could have only one winner. It was to be take all or lose all.[7]

Not democrats, but representatives of empire and ultranationalism dominated at Lausanne's negotiating table, and the epigones in diplomacy and academia largely followed their conclusions during the century after the conference. The Western powers—the national empires of Britain, France, and Italy—negotiated in 1922-3 with undemocratic, but militarily successful men from Ankara who almost all hailed from the cadres of the previous imperial CUP party-state. Although more or less involved in this regime's crimes and misrule, they claimed full sovereignty and self-determination in the name of a victimized and innocent Turkish nation. The Conference passed over the smaller and weaker peoples, natives of the same Anatolian soil, who were the targets of the genocidal Ottoman war decade (1912–22). The signing of the Treaty therefore was, depending on the perspective adopted, a day of glory or mourning, triumph or humiliation.

The Conference's fallout is still felt in the city of Lausanne to this day. Demonstrations take place on an almost annual basis, at times in the form of Turkish nationalist pilgrimages that celebrate Turkey's pride and sovereignty supposedly restored in 1923. To these demonstrators, the Lausanne Treaty ensured, in Kemal Atatürk's words of 1927, "the collapse of a great murderous plot prepared against the Turkish nation for centuries and thought to have been completed by the Treaty of Sèvres"—in their view, thus, "a political victory unprecedented in the history of the Ottoman era!"[8] More frequent in contemporary Lausanne, however, are the protests and expressions of mourning of the descendants of those who, in 1922-3, emerged from the negotiations as losers.

In Lausanne, the Western national empires sought untroubled post-Ottoman mandates, an unhindered concentration on Europe's urgent internal problems, and peace of mind regarding Ankara's previous alliance with Bolsheviks and its use of pan-Islamic currents. Italy and its new prime minister Benito Mussolini were absorbed with fascist reconstruction. Concluding a decade of war and genocide in the Ottoman world, and outlining the new post-Ottoman order in the Middle East, the Lausanne Conference endorsed an ethnonationalist response to the challenges of a multi-ethnoreligious society in Anatolia (Asia Minor). Despite their defeat in the Great War, it made former Turkish-Ottoman elites the diplomatic winners of the decade before, and in particular of the CUP-led domestic demographic and economic engineering. As for the Arabic parts of the former Ottoman Empire, it confirmed the 1920 Treaty of Paris-Sèvres and the San Remo resolutions on the mandates. France thus remained tasked with a League of Nations mandate for Syria, and Britain for Iraq and Palestine, comprising the conundrum to make the country a Jewish "national home," while leading the existing, mostly Arab, native population to autonomy.

Anti-democratic forces met with liberal-democratic national empires at the table of Lausanne. There, Ankara's nationalists, the Western allies including newly Fascist Italy as well as the Bolsheviks (these only for the Straits issue) sat together. British diplomacy embraced what it regarded as the lesser evil: not Bolshevism, but Italian Fascism and Turkism. Lausanne's endorsement of Ankara's field-tested ultranationalism, however, boosted authoritarianism, one-party rule, and the paradigm of ethnoreligious "unmixing of people" in the whole of Europe and beyond.

The Conference retroactively labeled "population exchange" the factual ethnic cleansing, starting in 1913, that it completed by a compulsory transfer of people, co-organized by the League of Nations and the International Committee of the Red Cross (ICRC). It accepted, in other words, the policy of Turkification of Anatolia implemented by the CUP regime and later continued by the emergent Ankara government under the label of "defense of national rights." This policy comprised the extermination of Ottoman Armenians, Assyrians, and Pontus Rûm (Greek-Orthodox Christians at the Black Sea) during and after the Great War; the forced resettlement of Ottoman Kurds (1915–17) and of further non-Turks; and the expulsion of the Rûm from Western Anatolia (1914 and 1919–22).

The Lausanne Conference excluded from its negotiating table not only Anatolia's smaller non-Turkish peoples, but also the neighboring Arabs, who still desired self-determination, and the Iranians, who wanted to have their say during the ultimate liquidation of the Ottoman Empire. Concluded by the era's potentates, the Lausanne Treaty cemented a precarious status for those whom it deprived of, or heavily restricted in, their collective and individual rights: native Christians, Kurds, and other non-Turks or non-Muslims that were excluded from, or marginalized within, the new Turkish nation-state. The long-prevailing diplomatic and legal interpretations of Lausanne in Turkey and internationally have underestimated the momentousness of exclusion, unaddressed violence and coercion, and of religious belonging (religion served as an almost unquestioned demographic core category in Lausanne). However, sharply divergent narratives on Lausanne emerged early on: on the one hand by unsatisfied pan-Turkish or Islamist groups, on the other hand by legal scholars and advocates of those excluded and disfranchised.

A scholar particularly concerned by the Armenian fate before, during, and after Lausanne was André Mandelstam, a Russian-Jewish pioneer of international law and former diplomat in Istanbul. In his major work on the Ottoman Empire, he labeled the CUP's extermination of the Armenians a *crime de lèse-humanité*, meaning a crime of the highest level.[9] Because of his empathy for the Armenians, he became a bogeyman for the CUP and Kemalists. Turkish nationalists hated him in particular as the author of the first draft of the 1914 Reform Agreement that they decried as a conspiratorial step toward Armenian autonomy (see Chapter 4), and as an international scholar who continued to fight, though without immediate success, for Armenian rights after Lausanne.[10] The "Armenian Home"—even in the modest form of a Turkish district for returning survivors—was the most sensitive topic at the Lausanne Conference. It came only briefly onto the negotiating table and was sharply rejected by Rıza Nur, Ankara's delegate in this matter who acted according to the instructions of his government.[11] The question of return went along with the inconvenient issue of returning genocide loot.

An elitist, discreetly triumphalist British narrative of the Lausanne Conference focuses on great successes achieved by Foreign Secretary Lord Curzon during the first half of the Conference. These consisted of open Straits, weakened Turkish-Soviet ties, an open door toward the mandatory future of Mosul, and burgeoning working relations with Ankara.[12] This narrative remained discreet because no one could deny the inherent moral defeat compared to the earlier ambitions. Britain had been an advocate of minority rights in the late Ottoman realm but was required to show its true colors in Lausanne—in other words, its prioritarian imperial interests. It thus abandoned, in the hour of crisis, its advocacy of minorities and its humanitarian self-expectation. Since the early 1910s, British diplomacy had clearly underestimated the power of Turkish nationalism. The Great War, fought by the imperial Young Turks in alliance with Germany, came at an unexpectedly high cost for Britain, absorbing almost a third of its combat strength. Defeated, but prepared for ongoing armed resistance, the former CUP cadres did not give up and successfully reorganized in Ankara.

The triumphalist Turkish narrative of the Lausanne Conference and its heroes goes back to the contemporary framing of history in the Kemalist press, domestic politics, politicians' memoirs, and, most importantly, Kemal Atatürk's account of contemporary history in his six-day speech in October 1927.[13] It sounded brilliant: after a disastrous Great War, the savior-leader led a new, young movement that departed in 1919 from a moribund Turkish-Ottoman Empire. In its quasi-holy war of "liberation," "independence," and "salvation," it defied the imperialist victors with their odious plans of partitioning the Turks' remaining heartland. Supreme commander Mustafa Kemal Pasha, who was labeled "Ghazi" (Muslim war hero) by the Ankara government, thus secured the "national territory" according to the 1920 "National Pact" that claimed Anatolia plus some adjacent territory. He saw himself as a defender of the country against "treacherous minorities" and "agents of imperialism," that is, indigenous non-Turks and Turkish liberals close to the West.

"National defense," according to Ankara's terms, comprised destroying the enemy, including "dangerous" non-Turkish peoples who claimed self-determination after the gospel of the League of Nations. An example is the attempt at autonomy by the Rûm of Pontus. "It was to be established on the most beautiful and richest shores of the northern Black Sea, but has been completely eliminated together with its supporters," Gazi Kemal boasted in 1923, after the conclusion of the Lausanne Treaty.[14] The Kemalists thus completed a regional genocide begun three years earlier by Atatürk's predecessor Talaat Pasha.[15] The language used by Rıza Nur—a minister in the early Ankara government—was equally exterminatory. According to his own complacent testimony, he ordered Osman Agha, a main perpetrator, "Agha, cleanse thoroughly the Pontus [. . .]. Destroy also the churches and take their stones far away, so that, just in case, nobody can say that there were ever churches here."[16]

Despite its loss of an empire and the sultanate-caliphate, the Ankara government stood in immediate ideological and personal continuity with the most committed nationalists among the late Ottoman elites, including the *génocidaires*. While Gazi

Kemal's circle demarcated itself from empire, palace, and dynasty, it continued to identify itself with Ottoman history. In his 1927 retrospect, Atatürk stated: "The questions brought forward at Lausanne's peace table did not exclusively concern the new regime, which was only three or four years old. Centuries-old accounts were settled."[17] In Lausanne, Ankara's delegation stressed the post-1918 defense of Turkish rule over Anatolia, which it termed self-determination. At the same time, it propagated an alleged ancient history of Ottoman victimhood at the hands of Europe. Thus, it succeeded in selectively reframing Ankara's core issues in Lausanne: Turkey's sovereignty, minimal minority rights, and the rejection of an "Armenian home."

Ankara's delegation in Lausanne not only successfully deflected attention from the Great War, CUP dictatorship, and mass crimes, which had stood at the forefront in Paris-Sèvres. It also proffered a narrative of national liberation that the CUP had first begun to articulate. National history was from now on seen to have culminated in the triumph at Lausanne, the diplomatic cornerstone of the Republic of Turkey that crowned the military victory in the Anatolian wars. Based on a new national understanding of history that had burgeoned since the early twentieth century, the magic moment of "Lozan" (Turkish for "Lausanne") not only contributed to rewriting contemporary history but also to setting the pillars for an endeavor that led to the Turkish History Thesis of the 1930s and made "Turanian" (proto-)Turks the indigenous population of Anatolia.[18]

Milestones of a Protracted Conference

When Swiss President Rudolf Haab inaugurated the Conference on November 20, 1922, he stressed the importance of a peace that would also satisfy the needs of the losers.[19] During the first days and weeks of the Conference, the speakers repeatedly ventilated lofty wishes for a world peace depending on the settlement for the Middle East. Often leading to heated exchanges, the Conference's first weeks addressed fundamental questions, including population transfer, minority rights, an Armenian home in Anatolia as well as the future of Northern Iraq (Mosul province).

Challenging the claim to unitary Turkish rule over Asia Minor and achieving robust minority rights would have required an *Entente cordiale* between the Great War victors and the readiness for an armed confrontation. This was, however, out of the question for national empires absorbed by their own consolidation after 1918. Aware of the disunity of the Western powers regarding Turkey and Europe, Ankara's delegation knew how to exploit the situation. Additional haste seized European diplomacy when on January 11, 1922, due to reparation claims, French troops occupied the Ruhr in Germany, thus drawing political and media attention away from the Oriental Question. On Germany, Turkey, and related issues of reparations, there was a serious rift between Paris and London. The dynamics in Lausanne therefore merged in complex ways with contemporary events and domestic politics.

Under the presidency of the British Foreign Secretary Lord Curzon, the conference emphasized during its first weeks humanitarian issues, minority rights, and the necessity of safeguarding a home for native Armenians in a part of Anatolia. By the end of 1922, however, faced with categorical rejection, the European insistence on Armenian and other minority rights and claims crumbled just as the Turkish delegates had anticipated, and the so-called Greco-Turkish population exchange as a compulsory measure was a done deal.[20] Ankara's men successfully insisted on establishing a unitary Turkey for Muslim Turks, by no means anything resembling a plural and democratic polity. A special convention, prepared in December 1922 and signed on January 30, 1923, made the transfer of 356,000 Muslim Greeks to Turkey, and of 290,000 Greek-Orthodox Ottomans (Rûm) to Greece, compulsory. Those Rûm that had fled or had been expelled already numbered around 1.5 million.[21] All of them lost their homes.

Talks preparing the population transfer had started before the Conference. League of Nations' Commissioner for Refugees Fridtjof Nansen had met with Hamid Bey in Istanbul on October 31, 1922, in order to prepare the negotiations. Hamid (Hamit Hasancan)—himself a member of Ankara's delegation in Lausanne—was Ankara's representative in occupied Istanbul. In line with a decade of Turkish ethnic cleansing, Hamid told Nansen during their preparatory Istanbul meeting that he was instructed by the Ankara government "to negotiate on the basis of a total and enforced exchange of populations, from which the population of Constantinople would not be excepted."[22] The majority in Ankara's National Assembly believed that non-Muslims had "no place in this country anymore." As a consequence, according to one deputy on November 3, 1922, with regard to the remaining Ottoman Christians in the country, "There is only one thing that can be done with them: exchange of populations."[23] Ankara's instruction to Hamid meant that virtually all remaining Christians were to be forced to leave their Anatolian home and that Ankara was ready to accept a (much lower) number of incoming Muslims from Greece.

Dozens of refugees died every day from exhaustion; many more would die during the months to come if resolute action was not taken. An expedited exchange, even if disproportional (i.e., targeting many more Christians than Muslims) and compulsory, would at least put a certain number of houses and parcels at the disposition of the refugees from Anatolia. Without exchange, Ankara would anyway pursue its removal and dispossession of Christians but without giving anything in return. Nansen's estimated figure of 850,000 refugees in Greece, in his report of early November, was expected to rise to much more than a million in December.[24] The only thing the Conference could finally mitigate was to exclude from the transfer non-Rûm Christians as well as those Rûm who were long-term residents in Istanbul.

In December 1922, the Turkish delegation successfully asserted that it would only recognize those groups as minorities which the Ottoman state had treated as non-Muslim *millet*, that is, Jewish, Armenian, and Rûm communities. This excluded the Kurds and other non-Turks or non-Muslims.[25] Only these weak—by then heavily decimated—groups would benefit from the minority rights to be laid out in the Treaty. This restrictive definition contradicted the minority rights and regime of the League of Nations, but it was critical to Ankara's project of forming a strictly unitary Turkish-Muslim state.

In contrast, the Treaty of Sèvres had planned a plural Anatolia and full-fledged minority protection, thus taking into account the historical diversity of the country. Insightful, progressive, and promising regulations, however, went along, inauspiciously, with imperialist deals, because "the Turkish settlement was regarded in Paris, not as an integral problem requiring solution in its own terms, but as the area of least resistance in which compensations could be found wherewith to bribe several esurient Powers to relinquish their claims in Europe itself." And these were "to be paid in Turkish territory for the sacrifices" demanded of them during the Great War, as Harold Nicolson, a diplomatic insider of the British delegation both in Paris and in Lausanne, astutely wrote.[26]

Sèvres' decisions on prosecution of war criminals, the restitution of genocide spoils, an Armenian state in Northeastern Asia Minor, a possible Kurdish state in Northern Mesopotamia, and—depending on a referendum—Greek rule over the region of Izmir were therefore ill starred and insufficiently supported. Led by the former Ottoman Foreign Minister Gabriel Noradunghian, exiled in Paris, the unofficial Armenian delegation had come to Lausanne well prepared. Under Turkish pressure, however, it was not given any official standing and admitted only to hearings related to a sub-commission. By January 1923, this delegation had to accept Lausanne's total abandonment of the idea of an Anatolian "Armenian home" and thus the complete failure of its main mission.[27] At the time, "Armenian home" meant nothing more than a Turkish-ruled small territory in Anatolia to which genocide survivors would be able to return, instead of a future as home- and stateless refugees that became reality after Lausanne.

The Armenian voice in Lausanne bore witness to unaddressed crimes and injustices, and to a tremendous refugee problem; it could not, however, inspire any call to action. The Armenian experience recalled unwelcome truths in a time that agreed on a forgetful peace and tried to suppress the horrors of recent history—believing this was the only way to move forward. Thus, when obligatory lip service was done, and some testimonies had been given for the record, no diplomat was willing and prepared to deal with the Armenians and related issues any longer. This remained the status quo for many decades to come. Two and a half years after the Sèvres Treaty, the "Convention concerning the Exchange of Greek and Turkish Populations," signed on January 30, 1923, terminated the millennia-old presence of Rûm in Asia Minor except for Istanbul, as well as the presence of Muslims in Greece with the exception of Western Thrace.[28] And, as Nur wrote triumphantly, "The Treaty of Lausanne has buried the Armenian question," and with this, it entirely disfranchised the survivors of the genocide.[29]

Most believed that *realpolitik* had to leave behind the Armenians as tragic casualties once and for all. In their eyes, the Lausanne Treaty achieved the necessary resetting and thus solved both the Oriental Question and the Armenian Question, albeit bloodily and costly. Others, such as Curzon, understood that the Conference fatally accepted evil, and that crucial questions of justice had therefore been postponed to a distant future. The Armenian delegate Alexandre Khatissian underlined in his serene retrospective, written in the late 1920s, the justice of the Armenians' main cause that was not lost but deferred to a far future. He agreed that there had been a number of illusions, miscalculations, mistakes, and misplaced or inflated expectations.[30] The atmosphere of the earlier Paris Conference had contributed to too much trust being placed in the victors of the Great War; it had gone hand in hand with unrealistic and immature political expectations in its immediate aftermath, which France and Britain attuned to their imperial visions. This unfortunate synthesis affected most non-Turkish nations looking to the West. Whatever the circumstances and the outcome, however, these groups were no less entitled to aspire to a new post-Ottoman age of self-rule and equal rights than any other.

One of the most heated debates—besides those on population transfer and minority rights—was that in the First Commission (for territorial questions) on January 23 regarding the province of Mosul. The question here was whether to annex the province to Turkey or to (then British-mandated) Iraq. Basic flaws in the historical underpinning of the Turkish position appeared when Chief Delegate Ismet declared Turks and Kurds to be from the same Turanian race and therefore to have been in perfect inherent harmony since the dawn of time. In ethnological terms, Erbil and Kirkuk were therefore to be recognized as entirely Turkish places. In the same breath, he claimed the Ankara government to be a perfect electoral democracy in which the Kurds were fully represented.[31]

In principle, Britain attained its main imperial goals by the end of January 1923, when Curzon put a draft treaty on the table, pushing for a rapid conclusion. The achievements by then included free passage through the Straits, Ankara's estrangement from Moscow, Ankara's approval to adhere to the League of Nations, and, pending further negotiations, the annexation of Mosul to Iraq. France, the main investor in the late Ottoman Empire, then still waited for satisfying compromises on the Ottoman debt and further investments, including railway concessions. The draft treaty took these into account. As for Ankara, the draft lacked balance in these hitherto little discussed matters; the Conference was interrupted on February 4, to resume again only on April 23.

Economic, financial, and strategic questions—not minority rights, the fate and possessions of Anatolia's non-Turkish natives, or the tens of thousands of refugees dying in the autumn and winter of 1922—turned out to be the thorniest issues. There, Europe resisted most strongly Ankara's expectations to make a *tabula rasa* of the late Ottoman situation. It is true that some delegates, especially Curzon and Rumbold, articulated sharp statements that named the breaches of taboo in fundamental issues such as the forced population transfer and the unpunished mass murder and expropriation of Anatolia's Christians. But these testimonies, or rhetorical performances, did not change the course of the decision-making.[32]

During the Conference interval, meetings in Paris and London dealt with the remaining bones of contention, as did turbulent debates in Ankara. There, spring 1923 saw important steps toward implementing Kemalist one-party rule. The circle around Gazi Kemal prepared the first general elections for June in a climate of intimidation and censorship. In the second half of the Conference, a more business-like atmosphere prevailed compared to the previous winter, although breaks and even an armed confrontation again shortly loomed. This second half of the Conference had to solve the remaining financial, economic, territorial, and legal questions, including the issue of foreigners' rights after the capitulations were abolished. From April 1923 until the conclusion of the Treaty, Horace Rumbold, former High Commissioner to

Constantinople, represented the British Empire in Lausanne, while Ismet and Nur again headed Ankara's delegation.

Ankara's delegation was adaptive to the era's prevailing vocabulary of a modern secular civilization with racial imprints. In exchange for the abolition of the capitulations and other legal restrictions of the Ottoman era, Ankara made an important pledge: to introduce modern law and equality. Throughout the whole Conference, it set out on a promissory narrative of Westernizing reform and the rule of law. However, driven by the desire for full national sovereignty and diplomatic success, it promised more than it could ever realize. Born as a post-CUP armed resistance against claims of non-Turkish Anatolian groups and their European backers, the Ankara government lacked a genuine commitment to constitutionality. During the whole century after Lausanne, it never could give itself a constitution based on a comprehensive democratic social contract; "there has not been a fully representative and inclusive constitution-drafting process in Turkish republican history."[33]

The reduction of the status and meaning of minority in December 1922 meant that only the former Ottoman *millets* were to benefit from all minority rights laid out in the Treaty, and even this conditionally. Ankara's delegation accepted foreign legal advisors for a five-year transition to a new justice system that would introduce full legal equality based on modern (European) law. Justice Minister Mahmut Bozkurt, who was in charge of the reforms from 1925, put it this way: "When we abolished the capitulations in the Lausanne Peace Treaty, we took it upon ourselves at the same time to establish a whole new Turkish judicial organization with a new legal system, new laws and new courts."[34] Lausanne Treaty Article 42 guaranteed the *millets'* own family laws. However, this article—as well as its special regulations that postulated a consensual drafting process in cooperation with the minorities in case of reforms— remained a paper tiger. By transferring the entire Swiss Civil Code, Ankara decided this crucial legal reform by itself, without consulting the concerned minorities or European experts. It pressured the intimidated minority representative to renounce on rights that the signatories of the Treaty should have defended—although, on a purely legal (versus factual) level, neither Ankara nor the minorities themselves could abrogate international law.

In his memoirs, Ismet Pasha was keen to emphasize that the foreign legal advisors, foremost among them the Swiss Georges Sauser-Hall, had no say in Turkey's reforms. Ultimately, they only served to "admit that the Turkish courts were working properly, as in all civilized countries, and that Turkish judges were competent in their duties."[35] The modus operandi of the law revolution is essential background for a notoriously dependent justice system. The rulers in Ankara craved immediate recognition as the representatives of a modern sovereign state, but they rejected consensus building and a true separation of powers. The "Law Revolution" (*Hukuk Devrimi*) of the 1920s, which also comprised penal and commercial law, was warmly received in Western capitals. But the façade of the "new Turkey" impressed more than its substance. Nevertheless, Ankara's new secularism based on the new civil law, which abolished the sharia, entailed some promising openings (see also Chapter 10).

Figure 1 Successful politics of force, power, and violence. Caricature "dedicated to the Lausanne Conference" and carrying its predominant—social Darwinist—message: "These problems do not fit into any formula. They must be solved by 'force'!" On the blackboard: "Peace = (straits + Mosul)/minorities by war, minus debt management and capitulations," *Akbaba* (Istanbul), January 22, 1923.

The Paradigm of Lausanne

At the heart of the Lausanne Treaty, there is no democratic consent but, unfortunately, coercion, violence, and an unspoken, era-defining genocide (see Figure 1). In July 1923, Carl J. Burckhardt, a young man from Geneva, traveled on an ICRC mission through Anatolia and met Gazi Kemal. Ten days after the signing of the Treaty of Lausanne and nine days before the Turkish president inaugurated the new parliament, he wrote to the poet Hugo von Hofmannsthal, his personal friend, about his observations in Anatolia.

He pointed to the "forced, monstrous exodus of the expelled Greek civilian population," Ankara's "narrowest nationalism," its "culture wars," the "terrible process of uprooting and expulsion of ancient peoples," and the "murder of Armenians, Kurds, and Circassians."[36] In contrast to the growing international admiration for Ankara's confident style and formidable supreme leader, Burckhardt did not share the slightest fascination with Gazi Kemal and similar emerging rulers. He later became a diplomat and ICRC president. "There is now a Turkish nation-state, ruled by a Jacobin dictator. [. . .] He will set a precedent. He is already writing the script of the near future. [. . .] He is ushering in a new era, more powerful ones of his kind will follow. [. . .] Of all the explosives [of our time], nationalism is the strongest."[37]

The Turkish example strongly impressed German contemporaries, who admired the revision of what they called the dictatorial Treaty of Paris-Sèvres in reference to the Treaty of Versailles.[38] They identified with their Great War ally's successful struggle against the Western victors. The German far right, including the early National Socialist German Workers' Party, embraced the methods of the ultranationalist formation of a new "Turkey for the Turks," as a contemporary slogan put it. With Lausanne, triumphant Ankara became the Nazis' number one paragon. By September 1923, Turkish nationalism had shown them "what we [Germans] too" must do "to set ourselves free."[39] The Turkish military and diplomatic success made them believe in the necessity of a reckless national savior and of eradicating "foreign elements." "For us Germans this heroic Turkish struggle is of utmost importance. We, too, must fight for our place in the sun again, whatever the cost [. . .]. Life issues are not solved by talk and majority decisions, but only by blood and iron."[40]

The genocidal Turkification of Anatolia is what the German jurist Carl Schmitt recorded approvingly, years before joining the Nazi party, as the "ruthless Turkification of the country," and what the German officer Hans Tröbst bluntly praised as "Turkish proof" in the Nazi magazine *Heimatland*. Both wrote during or shortly after the Lausanne Conference. Schmitt used his observation of Turkey as an incisive argument for rejecting pluralist democracy, political liberalism, and a constitutional polity conceived beyond the constraints of ethnicity. "The Turks have given proof that the purification of a people from its foreign elements is possible on a grand scale," Tröbst concluded. He was even more specific: "The bloodsuckers and parasites on the Turkish national body were Greeks [Rûm] and Armenians. They had to be exterminated and rendered harmless, otherwise the whole struggle for freedom would have been in danger." As a rule, "all foreign-born"—those religiously and ethnically singled out as "non-Turkish," although indigenous to Anatolia—would have had to die in the "combat zone." Tröbst assumed half a million Anatolian Christians killed in this way in 1919–22, most of them civilians or prisoners of war.⁴¹ This figure apparently came from Turkish insider circles, on whose side Tröbst had fought, and it captures the magnitude of victimhood even after the CUP genocides. Targeted after 1919 were mainly Rûm and Armenians, and Tröbst's figure comprises the slaughter of tens of thousands of Christians—many of them refugees from inner Anatolia—after the reconquest of Smyrna (Izmir), in September 1922, and the sending of thousands of Christian men from Smyrna to deadly labor camps, two months before the Lausanne Conference began.

In order to understand the actually existing and functioning Turkish nationalism at the time of the Lausanne Conference, one has to deal with Turanian racial ideology—just as one cannot understand German National Socialism without considering Aryan racism. There is an analogy with the Aryan supremacy obsession of the upcoming Nazi movement as well as an overlapping of anti-Jewish and anti-Armenian racism. This is most strikingly the case with Rıza Nur, the vice-chief of Ankara's delegation in Lausanne (see Chapter 6). From 1922, as we have seen, the German far right increasingly admired the successes of Turkish nationalism and looked for concrete recipes from the Turkish experience. In the immediate aftermath of the Lausanne Conference, legal scholar André Mandelstam rightly emphasized the gravity of "the implicit recognition [by the Conference] of a general right for all peoples to consolidate their existence through the destruction or violent assimilation of other nations."⁴² It became a paradigm.

The Swiss theologian Leonhard Ragaz noted shortly before his death in 1945: "Those atrocities in Armenia remind me strongly today, as I see them again in my mind's eye, of the Nazi atrocities which have now been revealed, leaving the world around me shaken. There exists an important connection between them."⁴³ For Ragaz and many other alert contemporaries in the 1930s and early 1940s, the Armenians were the obvious reference point and comparison when they learned about persecution of Jews and the Holocaust. In contrast to Germany, solidarity with the victims—not admiration for the revisionist victors—clearly prevailed in the Swiss public sphere, and the press was sensitive to all matters relating to liberties, pluralism, and minority rights. The plight of the Armenians touched hearts, and the crimes and fate they suffered remained burnt into public memory, driving long-lasting aid.⁴⁴

Karl Meyer, an insider and chronicler of the Swiss Federation of the Friends of the Armenians, reports how members of the Federation talked with Rumbold during the Conference. Rumbold was frank: "We cannot wage war for the Armenians. We do not want to deny our commitments, but we are not in position to fulfil them [. . .]. It is clear: the Armenians are sacrificed in the process [of compromising with Ankara]." Meyer concluded, "the Treaty of Lausanne is based on the fiction that Armenians do not exist. Thus, it serves neither peace nor justice. As a result, the situation of the Armenians became so tragic that it can hardly be properly imagined." A humanitarian leader, who worked among handicapped survivors in Lebanon for four decades after the Lausanne Conference, Meyer knew the situation better than others.⁴⁵ Another Swiss rejecting Lausanne's *realpolitik* and standing up for stateless Armenian survivors was pastor Antony Krafft-Bonnard. He was very active in Lausanne during the Conference and approached various delegates, among them Rumbold and Rıza Nur. Inspired by the

Gospel, he also demanded adherence to the "duty of humanity" after the Armenian Question was supposedly settled in early January 1923.[46]

Diametrically opposed to Krafft-Bonnard was Colonel Arthur Fonjallaz, Krafft-Bonnard's Vaudois compatriot. The chairman of a newly founded Swiss Society of Friends of Turkey, Fonjallaz played an active role behind the scenes and in the aftermath of the Conference. Beforehand, he had traveled in Asia Minor and published admiring pieces on Ankara's warfare. After the Conference, Fonjallaz organized a semi-official Swiss mission that proposed to establish lasting economic relations with Turkey and left for Ankara in September 1923. In December 1923, the Syndicat d'Entreprises en Orient SA was founded in the Lausanne-Palace as a direct result of Fonjallaz' mission. Making him its president, it brought together more than a dozen of the big names in Swiss industry. Subsequently, several Swiss companies successfully took root in Kemalist Turkey. Fonjallaz himself, however, the pioneer and great admirer of the early Kemalists and their new Turkey, lost his fortune in a series of failed undertakings. Although he had enjoyed Ismet's and Nur's proximity and sustained consideration in Lausanne, the establishment in Ankara was no longer interested in its Swiss admirer. In line with a political mindset that had emerged in his dealings with Ankara, the hapless businessman became one of the most high-profile fascists in Switzerland. He was not the only one to extend his veneration of Gazi Kemal (Atatürk) to Mussolini and, finally, Adolf Hitler.[47]

A Post-Lausanne Century

The publicly declared ambitions of the Western powers during the Great War and for the Paris-Geneva peace were, on the one hand, the liberation of formerly subordinate nations, in particular those brutally victimized during the Ottoman long Great War; and on the other hand, building up a League-based and law-based framework for all, small and large. In particular, this concerned the crisis-ridden world that the West has since then called the Middle East. The failure to meet these ambitions amounted to the collapse of the core message that had driven Western commitment during and at the end of the World War, and with this, a new world order not based on the power of violence, but law and democracy.

In the late and post-Ottoman world, this collapse resulted in the ultimate disintegration of the hopes for constitutional futures that had vigorously come to the fore during the 1908 Young Turk Revolution and reemerged after 1918. This double collapse and defeat was inherent in Lausanne's pact of power and interest, struck between Ankara's ultranationalists and Western Europe's remaining national empires. Lausanne thus opened the door for antidemocratic far-right currents in politics and diplomacy, starting with Turkism and Italian Fascism, and profoundly impacting Nazism. Ankara's National Assembly reestablished and rehabilitated leading forces that had carried Istanbul-based Turkey in the 1910s—a then-pioneering experience in imperial and genocidal single-party rule. Recognized by Lausanne, Ankara's National Assembly government became the first regime among interwar antidemocrats to be fully embraced by international diplomacy, despite its past and the *génocidaires* among its cadres.

Ankara used its multiple relations with, and its delayed membership in, the League of Nations as a means to domestically realize and internationally rubber-stamp its notion of state and society. This pioneering ultranationalist concept amounted to a radically homogenized, unitary, and, by the early 1930s, totalitarian nation-state. The League-supported "population exchange" of 1923 was the pivotal step toward the League's open abandonment of previously defended basic rights and principles, including freedom for small peoples and nations on their own soil.

This critical assessment is not to deny positive possibilities and steps during the formation of a "new Turkey." It is, on the contrary, essential to perceive gray areas, ambivalences, and paradoxes, even if the dark aspects need to be highlighted because of their democracy-obstructing long-term impact and their too-frequent white-washing. Insights into the paradox of ultranationalist Kemalists, who happened to admire democratic achievements, emerge if we look at the Turkish dealing with the Swiss host of the Lausanne Conference. Kemalist appreciation certainly went beyond the diplomatic courtesies of the moment and the momentous adoption of Swiss Civil Law. And it had to swallow the sharp contrast between Ankara's unitary state ideal and the highly diverse and federalist reality of the Swiss system.

To my understanding, the sustained Swiss references by Kemalists sounded Turkey's unmet constitutional challenges and hopes. They expressed the candid will to belong to the West, without being dominated by the West. Years later, Mahmut E. Bozkurt, Ankara's minister of economy during the Lausanne Conference, disarmingly confessed in his textbook on the "Atatürk Revolution": "In a political perspective, revolution or progress means making the people as sovereign as possible. For the Swiss it would be reactionary to follow us, whereas for us, it's politically a revolution to draw near to their constitution."[48] Although his adoration of Eternal Leader Atatürk blinded Bozkurt to real democracy, he knew that an active and participatory democracy, which gave the people the greatest say, was decisive for a progressive polity.

Ankara's success in Lausanne, in contrast, had encouraged personalized partisan rule, unseparated powers, and the belief in crude power. The Conference had left basic issues of contemporary history—such as dispossession, extermination, and the rights of small(er) nations—unclarified, and it thus left recent history demagogically exploitable. The suppression of dissent and the lack of fact-based clarification at the Lausanne moment in Ankara's National Assembly presaged a return of the repressed. Besides the unhealed wounds it left among non-Turkish people in and from Anatolia, this foundational moment therefore fueled conspiracy theories and soon also myth-based imperial nostalgia.

Lausanne is a Treaty to be peacefully but resolutely overcome from within by a new constitutional will and a spirit eager for new democratic contracts. Because of entrenched antidemocratic patterns, this overcoming from within demands hard democratic labor. Despite Lausanne's endorsement of an emerging one-party dictatorship, a democratic yearning—if weak and at times purely rhetorical—was there from the beginning. The Swiss press and the Swiss Federation of the Friends of the Armenians had sharply criticized the Ankara government, notably during personal interviews with the leaders of the Turkish delegation. Nevertheless, on the last day of the Conference in Lausanne, Ismet Pasha stated to a Swiss officer:

> I admire the Swiss people who have always concentrated their activity on the work and the arts of peace and who have always occupied a first place among the peoples in this field. [...] Through contact with them I have been morally supported in the defense of the vital interests of Turkey; because the principles I have advocated, especially that of national independence, are the same for which Switzerland has been fighting for centuries with success and which it has been able to adopt. I will never forget Switzerland, its institutions and its people, because Turkey can learn valuable lessons here.[49]

Updating and overcoming "Lausanne" today—in the spirit of these words—would mean a democratic, pluralist, and regionalist, possibly even federalist reconstitution for Turkey, even if such wisdom is a thorn in the side of unrepented heirs of unitary ultranationalists.

6

Rıza Nur

Cofounder of the Republic, Delegate
in Lausanne, Pan-Turkist

In the early 1920s, we meet a man in his forties, at the zenith of his active life, who enjoyed broad recognition in Ankara's National Assembly and held various ministries: education, foreign affairs, and finally health, and who was also active in diplomacy. Readers of this book have already met him, if briefly, in previous passages.

Dr. Rıza Nur (1879–1942) negotiated the Treaty of Moscow with the Bolsheviks in March 1921, together with then-foreign minister Yusuf Kemal (Tengirşenk).[1] Nur recalled this negotiation: "They wanted to befriend us in order to use us as a trump card against the British and French. We too used the Russian as a trump card. We knew, when required, we would break the bond." And he added: "We still wanted to occupy Baku. The main reason was to open the way to Turan."[2]

Although he served as the vice-chief at the side of Ismet (Inönü) Pasha, Yusuf Kemal's successor, he was considered the senior diplomat in Ankara's delegation at the Lausanne Conference, the one possessing the most experience and the most articulate ideology. Nur wrote extensive works of history before and even during the Lausanne Conference. However, his most popular books are his memoirs which—having fallen into disgrace in the Kemalist Republic of Turkey—he composed in exile toward the end of the 1920s. They have inspired counter-accounts to the national founding narrative of Kemalism in Turkey as well as conspiracy theories on the Lausanne Treaty.

After the publication of the memoirs and other writings in the 1960s, Nur was regarded by some as a martyr and prophet of suppressed truths, but by others as a baseless neurotic and fanatic. Opposite camps—Kemalists as well as their pan-Turkist and Islamist opponents—are, however, largely in agreement that Nur rendered much service in early Ankara. From a global history perspective, he must be recognized as a staunch and influential anti-Semite and anti-Armenian propagandist. He declared it "natural" that downtrodden people like the Armenians or the Jews were denied equal collective rights and had to suffer further disasters allegedly of their own making. The hand of his social Darwinist "god" himself brought this about:

The Almighty Force, who weighs and determines the fortunes of nations, filled all sorts of ancient and eternal pages of history. In this world, he destroyed two nations forever; he moved them from diaspora to diaspora; distributed them all over the world; and condemned them to live miserably. The first of these nations is Jewish, the second is Armenian.[3]

Political Surgeon, Pan-Turkish Ideologue

Nur's writings provide extraordinarily open and undisguised information about the thinking of influential elites at the time of Turkey's formation. He described himself as an extreme nationalist believing in Turkism (*şiddetli Türkçü nasyonalist*). In his diaries from the 1910s, Cavid Bey castigated this attitude as "müfrit nasiyonalism," that is, extreme or ultranationalism, finding it prevalent among CUP Central Committee members like Enver Pasha, Ziya Gökalp, Dr. Nazım, and Dr. Shakir.[4]

Nur is not only a main link between late and post-Ottoman pan-Turkism, and a central reference of this current to this day.[5] He became also a main reference for revisionist currents in relation to the Lausanne Treaty. These include groups of pan-Turkish, pan-Islamic, and neo-Ottoman inspiration. A pan-Turkist in the vein of Ziya Gökalp, Nur pursued the ideal of a great, strong, and culturally self-confident Islamic Turkey in equidistance from other powers. He is therefore a figure of reference for the Turkish current of Eurasianism to this day. Nur espoused more biologically underpinned racial thinking than Gökalp and pushed the idea of a superior "Turanian" (proto-Turkish) race. He was, by far, not the only one to make Turanian ancestry a central criterion of his political thought.

Developing a lasting influence, politician and author Rıza Nur is a significant figure during the years of transition from the Ottoman Empire to the Turkish nation-state. His person, his role in Lausanne, and his strikingly anti-Armenian social Darwinist approach to history shed much light on the political-historical thinking among the founders of the Turkish Republic. His thinking was mainstream, not marginal. And it was never fundamentally revoked. In particular, we find closely related ideas in Atatürk's historical and linguistic thesis of the 1930s. Nur's ideas have also considerably impacted the AKP (Justice and Development Party) ideology, especially since the 2010s.

Nur's tentative "party program" from exile, for a "total renewal of Turkey," dating from 1929, demanded Islam as the state's official religion; that women return to the hearth; the parallel use of both the Arab and the Latin alphabet; the restoration of the caliphate; the punishment of Kemalist leaders; the abolition of Kemalist (Atatürk-centric) national celebrations; the establishment of a "race directorate"; the establishment of missionary lodges spreading Islamic pan-Turkism; and a confederation of "all Turks." A first, more comprehensive public debate of Rıza Nur and his work emerged in the early 1960s, when his unpublished works were partly made known, although they still remained unedited.[6]

Rıza Nur can be termed a "political doctor": one among many politicized graduates of the Imperial Medical School in late nineteenth-century Istanbul who entered politics applying concepts of biology, surgery, and Darwinism to society. Let us think of cofounders or eminences of the CUP—such as Mehmed Shahingiray, Nazım, and Bahaeddin Shakir, who were a few years older than Nur. Like them—and like Yusuf Kemal who also hailed from Sinop at the Black Sea—Nur became a clandestine CUP member as a student in Istanbul. Like Yusuf Kemal, he entered the reopened Ottoman Parliament when he was only thirty years old. In 1912, however, Nur fell out with his party, whose leadership nevertheless supported him for further training abroad in Switzerland and Egypt. For several years, this left him ample time to write before joining Mustafa Kemal's movement and cofounding the National Assembly in Ankara in 1920.

Nur's Turanism and his glorification of Turkishness are influenced by contemporary Turkism and pan-Turkism, most evident in Ziya Gökalp's poetry and prose from the early 1910s (see Chapter 8). Minister Nur cooperated with Gökalp, the former CUP chief ideologue close to Talaat Pasha, after Gökalp was released from his internment in Malta. He commissioned him to conduct a study on the Kurdish tribes with the aim of using the expert knowledge for a rigorous policy of assimilation into Turkishness.[7]

Nur considered the Kurds to be Turanian and thus assimilable, in contrast to the Christian Armenians and Rûm, whom he portrayed as foreign bodies. As we have seen in the previous chapter, the argument that the Kurds were Turanian served the Turkish delegation in Lausanne as an argument for claiming Mosul. The Turanian argumentation, the Turanian idea of world history, and the claim of Turanian supremacy by Nur's cohort went, however, far beyond a few sparse examples. Strong emotions and identifications as well as aggressive feelings of supremacy grounded the contents of this ideology.

Nur's *History of the Armenians* versus His *History of the Turks*

The beginning of Nur's *Türk Tarihi* (History of the Turks), published by the Ministry of Education in 1924, reads as follows:

> The thing I am most proud of in the world is that I was born a Turk. I [. . .] have never seen such a heroic, brave, kind-hearted, intelligent and clever people as the Turks, never a nation with such a great and sublime history as the Turks [. . .] never one with all the abilities to rise to the highest position in today's world of civilisation. [. . .] Turkishness is for me an inextinguishable, inexhaustible love. It is delicious to be burned by this divine fire that seizes my whole being; it gives me pleasure and joy as it burns me. That alone keeps me alive.[8]

Türk Tarihi was published in 1924–6 in twelve (of a total of fourteen) volumes for the purpose of "national education," as it says in the introduction. In this work, Nur continued to uphold the "sacred idea of uniting all Turkish tribes in the homeland of Turan under one flag." He drafted a kind of nationalist history of salvation, dividing time into three major epochs: the pre-Islamic, the Islamic, and the present. History would culminate in a modern Turanian-Islamic synthesis, producing a Greater Turkey based on race and religion. This scheme is familiar to us from Gökalp's writings of 1917–18, and is still found in Gökalp's summa, his *Türkçülüğün esasları* (Principles of Turkism) of 1923. Gökalp died in Ankara in 1924, just as Nur's first volumes were published there.

Nur and other nationalists frankly admitted that the Turkish nation lagged behind in terms of civilization and education. But racial pride—pioneering civilizational deeds by Turanians in the history of humanity and the vision of a Turkish future in Turanian unity and great power—compensated for present Turkey's shortcomings. Grandeur and alleged Anatolian and Eurasian indigenousness underpinned the claims of the nationalist historians. They agreed with the Gökalpian doctrine of racial and national greatness: "The Turks' deeds in world history are so lofty that they cannot be compared to those of any other nation." Their narrative made Turks a heroic master race spreading from China and India to Europe, Arabia, and Africa. They also started to reject any association of the "Turkish blood" with the "yellow race," insisting on the Aryan origin of the Turanian proto-Turks.[9]

The outlines of Nur's Greater Turkey can be found on a map of "Great Turan" reproduced in *Türk Tarihi*. It stretches from the Balkans and Eastern Europe to China, and from the whole of Russia in the north to Syria, Iraq, Iran, and Afghanistan in the south.[10]

> In these lands lived the Turanian race, namely different tribes of this race, i.e. different Turkic tribes. Some of these tribes became Muslims and preserved their race well. Some of them remained Christians. Some of the Christians have preserved their Turkishness or their mother tongue, which is Turkish, but some have forgotten their language and their origin. The majority of Russians today are made up of these Christian Turks who have forgotten their Turkishness.[11]

Nur also classified the Chechens, Bulgarians, and Georgians, among others, as of the Turanian race and thus assimilable to Greater Turkey. But, as Nur later wrote in his memoirs regarding the Kurds, nations forgetful of their Turanian origin would have to be "purified of their own language and race with a consistent assimilation program." All non-Turanians were foreign invaders in the vast Turan. "The Turanian homeland was invaded by the Russians on one side, the Chinese on the other, and another corner by the Persians, and they represent the majority in those regions of our homeland. These peoples [. . .] came to us from other countries and remained as foreign bodies in the Turanian race."[12] In particular, the Armenians allegedly had migrated from northern Greece to Anatolia in antiquity and—the height of evil—had absorbed a Jewish tribe expelled from Palestine at Van.[13]

All these allegedly foreign nations in the Levant were "alien elements, a plague and microbes." It was "of vital interest and absolutely just not to let people of another race, another language and another religion live in our homeland," he wrote in his memoirs on the Lausanne Conference.[14] His idea of a purged state came close to what the Polish sociologist Zygmunt Bauman called a modern mass-murdering "gardener state." In Nur's case, "surgeon state" would be the appropriate term. He admitted that his *Türk Tarihi* was based on fragmentary research, but he stressed: "This book is enough for the present generation of Turks. It is very useful and necessary. Hopefully it will form a [first] basis [of national education]."[15]

Exterminatory racism is explicit not only in Nur's memoirs, and thus in a phase of his life in exile that could be dismissed as neurotic and not to be taken seriously. It is most explicitly embedded already in his historical works of the 1910s and early 1920s. In this and other respects, *Türk Tarihi* is to be understood in close connection with Nur's unpublished *Ermeni Tarihi* (History of the Armenians), which he began earlier and which it follows on from. According to the prologue dated May 1918, Nur wrote *Ermeni Tarihi* during the First World War in Egypt. But parts of it he added later. During the second half of the Lausanne Conference, he found time to complete the manuscript and commissioned a secretary of the delegation to edit the text.[16]

Minister and self-declared history teacher of the nation, Nur considered the Armenians "restless like the Jews. Both peoples are obstreperous. Their character invites disaster upon them. Thus, they were always crushed."[17] "It appears that being massacred is the Armenians' historical fate." "In all cases, the Armenians themselves caused their massacres."[18] Thus, according to an apparently inherent logic, Nur's love for a lofty, idolized Turkishness was fueled by the distinction from and the hatred and violent contempt for others. *Ermeni Tarihi* makes this matter of fact abundantly clear. For him, the least worthy and the worst "foreign bodies" for Turkishness were the Armenians. "They are like the Jews a wretched and dispersed people." "Like the Jews, they had to live under the domination of other nations [. . .] and could only commit themselves to commerce."[19]

For Nur, Jews and Armenians had been persecuted and massacred for thousands of years in world history through their own fault and according to social Darwinist laws of nature and history that favored the great and strong. "They [the Armenians] lack any rightful claim in the presence of the Turk."[20] He had only contempt for small and weak peoples, and this argument served him to deny the Armenians the right to any territory and self-determination in Anatolia and the South Caucasus. "The Armenian is weak and incapable. His impotence is established by his only 2000 years-old [political] life and fate. [. . . They] lack everything that would make them the lords of the land; also, they do not have the right to possess that territory."[21] In his excited disdain (and entirely inappropriate for a true historian and scholar in humanities), he declared, "The history of the Armenians is not important, because the Armenian people is not important. Since that is the case, the Armenians have not produced important events in their history."[22]

Nur openly endorsed the state's policy of extermination. "The Armenian had remained like a malign tumor in our body and needed to be removed by a minor surgery."[23] Rather surprisingly—in view of his at least partly physical-anthropological notion of race—he saw Islamization as a way of salvation for the otherwise doomed Armenians. "It is against nature that a Christian people, which is a minority only, lives in Asia. Such a people is like an alien body in Asia. For the Armenians, there is no solution except to bow to the unavoidable heavy consequences of this unnatural state; or to convert to Islam; or to disappear."[24] However, the quasi-equal weighting of race and Islam in Nur's ultranationalism is consistent with Gökalp's Islamic Turkism.

Nur's Political Peak and Turning Point:
The Conference of Lausanne

Nur was full of contempt for nations he considered unfit for war. Only victors had access to the negotiating table in Lausanne. He therefore scorned all unofficial delegates, including those from Syria and Egypt, but especially the Armenians. "They came to Lausanne from all over the world. A bunch of vagrants, policy buggers, poured into this city."[25]

On January 6, 1923, the British, French, and Italian delegates argued in the Sub-Commission on Minorities at the Lausanne Conference for a modest "Armenian home"—an autonomous province at most—under full Turkish sovereignty, a far cry from the independent Armenia projected in the Sèvres Treaty. The Sub-Commission also received an Armenian, an Assyrian, and a Bulgarian delegation to hear their requests regarding resettlement in Anatolia or, as for the Bulgarians, in Eastern Thrace.[26] Nur led Ankara's delegation in this Sub-Commission.

Before even listening to the representatives in the January 6 meeting, Nur furiously interrupted the procedure and left the room with his team composed of Mehmed Münir (Ertegün), Ahmed Cevad (Açıkalın), and Şükrü (Kaya). Münir, a future ambassador, had been Talaat Pasha's legal advisor at the Brest-Litovsk Peace Conference, and Şükrü, a future minister of foreign affairs and of the interior, had been Talaat's director in charge of the camps for deportees in Northern Syria during the second phase of the Armenian genocide. Before exiting Château d'Ouchy's meeting room, Nur shouted, "the Allies had to make such statements as they had incited these people against the Turks and were responsible for the present situation."

While still very agitated, Nur went to delegation chief Ismet, told the story, and proposed to go back to Ankara. But the latter responded, "Well done, I congratulate you." All in all, indeed, Nur had acted according to Ankara's Conference instructions.[27] Interestingly, Nur, notwithstanding his own hard-line position, felt ultranationalist pressure from Ankara, as he confessed three days later to an inquiring Antony Krafft-Bonnard. "But, please know that if we accept the [Armenian] Home here [at the Conference], we cannot go back to Angora. They would kill us there."[28] Rather than a subterfuge, Nur's words expressed realities of a formative nationalism, born in war, and confidence in its own military strength. It was characterized by an anti-Western and anti-Christian, especially anti-Armenian, stance.

While emotionally bound to ultranationalist pledges in Ankara and confessing social Darwinism, Nur highlighted in Lausanne "civilization," already a key term with Gökalp and the Young Turks. Civilizationism had played a major role in the context of peace planning at the negotiations in Paris and at the young League of Nations in Geneva. Nur and the other delegation members were convinced of the need for Turkey to adopt Western, and thus universal, modern civilization in order to be all the more culturally and politically independent vis-à-vis the West and the Soviet Union. In Lausanne, the problem was that civilization, democracy, and the secular rule of law were considered by most delegations to belong together.

Nur and Ismet "solved" the problem with promises and assertions. Both insisted that Turkey was already, or would soon be, a full democracy; that it had, or would soon have, a modern legal system; and that, thanks to the separation of state and caliphate, it was entirely modern and secular.[29] Since everyone around the table was eager for a peace agreement that would not be delayed any further, they were reluctant to question the lofty promises. Nur, in particular, used a—never fulfilled—rhetoric of freedom and democracy vis-à-vis Westerners:

> Our ideal was to recover our complete freedom. [. . .] Now, having peace in freedom, the new Turkey, a true democracy, which has chased away the Sultan and achieved the separation of Church and State, will be able to work productively. Turkey, having lost its non-native territories, is today within its ethnic borders, with a homogeneous population. This is the way we wanted it, and it is much better for our peace and for the tranquillity of the Armenians, who have a different political ideal, than to return to Turkey.[30]

Like many others from the far right and the far left, Nur claimed democracy although his political thought had little to do with a democratic social contract. Like Gökalp, he did not believe in a negotiated polity established by a democratic contract, but saw the nation predetermined by race, religion, and culture. This totally contradicted the constitutional ideal of 1908 that many Ottoman Armenians had embraced before the catastrophe of 1915. Turkey's "freedom"—recovered, as Nur told, in Lausanne after military victory in Anatolia—meant the undisturbed sovereignty of Ankara's ruling class, which had largely emerged from the defeated cadres and collaborators of the imperial Young Turk party-state.

Ankara's diplomatic success in Lausanne was also Nur's personal success. The delegation achieved more than many had believed to be possible, including hard-line positions that won the day. These positions of Nur and others regarded the minorities, the Armenian home, and the sidelining of moderate voices within the delegation. The success was there, though not the complete fulfillment of the maximalist demands as raised by many in the National Assembly. Nur summarized this somewhat ambivalent achievement in retrospect:

> We have given the nation the peace that we have sought throughout depressions, but that sometimes resembled a dream flying out of our hands. And this with great profit, with great honor. [. . .] This treaty [. . .] freed Turkey from every condition and made her a completely independent and European [Avrupâi] state. [. . .] However, this perfect treaty has a flaw. We gave freedom to the Bosporus [instead of full Turkish control], we could not give autonomy to Western Thrace, we could not get reparations from the Greeks, we could not take the Turks of Iskenderun into our borders, and Mosul was left to be settled later.[31]

Despite success, the Lausanne moment proved also a turning point for Nur and the members of the National Assembly close to him, the so-called Second Group. The First Group—the circle closest to Gazi Kemal—relied on the advantageous deal with the Western powers concluded in Lausanne to consolidate their position. Therefore, they rejected Nur's dream of an independent Turkish great power, anchored above all in

Asia and the Middle East, which retained the caliphate and used its authority to exert regional, "Turanian," and global influence.

Turkist Anti-Democracy Triumphing

Personal enmities and the power struggle between the factions in Ankara escalated during the Conference interval in March and April 1923 and led to politically motivated assassinations.[32] In addition to containment of hawks and too loud detractors of the negotiations in Lausanne, propaganda spread against the moderate members of the delegation, especially against the financial advisor Cavid, whom Nur had violently attacked at internal meetings of Ankara's delegation in Lausanne.[33] The political struggle in Ankara resulted in a purged new parliament, inaugurated in August 1923 to ratify the Lausanne Treaty.

Nur was reelected as deputy of Sinop in Turkey's first general parliamentary elections in June 1923, which took place in a climate of intimidation. He had to give up his post as a minister of health when the Republic was declared and a new cabinet chosen in October. The abolition of the caliphate and the growing repression of dissent alienated him from the Kemalist circle, though he had overall supported it during the entire Lausanne Conference. He finally began to fear for his life and therefore chose exile in 1926. In exile in France, he was feverishly active as an author, not only of his memoirs but also of Turcological essays, anti-Kemalist writings, an opera praising the *génocidaire* Topal Osman, and revised editions of earlier manuscripts, including a novel. Many manuscripts remained unpublished.[34]

In Europe, Nur maintained close contact with Reşid Saffet Atabinen, the former secretary-general of Ankara's delegation in Lausanne and later a member of the National Assembly who had previously worked for the CUP regime. Both had common ideas about history and the Turkish race. Atabinen joined the new Turkish Historical Institute (*Türk Tarih Kurumu*), founded in Ankara in 1931.[35] Under Atatürk's close supervision, the TTK team elaborated the Turkish History Thesis. From the early 1920s to the 1930s, Turanian (proto-Turkish) indigenousness and civilizational grandeur remained a cornerstone of Atatürk's mental map. Unlike Nur, however, he renounced the political pipe dream of pan-Turkism and a restored caliphate. Hitler admirer Atabinen highlighted the Aryanism of the proto-Turks and became probably the most zealous international advocate of the History Thesis until the 1950s.

As for Nur, he returned to Turkey after Atatürk's death and died in 1942. His "spiritual child" (*manevi evladı*) Nihal Atsız continued in Nur's pan-Turkist and anti-democratic footsteps, abandoning, however, the idea of a restored caliphate.[36] Like Nur, Atsız excelled in exterminatory racism: "If the Kurds run after the illusion of establishing a state, their fate will be to be wiped off the face of the earth"—just like "the Turkish race has exterminated the Armenians in 1915 and the Rûm in 1922."[37]

7

The Destruction of Dersim

Between March 1937 and September 1938, non-state-controlled parts of the Turkish province of Tunceli (formerly known as Dersim) were subjected to a military campaign that resulted in a particularly high death toll; many thousands of civilians fell victim to the violence. Contemporary officers called it a "disciplinary campaign" (*tedip harekâtı*, a term also used by the official military historian, Reşat Halli, in his 1972 account);[1] politicians and press described it as a Kemalist civilizing mission. "We open Tunceli to civilization," read the title of one book by a contemporary Kemalist.[2] In a November 2009 speech, however, Prime Minister Tayip Erdoğan, utilizing a more historically appropriate term, referred to it as a "massacre." In the current legal terminology, as applied since the 1990s, it must be named a genocide. In contrast to the 1925 repression of the Kurdish Sheikh Saïd rebellion and the 1921 Koçgiri uprising, it took place when the Republic of Turkey had already been consolidated. The campaign of Dersim was not a short-term reaction to a concrete uprising; it had been prepared well in advance. Mustafa Kemal Atatürk, the state president, personally stood behind it; he died soon after it ended.[3]

Context

The Republic of Turkey was founded after the 1923 Treaty of Lausanne, which had recognized the Turkish nationalist movement as the country's sole legitimate representative and admitted its victory in Asia Minor. The new Republic implemented revolutionary changes from above, including the abolition of the Caliphate in 1924, and the introductions of the Swiss Civil Code and the Latin alphabet in 1926 and 1928, respectively. Broadly acclaimed as a successful modern Turkish nation-state, the Republic rebuilt its international relations and succeeded, in a deal with France and the League of Nations (of which it became a member in 1932), in incorporating the Syrian region of Alexandretta into its national territory in 1938-9. However, the ideological climate of the 1930s was tainted by the racist undertones of radical Turkism (Turkish ethnonationalism). Cosmopolitan Ottomanism and Islam were radically erased from the political sphere and from intellectual life. The ideology of the new political elite—Kemalist Turkism—was tied to the single-party regime. Although triumphalist, it expressed the need for a connection to deeper roots and, by means of historical physical anthropology, made a huge effort to legitimize Anatolia as the national home of the Turks.[4]

The region of Dersim, renamed Tunceli in 1935, stood markedly at odds with the politico-cultural landscape of 1930s Turkey. In a 1926 report, Hamdi Bey, a senior official, called the area an abscess that needed "emergency surgery" from the Republic.[5] In 1932, journalist Naşit Uluğ, who acted as deputy from 1931 to 1935, published a booklet entitled *The Feudal Lords and Dersim*, which concluded by questioning how a "Dersim system" marked by feudalism and banditry could be destroyed.[6] After Hamdi, General Inspector Ibrahim Tali, Marshal Fevzi Çakmak, and Minister of the Interior Şükrü Kaya all collected information on the ground and wrote reports concluding that the introduction of "reforms" in the region was necessary.[7] The need for such reforms, together with military campaigns to implement them, had been a postulate since the nineteenth-century Ottoman Tanzimat. Several military campaigns had taken place at the time but had brought only limited successes. In the second third of the nineteenth century, parts of Dersim—along with other eastern parts of the Ottoman Empire that had, since the sixteenth century, been ruled by autonomous Kurdish lords—came under direct rule of the central state. In the republican era, this still depended upon the cooperation, that is, co-optation, of the local lords. The central parts of Dersim, by contrast, resisted both cooperation and direct rule until the 1930s. Dersim had nevertheless been represented by a few deputies in the Ottoman parliament in Istanbul and, from 1920 onward, the National Assembly in Ankara.

Dersim is a mountainous region between Sivas, Erzincan, and Elazığ.[8] Covering an area of 90 kilometers east-west and 70 kilometers north-south, its population in the 1930s, according to official contemporary estimates, counted nearly 80,000 people; one-fifth of them were men considered able to bear arms.[9] Dersim's topography was well suited to cattle breeding but only to limited agriculture. Its valleys, caves, forests, and mountains offered many places for refuge and hiding. They had been vital for the survival of Dersim's Alevi population, a Kurdish minority group that venerated the Prophet Muhammad's son-in-law, Ali, but whose "heterodoxy" had roots in pre-Islamic times. When the Ottoman state embraced Sunni orthodoxy, they refused the sharia and remained attached to unorthodox Sufi beliefs and practices that had been widespread in Anatolia and the Southern Balkans before the sixteenth century; these beliefs were then often linked to the thirteenth-century Anatolian saint Hacı Bektash. Since many of the Alevis had sympathized with Safavid Persia in the sixteenth century, they were forever stigmatized as heretics and traitors by the Ottoman state.[10]

In 1921, an uprising took place in Koçgiri, an Alevi region on the western border of Dersim. This was the first rebellion that had been shaped by Kurdish nationalism. The first language of the "Dersim Kurds," as they were called by contemporary observers, was not Turkish but Zaza (the main language) or Kurmanji. Nationalistic ideas had been influencing a number of Kurdish leaders since the early twentieth century. As General Fevzi Çakmak complained in his report of 1930, they had adopted President Woodrow Wilson's post–First World War principle of self-determination and linked it to Kurdish activism. Çakmak therefore demanded the removal of functionaries of "Kurdish race" in Erzincan.[11]

Though the declaration of a secular republic and the abolition of the caliphate in early 1924 had won over many Anatolian Alevis, those in the East remained largely distrustful. This divide roughly corresponded to that between the "Eastern Alevis" and "Western Alevis": converted by the sixteenth-century reformed Bektashi order, Western Alevis had been "domesticated" by the Ottoman state. The Turkish-speaking or Kurdish-speaking Eastern Alevis, meanwhile, did not belong to the organization of the Bektashis. Dersim was the location of many important places of Alevi religious pilgrimage, partly shared with local Armenians. Its "Seyyids" claimed descent from Ali (Muhammed's son-in-law and fourth caliph), and entertained a network of dependent communities in and outside of Dersim.[12]

Dersim was the only place more or less safe for Armenian refugees during and after the genocide of 1915, which mainly took place in the eastern provinces. The Bektashiye, however, were co-opted both by the First World War–era Young Turk rulers before 1918, and by the leaders of the National movement after 1918. In 1916, a Bektashiye leader had tried in vain to win over the chiefs of Dersim to fight side by side with the Ottoman army against the invading Russians. There were two limited uprisings by Alevis of Dersim, in which armed groups harassed the Ottoman army. They feared that they would suffer the same fate from the state as their Armenian neighbors.[13]

After the establishment of the new state in Ankara and the repression of the Kurdish uprisings of the 1920s, the capital's attention turned more and more toward Dersim, which was described as a place of reactionary evil forces, of interior and exterior intrigues, and hostage to tribal chiefs and religious leaders. It is true that Dersim could, in fact, be described as a premodern, tribally split society which became more and more isolated after 1920. According to Hamdi Bey, who visited Dersim in 1926, at the same time it became increasingly politicized, to the point of adopting openly anti-Kemalist Kurdish positions. Due to Dersim's growing social, economic, and military strangulation, sustained contacts with a world beyond Kemalism were no longer possible, not even with the most prominent post-Ottoman Kurdish-Armenian organization, Hoybun, founded in Syria in 1927.[14]

Dersim had a long history of banditry linked to its marginalization by the state and, consequently, to the region's long-standing economic problems; these were further exacerbated by the region's isolation and the bad economic conditions after the First World War in general. Yet, in the late Ottoman era, new currents and openings had begun to permeate Dersim's neighborhood. These included labor migration, emulation of the quickly modernizing Armenian neighbors, the desire for education and attendance at new Armenian, missionary, or state schools, as well as the spread of medical services in the region. Compared with the situation in the early Republic, late Ottoman Eastern Anatolia had been pluralistic, and culturally and economically much more dynamic.

On June 21, 1934, a Law of Settlement generally legitimized the depopulation of regions in Turkey for cultural, political, or military reasons. This law was conceived in order to complete the Turkification of Anatolia in the context of the new focus on Dersim in interior politics. According to Minister of the Interior Kaya's Gökalpian statement, the intent was to create "a country with one language, one mentality, and unity of feeling."[15]

Decision-Makers, Organizers, and Actors

During and after the Lausanne Conference, Rıza Nur, Ankara's social minister and vice-chief delegate, had contended that Kurds had "to be purified by a persistent assimilation program of their distinct language and race" and that it was "of utmost necessity that we annihilate all languages in Turkey and replace them with Turkish."[16] In 1930, former Justice Minister Mahmut Esat Bozkurt spoke of a war between two races, Kurds and Turks, and went so far as to say, "All, friends, enemies and the mountains, shall know that the Turk is the master of this country. All those who are not pure Turks have only one right in the Turkish homeland: the right to be servants, the right to be slaves."[17] In October 1935, Italy began a brutal invasion of Ethiopia, in which it used chemical weapons and killed hundreds of thousands of men, women, and children. Even though Turkey's and Italy's foreign policies contrasted, Mussolini's fascism was, according to Bozkurt—by then a Professor of the History of the Turkish Revolution and theorist of Kemalism—nothing other than a new version of Kemalism; in other words, both shared ultranationalist and social Darwinist convictions (see Chapter 10).

It was these elements that provided the context for a draft law, commonly known as the Tunceli Law, which was presented by Minister of the Interior Kaya in December 1935 and once again labeled the region a zone of "illness" that needed "surgery."[18] In terms of national security, there was no urgency. Non-military state officials that entered Dersim for administrative purposes such as the population census of 1935 remained unharmed.[19] With both parliament and the press being under the control of the Kemalist party, the law passed without opposition. Dersim, formerly part of the province of Elazığ, was established as a separate province, renamed Tunceli, and from 1936 ruled by the military governor and head of the Fourth General Inspectorate, Abdullah Alpdoğan. The other three General Inspectorates had served to "pacify" other regions in Turkey, judged to be a risk. Alpdoğan was the son-in-law of Nurettin Pasha, the general who had led the repression of the Koçgiri uprising in 1921, the destruction of Izmir in 1922, and had called for the "pacification" of Dersim. Reports made by Alpdoğan in 1936 emphasize the progress in instituting a military infrastructure, including gendarmerie stations, in the region. Roads, schools, and a railway to Elazığ were also established; this was considered a threat by many Dersimis.[20]

Hamdi Bey's report of 1926 labeled the attempt at peaceful penetration of Dersim using schools, infrastructure, and industry an illusion, calling for stronger measures to be implemented.[21] Against this background, actors on both sides were separated by a rift and unable to find a common language within the context of an unbalanced dialogue. Seyyid Rıza, a religious figure and probably the most important of the tribal chiefs, insisted on autonomy and the revocation of the 1935 Tunceli Law. He seems to have initially believed that Dersim could not be subdued militarily, and had worked for years, in some cases successfully, to unite the tribes.[22]

Following several incidents that culminated in tribal attacks against the new infrastructure in Pah and a police station in Sin in eastern central Dersim on the nights of March 20–1 and 26–7, 1937, the military campaign was launched. Having accumulated 8,623 men, artillery, and an air force, it was, by early May, vastly superior in numbers and resources to the forces of the insurgents. On May 4, 1937, the Council of Ministers, including Atatürk and Chief of General Staff Fevzi Çakmak secretly decided on a forceful attack against western-central Dersim; the aim was to kill everyone who was using or had used arms and to remove the population settled between Nazimiye and Sin. On the same day, planes dropped pamphlets promising that in the case of surrender, "no harm at all would be done to you, dear compatriots. If not, entirely against our will, the [military] forces will act and destroy you. One must obey the state."[23]

In the following months, the army successfully advanced against fierce resistance and ever-changing tribal coalitions that were led by Seyyid Rıza, the talented poet-activist Alişer, as well as allied tribal chiefs. Unity among the rebels was far from achieved; only a few tribes formed the hard core of the resistance. On July 9, 1937, Alişer and his wife were killed by their own people, and their heads sent to Alpdoğan. In July, Seyyid Rıza sent a letter to the prime minister in which he vividly described what he saw as anti-Kurdish politics of assimilation, removal, and, ultimately, a war of destruction. Via his friend Nuri Dersimi, who had gone into exile in Syria in September 1937, he also sent a despairing letter to the League of Nations and the Foreign Ministries of the United Kingdom, France, and the United States, all of which remained unanswered. On September 10, he surrendered to the army in Erzincan. Messages of congratulation were sent to Alpdoğan by Atatürk, Minister of the Interior Şükrü Kaya, and Prime Minister İnönü, who had visited Elazığ in June. Shortly before Atatürk's visit there, Seyyid Rıza, along with his son Resik Hüseyin, tribal leader Seyit Haso, and the sons of a few tribal chiefs, was executed. The executions had been hastily organized by Ihsan Sabri Çağlayangil, who later became foreign minister.[24]

Despite the setbacks of 1937, Dersimi groups resumed attacks against the security forces in early 1938, declaring that they all would perish if they did not resist.[25] The military campaign took on a new and comprehensive character as the government embarked on a general cleansing that aimed, as Prime Minister Celal Bayar stated in parliament on June 29, 1938, "to eradicate once and for all this [Dersim] problem."[26] In June 1938, units began to penetrate parts of Dersim between Pülür (Ovacık), Danzik, and Pah that had refused to surrender. Between August 10 and early September, a large campaign of cleansing and scouring (*tarama*) took place, costing the lives of many thousands of men, women, and children, including members of the tribes that had cooperated with the government.

Victims

According to the official statements, the military campaign of 1937 was aimed at bandits and reactionary tribal and religious leaders who misled innocent people. Clandestinely, however, parts of the general population of Dersim had been targeted from the beginning, at least for relocation in accordance with the 1934 Law of Settlement. This was especially true following the decision of the Council of Ministers on May 4, 1937. As had been the case in Koçgiri in 1921, those targeted feared that they would all perish like the Armenians if they did not resist.[27] The campaign of spring

1937 targeted the regions between Pah and Hozat in which most clashes had occurred. Its measures included the disarmament of villages and the removal of people, though most of the violence was directed toward armed groups. Halli, who amply cites military documents, scarcely uses the word *imha* (annihilation) for this period. This changed with the campaign of summer 1938, during which the population of Dersim, including in parts that had surrendered and had not been declared prohibited zones under the Law of Settlement, was subjected to extreme violence.

On August 6, 1938, the Council of Ministers decided that 5,000–7,000 Dersimis had to be moved from the prohibited zones to the west. "Thousands of persons, whose names the Fourth General Inspectorate [under Alpdoğan] had listed, were arrested and sent in convoys to the regions where they were ordered to go."[28] Those targeted for relocation included numerous families living outside of the prohibited zones or those living in areas outside of Dersim that were considered to be members of Dersimi tribes. Several notables living outside Dersim were killed in summer 1938, as were some young Dersimi recruits. For the killing of surviving "bandits," the prime minister, along with the interior minister, the minister of defense, and the Military Inspectorate proposed to implement the notorious "Special Organization" (*Teşkilat-ı Mahsusa/Özel Teşkilat*), which had gained its infamy during the First World War for its role in the mass killing of Armenians and, particularly, of targeted personalities.[29]

The first week of "cleansing" took place between August 10 and 17, 1938. According to the official military historian Halli, "thousands of bandits" were annihilated during this phase alone.[30] While Halli mentions no comprehensive number for the whole campaign, his detailed narrative does provide some precise figures; it also mentions dozens of incidents during which a "large number" of persons were killed. Based on this information, the number of deaths is likely to have been considerably higher than 10,000. An unpublished report by Alpdoğan's inspectorate, quoted in Turkish newspapers, mentions 13,160 civilian deaths and 11,818 deportees (*Radikal*, November 20, 2009). The high number of deaths, along with other ample evidence, proves that the killings were not limited to the insurgent tribes. A comparison of the censuses of 1935 and 1940 shows that the district of Hozat, with a loss of more than 10,000 people, was the most seriously impacted.[31] A proposed number of 40,000 fatalities seems, however, implausibly high.[32]

According to several sources, including Çağlayangil's authoritative testimony, the army used poison gas, imported from Germany, to kill people hiding in caves. Many others were burned alive, whether in houses or by spraying individuals with fuel. Even people who surrendered were exterminated. In order "not to fall into the hands of the Turks," girls and women jumped from great heights to their deaths, as many Armenians had done in 1915.[33] The suspicion of having lodged "bandits" or—according to witness accounts of soldiers—military units' desire for vengeance sufficed as justification to annihilate entire villages. Soldiers confirmed that they were ordered to kill women and children. One has to bear in mind that the Dersimis were seen—and declared by officers—to be Alevi heretics or crypto-Armenians. When gendarmerie posts were established in the 1930s, gendarmes even exercised control over whether or not local young men were circumcised, specifically targeting those that official propaganda had stigmatized as "enemies" and "traitors" since the Armenian genocide: "Was he perhaps a giavour, an Armenian?"[34] Dersim was not only a place of age-old Armenian-Kurdish coexistence, as we have seen, and of common Armenian-Alevi pilgrimage places and song traditions (*saz ve söz*), but it had also offered the most important sanctuary in Asia Minor during the genocide. Thus, many Armenians survived and remained there, finally suffering the onslaught in 1937–8 together with the other Dersimis.[35]

Witnesses

On September 27, the British Vice-Consul in Trabzon reported:

> It is understood from various sources that in clearing the area occupied by the Kurds, the military authorities have used methods similar to those used against the Armenians during the Great War: thousands of Kurds including women and children were slain; others, mostly children were thrown into the Euphrates; while thousands of others in less hostile areas, who had first been deprived of their cattle and other belongings, were deported to vilayets in Central Anatolia.[36]

This report is the exception to the rule; because all of Eastern Asia Minor, including Dersim, was effectively closed to foreigners, no other reports by foreign observers in or close to the conflict zone exist, to my knowledge.

Military, governmental, and Dersimi documents do survive, however. Some of these are located in the military archives in Ankara (ATASE), where they remain closed to independent research. This is true also for the relevant documents of the civil offices, which have largely remained under the control of the respective ministries and have not been transferred to the Republican Archives (BCA). However, a number of official reports have been leaked. They, along with Halli's military history, soldiers' testimonies, and witness accounts from survivors all agree that systematic massacres took place; soldiers and survivors specifically added that the targets included civilians, women, and children.[37]

Accustomed to looking up to the state and army as omnipotent entities, most soldiers feared speaking about their experiences even decades after the events:

> When we came to the headquarters, we learnt that discussions had taken place between the officers. A few said that that these people [women and children in Hozat who had not given information on the whereabouts of the men] had to be annihilated, others said that this was a sin. [. . .] They [finally] ordered us: "Annihilate all you can apprehend." [. . .] And that day we soldiers, in a horrific savageness and craziness, gathered the women, girls and children in a mosque—it was in fact not like a mosque but rather like a church—closed it, sprayed kerosene and easily burnt them alive.[38]

In the second half of the twentieth century, Dersimis themselves privately collected documents, conducted interviews, and created internet sites. More recent intensified work has added further material.[39] The year 2010 saw the launch of the "1937–38 Dersim

Oral History Project" at Clark University.⁴⁰ Others made insightful documentary films.⁴¹ A central archive dedicated to the documentation of the Dersim massacre, however, does not yet exist. The only Kurdish history dating from around the time of the events consists of a chapter in Nuri Dersimi's 1952 memoir, *Hatıratım*, which includes a number of eyewitness testimonies; the author himself had left Dersim before the campaign was launched.

Since the 1980s, this period has been the subject of a number of documentary novels and memoirs, including, for example, the work of Şükrü Laçin, a founder of the Turkish Workers' Party in 1963 who did not sympathize with Seyyid Rıza and Kurdish nationalism. In a book published in 1992, he recounts how he and people close to him lived during 1937–8. Laçin was born in 1924 in a village in the district of Mazgirt, south of Pah. Even though it did not belong to rebel territory, he and his family were removed and unable to return until 1947. In his sober retrospective, he describes how in summer 1938, the villagers had to surrender all weapons in their possession— mainly old sabers and knives—gather before a lieutenant, and listen to a nationalistic speech on the Turkish unity of the country. The lieutenant then selected nine young men, and, under the pretense that they still had weapons on their persons, took them with him. All were shot except for one man named Ahmed Korkmaz, a former soldier, who was saved at the last moment. Several functionaries, including Ahmed's former teacher, had spoken in his favor. Laçin confirms that the campaign of 1938 and the forced removal of populations covered parts of Dersim, such as Mazgirt, Pertek, and Nazimiye, that had not refused to pay taxes or enlist people in the army. He confirms that villages of the province of Erzincan in the districts of Refahiye, Çayırlı, Üzümlü, Kemah, and Tercan, where relatives of Laçin lived, were also targeted, because their inhabitants were Alevi Kurds and were said to have relations with Dersim.⁴²

Memories

In the years after 1938, the Kemalist party-state and its press continued to maintain the image and memory of a necessary and fully successful campaign of pacification, followed by sustained efforts at reconstruction. This is also the narrative of a book entitled *Tunceli Is Made Accessible to Civilization*, published by Naşit Uluğ, then the director of the daily *Ulus* newspaper, in 1939.⁴³ Evoking the punishment of "bandits" while avoiding any mention of mass killings, he presented a panegyric of a Turkish army toward which the nation had again to feel infinitely thankful. He also emphasized reconstruction efforts, which he illustrated using photographs and a plan that almost exclusively depicted military buildings. In his view, success, including a positive memory of the Dersim campaign, had been achieved once and for all; the Dersimis had been "made into human beings." Many surviving Dersimis themselves adopted the Kemalist view; orphans were taught to do so in state institutions or by adoptive parents. They tended to forgive Atatürk, who by now had become venerated across the nation as a father figure and "eternal chief" of the nation. They blamed ministers and officers for the dark side of the campaign. The Western and the Soviet press largely followed the Kemalist narrative of a civilizing mission against reactionary conservatives. Only the US press, loyal to its earlier critique of the Armenian atrocities and the Lausanne Treaty, seems to have voiced criticism of both the violent campaign and its undemocratic political framework; like the European press, however, it lacked independent sources.[44]

In 1937, the Armenian press published reports of heroic Kurdish exploits and resistance, and of the foundation of an independent Kurdish government. Such tragic yet heroic memories of Dersim in 1937–8 can also be found in the 1952 memoir of the Kurdish nationalist Nuri Dersimi, who had been in contact with Armenians since the beginning of his exile. Dersimi's texts, which underlined the barbaric aspects of the campaign, were seminal in the memory of the Kurdish nationalists. He was, however, also criticized by Dersimis as an instigator of armed resistance who left the country when it became dangerous.[45] Memories that depict the Dersim campaign as at least somewhat ruthless and misguided can also be found in letters sent by pious soldiers to the spiritual father of the *Nurculuk*, Said-i Nursi.[46]

The single-party regime met its end in the years after 1945. In 1947, the government repealed the Tunceli Law. Those who had been deported were allowed to return to their villages. The state of emergency that had been declared in 1936 was finally lifted in 1948. Memories that challenged those promoted by the former single-party regime, as well as ongoing realities in Tunceli, such as poverty, absence of schools and health services, and so on, could now be acknowledged. However, this could not be done freely. The army, the main agent on the ground, as well as the state and its founder, Atatürk, who was behind the Tunceli campaign, could never be openly criticized.

After 1945, Turkey, allied to the United States and NATO, stood under the shadow of the Cold War. Both right and left claimed Atatürk's heritage. They neither questioned the dark sides of the Kemalist "civilizing mission" nor its genocidal antecedents. During his stay at the Komintern in Moscow in 1937, Ismail Bilen, a member of the outlawed Turkish Communist Party, had, in line with Stalinist rhetoric, fully backed the Kemalist regime in its "politics against feudalism" in Dersim, although he had himself been imprisoned and exiled from Turkey.[47] Widely read in the 1970s and 1980s, Barbaros Baykara's novels on Tunceli/ Dersim in 1937–8 were still informed by this kind of state-centered, progressist narrative. However, within leftist circles, in particular among the members from Tunceli (of which Laçin is again an example), but also among those with Alevi and Kurdish backgrounds in general, the Dersim campaign has been remembered as a campaign of mass violence perpetrated by the state and its armies. Since the end of the twentieth century, a new, more independent-minded generation of writers, artists, and intellectuals has been looking back to the 1937–8 *Tertelê* ("massacre" in the Zaza language), beyond the previous ideological preconditions. Their newest studies, novels, and documentaries (see section "Witnesses" above) are based on carefully collected eyewitness accounts of the last remaining survivors.[48]

After the military putsch of 1980, which had crushed the Turkish left, critics of the state began to be more open to the Kurdish perspective, which pertinently stated that the Turkish nation-state had always reacted with extermination and denial (*imha ve inkar*) even against moderate Kurdish claims.[49] The dawn of the post–Cold War era saw a "renaissance" of long-suppressed ethnic and religious identities and histories, which in the late twentieth century led to the emergence of more detailed recollections of the

Dersim campaign, detached from Kemalist state ideology. Turkey's EU candidature in 1999 and the appointment of the AKP government in 2002 temporarily contributed to a more liberal period during which the military, the main contributor to the campaign of 1937–8, lost its hitherto sacrosanct, unchecked position at the top of the state.

On November 17, 2009, during the so-called Kurdish (democratic) opening, Prime Minister Erdoğan branded the events of 1937–8 a massacre. For the first time, the long-term memory of the Tunceli campaign as one of pacification and civilization was publicly challenged on a governmental level. Meanwhile, the former ruling party, the Republican People's Party, struggled to defend what for seventy years had been the official version of history. This version was now widely seen as unacceptable, as is evident in media discussions in and after autumn 2009, where it has been rightly viewed as ultranationalist. However, by the mid-2010s, the authoritarian turn in Turkey once again brought ultranationalists and the far right to the forefront in a coalition with the predominant Islamists of Erdoğan's AKP. The prime minister's critique in 2009 turned out to have been more of a political maneuver against the opposition party than a sincere introspection into Turkey's national history.[50]

Legal and Historical Interpretation of the Facts

In contrast to the aftermath of the Koçgiri revolt in 1921–2, there were no critical discussions in the Turkish parliament in the wake of the Dersim campaign in 1937–8; nor were there any legal claims for the officers in charge of the brutality and mass killing of civilians to be put on trial. In the case of Dersim, this was exacerbated by the fact that a legal(istic) framework for the campaign and the removal of the Dersimis had been established in advance by the Law of Settlement and the Tunceli Law, which was only repealed in 1947. This law gave Alpdoğan the authority to carry out executions without the constitutionally prescribed parliamentary votes. Other basic requirements of penal law, such as interrogation, communication of the indictment to the indicted, and the chance to appeal were also lacking.[51]

As was the case in other fascist and totalitarian regimes of the 1930s, legalism disguised the breach of fundamental law to the detriment of citizens or certain groups of citizens. Recently, lawyer Hüseyin Aygün filed a complaint for crimes against humanity in Dersim, where his relatives were killed in the village of Çamurek in 1938. The lawyer based his complaint on an official 1955 document that allowed surviving relatives of exterminated families to return from their exile in Kütahya. This document states that "The family members were totally annihilated." In early 2011, however, the court dismissed the complaint, arguing that the statute of limitations applies.[52]

Historical sociologist Ismail Beşikçi was the first scholar to research the Dersim campaign and to emphasize the legalist but illegitimate, anti-constitutional framework in which it took place. In his 1990 book *The Tunceli Law and the Dersim Genocide*,[53] he went on to label it a genocide. Arguing that the campaign's primary intention had not been the destruction of Dersim's population, but of its autonomous ethnic culture, anthropologist Martin van Bruinessen, in a 1994 article, proposed the label "ethnocide."[54] It is true that the Dersim campaign had in fact been rationalized as a civilizing mission. The intention of destroying the Dersimis as a distinct ethnoreligious group "in whole or in part" and of "forcibly transferring children of the group to another group" is, however, evident and well documented. The UN Convention on the Prevention and Punishment of the Crime of Genocide is therefore without doubt pertinent to Dersim in 1937–8. Beşikçi's position is certainly supported by later jurisdictions within comparable legal contexts, most notably the International Criminal Tribunal for the former Yugoslavia and its application of the Genocide Convention.

A conservative historiographical approach may limit the term "genocide" to those mass exterminations of the twentieth century that involved the eradication of large proportions of major ethnoreligious groups, as well as the destruction of the future of such groups within their habitats, as had been the case during the Armenian genocide and during the Holocaust. In both these cases, those responsible considered the targeted groups to be inassimilable to the nation and their removal to be necessary no matter the cost. The Dersim massacre did not decimate the entirety of the population; some groups were resettled, while others were able to remain in place. The 1938 extermination was first and foremost directed at those whose tribes and families were involved in the resistance. Others, however, were also targeted. These included relatives who were not in the resistance, and even people living outside of Dersim. In principle, however, the Kemalists responsible for the campaign considered the assimilation of the Dersimis into the nation-state a possibility. In any case, as a result, the area's informal autonomy and, to a considerable extent, its ethnoreligious habitat was suppressed. Deliberate mass killing according to ethnoreligious prejudice took place.

For political and diplomatic reasons, and because of simplistic notions of modern progress versus religious reaction in area studies, the dark sides of Turkey's foundation— from the Young Turks' single-party regime to pogroms against non-Muslims in the second half of the twentieth century—have long been under-researched both inside and outside of the country. The Dersim campaign remained under-represented in studies on Turkey regardless of discipline; one scarcely finds mention of it in the major university textbooks on Turkish history until the late twentieth century. With the exception of the translation of Beşikçi's book and a few articles and book chapters,[55] detailed research in Western languages remained non-existent until recently.[56] The contemporary Turkish output, as appears in the footnotes of this chapter, is, by contrast, much richer.

In the first decade of the twenty-first century, a fresh look at these topics and the Dersim campaign finally emerged. It also considered the consistently silenced Armenian perspective on Dersim—a dimension that Western scholarship failed to grasp for a long time. The lack of free access to the military archives, however, continues to seriously hamper comprehensive research on the Dersim campaign. These archives might be able to provide answers to questions regarding, for example, the hierarchical level at which the order was given to massacre people, including women and children; to what extent poison gas was used against people seeking shelter in caves; and whether there were, as it seems, absolutely no orders against—or punishments for—such extreme acts of brutality as burning victims alive, slashing open pregnant women, and stabbing babies. In many respects, the course of action recalled scenes from the

Armenian genocide two decades earlier. In contrast to Dersim in 1938, however, the regular army did not play the main role in that case.

From a state-centered nationalist viewpoint, the high number of civilian casualties was seen as collateral damage of a necessary campaign against reactionary rebels. Since the end of the twentieth century, however, scholarship has counteracted this by focusing on the deeply problematic aspects of the Dersim campaign and on the perspective of its victims. Considering it a consequence of the party-state's suppression of all opposition,[57] it recognizes its actions as ethnocide (i.e., the "deliberate destruction of Kurdish ethnic identity by forced assimilation"—Bruinessen) or as genocide committed against the backdrop of a colonialist enterprise (Beşikçi—bearing in mind that the Turkish political elite did not know "Kurdistan" any better than nineteenth-century European elites had known their overseas colonies). More recent interpretations, including this book, stress its roots in the genocidal logic of the CUP, which had given rise to the Kemalists. They thus also highlight its logical and chronological coincidence with the Turkish History Thesis.

The 1930s Turkish History Thesis exalted, in line with Gökalp, the essential value and superiority of Turkishness and the Turkish race and claimed Anatolia to have been the home of the Turks for millennia.[58] This was racial speculation that revealed an aporia of legitimacy and led to an ideological impasse in the form of ultranationalist Kemalism. It expressed the wish to make all remaining vestiges of non-Turkish presence and heterogeneous Ottoman coexistence disappear since they reminded state-centered elites of a period which they considered distressing and shameful—a period marked by the tedious "Oriental Question," in particular the Armenian Question, and by the lack of governmental sovereignty. It originated from the feeling that demographic engineering and military victory in the war for Anatolia had not provided sufficient legitimacy for unitary Turkish rule in Asia Minor. Both the Thesis and the Dersim campaign reveal a deep-seated and—due to the lack of a democratic social contract— well-founded fear of de-legitimization.

Part III

Revolution and Anti-Democracy
Biographical Approaches

Biographies based on ego-documents provide different, often more intimate insights into historical realities than abstract analyses. Part III uses biographical essays as a starting point to better understand *Turkey's violent formation*, thus deepening and broadening the approach already introduced in Chapter 6, and applied also in Part IV. The human beings focused in these political and intellectual biographies reveal "ordinary lives," but also exploits, extremes, abysses as well as paradoxes, ambivalences, and surprises. Their individual experience is key to a broader understanding of the era. In these approaches, it is as much about influential persons with an acclaimed afterlife like Ziya Gökalp, spiritual father of Turkish (ultra)nationalism, as about those deprived of glory, but who nevertheless left highly insightful legacies. Cavid Bey is a case in point. A committed Turkish patriot and several times a CUP minister, he never developed sympathy for extreme nationalism and the proto-fascism of the CUP party-state. He thus remained a child of the 1908 Young Turk Revolution in which the best minds had combined their patriotism with strong convictions of constitutional rule. After 1918, he counted among those who believed that the work started in 1908, but soon interrupted, had to be continued and accomplished.

8

Ziya Gökalp

Mentor of Ultranationalism, Advocate of Education

The most prominent influence on the driving ideological forces toward Islamic Turkism and pan-Turkism (Turanism) in Turkey from the early 1910s was Ziya Gökalp (1876–1924). In the short period between the constitutional Young Turk Revolution in 1908 and the First World War, Gökalp personified the ambivalent potential of these forces: peaceful on one hand and prone to war and violence on the other. One constructive element in his thinking was the drive toward modern education. This stemmed from the insight that an openly avowed deficit required a departure toward new horizons of knowledge. In his 1912 poem "Kızılelma" (Red Apple), Gökalp imagined an educational center next to Lausanne, from which progress would stream to Turkey.[1] With republican Ankara on the rise, a Kemalist interpretation of Gökalp's utopia, which had started with the *Foyers Turcs* at Lake Geneva, seemed to have been made real.[2] As we will see, however, the author of this peaceful, dream-like, and prayerful poem in that same year of 1912 also composed very martial verses. In 1914, he proved a fanatical propagandist for an Ottoman Great War that would not only open pan-Turkish expansion toward "Turan" (Caucasus and Central Asia) but also serve to make the country a unitary nation bound to one culture, one religion (Islam), and one language (Turkish). It appears that his intellectual attitude deeply blurred the line between education and indoctrination.

Topical Ideologist

Gökalp was a "radioactive brain," as Yahya Kemal stated after Gökalp's death in 1924.[3] For contemporary German scholars, he was a popular and efficient ideologue of the Great War, "the true father of Turkish nationalism," and the striking proof of continuity between the Young Turks and the Kemalists. Richard Hartmann and August Fischer had, in the early 1920s, gained these insights into modern Turkey's political thought, well knowing that Gökalp had "got drunk [. . .] with the ideal of the 'great eternal country Turan.'"[4] In a number of widely read poems from early August 1914, Gökalp had proclaimed jihad, prophesizing that "Russia will collapse and be ruined / Turkey will expand and be Turan!"[5] While Europe's prophets of the Great War are almost forgotten nowadays, Turkey's current president (2024), Recep T. Erdoğan, was jailed in the 1990s for publicly reciting inflammatory verses of Gökalp's popular 1912 poem "Soldier's Prayer": "The mosques are our barracks / The domes our helmets / The minarets our bayonets / And the believers our soldiers." He again recited the same poem in 2019.[6]

In the recollection of his confidant Falih Rıfkı Atay, a former assistant to Talaat and Enver Pasha, Mustafa Kemal Atatürk "warmed up late, but powerfully to Ziya Gökalp."[7] The well-known fascination with Atatürk in interwar Germany was intertwined with admiration for radical nation building in line with Gökalp's successful ultranationalism. Gökalp has been publicly owned by various politicians and intellectuals throughout the second half of the twentieth century. Most vocal were those belonging to the far-right MHP (Nationalist Movement Party/*Milliyetçi Hareket Parti*). Founded by Colonel Alparslan Türkeş in 1969, it has been the AKP's coalition partner since 2015. "The road of Turkish nationalism is one that draws strength from Ziya Gökalp Bey. [. . .] The main foundation has not changed: Turkification, Islamization, and modernization are the foundations that preserve their validity today," Türkeş publicly stated in 1974.[8] By the mid-twentieth century, Gökalp had earned for Westerners the scholarly label of "most original and influential among Turkish writers of the twentieth century."[9]

Erdoğan's public recitations betray a desire to bring back Gökalp's pre-1923 ideal—a modern, leader-led Islamic-Turkish state extending beyond the boundaries of the Treaty of Lausanne. As political scientist Tanıl Bora has emphasized, and as the following pages will illustrate, Turkish ultranationalism and radical political Islam share important common roots.[10] Gökalp is key to understanding the enduring lines of Turkish political thought. Assessing his role has, at times, proven difficult. Insufficient historical contextualization, often stemming from a lack of reliable knowledge about the dictatorial rule of the CUP, has led to difficulties in interpreting his character. In-depth research on the CUP and the Ottoman Great War, including the Armenian genocide, started only at the end of the twentieth century. Since Gökalp, at the height of his career, belonged to the CUP Central Committee, he cannot be separated from this formative situation, its interactions, and his related ideological output.

Other shortcomings in approaching Gökalp result from selective reading. Essays *and* poetry, from all periods, need to be taken into account. The latter has tended to be dismissed by sociologists as well as political scientists. However, his poems shed light on the convoluted prose of his articles; they frequently use, for example, terms such as "blood" and "Turkish race." His essays, meanwhile, do not.[11] Read together, one genre clarifies the other. In contrast to the essays, most poems are overtly nationalistic and written in an easily accessible Turkish. "*Türklük* is my ideal, my blood," reads a late occasional poem.[12] In many cases, polysemy and Sufi vocabulary add spiritual appeal. Given his varied contradictions and metaphorical shifts, as well as his opportunism and adaptive rhetoric, Gökalp can be thought of as much more of an ideologue than as a consistent thinker. What distinguishes him from other, comparable late Ottoman authors is (1) his position in the CUP; (2) the suggestive power of his poetry in combination with his prolific, sociopolitically influential prose; and (3) his ability to mirror and literarily capture the politico-historical dreams and aspirations of his cohort, while displaying his own mental path as a metaphor for the revival of the Turkish nation.

"Most attention to Ziya Gökalp has been paid in Germany," French orientalist Jean Deny observed in 1925.[13] In general, interwar Germany closely followed developments of their former Great War ally. Frustrated by the Paris-Versailles Treaty, many German nationalists admired and envied Turkey's timely revision of the Paris-Sèvres Treaty in Lausanne. This diplomatic success was followed in Turkey by a self-declared national revolution that won international recognition from Western powers. Germans of a right-wing orientation came to see contemporary Turkey as a role model in thinking and domestically implementing ultranationalism.

Gökalp sought proximity to power in various places: his hometown of Diyarbekir, in the first CUP seat, Saloniki, in the Ottoman capital, Istanbul, and finally, in the new capital, Ankara. As a member of the CUP's Central Committee from 1910 to 1918, he closely collaborated with his leading party colleague, Mehmed Talaat. Both were polyglot autodidacts without university diplomas. Ottoman-Turkish and French were the languages they most used, the latter being their interface to the West. Both lacked experience of life outside the Ottoman realm (except for Talaat Pasha's short travels as a politician to Europe, and his exile after 1918).[14] In contrast to the political networker, organizer, minister, and eventual Grand Vizier Talaat, Gökalp had benefited from a full and formative high school education. He was an avid reader and tireless writer from his teenage years onward. From the early 1910s, when he gave himself the pen name "Gök-Alp," meaning "hero (or warrior) of the sky," he proved to be a prolific author of essays and poems. Almost all of them carried his new gospel of Turkism (*Türkçülük*).

Gökalp published a poem under the title "Türklük" in 1911, shortly after he "converted" (to *Türklük*—a showcase "conversion," *ihtida*, to which we will return below). Proudly identifying as a child of the (mythic) ancestor Oghuz Khan, the poet expressed his longing for a mythic Turan and a golden age of khanates. This evocation of racial and mythical greatness not only addressed a susceptible Turkish readership but also imposingly and threateningly the Occident and the enemies of *Türklük*. Thus, the self-proclaimed son of glorious emperors rhetorically defied the high imperialism of contemporary Europe. Apart from its inherent violence, the poem programmatically presaged the Turks' imminent sociopolitical transformation from a tribe (*kavim*) into a vigorous modern nation (*millet*). It conjured up a revitalizing renewal; it thus challenged not only European talk of Ottoman decline but also intra-Ottoman expectations of doom, which were rooted in Ibn Khaldun's cycles of the rise and end of states depending on vital, or dying, bonds of solidarity (*asabiya*).[15]

Interpretations of Gökalp based on a primarily Kemalist viewpoint—that is, on his final output in Ankara—risk missing his expansionist pan-Turkism (Turanism). In the 1910s, Turanism had placed emphasis on political Islam and on the sultanate-caliphate. A comprehensive analysis of Gökalp's contribution to secularism in Turkey remains unsound if not linked to his imperative of a unitary state which initially, for him, constituted an Islamic state and khanate.[16] If made akin to secular democratic, or even liberal and humanitarian, principles, he becomes sanitized by later interpreters.[17] Until 1918, Gökalp propagated imperial expansion and domestic social engineering at the cost of non-Muslims and non-Turks. He mentored the first imperial single-party rule in the twentieth century. Minister Talaat and his "prophet" Gökalp put into force a synergy of radical ideas and politics. Instead of the notorious "CUP triumvirate,"[18] it is more pertinent to emphasize the "duumvirate" of the executive Talaat and the ideologue Gökalp. More than other CUP leaders, they both have left their deep mark on Turkey. Theirs is an influence that has lasted well into the twenty-first century, and their names are to be found everywhere in mosques, schools, streets, and neighborhoods.

If we look at the whole foundational era of post-Ottoman Turkey, from the 1910s to the 1930s, the trio composed of Talaat, Gökalp, and Kemal Atatürk is pivotal; all three were well acquainted with each other within the CUP. Kemal succeeded Talaat; Gökalp inspired both. Gökalp eventually proved to be one of the pioneering ideologues of twentieth-century "revolutionism from the right," a notion that overlaps with "proto-fascism."[19] In addition to essentialist ethnoreligious idealization and exclusion, he postulated the subordination of the individual to an army-like, hierarchical society. He also fueled the cult of heroic leadership and promoted the integration of organized religion into a unitary, leader-focused centralized state. As an adolescent raised in a religious family, he had experienced a deep personal crisis that led to his rejection of clericalism (see below). He gave up his insistence on the sultanate-caliphate only toward the end of his life. Nevertheless, he made Islam a lasting pillar of what he called his "religious Turkism." This was tantamount to a modern "political religion," even before the rise of what interwar intellectuals in Europe, theologians, and others called the "political religion" of Bolshevism, National Socialism, or Italian Fascism.[20] Unlike those ideologies, however, "religious Turkism" identified with and emphasized monotheism in its Islamic—i.e., allegedly supreme and ultimate—version.

Over the course of three decades, Gökalp's intellectual germination went in various directions. During cataclysmic times, his multiple experiences of loss were part of this journey. Perhaps the greatest of these losses was the failure of his grandiose pan-Turkic, pan-Islamic Great War visions that he had instilled in Turkey's youth in the 1910s. His disciple Muhittin Birgen, a lead writer of the CUP newspaper *Tanin*, put it this way in autumn 1918: "How many years I have said so many things to the people. Now everything has all at once collapsed."[21] In order to be credible for his broad audience after 1918, Gökalp was thus forced to reinvent himself. This did not require, however, a fundamental change of mind. With the exception of the top CUP leaders in Ankara, he was welcomed by his former circle of believers from Istanbul in Ankara. Here, considerably but by no means entirely altered political-mental coordinates prevailed, including Gökalp's Turkism.

Coming from Hamidian Diyarbekir

Gökalp was born in Diyarbekir where he attended the new governmental high school. He may have become a member of the CUP at that time with Abdullah Cevdet. He certainly was a member in 1896 while enrolled at the Imperial Veterinary School in Istanbul, where he met İshâk Sükuti.[22] Like Talaat, he was arrested during the Hamidian repression of the opposition in the 1890s but released after only ten months.[23] Without having finished his studies, he returned to his hometown and married the girl whom his conservative Sunni family had destined for him.

After the 1908 revolution, Ziya founded the CUP Diyarbekir branch, which was henceforth dominated by the Pirinççizâde family. Arif Pirinççizâde, Ziya's maternal uncle, was elected CUP deputy in November 1908; after his death in 1909, he was succeeded by his son, Ziya's cousin Feyzi. At first, the CUP's Diyarbekir branch followed the general constitutional interest. Two or three years later (i.e., after 1910) it became one of the most aggressively anti-Armenian agencies of the party, in line with the pre-1908 record of its founding group. In April 1909, many young branches in eastern Asia Minor, including Diyarbekir, Mamuretülaziz, and Urfa, still resisted the reactionary anti-Christian Islamism that had fueled a massacre of more than 20,000 Armenians and other Christians in the town and region of Adana. By 1912, the Diyarbekir group had not only affiliated with its local legacy of a new brand of anti-Western Islamism and anti-Christian mob violence—Diyarbekir had seen an atrocious anti-Armenian pogrom in 1895 with Arif among its ringleaders. It was now also part of the CUP, an intra-imperial party organization that, in 1913, went on to establish an empire-wide dictatorship.

In the immediate aftermath of the July 1908 Revolution, Ziya (then thirty-two years old) still subscribed to the vision of an "Ottoman America": a constitutional and federalist melting pot based on equality of diverse ethnic and religious groups. This may seem surprising, perhaps. Primarily, however, it stands as proof of a highly malleable mind. In the late Ottoman province of Diyarbekir, Turkish, Kurdish, Arabic, and Syriac speakers were living side by side. Ziya, of partly Kurdish descent himself, took an interest in diversity and studied Kurdish tribes and dialects. Thus, he temporarily kept his distance from the Turkish ethnonationalis that had already emerged in some circles of the anti-Hamidian opposition prior to 1908. He even explicitly denounced the fantasy of a vast Turkish-speaking Turan under the authority of a mythic *hakan* (ruler).[24] It was only a little later that he fully embraced this ideal. Turan-cum-*hakan* was to take for him the place of a grandiose but abstract mahdi (messiah). This was the new Turanist (pan-Turkish) gospel that Gökalp began to preach from the early 1910s.

By this point, Gökalp had settled in Salonica, becoming a prolific public intellectual and establishing himself as a member of the CUP Central Committee. He had come to fully recognize the attractive potential of an exalted modern ethnic Turkish nationalism for himself, his career, his peers, and his public. As we will see, he also found ways of merging this potential with traditions of imperial Ottoman supremacy and Islamic superiority. From then on, he insisted on referring to himself as "racially a Turk," and vigorously defended himself against being called "Kurd."[25] He purposefully submitted all of his scholarly efforts to Turkist presuppositions; this included a report on Kurdish tribes two years before his death. Thus, the *mefkûre* (ideal) of nation and liberty, which according to his own account had saved him from a deep personal crisis, got caught up in the maelstrom of his new ultranationalist political religion. Indicators of this could already be found in his writings in the immediate aftermath of 1908. "Our villagers mostly belong to the Kurdish people. They are ignorant, kneaded with tribal morality and completely devoid of national and patriotic feelings," he pejoratively wrote not long before he moved to Salonica, well in keeping with the Ottoman elite's haughtiness toward Kurds and the general population.[26] These and other similar lines testify to a rejection of, rather than a genuine interest in, what Gökalp felt to be the embarrassing otherness of Kurds. As early as 1909, Kurds, in his view, represented backwardness and a lack of national unity that had to be overcome. Civil liberty, human rights, and freedom were not values in and of themselves but means to an end: "Freedom (*hürriyet*) must spread to all social strata; every class should taste its flavor so that the nation can move forward. Because the freedom is only a means, the aim is the rise and progress of the nation."[27]

At the age of thirty-three, Gökalp settled in Salonica, then the seat of the Central Committee of the CUP that had organized the July 1908 "Young Turk Revolution." Despite its established name, this decisive turning point in late Ottoman history might be more accurately described as a *coup d'état* or *pronunciamiento* by clandestine CUP pressure groups, in particular young military officers. They helped the party reinstall the Ottoman constitution and, more importantly, control the sultan's politics, which they judged to be insufficiently forceful and patriotic. Sultan Abdulhamid II had suspended the first Ottoman constitution a little more than a year after its installment in 1876. The July 1908 Revolution introduced a short era of hope in the rule of law and democratic equality in the Ottoman world. There was no mass mobilization, however, to bring about a revolutionary change of the social fabric. It was only after 1913 that a groundbreaking transformation of society took place, enforced by the CUP single-party rulers. This was, however, the self-declared revolution of a meanwhile far-right party and therefore far from constitutional principles and human grassroots.

Inspiring the CUP: The Gök-Alp of the 1910s

Gökalp had come from his hometown of Diyarbekir in order to assist as a delegate of the Diyarbekir branch at the CUP Congress in September 1909. He became a close acquaintance of the Salonician group and, in 1910, a Central Committee member.[28] He met new, congenial friends and admirers, founding literary and philosophical journals with them. In line with his conversion from Ottomanism to (pan-)Turkism, he, along with most CUP leaders, believed in the superiority of Islam as "the most complete religion" and "highest level of human consciousness."[29] In 1912, Gökalp moved to Istanbul with the Central Committee. The Ottomans lost Salonica, a multiethnic, predominantly Jewish city, in the First Balkan War.

Compared to the CUP's previous propaganda, Gökalp's ideas were more inspired, innovative, and vigorous. He adopted the Turkist, Ottoman-Islamist, and state-centric centralist convictions that were predominant among long-standing Central Committee members, uniting them in a new synthesis. One new element was his emotive myth of an eternal Turkdom that would be revitalized by modern Western civilization: everything would become new and strongly national. He began using catchwords such as "new Turkey," "new life," "new family," "new law," and "new economy," labeling his proposed far-reaching societal changes in society a "social revolution" (*içtimâî inkılâb*).

In early 1915, he published his vision of a well-developed, corporatist Islamic-Turkish nation-state in Anatolia.[30]

Gökalp had taught sociology at a CUP school in Salonica and, in 1912, was given the chair of sociology at Istanbul University—the first such chair in Turkey. This afforded him the label of one of the founders of Turkish sociology. At the same time, he emerged as the revered leader of a new Turkist school of thought or "sect (*tarikat*)," as one of his many contemporary disciples put it. Gökalp was influenced by the then-famous French sociologist Émile Durkheim, a founder of modern sociology following in the steps of August Comte. Durkheim studied the ways in which new social institutions might help modern societies become more coherent and integrated. Gökalp, however, replaced Durkheim's concept of society with nation. He thereby perverted the concepts of a French-Jewish sociologist who leaned toward socialism, not ethnoreligious nationalism. At the University of Istanbul, the CUP headquarters, and frequently among guests at home, Gökalp shone as the star and "spirit" (*ruh*) who "gave the CUP a determinate social and political doctrine" after years of ideological vagueness.[31]

Gökalp saved, according to himself, an entire generation in search of an ideological orientation from the deadlock produced by the polarization of Ottomanism and Islamism. In his view, it was Islamic Turkism, with its ideal of Turan, that would provide this salvation. Based on this notion, he saw himself as a missionary called to teach a whole nation.[32] Starting with the educated elite, he succeeded impressively in his endeavor: in the early 1910s, the representatives of the Turkist movement "converted" (*ihtida*), as they put it, to the "social and national religion" taught by "the great Gökalp."[33] In the role of *pîr* (now an ideological rather than a spiritual guide), Gökalp stated in 1914 that "nationality is not determined by language alone but also by religion." In 1915, he declared that "religion is the most important factor in the creation of national consciousness as it unites men through common sentiments and beliefs."[34]

Within the Turkist movement, as well as in Gökalp's writings, (quasi-)religious vocabulary is essential, not accidental. It displays an impactful translation—or usurpation—of Sufi terms and mystical experiences into an ultranationalist language that exalts the individuals' merging into the modern national collective under the guidance of charismatic leaders. "Appeal is the property of the beauty (*jamâl*) and sanction that of the majesty (*jalâl*) of the [Turkish nation's great] Ideal [*Mefkûre*]. Through these two powers the ideals merge all individuals into a united, homogeneous, moral [national] oneness."[35] As historian and Iranologist Elton Daniel puts it, Gökalp's maxim "Ferd yok, cemiyet var; hak yok, vazife var" (There is no individual, there is society; there is no right, there is duty) appropriated the mystical belief in the annihilation (*fanâ*) of the individual in the whole. In this case, the "whole" symbolized a Turkish national society that was both a community of believers (*ümmet*) and of "blood" (common racial-cultural ties).[36]

Talaat and other CUP leaders frequently conversed with Gökalp. As the Turkish historian Enver B. Şapolyo, a disciple in Gökalp's circle, put it retrospectively, "Talaat Pasha and Enver Pasha adored Ziya Gökalp like a holy man [*walî*]. In every topic, his scientific opinions made him predominant in the Central Committee."[37] Gökalp's daughter recalled that her father had been "Talaat Pasha's closest friend. The Pasha visited us frequently with his friends and talked until late in the night. I was then a child. From time to time I entered the parlour and found my father always standing. He spoke and spoke all the time."³⁸ Intellectually, Gökalp prevailed over his colleagues in the CUP Central Committee. This was particularly true of his adversary Hayri Efendi, a comparatively conservative religious scholar who served at times as a *sheykhulislam* and as a minister of foundations. Hayri accused Gökalp of prioritizing Turkism over Islam—Turanism, including Turkish mythology, stood in tension to orthodox Islam—and resented the fact that the CUP ideologue enjoyed much greater influence than he did.³⁹ Gökalp, in turn, disdained Hayri as the representative of a religious elite and administration that stood at odds with the charismatic and *tarikat* (religious order) traditions in provincial Asia Minor that he identified with. Related to this was his penchant for popular Islam and the *gazi* ideal of a Muslim warrior's militant faith.⁴⁰

Gökalp remained deeply involved with ideological warfare. From early August 1914, he stood at the forefront of expansionist war propaganda. He made the public call to war a confession of faith in line with the Arabic phrase "Allahu Akbar" (God is the greatest). Transformed into a "national takbir" (*millî tekbir*) or the "Türk's Allahu Akbar" (*Türk'ün tekbiri*), it became a battle cry in the service of Islamic empire and Turan.⁴¹ It was in the same year that he published a volume of collected poems under the title "Kızılelma," or "red-gold apple." An old symbol of Turkish world dominion, this term would immediately have evoked in his readership the Ottoman mantra "The Muslims will conquer [very far] until Kızılelma."⁴² "Kızılelma" took its title from one of the collection's epic poems, first published in early 1913.⁴³ In this long text, Gökalp very probably alluded to his attempted suicide as an adolescent, making his personal affliction a metaphor for that of the entirety of Turkdom. He praised Kızılelma as a cure for Turkdom in its existential grief. For Gökalp, Kızılelma was the Turks' (abstract) messiah/mahdi, guiding their new departure toward Turan. He believed it was his generation's task to cultivate a great ideal (*mefkûre*): the creation of a new Turkey in Anatolia as the center of a vast, reacquired Turan. Anatolia (Asia Minor) was to become the "Turks' national home" (*Türk Yurdu*) and thus the cornerstone for the future of modern Turkdom.

Significantly, the collection started with the poem "Turan" (first published in October 1912). Turan suggested a potentially extreme irredentism, as Gökalp elevated it as the Turks' "enormous and eternal" fatherland. Imagined as historically predominantly Turkish, Turan's vague area reached from the Balkans to Central Asia and western China. The poem exalted "all old and recent victories of my elected, great and noble race" and the "heroes Attila and Genghis Khan," who "magnify my race with victory." It particularly honored the Ottomans' mythical ancestor Oghuz Khan: "In my arteries, he lives with glory and splendor."⁴⁴ Heroes in the image of Oghuz Khan loomed large in Gökalp's vision of leader-led corporatism. Ordinary individuals were called to obey but they were given little value and few rights.

Among Gökalp's magical and messianic notions of the early 1910s, "Turan" was the most suggestive term. He never abandoned it, even in his 1923 legacy to the Kemalist republic, the book *Türkçülüğün Esasları* (Principles of Turkism). By then, he had of course given unambiguous priority to *Türkiyecilik*, the fulfillment of a Turkified Anatolia. "Turan" in the war decade 1912–22 implied social engineering; society had to be cropped and cleansed, and new elements engrafted into it. "The people are the garden, we are the gardeners," reads a line in "Kızılelma." This statement could have been made—and probably was, orally—by Interior Minister Talaat, in order to justify the violent population policies that he started in late 1913. Turan was to be culturally unified and ultimately politically united with the Anatolian heartland. Not under any circumstances was Anatolia to be shared with non-Turkish natives or become the object of negotiations in their claims for cultural autonomy or self-determination. Gökalp's *mefkûre* did not envisage coexistence with others, their culture and language, in the "promised land."[45]

Gökalp, a Prophet of War and Military Spirit

The poems that Gökalp published in newspapers from early August 1914 promised rightful, vengeful, restorative, and expansive Ottoman-Islamic conquest, together with the emergence of a modern Turan. "The lands of the enemy will be ruined! / Turkey will grow and become Turan!" In his poem "Kızıl Destan" (Red Epic) of August 8, he led a chorus of anti-European *schadenfreude*: "The land of civilization will be red blood! / Each of its regions will be a new Balkan!" By mid-November 1914, jihad had officially been declared, and Turkey had officially entered the war.[46] For Gökalp and his wide readership, however, jihad had started much earlier, with the guerrilla war on the Caucasus border that the CUP, using its Special Organization, had launched in August 1914. On August 9, 1914, he wrote: "God's will / sprang from the people / We proclaimed the jihad / God is great."[47] Dysfunctional political ideas invested in the attempted conquest of the Caucasus were typically Gökalpian. A dictatorial state apparatus and its entirely censored press spread this ideology throughout the country.

The late 1914 campaign should have pushed into Central Asia. On November 11, 1914, a Central Committee circular sent to all CUP branches declared that "the national ideal of our people and country spurs us on the one side to annihilate the Moskowit enemy, in order to achieve a natural imperial frontier that includes all our [Turkic] co-nationals. Religion on the other side incites us to liberate the Muslim world from the rule of the infidels and to give the adherents of Muhammad independence." Gökalp's poems galvanized young military officers and a wide educated readership. They enthusiastically participated in what became a frustrated utopia that eventually turned to mass murder. Genocide targeted from 1915 the non-Muslim peoples that stood most in the way of both a unitary Anatolian state and a direct road to Turan.[48] In this Gökalpian spirit, Mehmed Reşid, the governor of Diyarbekir, was congratulated, on the Holiday of Sacrifice in October 1915, for having exterminated the Armenian and Syriac Christians in his province. Reşid's district vice-governor stated in his congratulatory telegram: "My greetings on your Holiday. I kiss your hands for having gained us the six provinces [with formerly Armenian population] and opened for us the road toward Turkestan and Caucasia"—that is, Turan's territory adjacent to Anatolia.[49]

When, in late August 1915, Talaat had succeeded in removing most Armenians from Anatolia, Gökalp rhapsodized in his poem "Talaat Bey":

You are the spirit who unites the souls
In you the committee sees his conscience
If it is a ship of salvation, you are Noah
You, if you were not, this nation would be orphaned . . .
You are of pure heart like a Turkish soldier
You are a hero free of arrogance and boasting
You are a statue of honesty as is Turkish history [. . .].[50]

The admiring and submissive spirit of devotion to utterly brutal—if successful—power defines Gökalp's hero-centered corporatism. He strove to appeal to the leaders, whom he effusively praised. Even though he was little involved in daily politics, he was constantly present at the center of decision-making, the headquarters of the CUP and its Special Organization in Istanbul.[51] In September 1915, around the time when his rhapsody was published, Mehmed Cavid Bey referred to Talaat, Gökalp, and a depraved situation in Istanbul in his diary, asking: "What becomes of the beautiful humanity in the hand of foolish butchers?" And later noting: "It throws one into despair to see the destiny of the nation under the influence of men with such a mind."[52] Cavid, who had served as finance minister several times, was the only prominent CUP member who consistently disagreed with the war- and death-prone attitude of his political friends, albeit mostly only in the privacy of his diary.

The sociologist Niyazi Berkes remarks that Gökalp "was the type of intellectual not infrequently found in the East: a spiritual guide, an inspirer, a *mürşid*," with "marked Sufi inclinations, and the influence of *tasawwuf* always remained conspicuous in his thinking."[53] Yet, this does not deny Gökalp's political impact and (co-)responsibility. A superficial historical grasp has long depicted him as a genius out of touch with decision-making, and overlooks, or at least underestimates, the real impact of an inspirer of his caliber. Although an admirer of potentates, he was not a weak sycophant but well aware of his influence. He knew how to manage the intellectual power that he exerted not only on an educated youth but also on leaders and functionaries seeking mentorship and susceptible to his appealing Turkism. Sidelining spiritual competitors like Sheykhulislam Mustafa Hayri or Said Halim, he imposed his Turkism authoritatively as the only viable version of modern Islamic-Turkish patriotism. On his advice, the interior ministry's Directorate for the Settlement of Refugees and Tribes undertook ethnographic and sociological investigations in Anatolia in order to prepare thorough Turkification. This went hand in hand with the Armenian genocide. Gökalp's own contribution was an inquiry into Kurdish tribes. Baha Said, a member of the CUP's Special Organization, conducted a study on "the characteristics of Turkish Alevis, Kızılbaş and Bektashis," which claimed that various religious—including Kurdish "heterodox"—traditions were of Turkish origin.[54]

The young journalist Zekeriya Sertel coordinated the CUP regime's "scientific" grasp on tribes. Sertel had belonged to Gökalp's circle since his years in Saloniki. In Istanbul, he collaborated with Yunus Nadi (later, the founder of the newspaper *Cumhuriyet* and the Anatolia Agency) and published the journal *Turan* with Reşid Saffet Atabinen.[55] As late as 1917, according to Şapolyo's recollection, Talaat Pasha declared, at a CUP meeting: "We came to lead this nation, but Anatolia has remained a sealed box for us," to which Gökalp answered: "We made a political revolution. [. . .] Yet, the greatest revolution is the social revolution [. . .] and this will only be possible by knowing the physiological and morphological constitution of society."[56] It was, in Gökalp's view, the duty of leadership to cull bad elements from society and graft on new ones in order to form a unitary body, a country in which "every individual has the same ideal, language, habit, religion."[57] Armed with knowledge of Western science and civilization, the state would then accomplish the superiority of the Turkish-Muslim nation. The non-negotiable requirement for national inclusion was Islamic Turkishness. This signified a merger of theological claims to supremacy with *völkisch* claims of cultural-racial superiority.

By mid-1917, the impending collapse of imperial Russia spurred renewed Turanist hopes. By autumn 1917, Gökalp was once again "preoccupied with the conquest of the Caucasus and the road to take toward Turan."[58] The Treaty of Brest-Litovsk opened a door to the area, which many Armenian survivors from Anatolia had fled to during the genocide. To them, Turan now posed a renewed exterminatory threat. In May 1918, a German general reported that "the aim of Turkish policy is the permanent occupation of the Armenian districts and the extermination of the Armenians. All of Talaat's and Enver's assurances to the contrary are lies."[59] As Cavid's diary reveals, Enver Pasha believed in Gökalp's Turan more naïvely than Talaat.[60] The Armenians stood in the way of the advance of "the Islamic Army of the Caucasus," under the command of War Minister Enver Pasha's half-brother. During the advance, Enver cabled to one of his generals that "it is unacceptable to offer an existence to the Armenians. All must be done in order to weaken them completely and leave them in an entirely destitute state so that their deprived life conditions prevent them from organizing themselves."[61]

A series of articles in early 1918 glorified the cultural, racial, religious, and economic unity of a Turan composed of "40 million Turks and Muslims." They made Istanbul, the capital of Anatolia's Turkish polity, Turan's "cultural center," its "seat of the caliphate," and "national Kaaba." They also envisaged cultural-religious unity as a harbinger of political unification. Gökalp's comparison between Anatolian Turkey and nineteenth-century Prussia, which had unified Germany, made this goal unequivocal.[62] Gökalp and the intelligentsia close to him spread their Turanist ideas via the new journal, *Yeni Mecmua*, which he and the CUP had established in July 1917. All publication costs were covered by Grand Vizier Talaat.[63] In his writings, Gökalp expressed his desire to see the "unity of [Turan's] Turks" form a "great Turkish nation" with a common "Turkish-Muslim ideal." He reasoned that "this age only grants nations that are big in number the right to live." Once "saved," Turan would be a great "organism" comprising all Turks, their sub-states, and their strong joint armies in Asia Minor, the Caucasus, Central Asia, and further afield. All residents would be Muslim, use the Turkish language of Istanbul,[64] and be led by one charismatic, eschatological leader-commander (*reis, sahib-kırân, kumandan*). As a result, all Turks would be "organized top-down like an army," living as obedient members of one state and one solidary society. Dissent would have to be severely repressed and divergent opinions or ideals "killed" (*öldürülmeli*). Thus, only the "Turkish-Muslim Ideal" (*Türk-Müslüman Mefkûresi*) would be left to live and prevail.[65] After all that had happened in Turkey by early 1918, readers easily understood that "killing" would not remain metaphorical but would target dissenters and dissenting groups in a very real way.

Significantly, the room in which *Yeni Mecmua* was produced was frequently used for meetings between the future political and intellectual elite of post-Ottoman Turkey, their ingenious master Gökalp, and his (senior) peers Ahmed Ağaoğlu, Yusuf Akçura, and Ali Hüseyinzâde. Attendees included Hamdullah Suphi (Tanrıöver), minister of education in 1925, Necmettin Sadık (Sadak), journalist, diplomat, and foreign minister in the late 1940s, Fuad Köprülü, nationalist history professor and foreign minister in the early 1950s, and Reşid Safvet (Atabinen), the secretary of the Turkish delegation at the Conference of Lausanne, deputy in Ankara, and international advocate of the 1930s Turkish History Thesis. Unlike the truth-seeking youth he had been in the past, Gökalp spoke with and for power; he turned toward, and believed in, leadership in the name of the Turkish nation. As Köprülü approvingly put it, Gökalp's rhapsodic poems for Talaat, Enver, and Atatürk "did all to intimately translate his own ardent and mystic spirit" full of "worship for [Turkish] heroes."[66]

Kemalist Principles of Turkism

As indicated, Gökalp never gave up on his Turanian dream. In the immediate aftermath of the World War defeat, he and the former top CUP luminaries continued to pin their hopes on CUP-led revolutionist Islamic militancy in the Caucasus, Central-Asian Turkestan, and Afghanistan.[67] Like Talaat, however, Gökalp quickly adapted to the new realities of an Anatolian resistance movement under Mustafa Kemal. This ambitious former CUP general now commanded the surviving party networks in Anatolia, including previously prepared underground cells (*Karakol*) and intact army units in eastern Asia Minor; he was also in charge of an ongoing cooperation with co-opted Kurdish leaders. Gökalp did not flee from Istanbul as Talaat and other top leaders had done. He was detained by the British in early 1919 together with a number of CUP members, including his cousin Feyzi Pirinççizâde, for crimes against humanity. After taking a number of British hostages, the Ankara counter-government obtained the release of their men in May 1921. Because Ankara carefully denied and concealed relations to high-profile CUP people, the star ideologue Gökalp had to first spend a year and a half back in his hometown of Diyarbekir, loyally supporting Kemal in his new weekly, *Küçük Mecmua*. Only then was he welcomed in Ankara and elected as a member of parliament.[68] Feyzi—a former deputy and leader in Diyarbekir's blood-stained CUP branch—served as a minister in the Ankara government from early 1922.

Gökalp proved his full allegiance through his pen. In 1923, he published his summa, *Türkçülüğün Esasları* (Principles of Turkism), which can be considered his post-imperial ideological credo. It rested on the unchanged foundation that "Turkism [*Türkçülük*] means exalting the Turkish nation."[69] From the very first chapter, his signature exuberant admiration for a "great genius" comes to the fore.[70] The first part of the book clarifies that defeat in the First World War had not made him give up on his dream of pan-Turkish unity: After the Turkification of Asia Minor, Oghuz union (*Oğuz birliği*)—unification with the Turkmen in Azerbaijan, Iran, Turkistan, and, implicitly,

Iraq and Syria—should follow. The unification of Turan was the third and final step; encompassing all Turkic peoples, it would reach as far as northwestern China. Gökalp compared his utopia of Turan to Lenin's communist society, which he also saw as lying in the distant future.[71] The gap between his exaltation of Turkishness and a universal socialist eschatology appears not to have bothered him.

"Turkism is neither chauvinistic nor fanatical," Gökalp professed in 1923.[72] On a superficial level, his 1923 definition of *Türklük* opened up toward a less exclusive conception of nation: "A nation is a society composed of individuals who are united by identical language, religion, taste and moral, that is of individuals raised under identical conditions."[73] In reality, however, this wording is not only as exclusive as any race-based definition of nation; it also puts immense pressure for assimilation on those who try to adapt and be part of the nation but will inevitably fail. The most problematic aspect of *Türkçülüğün Esasları* is the built-in rationalization of violence in the name of the Turkish nation. As is the case with many of Gökalp's texts, it is infused with social Darwinist contempt for minority populations and non-heroic individuals. Turkism radicalized premodern Islamic submission of non-Muslims by entirely excluding them from the "we" that Gökalp very frequently used, most notably in the phrases "our state" and "our history." As non-Turks, Muslim Kurds were soon to experience this chauvinism too.

Contemporaries rightly drew attention to Gökalp's racial self-redefinition, saying that, "by race, he originated from the Kurdish tribe of Zaza, but he Turkified himself to such a point that he never again spoke about the Kurds"—neither about the Kurdish future nor about his own Kurdishness.[74] Regarding his principles as compatible with universal standards, or his corporatism as meaningful for democracy and humanity, is impossible.[75] When trying "to find a basis of internationality to Turkish nationalism" based on Gökalp's principles, one is soon, in Niyazi Berkes's words, confronted with "fanciful utopias."[76] Domestically, he refused negotiation of social contracts because he rejected the equality of non-Turks. It was for the same reasons that he refused to regard the international order in constitutional, egalitarian terms, or on the basis of universal standards. His faith in a universal civilization devoid of universal principles obviously failed to meet such a challenge, as did some appreciative words on welcoming "original tastes" of different cultures or being "a bit humanity-oriented" (*biraz insaniyetçi*).[77] Based on the organicist concept of an Islamic-Turkish state and society, Gökalp's Islam promoted neither individual faith nor individual stances in relation to authorities. His 1918 poem "Duty" (*Vazife*) thus fully subordinates individual rights to a leader-led state and a God-like nation.[78] Religion, with all its spiritual and mental power, served as an indispensable cement for societal coherence in a unitary ethnostate.

In 1924, Gökalp was a member of the committee preparing Turkey's new constitution in the wake of ethnoreligious cleansing.[79] Making Islam the state's religion and Turkish its official language, it offered "all sovereignty unconditionally to the nation" (*millet*). Since the Enlightenment, the term "constitution" has, within a political context, referred to a fundamental social contract that, ideally, has been negotiated and agreed upon by all concerned individuals and groups in a territory, giving all of them a free voice. Gökalp's Turkism contradicted a democratic-minded social contract from the very start. For him, the Turkish *millet*, based on pre-existing Turkishness and Islam, possessed bonds stronger than any negotiated covenant. In essays published in 1916 and 1917, Gökalp castigated the reform efforts of the Tanzimat, arguing that those mid-nineteenth-century reformers had followed the pernicious idea of a constitutional monarchy, instead of a strong, corporatist sultanate-caliphate.

On reading the German sociologist Max Weber's thesis "The Protestant Ethic and the Spirit of Capitalism," he boldly—albeit without explicit reference to the author or the 1904–5 essay[80]—equated Protestantism to an Islamized Christianity "in total contradiction to the traditional basics of Christianity." It was this fact, he claimed, which led to the success of Protestant societies. This argument served to elevate Islam as the ultimate religion, the one that suited modernity better than all others: "The Islamic state means a modern state." He reproached late Ottoman reformers of the Tanzimat for alienating "our state from being an Islamic state" and for making it "inorganic" (*gayr-ı uzvî*)—instead of striving for a corporatist organism (*uzviyet*).[81] He argued that, in sacralizing instead of laicizing the state, Islam would be able to concentrate power more effectively. Since the merger of religion and state was its unique advantage, the modern future belonged to Islam.[82]

These arguments—put forward by Gökalp at the 1916 CUP congress—underpinned the institutional and legal reforms pushed by Talaat and Gökalp in 1916–17. The reforms resulted in removing the *sheykhulislam* from the cabinet and transferring the sharia courts, the pious foundations, and the religious schools (*madrasas*) to the ministries of justice, foundations, and education. The reforms also anticipated the establishment of Ankara's Directorate of Religious Affairs as a substitute for the Ottoman *sheykhulislamate* (religious administration). The substitution went hand in hand with the abolition of the caliphate in March 1924. Gökalp was again involved as a member of the relevant parliamentary commission, having revised his former insistence on the sultanate-caliphate.[83] The new Directorate of Religious Affairs subordinated and took charge of Sunni Islam. This was not a secular separation of state and religion. By contributing to the Directorate of Religious Affairs, which paid for mosques and imams via taxation, non-Sunnis were again—and are still today—sociopolitically discriminated against, as had been the case in Ottoman times. Gökalp's idea of national (*milli*) sovereignty and national polity was defined by pre-existing sacralized bonds of religion and culture. This precluded equality, the core principle of plural democracy. It prevented the negotiation of egalitarian social contracts among diverse populations and individuals in a given human geography.

Gökalpian Proto-Fascism

Kemalism remained Gökalpian, both in its philosophy and in its practical politics. For decades, this made the immigration and naturalization of persons who were not (1) Muslims and (2) Turkish-speaking almost impossible.[84] The self-serving appointment of foreign specialists, including academics from Nazi Germany, followed Gökalp's principle that a culturally distinct Turkish nation needed to boost its modern rise by assimilating Western civilization.

Gökalp's choice of primordial bonds over negotiated contracts appears connected to his lack of ability to dialogue. As his friend Yahya Kemal stated, the people around him faced a man who could not stop exposing his deliberations. He never truly listened to others or expected true answers from them. There was no opportunity for Socratic dialogue or wisdom.[85] He almost obsessively kept on developing his own concepts and arguments that centered around his unquestionable principles. In a similar lack of true dialogue, Atatürk tirelessly tried to base his supposedly unquestionable credo of Turkism on ethnohistory and linguistics, as anthropologist and scholar-diplomat Eugène Pittard reported from his astonishing meetings with him during the last decade of Atatürk's life.[86]

The leader Atatürk and the apostle Gökalp depended heavily on each other. Although less frequent and concrete than between Talaat and Gökalp, their interaction was profound, a case of strongly communicating vessels. Atatürk's inherently pan-Turkish History Thesis professed the Turks' civilization-bringing role in world history and their pre-existence in Asia Minor, thus perpetuating Turkish-centric myth-making mixed with positivist scholarship. The Kemalists' ethnocentric speculations left Gökalp's basic concept—the exaltation of Turkdom—unchanged. Though Gökalp had not made references to physical anthropology and racial craniology so influential in Atatürk's History Thesis, he was in line with the Turkish president's eclectic use of history and positivist science. Whereas the History Thesis placed great importance on common racial roots with Aryan Europeans, Gökalp distinguished between Turanians and Aryans.[87]

An essentialist understanding of nation is not compatible with democracy. Gazi Mustafa Kemal did by no means claim democracy when he established the Ankara government in the early 1920s. The core issue was the fight against those who challenged the own cohort's power claim, pride, and possessions.[88] He followed the concept of an authoritarian-led Turkish-Muslim nation, whose leaders claimed organic unity with, and representation of, the nation (*millet*) and people (*halk*) against outsiders, rivals, and adversaries. As the CUP had done in its wars since 1911, Kemal defended this concept in the hottest hour of his struggle, during the "War of Independence," in a close fraternity with Islamism and Sunni Kurdish leaders.

Although contexts changed, ideological and personal continuity from the 1910s to interwar Turkey prevailed. Inclusive-looking "ornaments" on the surface of Kemalist declarations and programs did not change the structural facts. To insiders, this was clear from the onset. "The CUP members have therefore never found odd the hero of the new national movement. They all rallied around him [Atatürk] with a national spirit and a national discipline that they had acquired in the twelve years before [since 1908]," wrote Talaat Pasha's intimate Muhittin Birgen, who later became a Kemalist disciple of Gökalp. "All CUP people who had well begun to identify with Ziya Gökalp's ideas during World War I, which were published in the name of the CUP, easily and logically rallied around Mustafa Kemal Pasha, to defend these [Gökalp's] new and solid principles."[89]

Whichever way we look at it, Gökalp offered very strong incentives for a totalitarian integration of state, religion, education, society, and the individual. Even though a few other names—such as anthropologist Şevket Kansu or Atatürk's adoptive daughter, the historian Afet Inan—added distinct color, the road to Atatürk's "Turkish version of totalitarianism"[90] in the 1930s was directly related to Gökalp. What the youth of the 1910s had embraced as the "religion of (Islamic) Turkism" including the adulation of heroes paved the way for the "religion of Kemalism" and the personality cult of Atatürk. A disturbing idolatry, complete with prayers, liturgies, and a temple (the Anıtkabir mausoleum in Ankara), this cult embodied all religious references invested in Turkism, albeit now centered on one national mahdi/messiah.

What was it that defines Gökalp as a seminal proto-fascist ideologue of Greater Europe? In historical discussions on fascism, there are evident geostrategic reasons for a differentiated assessment of Turkey. In the immediate aftermath of the Great War, the founding nationalist elites were allied to the Bolsheviks; they were labeled "revolutionary" by these radical leftists because they had joined in a common "anti-imperialist" front against Britain. After victory in their Soviet-supported war for Anatolia, the Kemalists again approached the Great War victors, who were now willing to compromise, at the Conference of Lausanne. Twenty years later, having remained neutral during the Second World War, they fully integrated into Western alliances. It is for this reason that Turkey is generally not counted among the fascist states. Some new scholarly approaches, however, have paid attention to the considerably fascist aspects in the foundation of modern Turkey.[91]

A deeper analysis that looks beyond diplomacy into the polity's fundamentals and construction reveals fascist core tenets in Gökalp and Talaat's working relationship, well before various fascisms came to the fore in Europe. It also provides an intriguingly different perspective on the long-term evolution of kindred patterns and ideologemes. The particular interwar and post-1945 contexts, including Western alliances, have not only contributed to Turkish longevity; they have also prevented a conceivable and possible domestic reckoning with the main tenets of what we might call the country's long-enduring "proto-fascism."

Patriot Cavid Bey

Victim of Judicial Murder in Ankara

The prominent CUP member Mehmed Cavid Bey was a skillful financial expert and negotiator, nationally and internationally. Although of weak impact in high politics and outvoted in, or excluded from core decisions of the CUP committee, he deserves careful attention. He even deserves—as this book's fresh approach to Turkey's formation intends to show—a profound reappraisal.[1] Cavid (1877–1926) was a nationalist, but never a Gökalpian Turkist. An agile cosmopolitan, he had espoused constitutional political thought, not the predominant essentialist credo of Turkism internalized by most of his cohort. By no means did he share their irredentist and restorationist imperialism. As a defendant in the court in Ankara that arbitrarily sentenced him to death, he said in his last defense on August 26, 1926, the day of his execution: "What this country direly needs are humans, not territory."[2] Cavid Bey's testimony, particularly his diary, is of inestimable value.

A Constitutionalist Turkish Patriot and His Unique Diaries

Constitutionalism—or more specifically, "constitutional patriotism" (*Verfassungspatriotismus*)—is a contemporary German term that is related, however, to the nineteenth-century notion of a "nation by will" (*Willensnation*), that is, a nation based not on an ethnoreligious identity primarily but on a consensual social contract, negotiated among all concerned people of a country and codified in a modern constitution. Ottoman constitutionalism originated in the Tanzimat but never became a predominant current, though it had grown deep roots in parts of the Young Turk movement—clearly so in Cavid's case and even more clearly for minority groups like the Armenians who relied existentially on the rule of law and democratic equality.

As explained in Chapter 8, Ottoman constitutionalism clashed with the essentialist Islamic nationalism of Ziya Gökalp. For a person of Cavid's intelligence and moral sensibility, essentialist identity was a no-go. His peculiar ethnoreligious background played a role in his independent-mindedness, even though he never delved into this identity issue. Outwardly a Sunni Muslim, Cavid was a *dönme* of the Sabbatian tradition and therefore widely treated as a crypto-Jew, "not an authentic son of the native land," according to a reproach by nationalistic journalists in late 1922. "Such news even during the conference is mischief and treason," he noted in his diary during the Conference of Lausanne.[3]

Like Mehmed Talaat, the CUP's central figure, Cavid belonged to the civil members of the party, not its predominant group of officers, including the officers from the Imperial Military Medical Academy, where the CUP was founded in 1889. Cavid is unique as a CUP leader because of his diaries that constitute a treasure not only of information by a CUP insider and minister but also of consistent contemporary critique. Dense and vibrant, his "ego-writing" started in the aftermath of the Young Turk Revolution, after he lost his first wife.[4] It ended on the eve of his trial and execution three years after the Lausanne Conference, that is, in 1926. Thousands of pages even in the printed version, his diaries cover the years 1909–24. Cavid was more spirited and critical, more communicative, frank, honest, and life-loving than most others. Besides being a well-informed interlocutor and diarist, he emerges as a voice of conscience and truth in critical situations. His voice mostly remained private, however, or sidelined by the decision-makers.

Like others in his cohort—of whom so many left memoirs, but very rarely, however, dense and authentic diaries—he also celebrated his patriotic ego from time to time, emphasizing tireless sacrifices for the national cause. Though thus in many respects an ordinary Turkish nationalist rooted in the CUP, he was different in that he could quite rightly claim a "treasure of honesty" (*sermaye-i namus*) for himself. In the seclusion of his diary, he boldly, proudly, and solemnly underlined this self-affirmation.[5] An exception among high-ranking CUP members, he categorically rejected entry into the Great War in autumn 1914, and felt horror at the anti-Armenian contempt and exterminatory hatred of his party comrades in 1915. Back in Istanbul from negotiations in Berlin, he accused his comrades in his diary—but nowhere else—at the end of August 1915: "Not only the political existence, but also the biological existence of an entire [Armenian] people you dared to destroy."[6]

Relevant also is Cavid's both personal and political *Şiar'ın Defteri* (*Notebook for Şiar*). Şiar is the name of Cavid's son, born in 1924 from his recent second marriage, when Cavid was fifty-five. In the form of letters to Şiar, which closely follow the toddler's development, this tender and family-centered writing reads like the continuation and conclusion of his diary. Its entries go from October 25, 1924, to June 10, 1926, the day of his detention in Istanbul, two and a half months before his death.[7] Cavid's diary offers insider knowledge on unofficial networks, statements, thoughts, and gatherings from both a Turkish nationalist and a cosmopolitan angle.

Cavid enjoyed excellent information thanks to his various interlocutors. Among them was a prominent acquaintance made during more than a decade of active political and public life in Europe and Ottoman Turkey. This comprised many personalities in, or formerly in, high positions. He cultivated a large network of acquaintances far beyond Near Eastern and Turkish nationalist circles. Because he mostly summarized his letters in his diary, the diary also gives insight into his rich correspondence. Cavid was committed to friendships beyond national borders and beyond camaraderie or functional networks. Most important was the long-standing CUP member and journalist Hüseyin Cahit Yalçın, who took care of his son after 1926.

Cavid's constitutional ideal became other-worldly in the 1910s, when pan-Turkism and war politics defined the CUP's party-state with which he closely colluded. As his diary proves, time and again, he therefore felt deep unease, but he kept loyal to Talaat Pasha, the CUP's informal head, Cavid's long-standing party "brother." Under Ankara's increasing power from 1920 and its growingly authoritarian, leader-centered rule from 1923, the Turkish polity again descended into a partisan autocracy, as chronicled in Cavid's diary. In this case, again, his opposition remained basically unspoken and limited to a private expression of opinion in his diary and in small circles of friends, while he no longer engaged in active politics. Nevertheless, this time, dissent drew him to the gallows.

A Revolutionary Young Turk

Cavid grew up in Salonica (Thessaloniki) in a family of merchants and finished the Mülkiye (Civil Servant Academy) in Istanbul in 1896. In 1902, he became a teacher of economics at the Salonica Law School where he met the one-year-older Mehmed Talaat, a young postal employee who desired to amend his rudimentary school education.[8] Together with others, they established a CUP cell and prepared for revolt against the sultan.

Toward the end of August 1903, Robert Graves, a young diplomat attached to the British Consulate in Salonica, received "a mysterious request that I would grant an interview to certain Turkish patriots who were in despair at the difficulties threatening their country, and wished to take my advice as to the course which they should pursue." Talaat, Mustafa Rahmi (Arslan), Ahmed Cemal (future Pasha), Hacı Âdil, and Cavid met with him. They were convinced "that the misrule of the Sultan Abdul Hamid had brought their beloved country to the verge of ruin" and "proposed to put themselves at the head of a revolt against his authority."[9] Thanks to collaboration with Young Turks in exile in Paris, the Salonica center grew to a hub capable of acting by 1908.

After the Young Turk Revolution of July 1908, the CUP dominated the parliament and pressured the government, but had no members in the cabinet. Talaat was in a strong position as a deputy and as a Central Committee member. When Grand Vizir Kâmil Pasha changed the war and the navy ministers and sent back the troops from Salonica to establish the governmental prerogatives against the intransparent power from the CUP in early 1909, he lost a vote of confidence. Committee control of the government became even tighter; criticism from both Islamists and liberals intensified. Since Kâmil was an Anglophile, British diplomacy was frustrated by the replacement of Kâmil by the CUP-friendly Hüseyin Hilmi Pasha. In early April 1909, Talaat, Rıza, and Cavid began to consider the formation of a revolutionary CUP cabinet.[10]

Public excitement and tensions in the army motivated soldiers and some officers from the rank and file in Istanbul to rebel on the night of April 12–13, 1909. They occupied the parliament and soon controlled the whole capital. Students of *medrese* (Islamic college) joined them in demanding the full implementation of the sharia and the banishment of Ahmed Rıza, Talaat, Cavid, Rahmi, and Cahit from the empire. As a consequence of this traumatic coup, the CUP Central Committee wanted to increase even more its control and influence. However, the CUP's *éminences grises* Dr. Bahaeddin Şhakir and Dr. Nazım first did not want the "young men" (Cavid, Talaat) to become ministers, preferring to insert them as counselors. Cavid was to assist the finance minister Mehmed Rifat. In June, he succeeded him, becoming the first CUP minister even before Talaat.[11]

The CUP in (partial) power went from crisis to crisis, internally and externally. In a general crisis in autumn 1910, it turned to Germany, the former sultan's special friend, the only European partner, in Cavid's words, not to set conditions "inconsistent with the dignity of Turkey." This turn was actively prepared by Ambassador Marschall von Bieberstein who, for this rapprochement, took the opportunity of Cavid's failure to get an important loan in Paris and London.[12] However, the international recalibration did not solve the CUP's problem of domestic political credibility. In March 1911, the committee therefore ordered the withdrawal of his CUP ministers Emrullah Efendi and Bedros Halajian. Cavid bitterly criticized the decision "to sacrifice" the Armenian Halajian and to not even give him the opportunity to resign himself, as Talaat had done. To exclude him in a critical time was "tantamount to hurting the [Armenian] group that is one of the most loyal to us," he confided in his diary.[13]

In spring 1911, the CUP was threatened by division. A group surrounding the CUP member and colonel Mehmed Sadık, a hero of the 1908 revolution, "seduced under the guise of religion a great many among our party members and those whom we trusted most." When Talaat went to talk with Sadık, there were "always the same fairy tales and nonsense: Freemasonry, Zionism, personalities." Sadık's group suspected, above all, Cavid, Talaat, and Cahid Cahit.[14] As a consequence, Cavid resigned on May 12, whereas Colonel Sadık was sent to Salonica for duty. Yet the crises continued, and the CUP's influence was shaken. Meeting his Swiss friend Louis Rambert in mid-September 1911, when Cavid had come back from travels in Asia Minor, both agreed that "everywhere in the country the minds were overexcited."[15]

Italy's invasion of Libya at the end of September 1911 increased nervousness. The CUP insisted on resolute armed resistance in Libya, at the same time seeking support from the Entente powers for what it considered its rightful cause. Cavid therefore wrote a letter to Winston Churchill, the newly appointed British minister of the navy. Halide Edib, a former pupil of the American College for Girls—the female figurehead of the Young Turk Revolution and, after 1911, of Turkism—translated the letter into English. The letter asked if the time had come "for a permanent alliance between our two countries."[16] With the letter to Churchill, Cavid and Talaat hoped to address a new First Lord of the Admiralty sympathetic with the CUP cause and their resistance against Italian invasion. Churchill's answer was polite but negative. This confirmed the reorientation toward Germany.

Dissidents, including Colonel Sadık's circle, who wanted an Ottoman Muslim alignment, on the one hand, and liberal intellectuals and representatives of non-Muslim groups, on the other, worked in favor of a new and strong party. The independent deputy Krikor Zohrab actively networked in favor of a liberal alliance. Cavid and the lawyer and Armenian writer Zohrab were friends. In a meeting in mid-October 1911 of Zohrab, Cavid, Talaat, and others, Zohrab insisted that constitutional rule be implemented, since in reality a regime depending on and in favor of the CUP existed, while pluralism was lacking, and the non-Turkish groups felt increasingly alienated by CUP chauvinism. Zohrab proposed cooperation and a coalition of the CUP and liberals, since they agreed on many important points. But after a meeting in their Istanbul Nuruosmaniye headquarters, the CUP refused to accept Zohrab's proposals.[17]

Although in sympathy with complaints by Zohrab, Cavid was not willing or able to clearly support him. In January 1912, Talaat and Cavid were again made ministers, and in spring, the CUP won a forced victory in an irregular election (*sopalı seçim*) that lasted bizarrely from February to April 1912, seeing mob violence and penal action by the CUP against adversaries. The backlash came in the form of a bloodless coup led by Sadık, which ushered in a liberal-conservative interlude until January 1913. Following the July 1912 coup, Cavid noted that "the general opinion now considers Union and Progress as broken down and feels great satisfaction from this consideration."[18] In its subsequent struggle for survival, the CUP involved the government in a race of populism and patriotic defiance in the context of growing tensions with Bulgaria and other Balkan states.

In defiant opposition, the CUP organized a huge meeting on Sultanahmet Square on October 4, 1912, where its leaders gave speeches shouting "War, we want war!"[19] On the next day, Hüseyin Cahid wrote in CUP's mouthpiece *Tanin* that "there is only one act, one vision that occupies the life and existence of the nation: war, war, war." Cavid alone, a charismatic orator, had the wisdom to absent himself and refused to speak because "as long as the state had not determined and decided on how to proceed, it was not appropriate to deliver speeches in public places." His diary entry on October 3 mentions an "enormous excitation" and a "war desire" that was difficult to stop.[20]

The Balkan Wars, to whose outbreak CUP demagoguery critically contributed, opened the road toward CUP dictatorship. In late 1912, Cahit and Cavid favored a new young and radical government, able to inspire—as they believed—new life in the country.[21] In January 1913, the violent coup led by Enver and Talaat inaugurated a five-and-a-half-year, German-backed CUP party-state. For the conservative Central Committee member Hayri, Cavid figured among the "men of revolution" (*inkılab erbabı*), together with Talaat, Cahid, İsmail Hakkı, Hacı Âdil, Enver, and Cemal. "We [Hayri and Necmettin Molla] came to the conclusion that Talaat, Hacı Âdil, Cavid, and Cahid were a calamity for this nation that they had subdued to their influence. My Lord, preserve this country, amen."[22]

German Ambassador Hans von Wangenheim, the successor of Marschall von Bieberstein in June 1912, was, in Cavid's words, an "utter Turkophile," although he had been adopting since late 1912 on behalf of Berlin a more positive attitude toward the Armenians and the reform question (see Chapter 4).[23] Cavid himself had many informal talks with German and other diplomats on this issue. Fully loyal to Talaat, Cavid used his persuasiveness to categorically refuse European control and draw Germany more to Turkey's side. He insisted that the CUP was committed to Armenian security and "willing to realize reforms in Armenia." He deployed a panoply of arguments to show that Armenian propaganda was at fault, Europe was not sincere, and Russia provoked troubles in the eastern provinces.[24] On December 28, 1913, in a critical phase of the reform negotiations, Cavid invited Vartkes and Zohrab to another debate and, as a result, exclaimed hopefully in his diary that on the matter of the European inspectors for seven oriental provinces, "we will be able to agree. The same is true for the issue of guarantees!"[25] But this proved presumptuous. A year and a half after his hopeful outline on the Turkish-Armenian future, deeply disillusioned, Cavid confessed in his diary in late August 1915, "We [CUP] have publicly proved [. . .] that we lack the capacity to rule." By then, all his fervent arguments of 1913 against foreign supervision had revealed themselves as hollow words. Leading the Armenian fellow citizens to death, "we have condemned everything."[26]

Cavid was neither willing nor able to exit the common political orbit and his dependency on Talaat. Following his friend's instructions, he became at times complicit in crime, for example that of violently ousting Rûm from the Aegean coast in spring 1914, when he published an appeasing article in the French newspaper *Le Temps*.[27] Even before the Armenians, Cavid thus proved wrong on the issue of the Rûm: in late 1912, he had pretended that the Rûm of Anatolia would live "in entire security" in case of a strongly Asia Minor–focused CUP policy.[28]

Member of a Dictatorial and Genocidal War Regime

Cavid was appointed the minister of finances in March 1914. On April 14, 1914, he returned to Istanbul from loan negotiations in Paris. A "general feeling of relief spread throughout the whole population," because he had succeeded in his negotiations for a substantial French loan of 800 million pounds, from which the commercial milieu expected a great boost for Turkey and Europe.[29]

But this was not counting on Europe's fragile balance. The July 1914 crisis opened the possibility of a general war, which the most influential CUP leaders considered an opportunity for Turkey. On the morning of August 2, 1914, Cavid suddenly entered Said Halim Pasha's mansion for a different affair and listened to the grand vizir who loudly read the unsigned war alliance treaty with Germany. All except Cavid were overjoyed that, at long last, they had concluded an alliance with a European great power. They felt ready to enter war, loyal to the letter of the alliance treaty. Talking in the evening in Enver's house, Cavid thought that "neither Talaat nor Halil had completely understood the treaty that they had decided to sign."[30]

On August 4, Talaat instructed the Ottoman delegates of the Greek-Ottoman commission for population exchange to abstain from any decision, since war promised new horizons, including revanchist reconquest of territory lost during the First Balkan War. Partly on Cavid's insistence, on August 6, 1914, Wangenheim accepted six far-reaching new conditions added to the August 2 treaty.[31] When Cavid accused Germany throughout his diary of having dragged Turkey into war, he lacked critical distance. He probably did not know-how much Enver and Talaat had insisted since mid-July 1914 on a war alliance vis-à-vis Austrian and German diplomats, advocating decisive military action by Vienna and Berlin. After a talk with Talaat on September 6, 1914, Cavid noted, "I said that I saw no interest at all now in making war against Russia, but Talaat, not less than Enver, wants to do so, even if without the Bulgarians!"[32]

True to his announcement, Cavid resigned from the cabinet after the Ottoman attack on Russia in October 1914. Said Halim, the grand vizir, was "weak-minded," Enver "entirely ignorant in politics and infantile-minded," and Talaat "imagined that everything could be resolved by boldness." The rule of these men "plunged the country into evil," Cavid noted on October 30, 1914, at last strongly critical of Talaat and, foremost, Enver.[33] He read Talaat's face, knowing that his committee brother lied when he spoke of a Russian attack. Yet, in an unshakable loyalty, he continued to assist Talaat in the future, out of, he believed, patriotic Ottoman duty. His diary reveals a schizophrenic situation from which writing gave him some distance, serving as an exercise in mental independence as well as a memory hook for daily affairs. Writing in private, he cultivated an individual *arrière-boutique* of his mind, as Michel de Montaigne put it in his famous sixteenth-century *Essays*.

Cavid was particularly disturbed by and revolted against an attitude of all or nothing, victory or death, among members of the Central Committee. He argued that nobody had the right to expect others to join in suicide. The diary of Krikor Zohrab, Cavid's Armenain friend, in an entry on November 3, 1914, notes that Talaat was "the foremost partisan of war" for "whom and his disciples, this war was *tout ou rien* [all or nothing]." Both friends discussed in the late evening of November 3, 1914, what they considered a Germany-centered, fatal "war psychology of Talaat and his followers."[34]

As the last of several committee brothers, Dr. Nâzım, a CUP hawk, approached Cavid to persuade him to revisit his decision and not to resign. Cavid's diary reports Nâzım's statements:

If the Central Committee has appointed me [Cavid] for a post but I opposed it, .[. . .] from now on, there could be given to any young man a revolver to kill Cavid Bey, because I was a fallen man for the fatherland, since my power was from the party [. . .] all people would now call me a "treacherous Jew" (in a way he [Nâzım] justified them) [. . .] there was no more place for me in the country.

When Cavid retorted that he would not act against his conscience but was ready for future service to the country, Nâzım "made do with the vulgar saying 'in this war we will perish or overcome.'" Cavid spared only a few words: "Wretched mind, ill-fated country." In the weeks after this encounter, Nâzım, himself of *dönme* (Sabbatian) origin, defamed Cavid everywhere as a treacherous Jew. Ridiculing him, he changed his name to "David" and even threatened to expel all Dönme because of Cavid's withdrawal.[35] Though he was a fervent patriot and at times a Jacobin-style radical (but not a chauvinist), Cavid strikes as a unique figure at the margins of the CUP war regime because he preserved basic principles of conscience and human dignity.

Deep distrust vis-à-vis Nâzım henceforth pervades Cavid's diary.[36] Talaat was saddened, as was Cemal, by the resignation of Cavid, whose intelligence refused the tale of Russian aggression and Talaat's unscrupulousness. "In Talaat's eyes, there does not exist any illegitimate action if problems are to be solved."[37] Cavid's rich diary documents well how Talaat's war dictatorship started in late 1914. When Enver's Caucasus campaign catastrophically failed and the Entente navy began to heavily bombard the Dardanelles on February 19, 1915, the CUP realized that the empire was on the defensive, definitively no longer in a dope-like dream of restoration and expansion. Pessimism now reigned widely, not only at the fronts and in the capital but also among those Ottoman representatives and allies whom Cavid met in Vienna and Berlin in early March 1915.[38]

Typically for the regime's gambling style, it was up one minute, down the next. The day of March 18, 1915, again retrieved the CUP from defeat and depression. This first important military success in the First World War against a naval breakthrough attempt by the Entente at the Dardanelles, pushed foremost by Churchill, galvanized the depressed rulers. The attackers suffered heavy losses. "This evening, we received the first good news. [. . .] This was glad tidings after long days of anguish and worry that depressed us. The issue of Çanakkale is not a near danger. We were delirious with joy," said Cavid. The committee members boasted about victory against the naval world powers and demonstrated everywhere the "firm conviction that Çanakkale could not be transgressed." They felt again safe and strong, ready for new action.[39]

When, after protracted negotiations in Berlin, an unsuspecting Cavid came back to Istanbul on August 19, 1915, he was surprised to find "a country very much decrepit materially and spiritually," as he noted on the day of his arrival. "Despite the [successful] defense at the Dardanelles, the morale is degenerate."[40] The elephant in the Room was the Armenians—meanwhile robbed, ousted, and murdered. "Apparently, nobody has the power to open the mouth and say anything. [. . .] The Armenian issue is horrifying. Nobody can say anything." Only then, Cavid realized that his leading political friends had implemented the "destruction not only of the political existence but the life itself of a whole [Armenian] people." He deplored this "monstrous murder and enormous dimension of brutality that Ottoman history had never known before even in its darkest periods." Yet, "despite all evils I do not want to give up my hope of a better tomorrow," he stated.[41]

Therefore, Cavid sided with the perpetrators, defended their arguments, backed their politics of "national" (Turkified) economy, and sought best loan conditions in his frequent negotiations in Berlin and Vienna. Vis-à-vis German foreign minister Jagow, he insisted in June 1916 that, even if badly handled in 1915, the Armenian issue was now finished for good and not to be revisited in any way; the German deputies had to stomach this.[42] In his repeated negotiations on loans and support, he capitalized on the psychological fact that in July 1914, Germany had shown vulnerability. "Once it saw trouble ahead, it remembered us." If it had wanted the alliance before July 1914, there would be perfect trust, Cavid reiterated to German diplomat Frederic Rosenberg, secretary for Oriental Affairs in the Berlin Foreign Office.[43]

Starting in early 1917, Talaat Pasha's grand vizierate—the peak of CUP party rule—combined reinforced Turkist indoctrination and ongoing Muslim self-assertion. From late 1917, after the Bolshevik retreat from war, pan-Turkish currents powerfully resurged. "We have not the courage to freely express our thoughts," Cavid wrote on the eve of Talaat's inaugural address.[44] The new grand vizier presented to the parliament his cabinet and his program, written by Cavid and Cahid Cahit on February 15, 1917, and the parliament gave its support without a dissenting vote.[45] Despite strong reservations, Cavid accepted, out of an unequal friendship, the invitation to be Talaat's minister of finance. "Based on our brotherhood, I request your consent [to the ministerial post],"

Talaat telegraphed to Cavid. A day later, on February 4, 1917, Cavid answered that "I accept [the post] as an act of friendship and self-sacrifice." He now orbited even more around Turkey's strongman.[46]

Cavid lacked the balance of serene emotional and intellectual distance. He contented himself with writing down his frustration in his diary, as shortly before entering the cabinet: "I have pity for Talaat. How much I had wished that in a cabinet, which for the first time is really ours, there [would be] nothing rotten and dilapidated. But what can I do? He does not want to give up his well-known evil principles and habits."[47] During war, German imperial nationalists like Vice-Chancellor Karl Helfferich had their like-minded, already much more radical counterparts in Istanbul, who placed their faith in Germany, thus empowering one another in radical thinking. "This evening, the Parliament has again witnessed the stupid thoughts of Bahâeddin Şhakir. War must be declared against America; no American spy [missionaries, teachers, doctors] has to be left here," Cavid noted on April 10, 1917, after American entrance into war against Germany:

> It throws one into despair to see the destiny of the nation under the influence of men with such a mind. [. . .] Ziya [Gökalp] too opined that the nation had to take a resolute stance against America and to march together with Germany, as if Germany will provide for everything. There was again the old refrain [from 1914]: "If we must die, let us die [. . .]." These wretched people do not know any relation with life outside Turkey and are unaware of what happens in the world. They imagine Germany to be as powerful as God.[48]

The Ottoman parliament decided to cut relations with America, to please Germany. Cavid and his friend Cahit were "voices in the desert crying out" against an interdependence with Germany under the factual dictator General Ludendorff that did not leave room for alternatives. Voiced in small circles and reaching his ears, such statements put the road that Talaat had chosen into question and made him visibly "feel sad." As a result, he again was able to bring the emotionally touched "dissidents" back into line with him and secure their continued services. Despite his insight and soul-searching, Cavid went as far as to actively back Talaat's and the CUP's will to abort any future Armenian autonomy. From spring 1917, he therefore drew Talaat's attention to the fact that the treaties with Germany guaranteed the Ottoman territorial status quo but did not prevent the possibility of Arab and Armenian autonomies and Armenian return. Thus, a stipulation must be added.

Cavid had correctly understood the repeated emphasis of German diplomacy since summer 1915, that it would not be able to defend Turkey during postwar peace talks in matters regarding the Armenians. This was the only consistent and sustainable point that Berlin made against the CUP's Armenian policy. Wangenheim, Germany's representative, had approved only a temporary removal of people from war zones in late spring 1915, by no means permanent dispossession. In vain, Cavid tried to add a stipulation against Armenian return, in accordance with the CUP policy of Anatolia's de-Armenization. Moreover, he was convinced and feared in November 1917 that "a democratic Russia will not conclude peace without having addressed the Armenian issue."[49] Yet, soon ceasing to become democratic, Bolshevik Russia sacrificed this issue, in which it first had shown loyalty to the 1914 Reform Agreement, and eventually allied with Ankara from summer 1920. In autumn 1918, Cavid again modified his position, as the power relations again fundamentally changed. He agreed that "the Armenians from the provinces of Anatolia" had "to come back to their homes," despite problems of restitution, partial destruction of homes, or the use of their properties by migrants, neighbors, or functionaries. He successfully defended this position in the parliament in mid-October 1918, after Talaat's resignation.[50]

In September 1918, Cavid had concluded, "This cabinet has no longer any right to survive. It failed in every challenge that it wanted to meet." A year earlier, he had already criticized Grand Vizier Talaat: "In contradiction to what we promised, we have not done anything to make law reign." Because "these words [of mine] made the grand vizier sad" and pessimistic, Cavid had then again felt compelled to support him.[51] While pessimism had again turned to (short-lived) high spirits when Bolshevik Russia retreated from war in late 1917, serious tensions with Germany, in view of the Caucasus and of territorial reacquisitions in the Balkans, emerged by late March 1918. Thoughts of a separate peace or degraded relations with Germany then came to mind, according to Cavid. He, in turn, added to the tension by pressuring Helfferich and Rosenberg to a full German relief of Turkey's debt. He overstretched the argument that preventing Turkey from financial collapse was in Germany's best interest. Secretary Rosenberg clarified to Cavid during the latter's visit in Berlin in September 1918 that the Reichskanzler was "saddened to see that the money which Germany had given us was used to annihilate Christians; [and that] this was part of the actual problem" between both governments.[52]

An overcommitted patriot depending on his party boss, Cavid could not cope with the elephant (of genocide) in the room of CUP politics. Talaat remained Cavid's "attachment figure," although he clearly suffered, not only under Talaat's disorganized and corrupt style but also, according to himself, under the undeniably evil aspects of this leader. However, in a leader-centered partisan polity deprived of democratic traditions and footing, Talaat had been the person of reference for a whole cohort. Even Cavid, therefore, tended to transfigure him after his death.[53]

Post–Great War Diplomacy and the Turning Point in Lausanne

After the end of CUP rule in late 1918, Cavid briefly entered the cabinet of Izzet Pasha. But being court-martialed and sentenced to labor, he hid in the house of his friend Nuri Pasha, before fleeing to Europe in September 1919. He organized his escape via Abraham Weil, an old acquaintance from the Régie des Tabacs.[54] From then, he mostly stayed in Switzerland and was the only prominent CUP leader accepted by the Swiss authorities, though under police observation. Talaat and others entered only very temporarily under pseudonyms and with false papers.

In Switzerland, Cavid kept in contact with the different diasporas from the Ottoman Empire, met personalities in transit, undertook many travels in Europe, kept a rich international correspondence, and worked for the nationalist cause. In early 1921, he was involved in the Rome and London conferences that started negotiations between the allies and the increasingly powerful Ankara counter-government. Abdülkadir Câmi (Baykut), Ankara's man in Rome in January 1921, alleged "extreme nationalism" among the Muslims in the eastern provinces to argue, in his conversation with Cavid, against any territorial concessions to the Armenians.

Cavid then advocated a "viable Armenia" side by side with "a viable Turkey" and possible compromises on Kars and Van.[55] But after Ankara and the Bolsheviks had divided the South Caucasus among themselves in 1921, he admonished the Armenian representatives to renounce their territorial rights enshrined in the Sèvres Treaty and to put trust in a renewed Turkey. "Based on a new constitution, all provinces will be given large administrative autonomy of which the oriental provinces will also benefit; but great Armenia is an illusion." For Armenians leaving Anatolia, "there will be reparations." Sure enough, as well meant as it possibly was, Cavid's advice proved entirely built on sand.[56] In the changed political atmosphere after 1921, Cavid lost sight of the supreme issue of justice, reparation, and prosecution for genocide victims. Cavid, too, internalized the apologetic reflex of his generation. He thus figures among early examples "of what now is called the culture of denial" in Turkish politics and public history.[57]

Cavid's diaries lament warmongering and extreme nationalism in his political entourage, which made his comparatively conciliatory prospects quixotic. In contrast to the (ultra)nationalist mainstream in Ankara, Cavid aspired to the rule of law, putting the fundamental challenge this way: "In order to ascertain its future, the country must exit its oligarchical state and subordinate itself to a democratic polity. If the Ankara government continues as an oligarchy, it will lead to the same negative and noxious consequences as did the Yıldız [Sultan Abdulhamid's Palace] and the Young Turk oligarchies."[58] A little later, in September 1921, he noted in his diary, "Ankara believes that all things can be solved by arms [. . .]. They have not made proof of any other skill than soldiering."[59] He was skeptical of the French policy of appeasement toward Ankara as practiced by Henry Franklin-Bouillon, whom he called an ignoramus of Turkey when the latter met Mustafa Kemal again in Izmir in September 1922, a year after the French-Turkish Accord of Ankara. "No doubt, he motivated them [the Kemalists] to even more extreme demands."[60] However, Cavid proved of short memory and weak judgment when resharing sweeping anti-Western outrage or even cultivating nostalgia. "In huge Turkey, in fact in the whole Near East, there is no man who can replace Talaat," he wrote in a letter to CUP mentor Ahmed Rıza at the end of 1921.[61]

Cavid came back to Allied-occupied Istanbul on June 29, 1922.[62] Although capable of sympathy with others and their needs, he also remained emotionally attached to the Turkish-Muslim cause during the final victories of the Turkish forces and the carnage of Izmir. "Everybody is satisfied and joyful. [. . .] The Rûm expected the reconquest of Istanbul a few weeks ago, but now, they see all their aims ruined. And what a great collapse! The Armenians are troubled and anxious. All the Turks—except Damat Ferit Pasha and his entourage—celebrate," he wrote on September 11, 1922.[63]

Invited by Ankara's delegation chief Ismet (Inönü) Pasha, Cavid joined the Near East Peace Conference of Lausanne as a financial advisor in early December 1922. In Lausanne, he belonged to a minority of those in the delegation who sought, above all, good compromises in view of building a respected, trusted, hopefully democratic Turkey. Growing apart from the delegation's majority, he complained that expertise and competences counted less than chauvinistic bravado and personal and party loyalties— like during CUP rule. For vice-chief Rıza Nur (see Chapter 6), Cavid was "the greatest traitor" who was working with the French enemy—and anyway *a priori* disqualified as "a Jew."[64] Nur and Ismet disliked, probably envied, Cavid's international prestige and rich personal and professional network. The Ottoman Public Debt Administration was a particular thorn in Ankara's flesh. Those in close touch with it for many years, like Cavid, who had various friends in Paris and elsewhere, were suspected of enriching themselves at the expense of patriotic interests.[65]

"Every minute I regret to have been drawn in this circle" of Ankara's delegation, Cavid confessed to his diary in Lausanne in late December 1922.[66] Two years later, he wrote, "Against this man [Ismet Pasha, meanwhile prime-minister] I nurture a limitless enmity and hate." The reason for this extraordinarily negative emotion was that Ismet brought the convenient libel of Cavid's treason in Lausanne back to Ankara. "Actually, this servile man implored me to assist him at the Lausanne Conference. But later, in order to silence an authorized voice who could expose the mistakes committed in Lausanne, he chose the easy way and accused me [. . .] of having created problems and virtually committed treason."[67]

Ankara's Scapegoat

In contrast to Cavid's relation with Talaat, ties with Gazi Kemal, Ismet Pasha, and their entourage in Ankara were marked by mistrust, jealousy, and rivalry. Since the early aftermath of the World War, there was the specter of the CUP's revival (*ihya*) of which Cavid wrote hopefully on several occasions in his diary, at times expecting a fusion or open cooperation of the unofficially ongoing CUP with Ankara's "organization in Anatolia."[68] In terms of cadres and main tenets, this CUP-Kemalist continuity and unity was anyway the case right from the start of the national movement in 1919. Mustafa Kemal's "we" in many letters and statements during these years rested on the CUP, of which he even pretended to be a founder and the main architect.[69]

But this self-assertive narrative served to claim the leadership of a unitary post-CUP power organization, establishing his emerging own new single-party as the only legitimate one. A late Ottoman soldier without a life outside the army, he never had experienced or even displayed curiosity for politics beyond a leader-led state. In other words, Kemal's problem with prominent CUP members based in Istanbul was his fear of capable rivals not entirely subdued. His exclusionary claim to power induced him to eliminate them in time. This had nothing to do with seeking more democratic ground or morally dissociating the new state from the main tenets of the former CUP policy in Anatolia. Kemalist political style was again ruler- and party-centered; its way to treat dissent was again through antidemocratic repression. Protracted dictatorships stand for the failure of dealing with and benefiting from human diversity, capacity, and competences.

The first half of the Lausanne Conference, including the following break, was arguably the critical crossroad that made Cavid appear as an enemy and traitor to Ankara's post-Lausanne establishment. In September 1923, Cavid noted, "Freedom of opinion amounts to treason for the rulers. 'If you do not think like me, you are a traitor and paid agent.'"[70] Cavid felt that they did not want "efficient professionals, but subservient henchmen." He inquired among close acquaintances of President Gazi Kemal and learned the arguments circulating against him. Besides his lack of subservience, there was the argument "that he had not adhered from the start to the national movement."[71] According to Ankara's nationalists, he should have joined them in 1919 instead of going to Switzerland.

As already alluded to, the Conference break from February to April 1923 saw a cluster of coercion, violence, and preparatory electoral manipulation along critical steps toward dictatorship in Ankara.[72] For admirers of Atatürk's genius from then to now, these were necessary acts combined by a strong man of unique intelligence who prepared incisive reforms. For more constitutional- and democratic-minded people, there loomed sultanic despotism, enlightened or not, reenacted in republican garb. Inspired by Nur, who then still supported Mustafa Kemal, propaganda spread in Ankara against the moderate delegation members.[73] During these same weeks of the Conference break, several meetings of long-standing political friends took place in Cavid's flat in Istanbul. In contrast to various other critics or enemies of Ankara's leader, the participants of these meetings were reform-oriented modernists ready to support Mustafa Kemal, without however wanting to totally submit to him. After several debates in Cavid's flat, they agreed in a meeting of April 8, 1923, on a reformist and comparatively liberal vision of the new nation-state whose capital should remain Istanbul.[74] Though not published, these views competed with Mustafa Kemal's election manifesto of April 1923.[75]

As transpires from his post-1924 diary, the *Notebook for Şiar*, Cavid enjoyed henceforth a mostly private life. Yet his political temperament lived on. He frequented his friends and Western personalities in Istanbul. He commented on the contemporary political developments in the *Notebook* vis-à-vis his son, the representative of a future generation. "In this era, which they label democratic and republican, we experience worse days than under the most horrible and accursed [sultanic] despotism. [...] I hope that in your time there will be no longer such a fake republic and false democracy."[76] In the intimacy of a dialogue with his baby in an emotional and subjective language, his testimony is to the point:

> On the occasion of the Kurdish uprising [of Sheykh Said] they have started to strangle the people's tongue [free speech and press]. [...] What a pity that the high and noble concept of [national] sovereignty has been perverted in our [Turkish] hands to a vile caricature. They have now opened Tribunals of Independence. The government deprives the newspapers and the associations of their rights.[77]

In Cavid's emphatic words, the voices of truth lapsed into silence. Everybody feared the politicized justice operated by speedy special trials. As under Sultan Abdulhamid, one was again hurrying to burn any literature or personal notes that could be used against oneself by the police and a travesty of justice performed by the special courts. Cavid destroyed possibly compromising letters and brought his pre-1924 diaries to a secure place. He even feared for the "mini-notebook" that he was writing for his son but decided to take it with him "until the last minute." He urged his son to always abstain from injustice and dirty intrigues. "Truth and justice shall be your emblem [*şiar*]."[78]

Three years after the Conference break, a trial took place in Ankara where Cavid was the indictment's key figure. The prosecutor presented Cavid as the head of a secret committee and the meetings in Cavid's flat three years earlier "as a sinister plot to undermine the new state."[79] Against any evidence, but manifestly politically motivated, the court insinuated Cavid to be the brain behind an assassination plot against Mustafa Kemal in Izmir in June 1926. Cavid was hastily hanged before midnight on August 26, 1926, the day of the verdict. The Ankara trial was a sequel to a trial in Izmir that had sentenced three men to death based on concrete evidence, and thirteen more by guilt of association or suspicion—all executed at public places in Izmir on July 13, the day after the final verdict. According to Andrew Mango, the supreme leader "spent the evening following the executions in his usual manner, drinking with his [subservient] friends. The anodyne effects of alcohol did not come amiss that night."[80]

The CUP- and Soviet-inspired 1926 trials unraveled promises made in Lausanne for a law-based independent jurisdiction. Repression and annihilation as a way of dealing with intellectual and political opposition went along with a growingly authoritarian, finally totalitarian rule that emerged in the decade after the Conference. The birth conditions of Republican Turkey, diplomatically underpinned in Lausanne, blocked the road toward democracy.

Murdering Cavid, Completing Gazi Kemal's Dictatorship

For Ismet Pasha, Turkey's plenipotentiary in Lausanne and president after Atatürk, Cavid's "fate" just represented "the worst possibility implicit in the nature of politics"— not the need to rethink a political culture that he naively took as "natural."[81] The experience of the honest dissenter Cavid, a private citizen after Lausanne, mirrors the making of a dictatorship that had bid its goodbye to residual democratic virtues. Sovereignty won in Lausanne required oligarchy at home, in order to be maintained within the labile compromises struck at the Conference of Lausanne. In 1926, Western observers well understood that Ankara's travesty of justice liquidated dissenters. However, having secured Mosul for mandatory Iraq by a treaty in June 1926, notably Britain played from then the game of Middle Eastern autocracy.

Contemporary Kemalist intellectuals bowed to power and to the political logics of violence, even those who were fully aware of the abomination of Cavid's killing. Some, at least, articulated pain in retrospective texts.[82] Most alleged, like Ismet, that this was the course of politics, or that violence in the name of "the nation" was imperative against "the enemies of the revolution." The partisan press took over and amplified the undignified discourse and rabble-rousing applied by the special court. They all made a bogeyman out of Cavid and "Cavidism."[83] Condoning scapegoating force and coercion amounted to a surrender to violence, slander, and lies. This matter of fact confirms the scapegoating logics of Turkey's problematic formation, as introduced in Chapter 1. Although a scandal, Cavid's judicial murder is a cornerstone of the new republic. In the retrospective of Falih Rıfkı (Atay), "It is a pity that the authority of the new regime rested on the scaffolds of Izmir and Ankara. However, this definitive purge [. . .] gave Mustafa Kemal the opportunity to complete the revolution that he had started."[84] Atay was among the journalists who had made Cavid a target of ultranationalism in Lausanne in December 1922. Close to Atatürk throughout the latter's presidency, he spent many nights drinking with him in the presidential Çankaya mansion. Mental anesthesia was the manifest corollary of violence and coercion applied against weaker, largely innocent people, while establishing an undemocratic polity.

No doubt, revolutionist ultranationalism devoured its own children during the 1920s; however, it also consumed many more innocents. Was there an inherent or "compensatory justice" in the execution of former CUP leaders or operatives like Dr Nâzım, Ismail Canbolad, Kara Kemal, Nail, and Hilmi? It is true that several participants in the April 1923 meetings like Dr. Nâzım and Kara Kemal had been deeply involved in Talaat's warmongering and anti-Armenian policy. But there is no consolation or higher logic in this thought. Ex-CUP cadres like Şükrü Kaya, Tahsin Uzer, Mustafa Abdülhalik, Feyzi Pirinççizâde, Ali Cenani, and Celal Bayar, who closely collaborated with Mustafa Kemal in top positions, had been no less involved.

The arguments on CUP misrule, proffered by the prosecutor in Ankara, were instrumental and arbitrary. They strike as particularly out of place in the case of Cavid who was placed in the center of the court's fabrication, but excelled as more democratically and constitutionally minded than those who charged him. Against the background of Young Turk and Hamidian rule, the recomposition of Turkish state power in a turbulent global era under one-man and single-party rule is understandable. But it was not a path to democracy, and it meant paying a high price in all things human for a hundred years to come. It reopened a field of politics for antidemocratic actors ready to destroy more hopeful departures.

10

Mahmut Bozkurt

Revolution, Racism, and the Secular Republic

"The most important task of the Turkish revolution is to eradicate the past and all its ideas," Mahmut Esat Bozkurt said in 1928.[1] Two years earlier, he had been the minister of justice who introduced the Swiss Civil Code, the backbone of the new Kemalist secularism, to Turkey. Bozkurt's prominent case demonstrates how the wish for modern national awakening, including secular democracy and lawfulness, merged with ultranationalism. The present chapter will elaborate on Bozkurt's "rightist revolution" in this vein. Despite its *völkisch* essentialism, it contained a few grains of universalism, and thus the potential to reach beyond the corset of its time. In his 1926 preface to the new Civil Law (a preface which also figures in following editions) Bozkurt stated: "The Turkish nation [...] must at all costs conform to the requirements of modern civilization. For a nation which has decided to live, this is essential."[2]

These words typically characterize the political thinking of a prominent Kemalist who displayed a marked "assertive secularism" and who sought a "total state monopoly on all religious activities, as well as on religious education."[3] As a right-wing revolutionist, he believed in modern progress, a nation defined by ethnicity, and the necessity of using force to achieve modernity. This short biographical study sheds light on deep ambivalences, providing insight into the three main stages of Bozkurt's life: his childhood in Izmir and education in Switzerland, his official positions in Ankara in the early years of the Republic, and his understanding of Kemalism in the 1930s. Bozkurt's ambivalence is reflected in the discrepancy between his ethnonational Turkist credo, partly fed by hatred and closely tied to his revolutionist project, and his longing for new horizons, which had the potential to break the prison of his radical Turkism, in which, however, he remained until his death during the Second World War.

Childhood, Adolescence, Early Influences

Mahmut Esat (1892–1943) was born into a family of landowners in the little town of Kuşadası, south of Izmir. His father was the president of the municipality of Kuşadası before being elected as a member of the Council of the Ottoman province of Izmir. Mahmut[4] attended primary school in Kuşadası and secondary school in Izmir. His school friend, Turgut Türkoğlu, who later also became a member of parliament in Ankara, recalled the young Mahmut's tremendous hatred of all non-Turks.[5] This hatred may partly be explained by his family history. His grandparents were *muhacir* (Muslim refugees) from the Peloponnese. His grandfather Hacı Mahmut told the boy patriotic stories full of painful losses. As Türkoğlu writes, these awakened the young child's love for his nation and fatherland.[6]

In 1908, the sixteen-year-old Mahmut Esat entered the University of Istanbul, where he obtained his Ottoman master's degree in law in 1912. It was there that he probably came across the Swiss law professor Eugen Huber's Civil Code (*Zivilgesetzbuch/ZGB*) for the first time. It was during this time that one of his law lecturers in Istanbul, the Ottoman Armenian former court president of Salonika, Haçeriyan Efendi, translated the *ZGB* into Ottoman and published it in the legal journal *Adliye Ceridesi* in 1912.[7] This forgotten, though at that time renowned, jurist can be considered one of the intellectual fathers of the Swiss-Turkish law transfer. Haçeriyan justified the great effort of translating the text all by himself in the following words:

> First of all, this is the latest civil law [. . .]. Moreover, it has benefited from the latest discoveries and advances in legal science. Third, Switzerland is a small and neutral state. It knows no internal turmoil. Its people are contented, quiet, frugal, hardy, and exceedingly developed in trade, agriculture, and commerce. I wanted to make the progress that this people has also achieved in the field of law, known to the Ottoman people.[8]

Similar arguments appear later in Bozkurt's work.

Thanks to his well-to-do family background, Mahmut Esat was able to finance what was then seen as the crowning achievement of academic training: studying at a French-speaking university in Paris or in Switzerland. Mahmut decided to pursue his doctorate at the University of Fribourg, where he first had to acquire a Swiss master's degree in law. The place where he lived and spent most of his time was Lausanne. As far as Bozkurt's socialization is concerned, it should be noted that he moved almost exclusively in circles of politicized Muslim men and rarely mingled with educated women. The only exception to this rule seems to have been his private tutor and landlady in Lausanne, Emma Jenni-Hoppeler, who, as he said, taught him French as well as "democratic politics," kindling in him a "love of republican" ideas.[9]

By 1911, a number of Turkish ethnonational clubs had been founded in Lausanne and Geneva, called *Foyers Turcs*. They were the vanguard of the Turkist movement in Europe and had close ties to the Turkist movement in the Ottoman capital, organized in *Türk Yurdu* and *Türk Ocağı* associations. In the early 1910s, this movement began to win over the majority of Turkish-speaking Muslims, as well as a few Jewish university students. It is not clear when exactly Mahmut Esat arrived in Switzerland, although he is known to have been there during the First World War and up until 1919. It is likely that he entered the country in 1913 or 1914, shortly after the March 1913 international congress of Turkists in Petit-Lancy near Geneva. The congress of Geneva-Petit-Lancy was attended by important spokesmen of the Turkist movement, among them Hamdullah Suphi, the long-standing president of *Türk Ocağı*, the predominant Turkist organization.[10]

The *Foyer Turc* Movement of (Pan-)Turkism

The *Foyers Turcs* of the diaspora constituted the formative microcosm that Mahmut Esat entered into on the eve of the First World War.[11] It was here that he developed his ideas before embarking on his political career in Ankara in 1920. The same is also true of Şükrü Saraçoğlu, Cemal Hüsnü Taray, and many other men who occupied important positions in public life in the early Republic of Turkey.

The goal and "ideal" (*mefkûre*) of the *Foyer* movement was to carry out a social revolution on ethnonational terms. Such a revolution was considered necessary in order to save the Turkish nation, which would otherwise perish. The dream of national "rebirth" was associated with the vision among *Foyers*' members of their own nation as the greatest victim in history, particularly of Russian aggression, of European imperialism, and of disloyal non-Muslim Ottoman citizens colluding with Europe. The *Foyers*, nonetheless, emphasized the constructive project: the effort required to achieve Western civilization and strength. Their members often condemned their own (Ottoman Muslim) failure. This sometimes went so far as to manifest itself in self-humiliation.

The 1913 congress in Petit-Lancy and the publications and minutes of the *Foyers* stressed the particular urgency to educate Turkish men and women, if possible, in Europe. One text already postulated the legal equality of men and women and the emancipation from Islam as a basis for the re-ordering of society.[12] On the other hand, Islam was very much in evidence as a major cultural ingredient for defining Turkishness. In the 1930s, by contrast, Kemal Atatürk and the Turkish Historical Society he established wanted to get rid of Islam once and for all and base Turkishness exclusively on "scientific," anthropological, ethnographical, and paleological foundations. Pre-Ottoman history nevertheless already played an important role in the historical construction of identity in the *Foyer Turc*.[13] The *Foyer* movement worked intensively on new interpretations of history. When the *Foyer* in Lausanne commemorated the founding of the Ottoman Empire on December 30, 1916, for example, Mahmut Esat made a fiery speech condemning historiography at home and abroad for failing to give due place to Turks and Turkish heroes, such as Sultan Selim I or Genghis Khan.[14] The depressing sight of the recent late Ottoman past was offset by a militant belief in the future of Turkdom according to the ideology of Gökalp, whom the students in the *Foyer* venerated. In this vein, the new Turkish identity-to-be was considered superior to all other identities. The ardent belief in it, and the project of a "New Turkey" closely tied to it, helped to surmount the difficult present reality of a declining empire. During the 1913 congress, which took place under the shadow of the Balkan Wars, hatred, resentment, and the call for revenge were all the more forcefully expressed.[15]

At the same congress of Geneva-Petit-Lancy, the participants declared their pride in having created a new national consciousness. They now called themselves straightforwardly "Turks." After a great deal of effort, they had shed the attitude of understanding themselves as *Osmanlıcı* or members of a multiethnic Ottoman nation.[16] Another topic of discussion was what one speaker called the liberation of the economy from the grip of the non-Muslims. This was a matter of much concern for Mahmut Esat, who would go on to serve as minister of economy in 1922–3. Like most of his *Foyer* colleagues, he saw the "class struggle" of the peasants and the workers as a struggle against what members of the congress labeled the Ottoman "Armenian profiteers," the Ottoman "Greek swindlers," and—only in third place—the oppressive Turkish landlords. The "class enemy" was closely associated with the ethnoreligious enemy.[17] The *Foyer* members talked about the urgency of saving Turkdom in Anatolia from the foreigners, among whom they included the non-Muslim Ottoman citizens.

All participants recognized, as the minutes read:

> how beneficial in political and economic terms it would be to create in Anatolia a homogeneous and concentrated unit of the Ottoman Turks. [. . .] a discussion on the topic of "tribal solidarity", during which the unanimous opinion of all congress participants crystallized that "Anatolia was the home-land which would guarantee the political existence of the Ottoman Turkdom." Fully convinced, the members of Türk Yurdu [thus] planned to make the Turks the owners of Anatolia and, supported by established men of various trades, to lead the way on behalf of the Turks who were as yet unaware of the salutary works aimed at guaranteeing their existence. And they swore solemnly that, being on the road towards the great national ideal, they would make Anatolia their national home.[18]

President of the *Foyer Turc* in Lausanne

Though he studied in Fribourg, Mahmut Esat joined the *Foyer Turc* in Lausanne and later became its president. He cooperated with his friend Şükrü Saraçoğlu, then president of the *Foyer Turc* in Geneva.[19] Şükrü, also a native of Izmir, belonged to the Izmir cell of the Young Turkish CUP, headed by Celal Bayar.[20] Many members of the *Foyers* in Switzerland lived, like Şükrü, on a scholarship awarded by the Ottoman state.

In a speech to the *Foyer* in Lausanne, its president Mahmut Esat exclaimed with an apocalyptic and social Darwinist undertone in spring 1918: "Shortly, the last hour will strike that will transform the face of the earth. Those who prepare for it now will be able to assert their right to live on that day. It is our duty to make the Turks ready for that day."[21] According to its minutes, the *Foyer* in Lausanne began to take the leadership of the movement for the "defense of the Turks' rights" (*Türk hukukunu müdafaa*) in Anatolia at the end of the First World War, when Mahmut Esat was its president. Those months were not only prolific in articulating visions of a "New Turkey" but also apocalyptically minded, albeit in a confident, proactive sense. Among *Foyer* members, there were little signs of crisis or despair like those felt among the Turkish-Muslim intelligentsia in Istanbul in late 1918 and 1919.[22]

In the discussions regarding the prospective Turkish nation-state in Asia Minor, well-known topics reemerged: the ultimate elimination of Christian influence inside and outside the territory on one hand, and the adoption of Ottoman Christian examples in education and economy on the other. In religious matters, the *Foyer* members ascertained that the nationalists should "not hesitate to guarantee our national organization under a religious [Muslim] cover, if necessary," in order "not to alienate the people from Turkism." A long struggle against the "religious conscience well rooted amongst us, but which harms progress" was predicted. Polygamy, the veiling of women, and arbitrary divorce by men were rejected. In those discussions, Mahmut Esat stated that "in religious matters, religion has to serve Turkdom, not vice versa." During the same series of sessions in May–June 1919, Aliçe Harun—a former Imam, who succeeded Mahmut in the Lausanne *Foyer's* presidency—said that "Religion must be put into a modern form and Turkishness must be freed from religious fanaticism. [. . .] Once the separation of the individual and the state will be recognized, this [religious] question will solve itself." As the minutes of the Lausanne *Foyer Turc* show, there was also already an ongoing struggle for a Turkish "purified" of Arabic and Persian vocabulary.[23]

In the months after the end of the First World War, the Turkish diaspora in and around the *Foyers* in Lausanne and Geneva produced an important quantity of propaganda literature in defense of the Turkish nationalist position on the future of Asia Minor. This agitation took place in cooperation with professional journalists and diplomats from the capital close to the CUP. Among them were Ahmed Cevdet (Oran), the owner of the journal *İkdam*, and Reşid Safvet (Atabinen), a diplomat and close collaborator of Talaat Pasha. In 1922–3, Atabinen served as the secretary-general of the Turkish delegation at the Lausanne Conference. Afterward, he was a member of parliament in Ankara and a founding member of the Turkish Historical Society (as we have seen in Chapter 6).

Beginning in the wake of World War defeat, one of the main aims of this propaganda was to prove by demographic and historical arguments the prerogative of the Turkish race to create a nation-state encompassing all of Asia Minor. In the Lausanne-based English-language paper *Turkey*, Mahmut Esat and his friends Şükrü Saraçoğlu, Yakup Kadri Karaosmanoğlu, and Harun Aliçe protested against British Prime Minister Lloyd George for his use of the term "Muslim Greeks": "we, who are Turks, from the points of view of blood, sentiment, conscience and all, and are wholeheartedly attached to our nation, we protest against the attributions of Mr. Lloyd George. There is no 'Mohammedan Greek' in our country. We are Turks not only by religion but mainly by race."[24]

In June 1919, Mahmut Esat and Şükrü Saraçoğlu secretly traveled from Switzerland to Anatolia in order to engage in the guerrilla war against the Allies in the region of Izmir. On May 19, 1919, shortly before his departure, Mahmut Esat had completed his doctorate at the University of Fribourg.[25] He returned to Asia Minor as the bearer of a revolutionary national project. In April 1920, Mustafa Kemal called him to Ankara for the inauguration of the new "Grand National Assembly of Turkey"—the counter-government to the Ottoman government in Istanbul—where he took a seat. In August 1921, Mahmut exclaimed in a long speech to the Assembly, "I hold that we are currently living the most important moments in our history."[26] Such superlatives are characteristic of Bozkurt's national-revolutionary self-confidence. When, in 1922, he was proposed to head the Ministry of Justice, he refused, saying that the situation did not yet permit the radical changes he had in mind.[27]

A Minister Introducing the Swiss Civil Code to the Republic of Turkey

Mahmut Esat's long 1924 article "The Principles of the Turkish Revolution"[28] glorified the War of Independence as a "holy revolution" needed to establish the nation's full sovereignty and achieve its final full accession to the community of Western states under the rule of modern law. In pursuing it, he argued, the Turkish Revolution was providing all oppressed nations, particularly the Muslim ones, with a good example. In a speech in 1930, he called the Turkish Revolution the greatest revolution in world history and praised its bearers, the Republican People's Party, for taking "the material and symbolic wealth [in Asia Minor] from the hands of the foreigners [non-Muslim Ottomans included] and [giving] it to the Turkish nation."

Except for the veneration of Atatürk, many elements of the history of the Turkish Revolution as taught in the universities after 1930 can already be seen in Mahmut Esat's article of 1924. Mahmut deplored the fact that the nation was not yet truly sovereign. He did not question, however, that this was linked to his own understanding of nation and people as limited to the community of the Muslim Turks, that is, the class that had ruled in Ottoman times (*millet-i hakime*). He was aware that neither the establishment of Turkish sovereignty over Asia Minor nor its Turkification had succeeded in making it a modern democracy. He thus postulated a third revolutionary stage for establishing the people's sovereignty in the political system and the economy.[29] This third stage failed to materialize, mainly because Bozkurt, in his worship of Atatürk, mixed democracy with an exalted leader-state that was supposedly organically connected to its people. Until his death, Mahmut Esat remained troubled by the consciousness that Turkey still had a long way to go to become a real democracy, as Switzerland, in his eyes, explicitly was.

When Mahmut Esat became minister of the economy in 1922, he said that he was close to the left wing of the CUP.[30] He showed a particular concern for the poorer classes and set up a system of loans for farmers. His first aim, nevertheless, was to fully Turkify the economy, in other words, to oust and dispossess the non-Muslims. This concern was clearly expressed, both by him and by President Gazi Mustafa Kemal, during and after the First Congress of the Economy in Izmir in February 1923.[31] In 1924, Mahmut Esat was appointed minister of justice. Two years later, he introduced the Swiss Civil Code into Turkey.

The young minister was full of verve at the time. He had two goals in mind: the creation of a unitary Turkish nation and its participation in what he considered universal Western civilization. The "Legal Revolution" (*Huku Devrimi*) served both goals. He abandoned previous civil law reform efforts and eclectic attempts to synthesize Islamic and European law, labeling them a "Tower of Babel." Within two years, supported by Gazi Mustafa Kemal (Atatürk), the head of state, and Prime Minister Ismet Pasha (İnönü), he introduced the Swiss Civil Code in an almost literal translation despite the resistance of emphatically Islamic deputies.

Mahmut Esat proved to be revolutionary as a minister of justice. This time, he directed his efforts against the "religious reaction" (*irtica*) that he largely associated with the Kurds, no longer against, by then, the largely reduced non-Muslims. The Kemalists had not accorded the Sunni Kurds the autonomy promised to them in return for their collaboration during the War of Independence. This brought about the great uprising led by Sheikh Said in 1925 that was motivated partly by religion (the caliphate had been abolished in 1924) and partly by Kurdish nationalism. Threatening the Kurds in particular, during a speech in 1925 on the projected new Civil Code, he declared, "The Turkish Revolution has decided to acquire Western civilization without conditions or limits. This decision is based on such a strong will that all those who oppose it are condemned to be annihilated by iron and fire. [. . .] We do not proceed according to our mood or our desire, but according to the ideal of our nation."[32] Later, during the Kurdish uprising of 1929–30, this prominent Kemalist spoke of a war between two races, Kurds and Turks, going so far as to say: "All, friends, enemies and the mountains shall know that the Turk is the master of this country. All those who are not pure Turks have only one right in the Turkish homeland: the right to be servants, the right to be slaves."[33]

Mahmut Esat leads us straight into the problematic core of the interwar Kemalist Revolution: a modernist project, it was, despite a few statements to the contrary, based on an underlying racial and ethnoreligious, as opposed to a civic and constitutional, understanding of nation. Thus, a profound tension existed between its ambitious claim to be part of the universal community of civilized states under the rule of law and the coercive, violent reality of its Gökalpian nationalism. Interestingly, the minister of justice took the ethnic and linguistic pluralism in Switzerland as a strong argument for the universal validity of its Civil Code.[34] However, he refused to recognize the significance of this pluralism, including political pluralism, in the functioning of those laws. In his view, the Swiss Civil Code was "the newest, the easiest to understand, the most democratic and the most practical of all civil codes in the world."[35] Reflecting on the vote in the Turkish parliament to accept the Civil Code on February 17, 1926, he wrote: "It changed the course of a thousand years of history. In the destiny of the Turkish nation began a bright morning, a new age."[36] Bozkurt's firm commitment to post-religious modernity was made evident in the *Esbabı mucibe layihası*, an explanatory introductory note to the new Code. Despite growing opposition from Islamic-conservative circles since the late twentieth century, it was, until the end of the century, still printed at the beginning of the Turkish Civil Code.

In the struggle for the new Civil Code, Mahmut Esat revived arguments from the *Foyer Turc* discussions of the 1910s that branded the traditional position of women in the Turkish-Muslim family as a scandalous "hostage situation." He fought for religious freedom (Art. 266) and even the freedom of Muslim women to marry non-Muslims, as granted by the Civil Code. It was these very freedoms, however, that remained largely theoretical in the decades that followed. Like Gökalp, Bozkurt considered civilization indivisible. He went further, however, in distancing himself from Islamic traditions. The Swiss Civil Code was for him "the purest cultural magazine and filtrate of Western civilization" and its appropriation was the revolutionary beginning of a new age.[37]

The justice minister's radical criticism nevertheless concerned Islamic institutions, not "Muslim matters of faith and conscience."[38] One of the deputies who vigorously supported him at the time was Yusuf Kemal (Tengirşek). In the 1910s, Tengirşek had been a doctoral student of law in Paris, from where he traveled to Switzerland for important *Foyers Turcs* meetings. In his memoirs, he wrote: "We made various promises [at that time] to strengthen the feeling of our Turkishness. For example, we pledged not to marry a non-Turkish girl and, if necessary, to kill those who wanted to hinder the progress we were working for and prevent Turkish girls from going to school."[39] The justice minister's writings lose none of the youthful indignation at the humiliating legal status of women in late Ottoman Muslim society.[40]

Did the Civil Code prove to be a stable foundation for a secular Turkish Republic, a firm pledge of Turkey's abolition of sharia and caliphate? It is true that the Code became the main pillar of a secular state and was increasingly integrated and adapted into Turkish society. For several decades, however, a worrying gap existed between the laws and their observance, most notably where legal marriage was concerned. There was a related problem: the hurried adoption of the Civil Code had from the start been part of a diplomatic deal made at the Lausanne Conference in 1923 (see Chapter 5). Only if Turkey introduced such a modern code would the Western powers accord the Republic full sovereignty without insisting on supervising its tribunals after the abolition of the capitulations (the legal privileges for foreigners in the Ottoman Empire). Thus, the nationalist elite's desire for power and sovereignty critically influenced the hasty legal revolution in 1926 and paved the way for an Islamist reaction in the long term.

Theorist and Propagandist of Kemalism

Mahmut Esat was minister of justice until 1930. His disappearance from the political scene coincided with the closing down of the extensive *Türk Ocağı* organization, that is, with its fusion into Mustafa Kemal's Republican People's Party in 1930-1. The *Türk Yurdu / Türk Ocağı* had been Mahmut Esat's intellectual home for nearly twenty years; on his return from Switzerland, he had continued to frequent them. After they were closed down, intellectual, cultural, and political life was increasingly totalitarian: controlled by the state and centered on its leader. Atatürk made great efforts in those years to promote the Turkish History Thesis and the Sun Language theory, both Turko-centric visions of human history—in an era of nationalist superlatives both in and outside Turkey.

While still a member of parliament,[41] Mahmut Bozkurt was appointed Professor of the History of the Turkish Revolution at Istanbul University. This new branch of study had been promoted by the government after its university reform in 1933. In 1932, he used the term "Kemalism" (*Kemalizm*) for the first time.[42] Together with Moïz Kohen Tekinalp, who in the 1910s and 1920s had also been close to the *Foyers Turcs*,[43] he then went on to become the most important theorist of this universally valid ideology, as he saw it. According to his logic, Atatürk was the greatest revolutionary in the world.[44]

In his book *Atatürk İhtilali* (The Revolution of Atatürk), Bozkurt defined revolution (*ihtilal*) as an event that produced a completely new situation by annihilating and replacing all that had been before.[45] The coercive construction of the new fully justified the destruction of the old and "bad." Seen in this light, it legitimized all the violence exercised by the CUP and the Kemalists. For Bozkurt, Atatürk entirely personified the Turkish Revolution and the Turkish nation. Bozkurt's quasi-religious cult of Turkdom and Turkishness (*Türklük*) fused with the cult of the leader-savior Atatürk. The supreme leader's career was associated with the War of Independence/Salvation (*Kurtuluş Savası*) and the revolutionary construction of the nation-state, that is, with the history of the Turkish Revolution as taught by Bozkurt. Thus, if Atatürk reigned, the nation reigned, and there was perfect "authoritarian democracy," with the chief taking his authority from the people.[46]

This was the idea of a *Führerstaat* (leader-state), but not democracy that breaks the power of individuals by checks, rules, and independent state institutions. In line with Gökalp's leader-centered corporatism, Bozkurt's conception of popular sovereignty and democracy therefore heavily suffered from leader worship. "The Turkish nation resembles a pyramid, its base is the people, at its top is the head coming from the people, who is called the chief in our country. The chief receives his authority from the people [*halk*]. Democracy is nothing but that." In Bozkurt's thinking, leader worship, ultranationalism, and violent revolution coexisted with the affirmation of democracy and universal civilization. No surprise, therefore, that he identified with Hitler and National Socialism. He viewed Nazism as a German liberation movement analogous to the Turkish one that had preceded it. He confirmed the view that "National Socialism was nothing more than a variant of Kemalism." "Hitler himself repeatedly said that he took Atatürk as his model."[47] However, this identification had its limits: Bozkurt's circle insisted on the independent Kemalist path and did not endorse the National Socialist war of expansion. Still, thanks to the Turks' success against the "imperialist" powers and the treaty they imposed at Paris-Sèvres, the Turkish experience, in Bozkurt's eyes, offered an ideal model of liberation for all nations oppressed by the West, particularly for those defeated in the First World War. He proudly cited Hitler's explicit affirmation of this position in a speech in the Reichstag.[48]

In sum, Mahmut Esat Bozkurt stood at the center of a social revolution that sought to completely renew both the normative and historical references of society. Legal and historical revolution were its two pillars. The first was about the definitive detachment from the sharia, a pillar of Ottoman society; the second was about the creation of a new identity that was no longer Islamic but was instead defined in racial terms by a contemporary history of national heroism and embrace of modernity.

Bozkurt's Janus Face

From the time of his arrival in Switzerland, Mahmut Esat was committed to a national project that was increasingly emerging in the formative microcosm of the *Foyers Turcs*. Asia Minor was to become the homeland of the Turkish nation—a nation now defined as the community of Turkish-speaking Muslims who all shared the same ideal of a strong, modern, and secular Turkish nation-state in Asia Minor. This was the goal Bozkurt and his peers aimed to achieve, and this was the meaning of the term "revolution" often used in the *Foyers*. In contrast to the founders of the CUP and the "first generation" (cohort) of Young Turks socialized before the end of the nineteenth century, they were no longer much concerned with saving a multinational empire.

Glorifying the Turkish ethnonation above all else, Bozkurt was by no means immune to racism and other forms of misanthropy. He frequently made enthusiastic statements such as "all for the Turks," "total Turkism," "first the Turks, then humanity, and finally the others,"[49] and the openly anti-Semitic "For me a Turk has more value than all the Jews of this world, not to say the whole world."[50] In line with Parvus (see Chapter 11), he occasionally employed a narrative of class antagonism in which a generic Turk figured as the proletariat. Nevertheless, the clear problem with Bozkurt's ethnonationalism was his unquestioning essentialist belief in a collective Turkish identity, which he took to be of superior and absolute value. At the root of this credo were the traumatic traces of the late Ottoman period, the *millet-i hakime*'s fear and hatred of the non-Turkish, non-Muslim "other," and the anxiety of the collapse of the Turks as a powerful political entity.

Ultranationalism and fascism were in general driven by hatred against real or perceived enemies and by fear or the real experience of loss, including the loss of cherished myths of superiority. Negative emotions thus defined the affective disposition of the actors. Ideologists like Gökalp, Bozkurt, and Atabinen portrayed conservative Muslims as "reactionaries," indigenous non-Turks as treacherous, Kurds as an inferior race, and Europeans as "imperialists." Referring to the near past, multiple enemy images thus framed the refoundation of Turkey as a nation-state. The makers of Republican Turkey could not emancipate themselves from this affective disposition and the ties that related them to the past. Bozkurt's character and political philosophy bespeak this disposition, and his exuberant nationalism excels with strong, at times racist enemy images.

He nevertheless conceived of "New Turkey" in contradictory, paradoxical ways as he almost always sought to put Turkish society in a universal frame. He wanted to conceive and shape it according to universal terms that, by definition, cannot be ethnocentric. For him, becoming part of a universally understood modern civilization was an ideal. In this—Kemalist—vein, Bozkurt could quite innocently write: "In a political perspective, revolution or progress means making the people as sovereign as possible. For the Swiss it would be reactionary to adopt Turkish norms. For us on the other hand it is revolutionary to implement theirs."[51] Looking back on his struggle for the introduction of the Civil Code, he wrote:

> Since the Turkish nation is and must necessarily be a member of the family of civilized nations, one must unconditionally, unreservedly adopt the legal systems of these countries. Just as the one who joins a club or party accepts and adopts the order and principles of the club or party, there is a compulsion for a state struggling to enter civilized society to adopt the requirements of that society.[52]

Bozkurt believed that the legal revolution, with its unreserved affirmation of modern European jurisprudence, not only enabled Turkey to acquire a modern understanding of the state, but also opened the door to reconciliation with Europe and eliminated "the centuries-long enmity between the Christian West and us."[53] In his eyes, the Swiss

Civil Code was the fruit of universally valid legal thinking. When its introduction was discussed in 1925, he argued that there was ethnic and linguistic pluralism in Switzerland; its civil law was therefore universal. Nevertheless, the concept of a modern plural society, which recognized and integrated different ethnic communities, remained alien to Bozkurt. For him, uniform law went hand in hand with aggressive secularization and homogenization—unlike the polyethnic Swiss original with its "soft secularism."[54] Despite its potential for further development, the Kemalist legal revolution therefore obeyed as much the political elite's desire of unrestricted sovereignty as it helped establish more individual freedom, equality, and rule of law.

11

Parvus in Turkey

A Merchant of Revolution and War

The number of those who resist the tyranny of Russia, who take up arms and throw dynamite, increases every day. When the Russians rise up, the Ottomans must rise up too, and when the Ottomans rise up, the Russians must do the same. The world is in turmoil. Besides Russia, the Spanish, Portuguese, Belgians and French are rising up.

Ottoman exile journal *İntikam* (Revenge) no. 30, Geneva, March 28, 1900

The ruling Young Turks regarded the Russo-German socialist Alexander Israil Helphand Parvus (1867–1924)[1] as an expert on economy and revolution whose contribution to their efforts they greatly appreciated. Intentionally or not, Parvus provided an intellectual foundation for the appropriation of leftist concepts by the right.

This adventurous and often solitary outsider was an influential figure not only in the Ottoman capital of the early 1910s. His record of both decisive agitation and widely read publications in Russia and Germany from the early 1900s is impressive. He exhibited a clever opportunism as he moved between concepts, models, and empires, and unlike many other socialists from tsarist Russia, he included the Ottoman capital in his transnational, cross-border area of operations. This chapter focuses on Parvus's multiple activities during his stay in Istanbul in 1910–15, and in particular his impact on the revolutionary introduction of an exclusively Turkish-Muslim "national economy" (*millî iktisad*) by the CUP party-state, the precursor of the Kemalist Republic of Turkey.

In the 1910s, there was a cluster of significant intellectual convergences between leftist revolutionaries and the Young Turk (CUP) rightist revolution.[2] Convergence included the concept of anti-imperialism, the desire for a strong state, support for world war as a catalyst of revolution and destroyer of the existing order, and, of particular importance, an identification of classes with ethnoreligious groups that justified ethnoreligious war and expropriation as forms of class struggle. This chapter seeks to explain the early convergences by considering the connections among émigré intellectuals of both the right and the left in the 1910s. Exploited by Parvus in his collaboration with the CUP, right-left synergy began to culminate in summer 1920, when the Bolsheviks embraced the Turkish-nationalist government in Ankara as a supposedly revolutionary and anti-imperialist ally against the West.

Parvus and the Link between Revolution from the Left and the Right

In the introduction to the first issue of *Die Glocke*, Parvus stated:

> We do not want to be influenced in our judgment by consideration for friends or comrades, not even by pity for poor and persecuted people. [. . .] We will express the whole, naked truth freely and plainly, without caring whom it benefits or whom it harms. Because knowledge is the highest contribution that an individual can make to the progress of humanity.[3]

He wrote these words at the end of August 1915, when the first phase of the genocide of the Armenian community in Asia Minor, a mass crime of hitherto unknown scale, was nearly complete. The influential agitator and conduit between Istanbul and Berlin was well aware of it.

What guided Parvus's intellectual activity and gave him a sense of mission and personal importance was his apocalyptic scheme of war-cum-revolution in the name of an abstract proletariat. This mission extended beyond ethics and compassion for "poor and persecuted people." While he emphasized this "lofty" goal, he did not, in fact, care about his own relation to, or the impact of his agitation on, the human realities in the trenches, in Ottoman Armenia, or elsewhere. Claiming the right to speak in the first-person plural, he argued that the iron laws of history and the aims of revolution demanded "our" sacrifices. In the early 1910s, having become a sophisticated though dissatisfied socialist intellectual in Germany, Parvus embraced the possibilities of influence, power, and enrichment that were offered to him in Istanbul during the Balkan Wars and the First World War. He treated these wars as means to achieve his final aim of world revolution. This, however, went hand in hand with enabling himself to live in luxury.

By way of introducing the respective Russian and Turkish revolutionary lexicons, this chapter will first go back to the revolutionary Russian and Ottoman student diasporas in Switzerland, where Parvus had studied before adopting German Social Democracy (SPD) as his social and spiritual home. The diasporas of education and political activism in Belle É—poque Switzerland were a hotbed for the elaboration of utopias, revolutionary activity, and networking by both the left and the right. This was the starting point for Parvus's career as a prolific socialist writer and activist.

Born Izrail' Lazarevich Gel'fand (Helphand) in 1867 to a Jewish lower-middle-class family in the *shtetl* of Berazino, east of Minsk, in what is now Belarus, Parvus gained notoriety in the SPD at the end of the nineteenth century under his pen name Parvus. An aura of fascination still surrounds his personality today. "In a world of mediocrity and a time of decadence, he was colorful, ambitious, theoretical, prophetic, extraordinary—a man of incredible intuition and intelligence," a Turkish academic wrote in the early 2000s.[4] Nevertheless, he was also vilified by former friends such as

Karl Radek, Leon Trotsky, and Rosa Luxemburg—most of them, like Parvus, Jewish émigrés from Russia—and by the National Socialists, for whom he was the Jewish prototype of both a Marxist revolutionary and a capitalist war profiteer. The present article seeks to clear Parvus's intellectual and political performance from its mystique, while at the same time avoiding such vilification.

Dividing his political and intellectual biography into pre-1910 and post-1917 periods, the article departs from earlier portraits by stressing Parvus's time in Istanbul as a pivotal and revealing episode that prepared him to become an agent of the German wartime government and its policy of backing the Russian Revolution of 1917. Contrary to what most earlier biographers have written, this sojourn in Istanbul was of decisive significance for Parvus's outlook. It offers crucial insights concerning the specific people with whom he maintained contact and the kinds of regimes and politics to which he was drawn.[5] Parvus mirrored, produced, and distilled a blend of leftist revolutionary discourses; he aspired to scientific truth, universalism, and a future without proletarian misery. Emotionally, however, he was—like Muslim émigrés from the tsarist empire and Ottoman leaders—inclined to a blanket Russophobia. Like Karl Marx before him, he looked forward to a world war that would destroy tsarism and international capitalism, which, he felt, had also held him back in his own life and career.

In the 1910s, Parvus changed from a revolutionary preoccupied with class struggle to a "geo-revolutionary." Thinking in more geostrategic terms, he set great store by Wilhelmine Germany's potentially transformative military power and a hoped-for German social democratic world mission. His dogmatically anti-Russian strategy of war-cum-revolution cost him the sympathy of many committed socialists, among them a few Ottoman Armenians, whose community was mortally threatened by this approach. In contrast to the ruling Young Turks, whom Parvus courted in the Ottoman capital and by whom he allowed himself to be courted, the Armenian parties cultivated strong ties with transnational socialism in the context of the Second International.[6]

As Heinz Schurer aptly argued, "The Russian revolutionary transformed into a German patriot did all he could to bring about the Russian defeat from within for the sake of a German triumph [in the First World War]. When the October Revolution came, however, the emotional attraction of the new Russia proved irresistible and Parvus violently swung back to his old country, only to be rejected."[7] Certain of eventual German victory and convinced that socialism would spread around the world after this triumph, Parvus found himself excluded from Bolshevik Russia, even though it was his initiative that had made Lenin's return from Zurich to St. Petersburg possible. In 1918, Parvus's political and intellectual life was thus a shambles. Instead of being a beacon of socialism and democracy, his adopted country—Germany—was in a sorry state, something to which he himself had unintentionally contributed. Now cured of his apocalyptic fantasies of war-cum-revolution, Parvus belatedly changed into a sober and farsighted political thinker, albeit one whose credibility and influence had dramatically declined.

Education and Activism in Switzerland

In the 1910s, Parvus became an advisor to the Young Turks and a contributor to *Türk Yurdu* [The Turk's Home], the most important Turkish nationalist review. During his studies in Switzerland, it had not been the Ottoman world and its small but growing diaspora that had primarily occupied him, but Germany and Russia. For their part, the Young Turks in Switzerland were impressed by the Russian revolutionaries and adopted as a slogan the declaration, "When the Russians rise up, the Ottomans must rise up too."

Israil Helphand was raised in Odessa, a cosmopolitan port city on the Black Sea, where he attended a Russian secondary school. Like the educated Ottoman youth and many other Russians, Jews and non-Jews alike, he dreamed of studying in Western Europe. In 1886, he had the chance to go to Zurich, where there was already a significant Russian community.[8] Eager to distance himself from his own background, he decided to study at the more conservative university of Basel, where the historian Jacob Burckhardt and the classical philologist and philosopher Friedrich Nietzsche taught, and where there were no communities of students from tsarist Russia or the Ottoman Empire.

The professor who appealed most to Helphand was the German economist Carl Bücher, a former journalist at the *Frankfurter Zeitung*, who left Basel for Karlsruhe in 1890. As Helphand wrote in his farewell address to Bücher, it was him to whom he owed his notion of scientific truth and his methodology, which included the comprehensive use of statistics. His studies and his doctorate in economics instilled in him a greater confidence in himself, his intellectual capacities, and his Marxist framework. His dissertation, however, had almost been turned down by "bourgeois" academia.[9] His socialist inclination also led him to enter into contact with Georgii Plekhanov, Rosa Luxemburg, Julian Marchelewski (Karski), and many others, all of whom were also residents of fin de siècle Switzerland. Yet, in contrast to socialists such as Luxemburg and Eduard Bernstein,[10] Helphand did not participate in the human rights movement that emerged in response to the anti-Armenian persecutions of 1895–6 and after. Anti-Russian and anti-British geostrategic thinking, together with state-sponsored anti-Armenian propaganda in the German press, largely prevented the German intelligentsia on both the left and right—and by extension Helphand, too—from developing a sense of solidarity with the victims.[11]

In the late Ottoman as well as the late tsarist empire, an educated and rebellious youth and its mentors were eager to revolt against the "imperial establishment" and its manifest injustices. Although there were some interactions and shared concerns, however, deep divisions between Ottoman and Russian revolutionaries predominated. Even if they lived side by side in educational and activist diasporas in Swiss towns, they did not collaborate. The exception were non-Muslim, notably Armenian socialists of the Second International. Switzerland was the preferred place for students and activists from Russia; in Alfred Senn's aphorism, the Russian Revolution of 1917 was made in Switzerland. Russian social democracy had been founded in Geneva in 1883 by, among others, the Marxist theorist Georgii Plekhanov. Five out of the fourteen congresses of the First and Second Socialist Internationals took place in Switzerland, as did the exile congresses of the SPD in the 1880s and most Zionist congresses. Even before organized socialism acquired its main hubs, Alexander Herzen, the so-called father of Russian socialism, had lived for a time in Geneva; it was there that he had published the first oppositional journal, *Kolokol* (The Bell). All this is well known and has been thoroughly researched.[12]

Less well known is the contemporaneous, though smaller, diaspora of Ottoman students and agitators in Switzerland. They were concentrated in French-, not German-speaking Switzerland.[13] This was a result of the Franco-centrism of the Ottoman Reform Age and the special place given to French as the "language of progress." By contrast, most social revolutionaries from Russia, including Parvus, respected German as the language of science, "civilization," and "high culture." The first Ottoman students in Geneva in the late nineteenth century experienced culture shocks and confusion upon their initial arrival.[14] When confronted with the atheism, nihilism, and anarchism of the revolutionary youth from Russia, they felt a deep disquiet. They were particularly disconcerted when these activists applied their concepts to Ottoman society, as the Armenian revolutionaries from the Caucasus were doing. At the end of the nineteenth century, Geneva was for a few years the center of the oppositional *Comité Union et Progrès* (CUP) that had been founded in Istanbul in 1889.

Originating mainly from the Caucasus and solidly established in the town and university of Geneva from the 1880s onward, the revolutionary Armenians were intimately acquainted with Marxism and the Russian revolutionaries. Beginning in 1887, they founded the revolutionary Social Democratic Party *Hntshak* (The Bell), followed by a journal of the same name, both inspired by Herzen's *Kolokol*. They were represented at the Second International by Georgi Plekhanov who lived in Swiss exile. In 1890, small circles of revolutionary students and populists (*narodniki*) from Tbilisi, Moscow, and St. Petersburg merged and founded the *Dashnaktsutiun* or Armenian Revolutionary Federation (ARF) in Tbilisi. An attempt at union with *Hntshak* failed, leaving the two groups distinct. The ARF, too, chose the city of Geneva as its Western center and published its monthly *Droshak* (Flag) there from 1891 onward. The ARF office in Geneva was responsible for ARF activities in most parts of the Ottoman Empire.[15]

In the late nineteenth and early twentieth centuries, there was a lively revolutionary spirit among Eastern European Jews in the Yiddish-speaking "Yiddishland" of the Russian and Austrian empires as well as among Armenians in the Russian, Armenian, and Persian Caucasus.[16] This invites us to rethink the often different and yet uniquely linked fates of the Jews and the Armenians, including the experience of genocide. Leftist revolutionary networks and interactions emerged in the tsarist empire and in revolutionary Russia, bringing Jewish and Armenian activists close together. Further west, in the Ottoman Empire, where leftist social revolutionaries played only a marginal role, this was rarely the case and after 1913, almost not at all. Here, especially in the capital Istanbul, both Ottoman Jews and Zionist representatives—as well as Parvus—sought and enjoyed the proximity of the CUP even after the party-state was established in 1913. Russian and Ottoman Armenians, in the European diaspora at least, served as the most direct bridge between Russians and Ottomans, and between revolutionary European, Russian, and Ottoman ideas and concepts.

Despite attempts at collaboration, however, relations between Armenians and Young Turks in Switzerland existed only on an individual basis, never collectively and politically. Nonetheless, the general revolutionary feeling did excite the Young Turks. They admired the revolutionary organization and enthusiasm of their fellow students from Russia, praising "the force that provides an Ottoman Armenian [. . .], or a Russian

Jew, with the courage to play with bombs," as Bahaeddin Şhakir wrote.[17] Moreover, they shared their resentments toward Russia and the European powers. They were definitely not ready to replace their religious creed with socialism, however, no matter how weakly they actually subscribed to it. Only Turkism—Turkish ethnonationalism— could take this role. It would begin to restrict and finally to replace religion a few years later. On a deeper level, there was a disparity between the two different political languages: the first, a secular, socialist millennialism that fundamentally distrusted the existing state and world system, and the second, a deeply internalized vision of a strong Ottoman state that had to be re-empowered according to a manifestly successful modern European model.

The ex-Ottoman Bulgarians might also have formed an important link between the Young Turks and Russians in Geneva. In the early twentieth century, Bulgarian students, numbering several hundred, formed the second largest group at the University of Geneva after the Russians. Among them were many active socialists. Some insights into the transnational socialist networks and their links in fin de siècle Switzerland can be found in the autobiography of the Bulgarian Christian Rakovsky.[18] While Armenians are mentioned, Muslim Ottomans are not. Rakovsky did, however, pay attention to the Ottoman world and clearly recognized the shortcomings of European socialism with regard to what he called "the Eastern questions." He, along with a number of Armenian socialists in Switzerland, must have been known to Parvus.

Around 1900, the Young Turks admired powers such as France, Britain, and Germany while hesitating to adopt radically revolutionary or anti-authoritarian theories. Instead, they hoped for a re-empowered Ottoman state that would occupy a respected place among the European powers. Their aims by no means included a world revolution based on intra-societal class struggle. It was only after the decisive turn to Turkism after 1910 that an important faction of young Turko-Muslim academics began to think in terms of social revolution and class struggle according to ethnoreligious lines. When, at the Second Congress of the Ottoman Opposition in Paris in December 1907, the ARF and CUP (at that time called CPU, *Comité Progrès et Union*) agreed on an alliance, it was a serious attempt to bridge the gap between the Young Turk desire for a strong modern state and the leftist-inspired Armenian revolution. "Revolution" was now pragmatically reduced to a reinstalled constitution and further Ottoman reforms, especially the rule of law in Eastern Anatolia. The alliance lasted until 1912.[19]

The Young Turks of the *fin de siècle* in Geneva were still seekers, not activists. Some twelve years later, the picture was different. By this point, the CUP had, via their new center of exile in Paris, become an elitist club of avant-garde activists on the road to establishing a single-party regime. By that point, activist students in the diaspora were clear about their goals: a "social revolution" in terms of Turkism (Turkish ethnic nationalism).[20] They were now organized in *Foyers Turcs* (*Türk Yurdu*), founded in 1911 (see Chapter 10). These were based on the same principles as the new Turkish Hearths (*Türk Ocağı*) in Istanbul and Asia Minor.[21] *Türk Yurdu* was also the name of the main paper of the Turkist movement that attracted a broad academic youth on the eve of and during the First World War. The *Foyers Turcs* and their journal *Türk Yurdu* stood close to the CUP, which partly financed them.

The objectives of these *Foyers* were now no longer concentrated on the future of the Ottoman Empire as a whole, as had been the Young Turks' focus twenty years previously, but specifically on that of the Turks. Moreover, the "great ideal" or "national ideal" (*millî mefkûre*) was to be reached by "social revolution" (*inkılâb-ı içtimâî*), a key term that the *Foyers Turcs* manifestly borrowed from the leftist social revolutionaries. An important related topic was the "liberation of the economy from the yoke of aliens," among whom the Turkists counted the alleged *comprador* bourgeoisie of foreign companies and non-Muslim businessmen. "Social revolution" meant the economic and educational empowerment of the Turkish Muslims, men and women, for the sake of a new Turkish nation in Anatolia.[22] In 1913, during the Balkan Wars, Turkism reached a peak in the European diaspora and in the Ottoman capital. Here, the socialist Parvus addressed the Turkists and influenced their ideal of revolution.

From Russia via Switzerland to Germany and Turkey

Like most students from the tsarist and Ottoman worlds, Israil Helphand believed that Western Europe was superior in terms of science, organization, and democratic character. With the exception of the last point—democracy—this corresponded exactly with what Ziya Gökalp termed modern Europe's universal civilization (*medeniyet*), an achievement that Turkey needed to obtain at any price.

Like Gökalp and the Ottoman Muslims in general, Helphand distinguished Europe's progressive civilization from its contemporary imperialist, capitalist, and colonialist aspects. At the time of the Second International, he, like many other socialists all over the world, believed in the superiority of the German Social Democrats and, hence, in their special mission to spread anti-imperialist socialism. After finishing his doctorate in Basel, he was—before Luxemburg, Radek, and Karski—the first socialist from tsarist Russia to begin a career in the SPD. Looking back, Parvus wrote in his autobiography that in the 1890s, "German Social Democracy became my fatherland."[23] Thanks to him, the German Social Democrats began to take the Russian Social Democrats, gathered around Plekhanov in Geneva, seriously and established contact with them.[24]

Parvus preached revolution in the *Sächsische Arbeiterzeitung*, castigating "opportunists," "reformists," and all other non-militant evolutionary "optimists" (who have not or only reluctantly embraced revolutionary violence). He attacked, among others, the respected SPD member Eduard Bernstein, a Jew from Berlin. Much later, however, he would express more pragmatic opinions that, in some ways, mirrored those of Bernstein.[25] The 1905 revolution, which caused him to return to Russia, distracted him temporarily from German affairs. He contended that the Russo-Japanese war of 1904–5 would "end with the breakdown of the political equilibrium in all countries." He saw this as the prelude to world revolution. As a member of the executive committee of the St. Petersburg Soviet—the organ that coordinated the workers' strike in 1905—he tried to light the fuse of revolution by provoking an economic collapse through mass strikes and other measures. The leaders, including

Parvus and Leon Trotsky (to whom Parvus had been a mentor), were arrested by the police, though they were able to escape after a few months of relatively mild confinement.[26]

What led Parvus to Turkey were his efforts to confront his own uncomfortable position of a revolutionary writer who lacked money, had failed as an activist in Russia, and remained a loner even within the Social Democratic Party of his chosen fatherland. Hastening to St. Petersburg in October 1905, he had left his loss-making publishing house and its debts to his business associate Karski in Munich, just as he had left his wife and his son without plans to provide for them in the future. Those German socialists who in this context demanded some *bourgeois* morality he snubbed as Philistines (*Philister*).[27] On his return to Germany, he was, for a short time, admired as a hero of the 1905 revolution and a near martyr of the tsarist regime, having adventurously escaped "the Russian Bastille" in 1907 as he proclaimed in the title of his commercially successful narrative.[28] As an "expert on Russia" who had a bone to pick with his native country, he contributed to a generalized view among German Social Democrats of Russia as "barbaric." He thus fueled their desire for a military crusade, as well as the spread of Russophobia even among moderate friends such as Adolf Müller in Munich.[29]

By way of Vienna, Parvus moved to Istanbul, where he arrived in the autumn of 1910. What attracted him to Turkey was, according to his friend Georg Gandauer, the possibility of studying the Young Turk Revolution, as well as the fact that Istanbul was "the center of multiple diplomatic threads and the place where Eastern problems were to be studied [and] from which already at that time the great crisis of imperialism, the World War, threatened to burst into flame."[30] Parvus in fact substantially changed his revolutionary ideas around 1910. He now became convinced that what was needed to precipitate the breakdown of the capitalist system was not, in the first instance, class struggle but rather a war between states. "War carries all capitalist contradictions to extremes. A *world war* can only end with a *world revolution*," he wrote in 1910.[31]

He now derided the attitude of Karl Liebknecht and his former close friend Luxemburg, both of whom remained loyal to the priority of class struggle over geostrategic *realpolitik*, as "revolutionism."[32] Anti-tsarist feelings continued to inform Parvus's thinking. Some of his anti-liberal resentments disappeared during his stay in Istanbul between 1910 and 1915, however, as he discovered a new world in which he felt free and at ease both economically and emotionally. He was listened to and admired. He began to enjoy the power of money and even the life of an *haut bourgeois* and *bon-vivant*. He became a successful merchant, an agent of the German embassy, an influential writer for a Turkish audience, and an advisor and mediator for the CUP. The CUP had organized the Young Turk Revolution of 1908 and forced the reopening of the Ottoman parliament. In 1913, it established a dictatorial regime that lasted until the end of the First World War. Parvus must have have been in some kind of contact with Mehmed Cavid Bey, the CUP's financial expert and minister of finances, and with Mehmed Talaat Bey (later Pasha), the predominant leader in the CUP Central Committee.[33]

Blurred Boundaries: From Leftist to Rightist
Revolution—and to World War

The Bulgarian socialist Rakovsky, an expert on contemporary Ottoman and Balkan issues,[34] introduced the greenhorn Parvus to the Constantinopolitan metropolis, just as he hosted Parvus's friend Leon Trotsky during the Balkan Wars of 1912–13. In his letters to the SPD leader Karl Kautsky in spring 1911, Parvus appears eager "to study a [different, Ottoman] world" and to promote socialism in the Balkans and the Ottoman Empire as a leading activist. "In comrade D. Vlachow [Dimitar Vlahov] I have found a man of quick comprehension and fine grasp of the [illegible word] questions of socialism. He would be for Turkey what Trotsky had been for the revolutionary struggle in St. Petersburg, only in different circumstances," Parvus wrote in a letter on April 3, 1911. Vlahov, an ethnic Bulgarian and member of the Ottoman parliament, opened a door to the political life in the capital for Parvus. "The arrival of friend Rak. [Rakovski] was timely. We are now inseparable, which reminds me of the beautiful days that I spent with Trotsky in St. Petersburg. We are becoming a force, but one that unfortunately lacks a social base. If only we had here the hundreds of thousands of workers of St. Petersburg."[35]

Not least for this latter reason, Parvus, in a distinct departure from his earlier *Sturm und Drang* period, began to concentrate on other activities. In the Ottoman capital, he was now not so much a spokesperson of the proletariat but rather a mentor to the educated Turkish elite, which perceived him as a sympathetic observer of the new Turkish nationalism. Nevertheless, there was, according to Armenian sources, a period in 1911–12 in which he still attempted to strengthen the socialist forces by bringing the Dashnaks (ARF) and Hunchaks (Social Democrat Hunchakian Party, SDHP) into an alliance for the 1912 elections to the Ottoman parliament. The CUP won the irregular elections (*sopalı seçim*) by means of violence and coercion. This was followed by a liberal-conservative coup in July, which deprived the CUP of its power until January 1913. In dire need of support, the CUP would have benefited from an electoral alliance. The SDHP leaders, however, did not trust the CUP's and Parvus's intentions. They consistently insisted on Armenian autonomy in parts of the eastern provinces. In their eyes, the socialist Parvus regrettably served an ultranationalist party "that had the Adana massacres on its conscience [as well as] murders, kidnappings and confiscations of property carried out to further the objectives of Turkish nationalism."[36]

As a holder of a European Ph.D in economics, Parvus became an attractive financial expert, banker, and merchant for the Young Turks of the CUP, especially in the context of the First Balkan War, which began in the autumn of 1912. For adherents of the new current of Turkism, he began to be a "European" (as he emphasized) mentor. "I wrote financial articles and was busy with founding banks. Once I made my first commercial gains, I put them aside because they were the lever for further advancement." The theorist of world-war-cum-world-revolution was turning, so other socialists claimed, into a war profiteer. "In time I acquired both the capital and the relations; when the World War began, the roads to capitalist accumulation suddenly opened wide to me. [. . .] The War has led many persons of liberal profession to commerce."[37]

Parvus's key to success in Istanbul was his ability to apply his economic concepts and intuition to the Ottoman situation. In the critical year of 1912, when the parliamentary system started to crumble, the Balkan Wars began, the ARF broke its alliance with the CUP, and Armenians appealed to the Great Powers for reforms in the eastern provinces, he was particularly adept in "speaking to the Turkish soul."³⁸ Yusuf Akçura invited him to edit the economic column of *Türk Yurdu*. This was a topic, he insisted, that was highly important but for which no Turkish author could be found. Parvus was recommended as someone who had already proven his skill at writing articles, notably for *Tanin* [Buzzing Noise], the CUP's main newspaper.³⁹

The first of a number of articles by Parvus in *Türk Yurdu* appeared in early spring 1912. In these articles, he reinforced the readers' feelings that Turkey was the victim of European imperialism and capitalism. He confirmed that the resulting financial penetration was as bad as a military invasion and that the Turkish-Muslim peasantry—the largest segment of the population and the group in whose name the Turkists had begun to speak—was in fact the most abused group in the empire. It was this Turkish peasantry, he remarked, that paid heavy and unjust taxes—"a peasant in Anatolia pays on average 30% more taxes than a peasant in Armenia"—and bore the duty of general military service, from which most non-Muslims had succeeded in liberating themselves. In contrast to the Christian-Armenian and Macedonian peasants, Parvus remarked, the Turkish-Muslim peasantry also did not enjoy the support and solidarity of its ethnoreligious elites and their political organizations.⁴⁰ In short, his arguments encouraged the Young Turks to become representatives of a Turkish ethnoreligious group. Though he avoided polemics against the non-Muslim subjects of the empire, Parvus's remarks concurred with the argument made by an early anti-Christian article in *Türk Yurdu* in September and October 1912. Supposedly also written by a European expert, it had urged "the Turks" to embrace imperial Turkism and empower themselves against the Ottoman Christians, whom the author depicted as economically successful spongers who lacked patriotism and worked only for the interests of their own communities.⁴¹

Parvus quickly learned the Turkish nationalist vocabulary, its *topoi*, catchwords, historical images, and—last but not least—its apocalyptic mentality, which regarded the task of becoming a modern nation as crucial for its continued existence. As he had done in his publications for German or Russian socialist readers, he combined the authoritative discourse of social science (though this time not openly socialist) with the attitude of a preacher and prophet. He addressed his readership with an insistent and direct "you," claiming for himself an imposing but somewhat mysterious and chameleon-like "we" that could stand for science, socialism, Germany, Europe, or simply, as a *pluralis majestatis*, for Parvus himself. (It never stood for the Jews, though he made use of Jewish networks in Istanbul, the Balkans, Europe, and Russia.) The results were lucid social analyses, powerful projections of the future, and passages of impressive rhetorical and even poetic power. Alongside these strengths, however, they displayed a know-it-all attitude and used facile demagogic arguments that were conditioned by the *Zeitgeist*, and by his own unacknowledged emotional ties.

It is instructive in this context to draw a comparison between his 1911 German address to the "proletarian youth" and his "letter to the Turkish youth" of June 1913.⁴² In both speeches, he positioned himself as an authoritative, scientifically minded teacher and as a senior advisor who knew the situation and needs of the countries' young while at the same time also equating himself to them. In the first case, he used the language of revolutionary socialism; in the second, that of anti-imperialist nationalism. In both cases, he encouraged the young to learn, be active, and defend the interests of their groups, which he represented as the chief victims of the present power structures. In the German case, he went further, urging the "proletarian youth" to behave like soldiers who place "the cause" above even their own lives—"bis in den Tod" (until death), as he declared twice at the end of the address. This rhetoric of victims resorting to violence and dying for the cause bears a striking resemblance to texts from other violence-prone ideologues. Particularly notable are Ziya Gökalp's martial poems of the 1910s.

In an address to "the Turks" during the final phase of the First Balkan War in April 1913, Parvus adopted an apocalyptic tone similar to the above-mentioned article of September 1912.[43] He strongly appealed to his readers. The Balkan states and the Great Powers, he wrote:

> want to annihilate you like the native Indians who perished in America. [. . .] They have closed all your roads and besiege you. If you cannot hold your positions and establish an economic force that meets modern demands, your death is certain. [. . .] Henceforth the last minute has begun. [. . .] If you do not work hard for the return of the Muslim refugees and for the protection of their property, you will have to leave Europe [the Balkans] completely and must assemble in Anatolia.[44]

Parvus thus contributed to Turkish fears of extermination and to the new discourse of Anatolia as the Turks' last resort and ultimate home. He thus contributed to the prevailing feeling of the time "that in order to avoid being exterminated, the Turks must exterminate others," as the Turkish author and (relatively liberal) nationalist Halide Edip put it in retrospect.[45]

Parvus—the European expert, socialist theorist, and clever master of rhetoric—identified the Turkish-Muslim peasantry as the class that more than any other deserved to benefit from a social revolution. He called upon the Young Turks and Turkists to identify with this class—which at the same time he presented as the "people" and the core of the "nation" (*millet*)—and to liberate their economy from imperialist exploitation. All this was a strong stimulus for the Turkists' "social revolution" and had a strong impact on the concept of the "national" (Turkish-Muslim) economy, *millî iktisad*. After 1913, the CUP coercively implemented the ideal of *millî iktisad* against foreigners and non-Muslim citizens in the Ottoman Empire, branding both groups as alien exploiters. In this way, the spiritual fathers of Turkish nationalism absorbed the revolutionary and anti-liberal elements of socialism. Parvus served as an intellectual catalyst for this process of war-based revolutionary nation building.

During his time in Istanbul, Parvus himself maintained a more or less socialist superstructure in his writings. His audience, however, received his messages in a way that amplified the seminal impact of Turkism. Also contributing to this trend was a Russian Muslim intelligentsia based in Istanbul, most of whom had, like Parvus, enjoyed a modern education in Russia and Western Europe. The most well known among them were Ali Hüseyinzâde (Turan) from Baku, Ahmed Agayef (Ağaoğlu) from Shusha in Azerbaijan, Yusuf Akçura from Simbirsk on the Volga, Ismail Gasprinski (Gaspıralı) from the Crimea, and Mehmed Reşid Şhahingiray from the Caucasus, who had been one of the founders of the CUP in 1889 and, after 1913, became a fanatical anti-Rûm (Greek-Orthodox) and anti-Armenian governor. Hüseyinzâde, Agayef, and Gasprinski were all contributors to the journal *Türk Yurdu*, of which Yusuf Akçura was the director.

Ali Hüseyinzâde was a student at the Military School for Medicine in Istanbul, where he began to open the eyes of his Ottoman fellows to the trans-imperial Turkish world (*Türk âlemi*). Close to the CUP, he had fled from the Hamidian police and published the journal *Füyuzat* (Enlightenment) in Baku in 1906–7. This journal coined the seminal slogan "Europeanize, Turkify, Islamize," and called for a correspondingly anti-Hamidian revolution in Turkey. After his return to Istanbul in 1911, Ali Hüseyinzâde was appointed a senior consultant and, on Talaat Bey's initiative, elected to the CUP Central Committee. It was in that same year that he became involved in the *Foyers Turcs* and *Türk Yurdu*. Parvus must have known him and have regularly interacted with the Russian Muslim intelligentsia in the Ottoman capital.

Though they had no particular affinity with socialism, these politicized intellectuals shared Parvus's distinctly anti-tsarist and anti-imperialist sentiments, as well as his desire to make a clean sweep of the existing power relations. While Parvus fully cooperated with rightist modernizers, he did not openly advocate an ethnoreligious national revolution himself. Yet, he did not oppose or warn against interpretations of his message that took an ultranationalist or *völkisch* form. In his articles, he maintained an internationalist vocabulary together with abstract notions of history and class relations, all the while careful to always include some statistics as proof of the scientific nature of his writing. Parvus contended that the neglect of Turkey's working class by the country's intelligentsia and political class "was the reason why the civilized world has received the impression that the Ottoman Christians struggled against Turkish domination." Once the Turkish elites showed solidarity with the peasantry and state policy took the people's interest into account:

> the Turkish question, that is, the question of Turkish nationality and of the national renewal of the Turks, will join the Bulgarian, Armenian, and similar questions, and the civilized world will be obliged to deal with the Turkish question just as it has done with the others. In that situation the struggle between the different [ethnoreligious] elements will lose the violence it now has, because then the general relation between the interests of the popular classes will become evident.[46]

It is thus fair to say that Parvus maintained a universalist framework of inter-ethnic popular solidarity in his articles in the Turkish press. Moreover, as a European "friend of the Turks," he enjoyed considerable goodwill and did not abstain from criticizing the CUP—at least not in the comparatively open political atmosphere before the definitive establishment of the CUP's one-party regime in the summer of 1913. He thus postulated a constructive continuity in parliamentary and democratic life. Emphasizing democracy and the positive sides of "the civilized world" (Europe), he underlined Turkey's need to receive its fair share of European capital and outlined the positive impact that a peaceful, prosperous, and balanced Europe could have on Turkey in the future.[47] The question, however, is which of his messages—peace or revolution-cum-war—proved the most compelling in the "hour of truth" of 1914, when Europe collapsed. At that moment, the influence of the merchant of revolution and war reached its peak. He began to play a seminal transnational role between Istanbul, Berlin, and St. Petersburg.

Great War: The Peak and Dead End of War-cum-Revolution

Though somewhat suppressed after the 1905 failure in St. Petersburg, Parvus's desire for revolution and action, together with his emphatic approval of war as a factor in revolution, reappeared in force in August 1914. War was also desired by important CUP representatives, among them by the thirty-three-year-old minister of war and member of the CUP Central Committee, Enver Pasha, and his dominant associate, Interior Minister Talaat Bey. Most CUP leaders easily identified with the anti-Russian aspect of the German-Ottoman war alliance. A CUP circular of November 1914 reads:

> The national ideal of our people and our country drives us to annihilate the Muscovite enemy on the one side, in order to obtain a natural imperial frontier that includes and unites all our [Turkic] national comrades; on the other side our religious sentiment drives us to liberate the Muslim world from infidel domination and give the followers of Muhammed independence.[48]

From August 1914, pan-Turkist, and to a lesser extent, pan-Islamist war propaganda ran at full strength in the Ottoman capital. Using anti-Russian clichés and ideas about the clash of races and religions, it conjured up images of a "Great Turanian Empire."[49] Arguing in terms of geopolitics and (only to his socialist readers in Europe) global revolution, Parvus fully participated in both anti-Russian and anti-British war propaganda, as well as in the CUP's struggle for national-imperial sovereignty through war. He portrayed Britain as the jealous enemy of modern Germany and, above all, as the greatest enemy of the Ottoman Empire, which it planned to dismember.[50] Even before 1914, he had confirmed his readers' widespread opinion that when European financiers and diplomats demanded reforms, they "only wanted to break off something from the Ottoman Empire and to live at its expense."[51]

The CUP had used the same language when international diplomatic negotiations produced the reform plan for the Kurdish-Armenian provinces in 1913–14 (see Chapter 4). Parvus was well informed about the Armenian problem in Ottoman Eastern Anatolia. During his first years in Istanbul, he maintained contacts with leftist Armenian politicians and often visited the editorial office of *Azadamard* (Fight for Freedom), an Armenian daily.[52] In early January 1913, shortly after discussions about reform had reemerged in Europe, he published an article in a German newspaper that openly identified the real problems: a terror-stricken Armenian rural population subjected to increasing aggression by Kurdish chiefs and landlords, and an Ottoman government that made many hollow promises but failed to prosecute crimes, instead coopting and arming the Kurds, whom "it considered the state-supporting element because they are Muslim."[53] Did Parvus contribute to the general shift in Germany's official stance? It is true that during the first half of 1913, German diplomacy underwent a fundamental change with respect to its hitherto conniving approach to the Armenian question. It now regarded the Armenians' main demands as justified and suggested that the "German press would have to give up its previous negative attitude towards everything Armenian."[54] Articles sympathetic to the Armenians all of a sudden began to appear in the German press in the spring of 1913;[55] Germany, along with Russia, became a crucial partner in the reform negotiations in the second half of 1913 that led to the reform plan of February 8, 1914.

Parvus, however, did not support the reforms; only later did he enter into direct contact with Hans von Wangenheim, the German ambassador in Istanbul. The main reason for his contradictory stance on this core issue of the Eastern Question before the Great War was, once again, his anti-Russian attitude. This attitude finally led him to give unrealistic and dangerous advice to the Ottoman and German governments in summer 1914. He proposed a comprehensive scheme of uprisings in tsarist Russia involving ethnoreligious minorities and proletarians in collaboration with the Triple Alliance. These were to include Armenian-supported revolts in the Caucasus. In partial collaboration with Dr. Max Zimmer of the German embassy, he supported efforts of the German Foreign Office (GFO) to organize pro-German national movements in Bucharest, Sofia, Ukraine, and Georgia.[56] Whether on Parvus's advice or not—we lack concrete sources to say with any certainty—the CUP invited the ARF to lead an anti-Russian guerrilla war aimed at preparing the Ottoman conquest of the Caucasus. By summer 1914, however, the Armenians had lost all trust in Parvus, seeing him as an agent of the CUP as well as Germany.[57]

Despite the ARF's refusal to take part in what it saw as suicidal, attempts at revolutionizing the Caucasus began in early August. In October 1914, a seminal German memorandum by Max von Oppenheim, a collaborator of the GFO, entitled *Revolutionizing the Islamic Possessions of Our Enemies*, once again referred to the Armenians and other Eastern Christians in derogatory terms—as if German diplomacy had not reassessed its attitude toward them and self-critically reconsidered such language.[58] In August 1914, Germany abandoned its commitment to the reforms it had embraced only a few months earlier. The Ottoman government, too, suspended its reform obligations. In September, it announced the abrogation of the capitulations (the tax and legal privileges afforded to foreigners). It also succeeded in obtaining large sums of German money in order to prepare for an attack in the Caucasus. In a GFO memorandum in early 1915, Parvus detailed his scheme without reassessing the Caucasian part that put the Armenians at risk.[59] It is true that Dr. Johannes Lepsius, the president of the German-Armenian friendship association, also called on the Ottoman Armenians in December 1914 to support the war effort. Yet, unlike Parvus and the CUP, he limited this appeal to Armenians on Ottoman territory, in accordance with the ARF's official position.[60]

Parvus had supported the repudiation of the capitulations and the cancellation of the *Dette Publique* (service on the Ottoman debt). He fully backed the anti-Russian war effort and the insurgency scheme. He pleaded with Germany that it was their duty to destroy and partition the tsarist empire and thereby bring about revolution and democracy. "Russian democracy can only be achieved through a complete destruction of tsarism and the dismemberment of Russia into small states," he stated in his meeting with Wangenheim in early 1915.[61] In the same sense, he spurred on his socialist comrades in Germany to give full support to the war effort, thus contributing strongly to the *Burgfrieden* (national unity across party lines) in Germany. For his Turkish audience, he painted a picture of a strong, modern, Turkish-led Islamic empire that extended from Edirne to Basra and blocked Russian expansion to the South.[62]

Principally, Parvus was probably correct in his assessment that the Russian autocratic state tradition needed to be dismantled and the empire fragmented to make room for smaller democratic polities. But the violent means he chose to achieve this goal led to the contrary. Just as he had anticipated the World War, it now galvanized him in the role that he had assigned himself. Back home in Germany in early autumn 1915, he wrote in his newly founded journal, *Die Glocke: Sozialistische Halbmonatsschrift*: "I made the war the starting point of our tactics. Above all, the military might of tsarism, that strongest foundation of reaction, had to be brought down. For this purpose, the excellent military organization created by the German general staff had to be used."[63] Although former friends accused him of having become a warmonger, there were many German socialists fascinated by what they saw as his intellectual brilliance, his personal success, and the cunning he exhibited in *realpolitik*.[64] The GFO meanwhile believed it could use Parvus for its own agenda. In Germany, he not only founded his own publishing house but also engaged in a profitable, though partly illegal, commerce between Russia, Germany, and other countries.

Thanks to his pro-German commitment in Istanbul, he was also an important contact for the GFO on European matters, as well as for the political section of the General Staff, especially with regard to Russia. Though based on a much earlier idea, his scheme of using the World War to revolutionize Russia only crystallized after the summer of 1914. He presented an elaborate plan to the GFO in early 1915.[65] In spring 1917, Chancellor Theobald von Bethmann Hollweg finally realized how favorably a revolution in Russia might affect Germany and ordered the embassy in Bern to contact Russian exiles in Switzerland to offer them transit through Germany. Parvus was now able to fully play the role of intermediary. German agency, German money, and Parvus's networking were decisive factors in Lenin's journey to Russia and the making of the Russian Revolution.[66] Lenin himself, however, refused to meet the now disreputable Parvus personally.

In September 1917, Parvus co-organized a mainly socialist peace congress in Stockholm, the so-called "Third Zimmerwald Conference." Mainly prepared by the International Socialist Committee, it was meant to be the last socialist anti-war conference, specifically intended to bring about peace by means of a democratized, revolutionary post-tsarist Russia. Although neither Parvus's nor the CUP's warmongering had anything to do with peace-seeking internationalist socialism, Grand Vizier Talaat Pasha did not want to miss any diplomatic opportunities. He therefore made up a fake Turkish Socialist Party with its own seal and prepared to send CUP intimates—Ali Hüseyinzâde and Nesim Masliyah, members of the Ottoman parliament whom he labeled socialists—to Stockholm. Armenian socialists from Geneva protested against this act of "pseudo-socialist cynicism" on the grounds that Talaat above all intended it to neutralize Armenian voices. Turkey's Austrian allies, meanwhile, wanted the Ottoman delegates to contribute to the failure of the congress by making maximalist demands, such as the maintenance of the Ottoman Empire in its entirety. In the end, the Turkish delegation was not admitted.[67]

Bitterly disappointed that the Bolsheviks were rejecting him despite his decisive contribution to the making of the October 1917 revolution, Parvus turned fiercely against them. He now began to place even more emphasis on democracy including elements of private enterprise, which, in an unusual move, he now saw as the cornerstone of the success of socialism.[68] This was the same man who, in the months after the February revolution of 1917, had breathed fire and brimstone against Aleksandr Kerensky's leftist-liberal government.[69]

Belated Conversion from Warmongering Apocalypticism

Sincere or not, Parvus was too late to be taken seriously by most of his contemporaries when, in 1917, he began to formulate an eloquent, albeit Eurocentric, lament for the insane consequences of the World War—a war whose historical and revolutionary necessity he had been inculcating in his readers for years.

"All parties had calculated wrongly," Parvus wrote in summer 1917, complaining of the monstrous destruction caused by the ongoing war. He began to anticipate the even more catastrophic consequences that Germany's defeat would have for Europe, as well as what he thought would be its unavoidable retaliatory mania in its aftermath. Yet he offered no *mea culpa*, nor did he question the propaganda for a German victory by which he had promoted his insane concept of a German-Ottoman war of destruction against Russia. Like most other responsible players of the 1910s, he was unwilling to account both for what had gone fundamentally wrong and for his own inflammatory role in precipitating this outcome. On the contrary, after the war, he did not abstain from glorifying, somewhat presumptuously, "the struggle we have risked" and the "responsibility we have assumed."[70]

Nevertheless, he reassessed his political thought in the light of the postwar situation. In an address "to the French Germany-haters," he insisted that if the German Empire were destroyed, if reparations were too heavy, and if Western Europe, in particular Germany and France, did not cooperate against the Russian peril, the Germans would become the organizers of the next world war. Once again, Russia—this time, Bolshevik Russia—was Parvus's chief enemy. Interestingly, Turkey once again disappeared from Parvus's world view. Turkey would have been a relevant lesson in applied national "social revolution," the ideology of which was, as we have seen, indebted to Parvus's earlier writings for the CUP.[71]

The German friends of the CUP regime in Istanbul had included such politically diverse figures as the Turcologist Ernst Jäckh, the Orientalist Max von Oppenheim, the left-liberal politician Friedrich Naumann, the journalist Erwin Nossig, as well as officers such as Enver Pasha's friend Hans Humann. Parvus was part of this circle, in particular of the CUP's war party led by Enver and Talaat. His dizzying political network and field of action during the First World War was mirrored in post-1918 Germany by the paradoxical interactions between right-wing German officers, incriminated CUP members in exile, revolutionary socialists from Russia, and politicians of the Weimar government.[72] For many of them, Parvus's villa in Berlin was a hub. Although he remained loyal to the socialist world view in theory, he had, in late Ottoman Turkey, contributed to bringing together coercive leftist and rightist concepts of violent revolution. This syncretism was reflected in his intellectual and political networks and eventually entered Kemalism, in particular through the lasting concept of the national economy or *millî iktisad*. As already mentioned, it also prefigured the Bolsheviks' embrace of Ankara as an anti-Western ally—and thus a concubinage of convenience between communists and ultranationalists struggling to establish their power under the guise of anti-imperialism.

Parvus excelled as a suggestive mentor and missionary, an effective agitator, and as Scharlau and Zeman have underlined, a very clever merchant of war.[73] His aspiration to qualify as a thought-provoking scholar of the social sciences, a true-to-life journalist, or a critical witness of his time, was to remain overshadowed by his distorting ideological commitment to war and his penchant for life in luxury. Though clad in scientific language and an impressive body of written work, his fantasies of war-cum-revolution, along with his sweeping notions of history, class, and society, distorted Parvus's grasp of the realities of human and social life. The idea of "revolution" in fact proved to be a contributing factor to the Great War, not an antidote to it, despite the impressive forces for peace that existed among socialists. Thus, the pervasive willingness to promote violence that fed the First World War emerged not only from the right but also from large parts of the left. More than any other non-state actor, Parvus explored the possibilities of a left-right synergy for revolution and geostrategic transformation in the 1910s.

The world that he knew, and that he tried to dominate intellectually, was the economic and political power game of the "Old World" of Europe, Russia, and the Ottoman Empire. He was not familiar with the historical forces at work in England, let alone the United States. America's synergy of modernity and millennialism, and its distinctive notions of historical progress and Jewish-Christian relations, would have profoundly called into question the resentfulness of his Eurocentric, secular-apocalyptic, anti-*bourgeois* approach. Parvus lacked critical analysis of his own emotionally formative experiences in late tsarist Russia, including those in *shtetls* that were undergoing existential crisis, new social rifts, and an apocalyptic mood. Opting to study in Basel, not Zurich or Geneva, he tried to detach himself to a degree from these and similar dynamics within circles of the diaspora. His emotional intelligence, however, obeyed anti-Russian impulses, which he could easily connect to those of the political elite in Istanbul.

Enriched during war, the merchant of revolution could easily afford to buy a villa in Wädenswil by Lake Zurich, where, from November 1918, he intended to enjoy the sunset of his life away from the depressing devastation of war. Notorious and disliked by the local people, however, he was expelled in early 1920. Thus, he went to spend his last years in a villa in Berlin,[74] where he died in 1924. His friend Jäckh, on the other hand, was given the chance to leave the Old World in the wake of its seminal catastrophe. In the United States, Jäckh discovered a different world, one that allowed him to make a new personal, intellectual, and scholarly life for himself. Thus, he conceived a trans-Atlantic, anti-Soviet alliance and founded the Department of Near Eastern Studies at Columbia University in New York. After having believed in and advocated the transformative military power of Wilhelmine Germany, Jäckh put his trust successfully in the new trans-Atlantic superpower. Both in his trajectory and in that of Parvus, one may discover seeds of American neoconservatism.

It is true that Parvus had been a vociferous patriot of his adopted country, to whose power he had tied his political thinking in the 1910s. Like ex-Trotskyite neo-conservatives a generation later, he had been a fervent supporter of the Russian Revolution before turning vociferously anti-Bolshevik. In contrast to other intellectual supporters of war-cum-revolution in the 1910s, especially those on the right (e.g., Filippo T. Marinetti), he had not been fascinated by any personal experience of war. Cured, moreover, of his militaristic brand of socialism after the World War, Parvus became a mostly sober and at times lucid voice for a humble German pragmatism and for European cooperation. Now pointedly anti-Bolshevik, his efforts concentrated on European recovery, prosperity, and reconciliation. Even if he still adopted the tone of a prophet, he now did so in a more thoughtful fashion that focused on the peaceful reconstruction of Germany and on what he knew to be the virtues of Germany's hard-working, moderate Social Democracy.[75] This was a valid but (too) late plea for a potentially peaceful European future after the Great War. It almost completely lacked, however, historical introspection and soul-searching.

During his past as a missionary and merchant of socialist revolution, especially in 1914–17, Helphand Parvus had pushed his luck, played for high geopolitical and social-revolutionary stakes, and, measured against his own goals, failed. Neither his German nor his Russian hopes had materialized. One area where he had a successful and lasting impact, however, was the conception and establishment of the Turkish national economy. Born of his undogmatic and unprincipled flirtation with power, it transferred aspects of leftist thinking about social revolution to the right and the right's religious-racial concepts. This Turkish development of the 1910s anticipated a menacing evolution that would later occur, in an even more radical form, in his adopted German homeland, which had suffered more lasting wounds from the Great War than had Parvus himself.

Part IV

End of Empire, Time of Genocide

Turkey's and Germany's Affinity

Germany and Turkey share a painful and shameful story: the Armenian genocide and Germany's supporting role in it. During the Great War, imperial Germany and imperial Turkey were bound together by war goals, war constraints, war propaganda, and denial of domestic mass murder in Ottoman Turkey. On many levels, this fatal bond impacted both countries for decades. From August 1914, Berlin sided with and depended on the warmongering hawks of the CUP, Istanbul's "war party" that, as CUP insider Cavid repeatedly noted, consisted of minds marked by "chauvinism" (şovinizm) and "extremist nationalism" (müfrit nasyonalizm).[1]

Though with different ultimate goals, as revealed in Chapter 11, Parvus had, like the other Germans promoting war in Istanbul, embraced the imperialist agenda of a German-led "Greater Central Europe" whose influence would extend to Russia and to the Ottoman world.[2] For them, Germany—in particular, the German economy, culture, and science—deserved first place in the world. This was also the position of Parvus, even though he placed German domination within the context of a Euro-centric history of progress toward global socialism. Although it was at total war and under military censorship, Wilhelmine Germany left more room for dissent, civil engagement, and democratic agency than Imperial Russia and Turkey, as proven by the lives of deputy Matthias Erzberger and pastor Johannes Lepsius.

The more than four-year tie-up with the CUP regime for better or worse left its fatal imprints on both sides. Many Germans, also beyond the far right, admired the successful Turkish resistance, revisionism, and nationalism after World War defeat. The example of seemingly brilliant and promising success set by the former wartime ally in the larger context of the Lausanne Conference fueled revisionist and exclusionary social Darwinist nationalism in Germany. In particular, it facilitated the acceptance and internalization of related exterminatory policies. The former wartime ally was a prime example of how a treaty revision, a radically nationalist future and international reintegration could be enforced despite defeat in the First World War. This seemed to most Germans to be a positive path, in contrast to the fascinating but threatening rise of anti-Western Bolshevism.

12

Johannes Lepsius

A German Patriot and Protestant Internationalist

Johannes Lepsius was a prominent but somewhat different child of the German Empire, which makes him particularly interesting for a historical study. He knew how to use for his goals the cultural, political, and journalistic opportunities and the related networks, notably of churches, in the Wilhelmine Empire. As a key to understanding his prominence and achievements—including as a voice of truth and humanity during genocide—I have proposed to focus on him as a German member of the Protestant International of the nineteenth and early twentieth centuries.[1]

Johannes Lepsius's informal but active affiliation with an informal Protestant International placed him, like few other Germans of his time, in a global interaction. At the same time, this put him in a tension between patriotism and belonging to a dynamic transnational network. This was comparable to the situation of Social Democratic members of a Socialist International or of Christians belonging to the Catholic Church, but it led to even more serious tensions. Otherwise dominant dynamics in Berlin and Belle Époque Europe found themselves relativized by his affiliation to a Protestant International, however much Lepsius identified from his youth with the Kaiserreich and Martin Luther's Protestantism.

Johannes Lepsius participated in an informal movement that, from the late eighteenth century onward, claimed to be Christian, modern, and missionary. He was part of a transnational, predominantly English-speaking network of individuals and nongovernmental organizations whose spokesmen saw themselves as the vanguard of a future global society. In the early nineteenth century, this went hand in hand with a distinct Christian Zionism *avant la lettre*. One might regard the Calvinist International of the sixteenth and seventeenth centuries as one of its precursors, which, however, was not yet missionary in orientation but was primarily concerned with transnational self-preservation after the break with Catholicism.

Near East Millenarianism

I first encountered the retrospective term "Protestant International" as a student with the missionary historian Paul Jenkins, the co-supervisor of my licentiate thesis in Basel. Jenkins was studying, among other things, the trans-European cooperation of the Church Missionary Society with the Basel Mission in the first half of the nineteenth century. Basel formed a continental European hub of this International in the nineteenth century because of the Basel Mission and related organizations.

Johannes Lepsius came into contact with this network as a young assistant preacher in Jerusalem in the mid-1880s, where he also came into contact for the first time with Armenians, the ethnoreligious community in the late Ottoman Empire that participated most in the globalization of the nineteenth century. In Jerusalem, he married Margarethe Zeller, the granddaughter of Bishop Samuel Gobat, who had died a few years earlier. A native of the Bernese Jura who had been educated in Basel, Gobat had led the Prussian-British bishopric of Jerusalem for a third of a century. This bishopric stood for transnational Protestantism as well as the new symbolic and utopian meaning of the Ottoman Bible lands for the modern West in a time when faith and religion were losing ground in European public life to secular ideologies. But in turn, a religiously rooted, Middle Eastern–centered, utopian-apocalyptic spirit was having a powerful impact.

The Ottoman Empire had faced an existential crisis since the late eighteenth century; diplomacy called it the Eastern Question or Question d'Orient. Missionary-minded circles, mostly belonging to the Protestant International, interpreted this crisis as the historical hour when biblical prophecy would be realized in a modern framework. In the late Ottoman Empire, Americans formed the leading elements of the Protestant International. Until the First World War, the United States was present in the Near and Middle East mainly through missions, also increasingly economically, but hardly politically or militarily.[2]

Near East–focused millenarianism was a central component of the beliefs and ideas of the Protestant International. It was not, or not only, the vague intuition of an *ex oriente lux* (this is the title of a volume published by Johannes Lepsius in 1903)[3] or the dazzling, multi-layered phenomenon of a *holy land mania*, especially but not only American, as Hilton Obenzinger has called it.[4] For in the nineteenth century, a stream of pilgrims of various denominations arrived in Palestine by steamship on an unprecedented scale. At the center of Near East–centered millenarianism was the expectation of a global kingdom of God that would flourish from the Near Eastern Bible lands. American millenarianism, in particular, was and is a synthesis of modernism and millenarianism that, from the late eighteenth century onward, closely paralleled the previously more marginal Protestant vision of the "restoration of the Jews to Palestine and to Jesus" (see Chapter 2). Only then did American millenarianism— the commitment to a kingdom of God on earth which, according to Helmut Niebuhr, characterizes American Christianity[5]—become Near Eastern millenarianism.

The American Board of Commissioners for Foreign Missions (ABCFM) was the first American overseas mission, founded in 1810. It combined its goal of evangelizing worldwide and working toward the kingdom of God—or rather a modern republic of Jesus on Earth—with a vision of Jewish return and conversion. The service in Boston in the fall of 1818, before the first American missionaries were sent to the Ottoman Empire with Palestine as their destination, spoke a clear language in this regard. Carl F. Ehle, who studied Christian Zionism in the United States, called this vision and the self-commitment associated with it, "endemic to American culture."[6]

In short: In the horizon of an acute crisis of the Ottoman Empire and thus of an omnipresent Eastern Question, the talk of the fall of Islamic rule, of the reorganization of the Near East, and of the founding of a Jewish community in Palestine had been intensifying since the end of the eighteenth century. For this was the prerequisite for the modern millennium, and preparing it was considered the noblest task of American mission overseas.

Lepsius's Millenarianism and the German Orient Mission

We find Johannes Lepsius at the end of the nineteenth century involved in Middle Eastern millenarianism and in the network of the Protestant International. However, it was with a "German accent," to which I will return. The expectation of a kingdom of God on earth was not self-evident for an academic from an upper-middle-class background, although Dr. Lepsius served as a committed village pastor at that time. But he sought to clearly distinguish himself from both the Lutheran church orthodoxy, as he called it, and a modern European theology without a kingdom of God on earth. In the process, the Middle East captivated his global political and eschatological attention.

In 1900, Lepsius founded two magazines with the significant names *Der christliche Orient* and *Das Reich Christi* (*The Christian Orient* and *The Kingdom of Christ*). In them, and elsewhere, he wrote that humankind could reach its goal by no other way than the way of history, or historical evolution. The "Kingdom of God" is in constant realization until all peoples on earth are united in one kingdom of righteousness under one head, the king of Israel and ruler of the world, he wrote. To the dualistic-spiritualistic worldview of orthodoxy and modern theology, the message of a real kingdom of God on earth, and thus also the supplication in the Lord's Prayer, must remain a folly. As long as the people of Israel lived in dispersion, the fulfillment of the prophecy of Christ's kingdom was out of the question.[7]

It is hardly surprising that Lepsius was extremely interested in the then emerging Zionism and that in 1897, according to the local press,[8] he was one of the diligent visitors at the First Zionist Congress in Basel, a city with which he was already connected by various threads. Fifty years earlier, in the middle of the nineteenth century, a settler from Württemberg in Palestine, a forerunner of the German Templars, had noted in a letter that he considered it a high honor to be allowed to be a farmer and vineyard keeper of the now believing Israelites gathered again in Palestine in the soon to come kingdom of Christ.[9]

More than these and similar pietistic currents and precursors, Johannes Lepsius, like the Americans, fully affirmed the globalizing as well as the scientific and technical aspects of modernity. To subdue the earth was a sacred duty. God's polity, the kingdom of God, means nothing else than the rule of God over man and the rule of man over the earth, Lepsius insisted. Therefore, contemporary humankind spans a fine network of spirit and electricity over the entire surface of the earth, so that the head and heart of man can impose their will on the entire body of the earth.[10] Actually, the World

Wide Web and digital technology largely fulfilled these words spoken over a hundred years ago.

The Protestant International and its missionaries to the Ottoman world became increasingly committed to reforming, democratizing, and modernizing the Ottoman Empire—or "leavening the Levant," as they put it[11]—by their updated gospel. Their initial missionary strategy in the first third of the nineteenth century, focusing on converting Jews and Muslims in Palestine, had all in all failed. The ABCFM therefore turned to Oriental Christians, especially Armenians. It sought to build them up as forces of the future in a thoroughly reformed Ottoman and globalized world, rather than, as before, in an apocalyptic, soon-to-be post-Ottoman world. Since the Ottoman Reform Era (*Tanzimat*, considered starting in 1839), the ABCFM successfully engaged in education and health care, where it created lasting modern institutions. After the Young Turk Revolution of 1908, it intensified its commitment to reform, now again increasingly seeking to involve Muslims. Lepsius's project of an Islam seminar in Potsdam crystallized in those years.[12]

The American missionaries in the Levant had started without or with little diplomatic support. The first US embassy in the Ottoman capital opened only in 1906. The ABCFM members combined their commitment to Turkey after the 1908 revolution with the goal of a democratized and federalized Ottoman constitutional state. Therein lay evolutionary and revolutionary elements of a republican US civil religion compatible with faith in the Bible, and thus with a millenarianism of the Protestant International, which had roots in a few corners of modern continental Europe, such as Basel and Geneva. For German Lutheran Protestants, *Reich Gottes* (Kingdom of God) thought was inscribed with loyalty to the prince. When, in the Lord's Prayer, the request for a kingdom of God on earth was expressed, it resonated less with the idea of a modern, still utopian global republic of Jesus than with that of a quasi-fairy-tale kingdom that could hardly ever be of this world.

The two German missions, the *Christliche Orient-Mission* of Johannes Lepsius and the *Hülfsbund für christliches Liebeswerk im Orient*, which had begun at the end of the nineteenth century as Armenian relief organizations under American mentors, were increasingly concerned after 1908 to distinguish themselves as German organizations. Especially since, in contrast to before, supportive interest in them as cells of German influence was now germinating on the part of the Wilhelmine Empire.[13] For the mission director, theologian, and patriot Lepsius, a dream seemed to be realized in those last years of the Belle Époque. Namely, that finally Gospel and German fatherland, Orient mission, and Orient policy of German provenance reconciled to bring peace on the Ottoman-Armenian field of work, where his own small *Orient-Mission* was active. Henceforth, it seemed, it would thus be able to work together with German power for a common Orient project with millenarian dimensions.

The background for hoping for this cooperation was the remarkable pro-Armenian turn of German diplomacy at the beginning of 1913 in connection with the newly gained German insight into the necessity, according to the then Ambassador Wangenheim, of radically modern, constitutional reforms for the Ottoman eastern provinces.[14] Article 61 of the Berlin Treaty served as the basis for the reform postulates. German diplomacy took this turn in the context of a reformulated Baghdad railway

(*Bagdadbahn*) to influence policy. It was now—temporarily—much more sensitive to and inclusive of the Armenians (see Chapter 4).[15]

Cataclysm

The July crisis of 1914, the enthusiastic self-righteous affirmation of war in August— also by Johannes Lepsius—and the ensuing Great War have become the historical hour of truth for Europe, the Ottoman world, and the Protestant International. It shook up previous sublime values and credos, putting them through their paces. After the Great War, futures could no longer be projected in the same way as before 1914. The millenarianism of the Protestant International lost much of its coherence, its inherent optimism, and also many of its transnational networks.

It took until June 1915 for Lepsius to find his way back to his real task: to recognize the Armenian victims, to side with them, and to radically question the German war policy on the side of the CUP.[16] His Near East mission had always practiced solidarity— it began, after all, as Armenian relief. In its beginning in the 1890s, it went along critical contemporary analyses time and again. In this vein, Lepsius's *Indictment against the Christian Great Powers* of 1896 and *The Report on the Situation of the Armenian People* of 1916 stand out.[17] Both books were energetically researched, lucidly prepared, and efficiently addressed. For Lepsius, reporting—saying what is going on in a situation of extreme violence—went hand in hand with principal and practical solidarity with the victims. This combination makes up Lepsius's outstanding achievement in connection with the Armenian genocide.

In all of this and despite remarkable achievements, there remained an aporia for Lepsius's experience as a Protestant in the Second German Empire. There was no doubt for him that believing in the God of the Bible and being a Christian necessarily involved a prophetic and thus political dimension. But his commitment collided at times with his patriotism, and his millenarianism could not (entirely) escape the Wilhelmine urge for world recognition via oriental politics. The tension between faith and fatherland caused him extraordinary trouble in the last decade of his life, making it largely impossible for him to anticipate the future in any reasonable and confident way. This was his reality, and it was indeed a fatal, wide-ranging reality in Germany from the 1910s onwards.[18] Lepsius's problem was exacerbated by the fact that the universal visions of the Protestant International had largely collapsed in the late 1910s. Its evolutionary, progressive, so-called postmillennial, modernist eschatology literally lost its language during the World War. The missionary Protestant International itself, as it existed since the late eighteenth century, came to an end.

While the League of Nations adopted many secular tenets of the Protestant International, notably with regard to the Near East, the League's *political project* was dead within three years of the League's foundation (see Chapters 1 and 5). It is true that networks, which went back to the Protestant International, continued to make impressive achievements in the interwar period, for example in the supradenominational Near East Relief, which American missionary circles had founded in the fall of 1915. But the language and concepts of the Protestant

International, together with President Wilson's Middle East policy defined by missionary circles, did by no means prevail. Democracy, justice for war crimes, safety and self-determination for small peoples, a comprehensive US mandate to this end, and a modern Middle East confederation remained all wishful thinking. Darker, so-called premillennialist scenarios of the end times, which gave far less room to the active human advancement of a republic of Jesus on Earth, soon began to dominate American apocalypticism.[19]

In Lepsius's words of 1919, Jesus left not only the Paris Peace Conference but, having become a strange stranger, the world altogether.[20] For Johannes Lepsius at the end of the 1910s, main references fell away almost completely: the German Empire, the Protestant International, his Near East millenarianism, and his practical missionary project.

"Root Web of the World War"

After the Great War, Lepsius's earlier talk of the millennium was hardly any more suitable for projecting the future. He could no longer pick up where he left off. The language of the Protestant International, as he had adapted it to his German world, had faltered after the experience of total war. Christian talk of the millennium to be created had all but dried up. This applied especially to the Near East, where the Armenians, the main recipients of modern missions, had been the victims of extermination. Nevertheless, Lepsius continued looking for new and better horizons, for the possibility of another, peaceful world order.[21]

Lepsius's notions of world history and eschatology were fragile and questionable since he formulated them at the end of the nineteenth century. In some of his publications, there are, to put it mildly, ambivalent passages interspersed with German cultural Protestantism. Together with the philosopher of history Houston Steward Chamberlain, he then saw the Germanic peoples as being called to bring Christianity to rule in the world. In the same vein, he had equated Christian global culture with the kingdom of God, calling Germany, England, and the United States Protestant empires that ruled the world thanks to the spirit of Luther and Calvin.[22] All of these were elements of Protestant culturalism against which Karl Barth's dialectical theology took a resolute stance a few years later.[23] The First World War indeed falsified many things, and also for Johannes Lepsius.

All the more he sought to understand why the seminal catastrophe had happened, in whose center stood his beloved Germany. In his own words, he strove "to dig out the whole root system of the world war in the decades before the catastrophe and to expose the course of the gigantic roots from which the world ash of the war grew." He wanted to "present the history of the last ten years in a completely objective account to the whole world."[24] This could not be done in this way—certainly not in the German situation at that time and in this totality, and above all not with the (partly) apologetic intentions of Lepsius. He remained fixated on the trauma of the Great War in which he, too, had lost a beloved son at the front.

His wish of "a completely objective representation" of the origins of the war was informed both by the myth of German innocence—the *Kriegsunschuldlegende* so typical of the "Weimar consensus"—and the myth of a definitive and objective public historiography. Early on, he felt the danger of radicalizing German protagonists who considered previous politics as much too meek, wanted "to turn the tables," and argued that "we Germans will then be the aggressive nation and again turn the fortune."[25] From the Lausanne Conference onward, Turkish nationalists looked down on democratic-minded people's belief in Germany in "salvation not by force but politics, thus duping themselves." They felt sorry for Germans who had gotten into a predicament and lost sight of the supposed iron law of the "merciless struggle for life in international politics."[26]

Lepsius could not contribute to a substantial change of mentality in post–Great War Germany. Why? Insisting on representing German foreign policy since Bismarck as fundamentally peaceful,[27] he did not take the case of the Armenians—fright over the genocide together with the frank confession of co-responsibility, failed help, and untruthfulness—as the implacable lever for a German *metanoia*. Even if in a somewhat original interpretation one considered with Lepsius the *Bagdadbahn* as a genuinely peaceful project and true alternative to sea-based imperialism, German failures in 1914 and 1915 were reason enough to engage in soul-searching without any complacency.

Nevertheless, Johannes Lepsius achieved something historically significant in the last decade of his life. Apart from Armenians themselves, very few people at the time were tackling the task of coming to terms with contemporary Ottoman-Armenian history. It was this task, and the empathy it entailed, that set limits to Lepsius's own resentment of Germany's fate. "As bad as it looks in our own fatherland, even our misery does not come close to this murder of a nation [Völkermord] that the Young Turks have on their conscience," he wrote in 1919 in the preface to the second edition of his fundamental report of 1916.[28] This solidarity and also a good portion of humor time and again prevented cynicism from arising—although very many things, including his German patriotism, Near Eastern millenarianism, and Christian Zionist visions had almost completely broken down.[29]

Ambassador Wangenheim and the CUP

Sliding into Moral Defeatism

From July 1912 until his death in October 1915, Baron Hans von Wangenheim was the head of the German embassy in Istanbul, one of the most important political hubs of the Belle Époque. If his term in office was successful, he could hope to become head of the foreign office or to receive some other important assignment in Berlin. During the July crisis of 1914, he opposed a war alliance with Ottoman Turkey, but was persuaded otherwise following a hint from the emperor. Soon, he came to enjoy the part of warmonger and most powerful European ambassador in Istanbul before his noiseless personal and political downfall in the summer of 1915. He embodies an early, pervasive loss of moral compass in German political life at the beginning of the World War era.

In 1913, Wangenheim had arrived at the insight—albeit not very firmly established— that Germany and Russia should jointly campaign for reforms in Eastern Anatolia in order to guarantee the safety of the Ottoman Armenians and a common Ottoman future (see Chapter 4). There was talk of "Armenian reforms." This new insight broke with Germany's previous policy regarding Turkey, within which the understanding of the "Armenian Question" had followed the official Ottoman view of foreign-controlled subversion. The relevant Reform Agreement was signed on February 8, 1914. In line with his war policy, Wangenheim lost sight of both the Agreement as well as the Armenians and the Ottoman Christians as a whole. When various personages solicited him for protection of the mortally endangered minority in spring 1915, he declared that he was not responsible for a *nobile officium*, as he termed it, whose content, that is, humanity and Christian solidarity, was beyond military logic.

Toward the end of May 1915, Wangenheim granted the ally a geographically and temporarily limited resettlement of "politically suspect" Armenian families. When he became aware of the actual policy of comprehensive eradication shortly afterward, he was overcome with fury but did not know-how to react adequately. Mentally weakened and emotionally devastated, he was put on leave for weeks. He ultimately suffered a stroke and died in the autumn, a shadow of his former self. In spite of Wagenheim's support of Turkey's policy of denial and of cynical statements by several of its representatives, Germany in principle expected that the surviving Armenians would be resettled in their homeland and their property returned after the war. This expectation caused the reigning Young Turks in Istanbul lasting worry.

Fruit of Haste with Fatal Consequences: The 1914 German-Ottoman War Alliance

Compiling a minimum of biographical information on Wangenheim is no easy task. While his name recurs in literature, memoirs, and archives in connection with the fateful first year of the World War in the Ottoman Empire, he has been forgotten as a person, an instigator of projects, and a figure of German history. Indeed, his ideas have long since become historical footnotes. In contrast to Wangenheim, there is a wealth of information on Young Turk collaborators and opponents. The Ottoman Empire was headed by a committee named "Unity and Progress" (*Comité Union et Progrès*), whose leading figure—as the readers of this book already know—was the interior minister of the time, Talaat Bey (later Pasha). This revolutionary-minded *komiteci* (committee militant) became Wangenheim's principal addressee, although both often communicated via third parties as well, namely Enver and Cavid.[1]

As opposed to Wangenheim's ideas, central aspects of Talaat's ambitions have, in the long term, been realized. This difference in success correlates with a fundamental difference between German and Young Turk war objectives. In contrast to the former, the latter had both maximal and minimal goals. The latter they defined as existential. As they had long been concerned with scenarios of political ruin, even a lost World War did not spell the end of all their plans. Ever since the trauma of the Balkan Wars of 1912–13, the Young Turks had pinned their hopes on a right-wing revolution, that is, a social revolution in favor of Turkish Muslims. At the expense of all non-Muslims, Asia Minor should become the national home of the Turks. At the same time, the empire outside Anatolia ought to be preserved and, as of August 1914, expanded eastward toward "Turan" with German backing.[2]

Talaat's friend Ziya Gökalp, an influential member of the committee and ideological father of Turkish-Muslim nationalism, exalted the term "Turan" to signify a mythically elevated Turkish primal home beyond the Caucasus. In autumn 1914, "To Turan" became the battle cry of a young generation of officers, civil servants, and intellectuals enthusiastic about the Great War. This suited Wangenheim just fine, as he urged quick anti-Russian action in the Caucasus. In August 1914, the German-Ottoman war alliance spurred his illusion of a quick victory. Indeed, the committee had been organizing attacks in the southern Caucasus and northern Persia since August 1914— three months before Ottoman Turkey officially entered the war. These strikes involved units of its Special Organization along with locally recruited men whose ideological base consisted of a mixture of Turanism and pan-Islamism.

Wangenheim fought for more German influence in the late, possibly soon-to-be post-Ottoman world in order to promote Germany's supremacy on the European Continent and its high standing in the world. Committee politics were alien to him. Before 1914, his projection of the future of the Middle East partly contained constructive responses to late Ottoman challenges and deficits of other European powers' Middle Eastern policies. This is particularly true for the enduring infrastructure project of the Baghdad railway. Initially cautious in his approach, and then, in late July 1914, more proactive, the German diplomat, unfamiliar with his ally, maneuvered himself into a political dead end. German policy toward Turkey during the Great War was characterized, on the whole, by fundamentally untruthful communication on various levels. This exacerbated deficits that were already inherent in the German political system before the July crisis, and contributed to the Wilhelmine Empire inadvertently losing its own constitutional substance, which as yet was fragmentary and fragile.

Germany turned into the epitome of the (self-)destructive loser, not just from 1914 to 1918, but with regard to the whole World War era. By contrast, and in spite of their defeat in the Great War, the Young Turks and their Kemalist successors emerged as (limited) winners, albeit as unscrupulous ones, whose foundation was therefore fragile in the long term. Paul Rohrbach, an employee at the Foreign Office and member of the German-Armenian society, wrote to Ernst Jäckh on September 21, 2015: "The news we receive here of the eradication of Armenia are dreadful [. . .] Enver has coldly confirmed to Lepsius that they now wanted to finish off the Armenians once and for all. Morally, this breaks the backbone of the German-Turkish alliance."[3] This political and ethical fracture coincided with the personal breakdown of the German ambassador in Istanbul.

Like Jäckh and Wangenheim, Rohrbach had been banking on a Turkey reinvigorated by German aid as the key to German world power and Middle Eastern predominance. A vociferous publicist of German-Ottoman war policy, his addressee, "Türken-Jäckh" as he was called by contemporaries, could be described as one of the early carriers of that underestimated German fever for Turkey explored by Stefan Ihrig in his recent publications.[4] Young Turkism and Kemalism have long been deemed exotic or marginal by Western academic history. However, they appear to have been the sole immediate models of total national revolution to German nationalists, who saw their systematic unscrupulousness both domestically as well as outwardly as a prerequisite for viability. "Turkish recipes" became the obvious choice. During the interwar period, the "Kemalist Revolution" and Ataturk's "New Turkey" were deemed astonishingly successful not only by them, but generally in the West.

Because he was following a rash and hubristic agenda, Wangenheim was taken in by hitherto unknown *komiteci* at the head of an empire. Their front lines were not restricted to those of a conventional war but extended to the interior in a revolutionary way. Politically, this was uncharted territory. Wangenheim stumbled, while others, in particular officers such as his naval attaché Hans Humann, succumbed to the fascination of ruthless revolutionaries and seemingly expedient mass violence even against civilians.[5] To stay with the metaphor, Wangenheim, proceeding at the pace which he had chosen at the emperor's command, had run the risk of stumbling and not regaining his footing. This was, indeed, to be his fate.

Less exposed than Rohrbach, Lepsius, Erzberger, and others, opportunists such as Jäckh could "reinvent themselves," without assuming responsibility for the ethical fracture of 1915, or even beginning to face the heinous crime for what it was. Rohrbach resigned from the German-Turkish society, which Talaat and Enver also were members of, telling board member Jäckh that "Germany's name would remain besmirched" as long as Turkey did not make atonement, and that if no atonement was made, he would cease "to be German in the political sense." Meanwhile, an increasing number of frustrated Germans began adopting Young Turk methods as unavoidable tools for political success.[6]

The Mantra of a Renewed Turkey and the Weakness for *Komiteci* (1913–14)

A German Oriental policy that had remained utopian prior to the World War can be summarized as the convergence rather than the divergence of Wangenheim and Lepsius, of a politics of interest and of nation building inspired by Christian and humanitarian ideas. The above-mentioned Reform Agreement of February 8, 1914, and a concomitant constitutional prospect for the Ottoman state would have provided the framework. The backbone of Germany's politics of interest had been the *Bagdadbahn* (Baghdad railway project) and further infrastructural, economic, or cultural projects. Unlike the other railways, which tended to serve narrowly defined interests of foreign powers in the vicinity of Ottoman ports, the Baghdad railway fundamentally improved the infrastructure of the Ottoman world.

Wangenheim had been transferred from Athens to Istanbul in June 1912, succeeding longtime ambassador Adolf Marschall von Bieberstein. After a couple of months' settling in under the leadership of Grand Vizier Muhtar, and later, Kamil Pasha, Wangenheim saw himself confronted with demands for reform made by the Armenians to the liberal-conservative Ottoman government, of which he first informed Berlin on January 2, 1913. On January 10, 1913, he received instructions from the undersecretary of state in the Foreign Office, Arthur Zimmermann, "not to leave the fate of the Armenians to the Triple Entente alone." Consequently, he took up the challenge of involving himself in the "Armenian Question."[7] He revised Germany's previous attitude and its underlying views—including Germany's previous extenuation of the massacres under Sultan Abdulhamid II—and wrote detailed reports with historical references.

In the words of the Austrian ambassador Pallavicini, Wangenheim had, by spring 1913, already laid the foundation for a new "German policy towards Turkey."[8] As far as the conflictual establishment of the military mission under Liman von Sanders in late 1913 and the negotiations toward the agreement of February 8, 1914, were concerned, he did not remain unsuccessful. As of late 1913, he enjoyed a strong position in every quarter. He distanced himself from his predecessor by demanding that Germany's "Anatolian efforts" should no longer rest on "feet of clay," but on a broader, political as well as cultural foundation.[9] Unlike Pallavicini, Wangenheim believed that Turkey could regenerate and regarded the committee as the solid core within the state.[10]

The mantra of reinvigorating Turkey, which young, energetic committee members, along with Germany, had committed themselves to, had stirred within Wangenheim ever since the committee had seized power for good in a coup in January 1913. Only by the committee "could Turkey be expected to be saved," and only with its aid could "Germany implement its plans here," Wangenheim wrote on August 8, 1913.[11] He admired the audacity of the *komiteci*, who had disregarded the London Treaty of May 30, 1913, and had reconquered Edirne, which had been lost during the First Balkan War, in July. He expressed his fascination for Talaat to Cavid, the minister of finance: "He has accomplished the matter masterfully and has performed a true masterstroke."[12]

However, the ambassador kept his distance for the time being; he wanted to be able to work with a different government again, too, should the need arise.[13] In a private letter to Foreign Secretary Jagow, he explained his sympathy for the Turks as not arising from emotions, but from "cool political calculation" alone. However, the letter reveals romantic essentialist ideas concerning the national character of the "Turk" as the "only gentleman of the Orient" and an affinity toward Sunni Turks loyal to the empire.[14] A year later, in August 1914, Wangenheim expressed the belief that true friends of the Germans could only be found among the Turks, not among the Greeks or Levantines. He considered Enver, Talaat, and Halil to be Germanophiles from the depth of their hearts, not just out of self-interest.[15]

Until the assassination of Grand Vizier Mahmut Şevket Pasha on June 11, 1913, it was he that Wangenheim had primarily dealt with, followed by his successor Said Halim, whom he perceived as strongly dependent on the Young Turk committee. However, Wangenheim barely knew the inner workings of the committee. Thus, in late 1913, he considered Cemal to be the decisive figure within the committee when it came to the question of reform, and in April 1914, he believed Halil to be its most influential figure regarding foreign policy. He seems to have remained unaware of Talaat's dominant influence, both with regard to the latter two aspects, as well as within the committee as a whole.

With his new commitment to the Armenian Question, the continuation of the Baghdad railway, and a renewed, ambitious military mission, Wangenheim had opted for increased German involvement. However, he remained aware of the limits of German "Oriental policy" and showed himself willing to compromise when dealing with fellow ambassadors, among whom he strove for pre-eminence. He was particularly careful to duly coordinate his efforts with Great Britain and Russia. In spite of his new interest in the Armenians, he continued cultivating Germany's special friendship with Ottoman Turkey's rulers. Talaat's confidant Cavid, who was the minister of finance in 1913–14, judged him to be "extraordinarily Turkophile."[16] Like the Austrian military attaché Joseph Pomianowski, Cavid deemed the German minister manipulable and not very competent with regard to the Armenian Question. As opposed to the majority within the Young Turk committee after 1912, the "crypto-Jew" (*dönme*) Cavid placed value on a peaceful and equal common Ottoman future that included the Armenians.[17]

In spite of supporting Ottoman objections during the negotiations, Wangenheim believed in securing an Armenian future as part of the agreement of February 8, 1914. To many serious observers and protagonists, it seemed a sound compromise and a worthwhile investment in a lawful Ottoman future. When he was simultaneously gripped by the European war fever and a fever for Turkey in late July 1914, however, Wangenheim began to lose touch with reality. "As far as the defense of Armenia is concerned, we'd become allies of England," he mused on July 31, 1914. On the same day, he urged for the conclusion of an alliance with Turkey, which was directed against Russia and therefore also against the Entente and Great Britain.[18]

A forced war against the Russian Caucasus did not simply imply the cancellation of Germany and Russia's joint support of the "Armenian reforms"; it acutely endangered the multiethnic region where these were to be implemented. This was, however, in the interest of the committee, which had become hostile to the Armenians and in the meantime had come to prefer local Sunni strongmen to its former ally of the 1908 revolution. Only very reluctantly had it acceded to the Agreement of February 1914.

Playing the Wrong Part: The Ambassador as Warmonger

Until the 1914 July crisis, the CUP Central Committee had been a more or less impersonal "black box" to Wangenheim, of which he wrote that it was a "group where ideas, but not personalities reign."[19] The inner web of its interpersonal relations was unknown to him. He held himself politely, yet benevolently aloof from the committee, which can be described as a German patronage of CUP Turkey based on mutual interest. Initial advances by the heads of the committee, who approached him about an alliance during the July crisis, were met with a cool reception.

This habitus of Wangenheim relied on a peaceful Oriental policy. When Emperor Wilhelm ordered him to cooperate with the Young Turks, who were keen on an alliance, it changed abruptly. At the same time, Austria had advocated joining forces with Istanbul in order to teach Serbia a lesson. Talaat, Enver, and Grand Vizier Said Halim strongly encouraged Pallavicini to do so. By presenting the prospect of an Ottoman rapprochement with the Entente, Enver and Talaat deliberately added fuel to the Austrian flames and put pressure on Germany. On August 2, Said Halim and Wangenheim signed a highly secret treaty.[20] Thenceforth, Wangenheim was the servant of an alliance and war policy which not he but Enver and Talaat had suggested, and which his master, the emperor, had imposed.

Wangenheim's communication with Talaat and Enver increased. The former diplomatic distance melted away. Time and again, Wangenheim lost his temper. On the one hand, Berlin had instructed him to persuade Ottoman Turkey to take military action against Russia and British-administered Egypt as quickly as possible; on the other hand, he was expected to contribute to Turkey's successful total mobilization and further consolidation. Constantly involved in negotiations, he had to accede to far-reaching demands for financial aid and arms deliveries. When Talaat unilaterally canceled the capitulations on September 9, 1914, thereby reaping the first fruits of the war alliance without prior consultation, Wangenheim was infuriated. At his meeting with him on the same day, Cavid saw himself "face to face with a rabid dog," as he noted in his diary. "He didn't speak but barked."[21]

Germany's ally had achieved one of the central goals of the partnership it had initiated: a hitherto unknown authority. "Henceforth, the temerity to act domestically and outwardly was gone and the government saw itself as a [sovereign] government," Muhittin Birgen, the editor of the Young Turk newspaper *Tanin* and later advisor to Talaat, wrote.[22] In addition to canceling the capitulations, the government did not hesitate to suspend the Reform Agreement in August/September 1914, block the Dardanelles, and prohibit foreign postal services. In order to stay true to his pre-war version of German Oriental policy, the German ambassador would have had to adhere to the Reform Agreement. However, he was anxious to respect the Young Turks' insistence on sovereignty in order to enforce the military priorities demanded of him.

In an amendment to the treaty of alliance on August 6, Wangenheim had taken it upon himself to give permission for the committee's irredentist war of conquest and "Islamic revolutionization" in the Caucasus to go ahead. The amendment to the treaty euphemistically stated that "Germany will procure a minor border revision on behalf of Turkey, which shall bring her within direct contact with the Muslims in Russia."[23]

The committee was aware that observance of the treaty demanded partaking in the war and not simply conducting irregular actions. Therefore, the official entry into the war could not be drawn out for very long. In October, the leading committee members and Wangenheim agreed on a naval attack in the Black Sea in order to provoke an open war with Russia. Thenceforth, the German ambassador enjoyed a more powerful position in the Ottoman capital than ever before.[24] In return, he offered compliance when it came to the Young Turks' domestic activities.

Turkey had made it quite clear that it counted on German victory; at the same time, Germany was evidently dependent on Turkey. Wangenheim's manifest desire for quick Ottoman military operations cleared the way for demands from the ruling Young Turks who knew how to use German dependency to their advantage. Since August, Wangenheim had believed in "revolutionary Islam" as a quick super-weapon outside Europe. He thus began to push for overambitious military plans to advance into the Caucasus and beyond the Suez channel.

Max von Oppenheim's programmatic treatise on *Revolutionizing the Islamic Possessions of Our Enemies*[25] portrayed jihad as a fantastic weapon. Oppenheim led the Foreign Office's propagandist Intelligence Bureau for the East, which had been founded in 1914. Drawing on anti-Oriental Christian stereotypes, his article documented how quickly German Oriental policy departed from the spirit of the Reform Agreement, which, indeed, had remained alien to many in the first place, among them the assiduously collaborating guild of professional Orientalists. Carl F. Lehmann-Haupt, a historian of the ancient Middle East and friend of Lepsius, remained a lone warrior in a discursive context where anti-Christian and/or anti-Jewish gibes as well as a culturalist flirtation with imperial Islam and ancient Oriental myths and empires prevailed.[26]

As late as the embassy's New Year's reception, Wangenheim reassured a representative of Armenian patriarch Zaven that as long as Germany remained Turkey's partner, no Ottoman Armenian had anything to fear. Shortly before, he had assured the patriarch that although the Reform Agreement might have been postponed, it was not canceled; in truth, Talaat had annulled the treaties with the reform inspectors via a cabinet decision and sultan's decree on December 29, 1914, thereby effectively abandoning the contract.[27] When Zaven visited him on February 20, the ambassador again confirmed Germany's commitment to the protection of the Armenians and to reforms following the war.[28] Fixated on war and an inflated sense of global standing, Wangenheim's perception, thoughts, and words became increasingly incoherent. Taking euphemistic Ottoman telegrams at face value, he attempted to deceive himself and colleagues in Istanbul about the catastrophic defeat of Enver Pasha's Caucasian campaign in late 1914, which he had pressed for.[29]

Into the Abyss—Politically, Morally, and Personally

In autumn 1914, a reluctant Wangenheim had been assigned a military role and had thus achieved an extraordinary position of power, which involved the privileged interaction with Young Turk partners. Their way of communicating, however, was unfamiliar to him; this was further complicated by the war. The Ottoman Great War was more total than the one in Europe in that the Young Turk committee government opened fronts both outwardly and domestically. Total war of the military kind—mass destruction, mass killings, the use of poison gas as well as submarine attacks, even against civilian ships—was demonstrated to the world by Europe with increased intensity up until spring 1915.

The committee government had a lot to gain both domestically and abroad. Defeats at one front could be compensated with successful measures at another. Stratagems of a war thus redefined included forced mass migration, expropriation, as well as the massacring of the state's own citizens and the plundering of their property. This understanding of a total world war, in which genocide became an option, remained alien to Wangenheim.[30] A self-determined policy toward the committee and its multifront fighting would, however, have required skepticism and an anticipation of the worst possible outcome.

Interior Minister Talaat, by contrast, had a precise idea of the possibilities of forced resettlements; he was well aware of the fact that if their goal was to be the Syrian desert, they would end in death. Local CUP gangs had successfully driven up to 200,000 Rûm (Christian-Orthodox citizens) from the Aegean coast in spring 1914 and settled Muslim refugees from the Balkans in their stead. These actions were implicitly justified by Talaat in parliament at the beginning of July 1914. A similar, intensified course of action was therefore to be anticipated, as was its deadly outcome provided there were no foreign ships at hand to bring the victims to safe shores, as had been the case on the Aegean coast.[31] Unlike his more critical contemporaries, Wangenheim seemed to have accepted Talaat's justification of spontaneous rioting on the part of frustrated Muslim refugees from the Balkans and to have ignored the demographic engineering the committee had accomplished by this move.

Those who followed publications in the capital, however, knew that the committee—in accordance with the rapidly growing *Türk Yurdu / Türk Ocağı* movement—wanted to free Anatolia from foreign interference and make it a safe haven, that is, the sovereign national home, *Türk Yurdu*, for Turkish-speaking Muslims. This was the CUP's minimal goal and concerned domestic policy. After the outbreak of the World War, it took a back seat to the Ottoman campaigns in the Caucasus, Northern Iran, and Egypt. From the Young Turks' point of view, these pursued the empire's maximum expansive and restorative goals. Wangenheim must have known that by 1914, the CUP's and the Turkist movement's ethnoreligious, primarily Muslim and Turkish concept of nation fundamentally differed from that of the Ottoman constitution of 1908.

A new, immediate threat to the empire—not just in the East, but in proximity to the capital where the Entente was attacking—was added to the defeats in the expansive and restorative campaigns, along with a long, religiously polarized Eastern Front that ran right through the civilian population. All this contributed to the Young Turks' minimal goal of *Türk Yurdu* taking center stage again in March 1915, together with defending Istanbul. In letters to the governors and the army on April 24, 1915, Talaat therefore conjured up the threat of a general Armenian uprising and of Armenian autonomy in Anatolia. According to him, they endangered the future of the country, in other words, the minimal goal. As late as the end of March, Talaat had described disturbances in Zeitun as isolated instances to embassy employee Mordtmann. In spring 1915, local army reports repeatedly denied there was a general uprising.[32]

In March, April, and May 1915, Wangenheim received a wealth of information from his consuls, staff, and from Zaven, as well as from Lepsius's network—all of whom drew attention to the threat that the Armenians stood under. The German embassy also possessed a report by Dr. Liparit Nasariantz, a cofounder of the German-Armenian society, which emphasized that as a result of the World War, Germany had become the only European great power that could assume responsibility for the Christians in the Eastern provinces.[33] Wangenheim did not simply discount these reports but disastrously counterbalanced them with statements by the Turkish ally. In mid-April 1915, at pains not to disgruntle the committee, he therefore argued:

> But the present hostile mood towards the Armenians within government circles further limits our efforts for the Armenians and calls for particular caution. Otherwise, we run the risk of jeopardizing more immediate interests for a possibly hopeless cause.[34]

This was an embarrassing admission of defeatism. Wangenheim declared the protection of the endangered Armenians and Germany's own ethical standards "possibly hopeless" and therefore dispensable. He renounced the *nobile officium*, as he called it in the same letter, from the outset. In accordance with, as he believed, pragmatic German interests, the ambassador held on to his unguarded purposeful optimism, softening critical messages. Out of fear of mistrust and conflicts, he gave the Germanophiles on the committee undue credit, even with regard to the sensitive Armenian Question. He did so at least as long as he believed he could still somehow argue for a reassuring, militarily strategic version of events. This timespan was sufficient for Talaat to eliminate Armenian elites and set wholesale deportations in motion.

In late May 1915, Wangenheim's misguided communication with Enver and Talaat culminated in his granting Enver's request:

> to close large numbers of Armenian schools, repress Armenian newspapers, prohibit Armenian postal correspondence, and to resettle all not entirely blameless families from presently insurrectionary Armenian centers in Mesopotamia in order to contain Armenian espionage and to prevent renewed Armenian mass uprisings, using the state of war emergency.[35]

Around the same time, the ambassador's office deigned to draft an entirely apologetic response to the Entente's declaration of May 24, 1915, which held the members of the committee government responsible for crimes against humanity. In this draft, Wangenheim identified with the committee's position and pointed to disloyal Armenian activities influenced from abroad.[36] He placed himself in the same leaky boat as the committee, as far as honest history was concerned.

Little Acceptance, but Hardly Any Escape
Routes: Turkey Policy 1915–18

Only a few days later, Wangenheim's bearing and discourse became untenable. The views hitherto presented were immediately falsified in light of news from the provinces and frank conversations with committee members. Wangenheim now abruptly reversed his narrative, exposing the Young Turks' Armenian policy as the extermination of the Armenian race in the Ottoman Empire.[37]

In June 1915, Wangenheim's self-conception as representative of the German allied power, and co-architect of a new Oriental policy since 1913, totally collapsed. His martial star—the destiny that Emperor Wilhelm had bestowed on him in July 1914 by instructing him to go ahead with the war alliance—faded too. US Ambassador Henry Morgenthau's diary entry for July 12, 1915, records that Wangenheim had had a nervous breakdown and was therefore unable to work. Not long after, a burn out, an imminent vacation, longing for peace, and the intention of lodging a complaint with the committee government because of the Armenians, are also mentioned.[38] Having repressed any thoughts of the worst possible, albeit predictable, outcome, Wangenheim, as well as his superiors, was at a loss. Cynicisms began to creep in. Despite a sense of profound shock, the only viable option seemed to be superficial damage control and half-hearted protests. Adequate, courageous decisions designed to save what was yet to be saved did not even come into consideration.

Depending on individual efforts, and provided it did not offend the committee government, Germany offered modest support to humanitarian ventures, albeit only to low-profile aid by NGOs.[39] To the worst case of the Young Turk genocide, the Foreign Office thus added the worst case of a political culture, which not only failed to spell out what had happened but laid the blame on the victims and only sought to limit the reputational damage caused. It intended, as Undersecretary of State Arthur Zimmermann wrote in early August 1915:

> to demonstrate that a widely dispersed, subversive Armenian movement indeed existed in Turkey, whose suppression was a dictate of self-preservation to the Porte, and that the Armenians are being incited to their highly treasonous activities by the Entente Powers, who therefore bear the moral responsibility for the consequences.[40]

Talaat had failed to provide any evidence to support the general mistrust toward the Armenians. Mild protests, which did not call the alliance itself and Germany's massive material support of its ally into question, caused little or no pain to the committee government. Returned to his post for a brief spell in October 1915, Wangenheim made reference to social Darwinist patterns in order to prove the impossibility of Armenian-Turkish coexistence. He proposed to Morgenthau that those who had so far survived be sent to the United States or Poland, in order that they might yet be saved. As was suggested to him by circles close to the embassy, Jews from Poland could be resettled in regions from where the Armenians had been removed. More than ever, he saw final victory as the only solution.[41]

In autumn 1915, the ambassador was but a shadow of his former self. To Morgenthau, he seemed like the sinister Germanic god Wotan. Wangenheim's influence on the committee, which he had built up during the 1913 negotiations on a reform agreement and had fully enjoyed as Germany's representative during the first months of the war, had dwindled. Two strokes put an end to his life in October 1915.[42] Even though the German conception of a world centered on the Levant had collapsed with Wangenheim, Berlin continued its collaboration with Ottoman Turkey as though nothing had happened. In fact, it even expanded it.[43]

If we readjust Zimmermann's words, the Foreign Office had, in accordance with Young Turk propaganda, shifted "the moral responsibility" onto the Entente.[44] In truth, Germany had, to paraphrase Rohrbach, morally broken its own neck and backbone. Ever since its proactive approach in late July 1914, it had thrown in its lot with the committee government. In spite of the extreme developments on the part of the CUP party-state, it was neither willing nor able to revise this bond. Against its better judgment, it at least partly adopted a propagandistically distorted depiction of the fate of the Armenians. As it turned a deaf ear to the *Zivilisationsbruch* and destruction of the Ottoman social fabric by the CUP, it rendered itself susceptible to the kind of behavior patterns, ideology, and historical misrepresentation that coincided with the brutal end of Ottoman coexistence.

A Conscience Buried but Not Silenced

The CUP coup in January 1913 stood in stark contrast to the Ottoman spring of the 1908 revolution, which had enjoyed broad consent and had claimed to guarantee an Ottoman future on the basis of constitutional patriotism. Ever since its authoritarian successes in 1913, the committee pursued a policy that can be conceived of as a right-wing revolution. A regime of determined committee members wanted to re-mold the existing society in the Anatolian heartland in favor of its Muslim community and, from August 1914, to restore and expand the remaining territory of the empire. From July 1914 onward, in his sudden war fever, Wangenheim had forged a close bond with this policy of imperial ultranationalism. Berlin carried this close cooperation on for four years.

Some critical arguments existed within the Foreign Office itself, even if mostly at its margins only. Voices of reason criticized the haste, the excessiveness, and the precarious foundation of the war alliance. They particularly condemned the unprecedented crime of 1915 and refused to buy into its logic. They remained subdued, however, and barely audible from the outside. Compliant and ready to back Turkey's propaganda of denial, Germany conveyed the impression of having more or less been forced to give its blessing to the CUP's Armenian policy. Nonetheless, Berlin never revised its position that it had only ever agreed to limited and temporary resettlements, as Wangenheim had fatally done on May 31, 1915. Time and again, Matthias Erzberger and other representatives indicated that they could not and would not defend Turkey's Armenian policy at a peace conference in the wake of the World War.

Personalities as disparate as Erzberger, Lepsius, and Rohrbach, who were all associated with the Foreign Office, regarded the return of the Armenian survivors and the restitution of their property as the minimal standard of atonement or redress. This was not the case for Wangenheim, whose ethical defeatism in spring 1915 evolved into confusion, cynicism, and extreme views before his untimely death in October 1915. During the final year of the war, franker statements in the Reichstag concerning the Armenians, as well as serious German-Turkish conflicts in the Caucasus, gave rise to Turkish fear that Armenian life could bud once more with German support. Up to the end of the World War, this frequently caused anxiety in Talaat's circle.[45]

Democrat Matthias Erzberger and Turkey

"Turkey has become a burden to us. The relevant French, English and American publications on the slaughter of the Armenians make us German democrats blush with shame. Therefore, it will be difficult for Germany, and in particular for us German democrats, to defend Turkey once peace talks with the enemy begin. Unfortunately, Turkey now bears a major blemish."[1] Thus Matthias Erzberger (1875–1921), a democratically minded member of the Reichstag, confronted Muhittin Birgen, editor-in-chief of *Tanin*, the most important Young Turk newspaper. Birgen simultaneously functioned as advisor to Grand Vizier Talaat Pasha, who also arrived in Berlin at the time and showed himself concerned upon receiving Birgen's report of his conversation with Erzberger.[2]

According to Birgen, Erzberger had, in the summer of 1917, become the leader of a democratic and socialist opposition, which had been weakening the government ever since, and had been distancing itself from Turkey because of the Armenians. To him, the latter was a sign of German confusion. "We Turks have a clean conscience and know ourselves to be free of sin," he apparently told Erzberger.[3] In his memoirs, which stem from the 1930s, the heyday of Turkish ultranationalism, Birgen deigned to observe that Erzberger had paid for his lack of realism by being assassinated.[4] The prevailing opinion among nationalists, both in Turkey and abroad, was that the Armenian issue, as discussed in certain German circles, was an example of misplaced humanity for victims who had deserved their fate. In their view, the issue was resolved once and for all when the Treaty of Lausanne had approved unitary Turkish rule in Asia Minor in 1923 and had thus, implicitly, endorsed the methods by which this rule was achieved.

Since 1989, knowledge on the Armenian genocide has grown markedly. Outside Turkey, the Armenian Question has increasingly come to be understood as an unmet crucial benchmark for human rights standards in wider Europe; the treatment of the Ottoman Armenians during the First World War is broadly recognized as an incisive crime against humanity. All ethicality consists of granting the Other a future, both individually and collectively. The existence and future of the late Ottoman Armenians in the regions they had inhabited for millennia were gravely endangered. Since the late nineteenth century, large sections of the European and American public had, for good reason—and also due to a sense of Christian solidarity—started to become aware of the Armenian plight. This inspired a supra-confessional human rights movement that reacted to the mass murders of the 1890s under Sultan Abdulhamid. In the Berlin Treaty of 1878, European diplomacy had committed to ensuring that reforms for the security of the Armenians be implemented—wherein it ultimately failed completely (see Chapter 4).

For the politician Erzberger, German interests held primacy throughout the first years of the First World War. That these could in no way be reconciled with the acceptance and concealment of Turkey's treatment of the Armenians only became clear to him in 1917/18. At the time, he began to distinguish himself with noteworthy insights, statements, and decisions, which also made a lasting impression on Young Turk representatives. My elucidations here focus on the journey that led him to this point. Did it require foreign publications, the imminence of defeat, and the threat of peace conferences for the prominent politician to distance himself from genocide and to recognize it as a universal iniquity? The fact is that he did. He, the "man of the moment, was preparing for an important role" according to Birgen.[5] He signaled to the Young Turk regime that a democratic Germany would adopt an unambiguous stance with regard to the extermination of the Armenians. Insights regarding foreign policy played a central part in his transformation process.

I would like to raise the argument that—apart from his insights concerning Belgium and Alsace-Lorraine, which Klaus Epstein already pointed out fifty years ago[6]—the crimes against the Armenians played a key role for his reorientation, and that his becoming a democrat coincided with his unequivocal condemnation of these crimes. His conversation with Birgen may serve as early proof for this argument. The Armenian Question also figures prominently in Erzberger's memoirs, published in 1920. Before focusing on Erzberger's attitude toward Ottoman Turkey and the Armenians beginning with the eve of the Great War, this chapter offers a few insights into his early career.

The Young Politician

A devout Catholic, Matthias Erzberger had initially been a teacher before becoming a journalist and, as of 1903, a Reichstags deputy for the Center Party. Even though there had been a Catholic, predominantly French-speaking branch within the philarmenian movement in Europe since the late 1890s, Erzberger does not seem to have been affected by the Armenian aspect of European and late Ottoman history. This sets him apart from individuals such as the socialist Reichstags deputy Eduard Bernstein or the Protestant publicist Johannes Lepsius. Only during the First World War, and even then only after the decisive spring and summer of 1915, is Erzberger recorded as having become involved in the question of Armenian existence and future. Therefore, he only becomes genuinely significant to the topic of this chapter as of autumn 1915, and particularly with his visit to Istanbul in February 1916.

Thus, the young deputy's attention seems to have been drawn to the Armenian Question, and the Ottoman Empire as a whole, relatively late. In an article published in the Munich newspaper *Allgemeine Rundschau* in the autumn of 1911, he sided with Italy when its army invaded Ottoman Libya. He declared Turkey an alien element within Europe and expressed a desire for a Christian restoration of the Mediterranean world. "In Tripolis, Italy acts as an agent of culture and progress. Wherever Islam sets its foot, the grass grows no more [. . .]. Italian culture ranks far above Turkish maladministration [. . .]. If Italy contributes to all Mediterranean countries becoming Christian again, it must have and expect the sympathy of all Christians."[7]

This was a superficial, culturalistically and religiously tinged statement. It went in line with anti-Islamic crusading rhetoric still common at the time, although it was fundamentally questioned by socialist and pacifist thinkers in the West as well as by a few missionary voices within the Ottoman Empire. Italy's brutal colonialist invasion of Libya further poisoned interreligious coexistence in the late Ottoman world and ushered in a final Ottoman decade that led the empire via the Balkan Wars of 1912–13 to the seminal catastrophe of the Great War. Since the summer of 1913, the Ottoman Empire had been headed by a dictatorial party-state under the conspirative CUP. It included young *komiteci*, who saw themselves as revolutionaries, first and foremost among whom were Interior Minister Talaat and Enver, the minister of war. Both were roughly of the same age as Erzberger, who, on the eve of the First World War, was still under forty years old. In the early 1910s, Erzberger belonged to the political mainstream, that—harsh as it might sound—shared responsibility for the catastrophe of 1914. In the aforementioned article from autumn 1911, he commented, "Tripolis has shown with full force that the interests of nations are not decided upon by way of law, but through military strength alone. [. . .] The idea of disarmament and arbitral tribunals has been set back by decades by the Tripolis war." Smugly confident of Germany's own strength, he also commented that the Turkish state, in contrast to Germany and Italy, was not fit to survive.[8]

By 1914, Erzberger had barely acquired any knowledge of his own concerning Ottoman affairs. Therefore, he used simple points of reference such as his own animosity toward England, loyalty toward the pope, and obedience toward the government. As Klaus Epstein already recorded fifty years ago, "Erzberger's views on foreign policy were no wiser than those of most of his contemporaries."[9] At their party conference in September 1911, the German social democrats, and in particular August Bebel, warned of the danger of a world war and advised against German saber-rattling during the Morocco crisis that preceded Italy's attack on Libya. In response, the Center politician branded them traitorous revolutionaries.[10] On that occasion, he adopted a pose that can best be described as a strongman act.[11] Again and again, he resorted to swagger, in particular against England, and took the stance that as a sovereign world power, Germany had to rely on military strength, population strength and increase, a lead in armaments, and the sword; in short: power, not law.

Entering the First World War

The outbreak of the First World War produced excessive expectations and an exalted rhetoric imbued with religious overtones. Erzberger was no exception. Albeit a Catholic, he immersed himself in what Manfred Gailus termed the "national Pseudo-Pentecostal experience of August 1914."[12] His hyper-annexionist memorandum of August 1914 declared military and economic supremacy over Continental Europe the German war objective. Interestingly, it does not include any considerations regarding the Ottoman world (with the exception of North Africa). This stands in contrast to the similarly exaggerated expectations of Ernst Jäckh and Friedrich Naumann, for example, or Paul Rohrbach and Johannes Lepsius, who all prominently included the Ottoman sphere as a prospective zone of German influence.[13] It was only when he became head of foreign propaganda in August 1914 that Erzberger began to shift his focus onto Turkey and the Caucasus and concern himself with foreign policy more intensely, as his biographer Epstein noted.

The boundary between foreign propaganda and intelligence activity seems to have been blurred. Thus, Erzberger had, since the outbreak of war, been in contact with Dr. Paul Schwarz, who served as consul in the northeastern Anatolian city of Erzurum and was charged with organizing guerrilla attacks. On September 14, 1914, he wrote that the aim was to sabotage oil supplies in Batum as well as the transport thereof by railway. In order to sabotage the oilfields in Baku, Schwarz considered it necessary to "lobby the Armenians" for help. On December 30, Erzberger proposed using a well-known Lazarist priest of Armenian descent for this purpose. In a concluding report to Erzberger dated May 20, 1915, Schwarz wrote of sixteen persons whom he had trained and who had successfully carried out three acts of sabotage against Azerbaijani Oil facilities.[14] This was dangerous territory—not because of the comparatively harmless acts, but because of the German and Young Turk insistence on drawing the Armenians into a guerrilla force on Russian terrain and hence into a conflict of loyalty. At the time, Armenian and incidentally also Jewish representatives pleaded with their kinsmen to remain loyal toward their respective states of residence and citizenship.

The acts of sabotage in the Caucasus were linked to expansive pan-Turkish hopes and served the preparation of a related military campaign. In addition to the secret German-Ottoman treaty of August 2, 1914, German diplomacy had granted the committee government an adjustment of the north-eastern border in such a way as would connect Turkey directly with the Russian Muslims. Recent studies have shed light upon the intense pan-Turkish (Turanist) war propaganda which started in August 1914, as well as the broad affirmation of the war effort among Muslims, who greeted, or resigned to, dictatorial rule in the name of Islam and the sultanate-caliphate. Right from the start, the war propaganda almost entirely excluded the Ottoman Armenians and other non-Muslims. From 1913, the CUP's intensified Turkism was connected to the agenda of transforming Asia Minor into a *Türk Yurdu*, a sovereign national home for the Turks. This minimal goal of the First World War became all the more central when Enver Pasha's Eastern Anatolian-Caucasian campaign failed catastrophically at the beginning of 1915. Instead of an Ottoman breakthrough into the Caucasus, a lengthy Eastern Front stretched all the way from the Black Sea through Eastern Anatolia to Northern Persia from the winter of 1915. It was toward this front that Enver's brother-in-law Cevdet had undertaken a failed yet fateful advance in that same year.

Erzberger knew little of these matters. Otherwise, he would hardly, on January 4, 1915, have passed on an unrealistic paper entitled "A Solution to the Armenian Question" to legation councilor Frederic Rosenberg, who had been in charge of the so-called Orient Portfolio in the Foreign Office since 1910.[15] Its author, an anonymous, presumably Armenian Father, proposed establishing an Armenian Principality of the House of Savoy under German protection and Ottoman sovereignty in Cilicia; this should also have won over foreign Armenians to the cause of the Central Powers. However, the

CUP government's thrust of policy was entirely different. With additionally recruited special forces, it opened a campaign against its Armenian citizens in spring 1915. In official terms, this constituted a program of "sending away," *sevkiyat*, of the Armenians. In reality, however, most were not sent to new areas of settlement, but to their deaths.

Belatedly Recognizing Massive Evil

One and a half months before the onset of the total and systematic destruction of the Armenian community, the archbishop of the Mekhitarists (Armenian-Catholic monks) in Venice petitioned Erzberger for preventive measures against impending mass murders. In doing so, he pointed to messages from an Armenian bishop in Anatolia. Judging from the relevant files among Erzberger's papers,[16] his only reaction seems to have been to hand over the letter to the Ottoman ambassador in Berlin. In his immediate response, the latter vehemently denied any anti-Armenian intentions on the part of his government or among the Turks. Unlike a small minority of Germans such as Consul Walter Rössler in Aleppo, Erzberger did not grasp the severity of the situation. Rössler, by contrast, informed the chancellor on April 12 that the vali of Aleppo had urgently requested German intervention, as his colleagues on the committee were planning evil against the Armenians and thus, he felt, also against his fatherland.[17] Indeed, time was running out for a decisive German confrontation with the CUP government on behalf of the Armenians. Far from being challenged, though, the rulers in Istanbul instead sought and received the Germans' blessing for resettlements—apparently necessitated by the war—from the German ambassador Wangenheim.[18] Thus, they possessed the means for comprehensive demographic engineering—a policy of resettlement and ethnoreligious homogenization in Asia Minor (Anatolia)—without fear of being troubled by their senior partner. All subsequent half-hearted attempts at protection failed as they appealed to a Young Turk sense of goodwill that, in this matter, simply did not exist.

Even on October 21, 1915, when the first phase of the genocide, the removal of the Armenians from Asia Minor, had largely been concluded, Erzberger refused the request of a Father from the Bernese Jura who asked him to act on behalf of the persecuted Armenians. "A punishment of the Armenians" had been necessary, he stated, because they had not acted loyally. At the same time, he railed against England, which apparently used Armenian reports of atrocities for propaganda purposes. Judging, again, from files among his papers, he adopted a German Catholic position, which tried to distance itself from the Protestants, and accordingly also from the best-informed German voice with regard to the Armenians, Johannes Lepsius. Thus, it was Father Joseph Froberger, formerly the superior of the German province of Africa missionaries Pères Blanc from 1905 to 1910, who on October 15, 1915, informed Erzberger of the latest developments; among them was the assembly of Protestant Missionary and Church representatives convened by Lepsius in Berlin on the same day. For Froberger, there was "a veritable contrast between Catholics and Protestants in the [German] national understanding of this [Armenian] question."[19] Against this background of *Kulturkampf* and the resulting fear of anti-Catholicism, German Catholic representatives such as Froberger and

Erzberger seem to have attempted to be more nationalist than other Germans in the critical hour of the war.[20]

Their argumentation had a soothing effect; it culminated in the message not to endanger the alliance with Turkey on any account. At the same time, they depicted the Catholic Armenians—as opposed to the Apostolic, i.e., Orthodox, and Protestant Armenians—as entirely loyal.[21] The Vatican delegate to Istanbul, Angelo Dolci, had already argued in this way in a letter to the grand vizier in early July 1915, distinguishing the Catholic Armenians from all others by virtue of their loyalty.[22] Instead of facing the anti-Armenian measures for what they were—the destruction of the Christian-Armenian community as a whole—this approach facilitated the *divide et dele*, that is, the "divide and destroy" policy of the committee regime. In the end, this did not help the Catholic Armenians either in most cases.[23] In spite of this approach, the Catholic petition to the chancellor of October 29, 1915, signed by Erzberger and two further representatives, was at least written on behalf of all Armenians.[24]

In the autumn of 1915, urgent letters from, among others, Catholic Fathers and eyewitnesses, began reaching Erzberger. They included a letter written by a certain Father Dr. Straubinger from Istanbul, which the deputy forwarded to Rosenberg. Straubinger realized that the national rebirth of the Turks, for which there was such enthusiasm among academics in Germany, meant the demographic Islamization and formation of a unified Turkish-Muslim state, which would involve the systematic robbing and murdering of Christians. Erzberger adopted Straubinger's proposals of November 25, 1915, and their further elucidation in a letter of January 18, to focus German aid on the Catholic Armenians, when he traveled to the Ottoman capital in February 1916.[25] There, he held talks with the heads of government, Talaat and Enver. He also made the closer acquaintance of the German ambassador Wolff-Metternich, a Catholic and former ambassador to London, who was receptive toward the Armenians. Ever since taking office in November 1915, Wolff-Metternich had written openly about the CUP government's extermination policy in his internal correspondence. As Berlin barely supported him beyond trying to boost Germany's image, his attempts at opposing anti-Armenian policies remained unsuccessful.

At the time, Erzberger believed that his requests for the termination of the Armenian persecution, the resettlement of the survivors, and the reopening of their churches had been granted, and that anti-Christian violence in Syria was out of the question. Wolff-Metternich, however, was skeptical of the CUP ministers' assurances.[26] In truth, the second phase of the genocide had been underway in the Syrian desert camps since autumn 1915 and continued unhindered until the beginning of 1917. The consul in Aleppo, as well as German-speaking Protestant missionaries and eyewitnesses, had informed the Foreign Office about these developments early on.[27]

The "memorandum concerning the measures in favor of the Christians in Turkey," which Erzberger delivered to the Foreign Office and, as agreed in Istanbul, to the CUP government at the beginning of March, focused on the Catholic Armenians. Once again, it emphasized their "aversion against nationalist endeavors." This distinguished them in a positive way from the Orthodox Armenians, the bearers of an idea of Armenian national independence, as well as from those who had been educated in American missionary schools and who had adopted a democratic and enlightened outlook. Erzberger's proposals of having the surviving deportees taken care of by the mission of the Order of the Knights of Malta and resettling them in isolated villages along the Baghdad railway were, therefore, in fact restricted to the small Catholic minority. The dictatorial committee, however, was not even prepared to compromise when it came to this group—so little did it value its ally's belated attempts at protection. It correctly assumed that the German partner would anxiously cling to the alliance and to the concealment of the as yet not properly named matter both at home and abroad. In a meeting of the budget committee of the Reichstag on March 31, 1916, Erzberger bade "not to discuss the Armenian question in public, as this could result in yet more harm being done to the Armenians."[28]

Johannes Lepsius, by contrast, had been speaking plainly and publicly about the systematic extermination of the Armenians since the summer of 1915.[29] A year later, in the summer of 1916, Erzberger began taking Lepsius seriously in so far as he sent the latter's newly published, well-researched book, *Report on the Situation of the Armenian People in Turkey*, to Wolff-Metternich. In his accompanying letter of August 1, he commented:

> The effect of this memorandum is considerable. In the many letters which I receive from deputies of all parties and from different camps, the strongest indignation and the greatest outrage about Turkish behavior is expressed. I fear there will be an explosion in the autumn session of the Reichstag, and be it in the budget commission alone, which will debate the new Turkish treaties.[30]

Repositioning and Soul-Searching

This "explosion" did not occur. Erzberger's words to Wolff-Metternich might have indicated a clear starting point for his dawning insight that the destruction of the Armenians constituted an atrocity from which a democratic Germany had to distance itself by all means. During the year 1916, however, the Center deputy still treated the Armenian Question according to his previous concepts, interests, and networks, without any awareness of an irreparable moral rupture. When he and Wolff-Metternich made a considerable, yet vain effort in the late summer of 1916 to purchase the Cenacle, the site of the Last Supper on Mount Zion in Jerusalem, for the German Catholics, they did not refrain from arguing that this would assuage German indignation about the persecution of Christians in Asia Minor. This was indeed a far cry from confronting evil and helping victims. The CUP government's talks with Erzberger and Wolff-Metternich in this unfortunate and indeed shameful context are even recorded in early Kemalist historiography.[31] From September 1916 to January 1917, Germany contractually tied itself ever more strongly to the common war effort and a common future with the CUP party-state. It backed the latter's desire for unrestrained sovereignty and the preservation of the Ottoman Empire's territorial integrity.

In September 1916, German diplomacy also granted the CUP rulers' request to recall Ambassador Wolff-Metternich, who had called attention to the persecution of the Armenians several times. Simultaneously, dictatorial hardliners gained power on both sides, that is, Mehmed Talaat on the one hand, whose close circle had enjoyed unchecked power since 1913, and General Erich von Ludendorff on the other. Ludendorff, together with Paul von Hindenburg, had replaced Erich von Falkenhayn as head of the *Oberste Heeresleitung* at the end of August 1916.[32] While an officer thus became *de facto* dictator in Germany, a civilian politician and *komiteci*, who was interior minister and, from 1917 also grand vizier, dominated the Ottoman state. Thus, the course was set for the antidemocratic, militaristic developments which took place in Germany in 1917 and from which Erzberger began to distance and thereby reorientate himself. He became an outspoken opponent of unrestricted submarine warfare, which Ludendorff had wanted, and launched the resolution of July 1917 for a negotiated peace. He showed the courage to say that "only a political idiot can define the war objective in 1917 in the same way as in 1914–15."[33]

Nevertheless, in the winter of 1918, Matthias Erzberger considered the Treaty of Brest-Litowsk with its massive German annexations in Eastern Europe to be reconcilable with the resolution, and accordingly also the Treaty's Article 4, which denied Russia the northeastern tip of Asia Minor (which it had won in 1878). The Ottoman advance soon followed, endangering the survival of the Caucasian Armenians. That region thus also threatened to become "free of Armenians" (*armenierfrei*), as the phrase went among Germans in Ottoman Turkey. It was only then that the Reichstag began to ask about the fate of the Armenians. In 1916, Karl Liebknecht alone had asked this sensitive question, and thus almost exposed himself as a traitor to the war effort. Independent social democrats in particular now began championing the Armenian cause, declaring that they would "no longer allow themselves to be censored when debating the highly important Armenian question." Erzberger, too, now followed this course. He opened himself to criticism, however, when he did not follow their example of arguing against Ludendorff's maximalist treaty, which obviously threatened the Armenians.[34] "Undeniably, 700,000 people perished [in 1915–16] as a result of the atrocities against the Armenians," he declared on March 21, 1918, eighteen days after the Treaty of Brest-Litowsk had been signed in the budget committee.[35] Even if this number of victims is too low, it went far beyond what denial propaganda in Germany had hitherto permitted to say.

In the interfactional committee, as part of which the government majority, consisting of SPD, Center, and FVP, had been convening since July 1917, the Armenians only became the topic of discussion on June 19, 1918. By then, the Foreign Office had confirmed the advance of Ottoman troops in the Caucasus far beyond the boundaries agreed on in the Treaty of Brest-Litowsk, upon which Erzberger accused the ally of breaking its stipulations. "Over one million Christian Armenians are exposed to the Turkish bands without protection. These people's lives can only be saved if the Turkish armies are withdrawn," he said. As for Talaat Pasha's assurance to protect the Armenians, he held that "a Turkish promise is worth nothing."[36] In his memoirs, he wrote that he had advocated sending German officers to the Caucasus to prevent further anti-Armenian atrocities in the wake of the Russian retreat and the Ottoman advance.[37] Nonetheless, the Armenians in Kars and Ardahan were, in the words of the German consul for that area, Otto von Wesendonk, exterminated.[38] It was a little later, in July 1918, that the chancellor let the Turkish ally know that he was "saddened to see that the money which Germany had given us [Turks] was used to annihilate Christians; [and that] this was part of the current problems between both governments." In August 1918, Erzberger told Birgen that the foreign publications concerning the destruction of the Armenians "made us German democrats blush with shame."[39]

A Perceptive Democrat at Last

In spite of some late attempts and statements, Matthias Erzberger did little of effect for the Armenians all in all. Moreover, in 1915–16, his understanding of ethics and contemporary history did not allow him to speak clearly and resolutely, as deputy Liebknecht or the "lonely caller in the wilderness," Lepsius had done. As an uncritical supporter of the Treaty of Brest-Litowsk, he remained inconsistent concerning the protection of the Armenians even in 1917 and spring 1918. Nevertheless, the Armenian Question acquired central importance to him when he became one of Germany's few politicians with feasible ideas as to what a democratic future should look like after the catastrophe of the Great War.

Erzberger's becoming a democrat coincided with his acknowledgment and condemnation of the anti-Armenian atrocities. Thus, the former annexationist and propagandist of German hegemony developed into an advocate of a negotiated peace; the Catholic and dynastic networker became a democrat, and ethically sensitive in the field of international relations. As opposed to many anti-American voices in Germany, he ultimately paid respect to the Protestant US President Wilson and his ideals of democracy and a League of Nations.[40]

After the World War, the thoroughbred politician Erzberger publicly concluded: "The Armenian question is undoubtedly one of the darkest chapters in the annals of European guilt."[41] Even then, however, he showed difficulty in linking the ascertainment of the Young Turks' sole or primary guilt to the inevitable examination of Germany's share of the responsibility. Doing so would have meant deconstructing the convenient Weimar *Kriegsunschuldslegende*—the myth of Germany's innocence regarding the war—to its core. Neither Erzberger nor the notables of the Weimar Republic had the heart to admit publicly that Germany, the senior partner of the Young Turk committee government, had failed the Armenians more than any other European power.[42]

Germany and the Armenians

A Fatal Failure

Was the Armenian genocide a genuine project of the reigning Young Turks, or was there driving German agency and doctrine, *ta'lim-i Alman*, as many local Ottomans said? Was Ottoman Turkey's ally in the Great War instrumental in and co-responsible for the Great Crime (*Metz Yeghern*) against the Armenians? Was there a road, a German road, from the Armenian death camps in the Ottoman Syrian desert in 1915–17 to the eastern European extermination camps in 1942–5: a twisted road from Der ez-Zor to Auschwitz? Did the Old World's seminal catastrophes after July 1914, its *descente à l'enfer*, follow the compelling logics of good and evil forces, with the German state being a main actor of evil?

The US Ambassador Henry Morgenthau and the Entente powers, as well as some later historians "overplayed the [evil] influence of Germany in Istanbul," according to British historian Donald Bloxham. Vahakn Dadrian, a pioneer of Armenian genocide studies, meanwhile, insisted on "German complicity, namely, the willingness of a number of German officials, civilian and military, to aid and abet the Turks in their drive to liquidate the Armenians." Others have argued similarly.[1] Both arguments are true. A number of officers and propagandists more or less openly supported the comprehensive removal and extermination of the Armenians in Asia Minor. This was not, however, endorsed by German diplomacy. Nevertheless, Germany lacked the will to prevent genocide. It therefore fatally failed the Armenians in the darkest chapter of the Great War and, in the words of a German Foreign Office collaborator, broke its own moral neck.

The German debate on failing the Armenians is as old as the famous question regarding culpability for the beginning of the Great War. Although intensely discussed during and shortly after the First World War, the general *Kriegsschuldfrage* (question of war guilt) was largely re-admitted into academic debate a few decades later.[2] German involvement in the Armenian genocide, by contrast, only began to be discussed again at the end of the twentieth century. Even then, it was not historians employed at universities, but a retired journalist, Wolfgang Gust, who in the early 2000s edited the critical German state documents on the Armenians dating from the 1910s. This highly important documentation of the Armenian genocide sheds a great deal of light on our main issues—Germany's involvement in the Armenian genocide and the extent to which the experience of this genocide influenced German political thinking in the run-up to the Second World War.[3]

Allied with a Dictatorial Regime of Self-Declared Revolutionaries

First, let us understand the background for the German-Ottoman war partnership, concluded in 1914, which proved to be a decisive setting. Sporadic German-Ottoman interactions during the nineteenth century intensified after the Congress of Berlin, which Chancellor Bismarck convened in June 1878.

After the British had won a foothold in Cyprus at this Congress and, in 1882, invaded Egypt, the Ottoman Sultan Abdulhamid II sought alternatives to British support for the late Ottoman status quo. In 1883, the Germans sent a military mission under Colmar von der Goltz to reorganize the Ottoman army which had collapsed in the Russian-Ottoman war in 1878. Both German military doctrine and German arms began to permeate the Ottoman army. Goltz's seminal book *Das Volk in Waffen* (The People at Arms) was translated into Ottoman.[4] Even more importantly, a huge politico-economic project began to crystallize at the end of the 1880s.

The famous *Bagdadbahn* (Baghdad railway), financed by the Deutsche Bank, a project of economic and industrial penetration, was for its promoters an alternative to the colonialism-imperialism practiced by Germany's senior rivals, Great Britain and France. Rightly or wrongly, the Wilhelminian elite—the elite of the *Kaiserreich* of Emperor Wilhelm II—felt it was deliberately excluded from enjoying its own portion of *Weltgeltung* and *Weltmacht* (global standing and power) that it claimed to deserve according to its economical, civilizational, and military weight. The 1904 Entente Cordiale between France and Britain, including Russia in 1907, was perceived as an alliance among established powers that again proved unwilling to integrate newcomers. Anti-Russian and anti-British feelings, along with the conviction that Germany deserved a brilliant, world-shaping future, were not limited to right-wing and liberal nationalists but were also shared by socialists at that time. This was, according to Marion Dönhoff, a fatal *Grossmannssucht* (although less so in the case of the socialists).[5]

The close cooperation with the Ottoman Empire at the end of the nineteenth century germinated as an answer to German ambition and frustration. Bismarck himself had been skeptical about German involvement in the "Orient." He judged the Oriental Question to be a bottomless pit and viewed Article 61 of the Berlin Treaty, which was intended to guarantee safety for the Armenians in the Ottoman eastern provinces, their main region of settlement, as purely "cosmetic."[6] The multireligious and hierarchical, largely agrarian Ottoman Empire suffered an existential crisis that had begun in the late eighteenth century and could not be remedied by the mid-nineteenth-century Tanzimat reforms. It dramatically worsened during the 1870s and the Russian-Ottoman war of 1877–8. Marked by the loss of territory in the Balkans and eastern Asia Minor, the young Sultan Abdulhamid II was determined to save the state by means of a more authoritarian rule involving state-sponsored Islamism and reforms within a "reactionary" and "despotic" framework (as it was labeled by his domestic critics underground). His politics of Islamic unity concerned an imperial interior that, since the Berlin Treaty, had become demographically much more Muslim and geographically more Asiatic. In diplomacy, the sultan skillfully exploited both the growing inter-European competition and German ambitions.

Abdulhamid risked diplomatic isolation when the press in the West depicted him as the red sultan (*sultan rouge*), the ruler responsible for large-scale anti-Armenian massacres in 1894–6. The main massacres in Anatolia in autumn 1895 began precisely after the sultan had signed, under international pressure, a reform plan for the Ottoman eastern provinces of Asia Minor, according to Article 61 of the Berlin Treaty. They cost the lives of about 100,000 Armenians, mostly men and boys, who were killed in a wave of pogrom-like atrocious violence perpetrated by groups who had generally organized in mosques, and whom the local authorities tolerated or encouraged (see also Chapter 3).[7] The Armenian massacres of the *fin de siècle* were to remain in Western cultural memory up to the Second World War, a pivotal reference for mass violence against civilians in which state and local actors had collaborated.[8]

Sultan Abdulhamid was particularly content in October 1898 to receive the German Kaiser Wilhelm II in his empire, and thus secure his diplomatic rehabilitation. By then, British-led diplomacy had failed in orchestrating a strong response to the mass violence that had shocked a large Western public and those in the Ottoman world who did not identify with Sunni supremacy.[9] British diplomacy, Christian groups, and transnational humanitarian agencies argued that the reforms agreed upon in Article 61 urgently needed to be implemented. Among the humanitarians, one of the most articulate was the German pastor Johannes Lepsius, a vociferous critic of European diplomacy (see Chapter 12).[10]

The reform plan of 1894–5 was not implemented despite or, fatally, because of the massacres. Germany was in the forefront of those powers that ostentatiously put their interests above an international consensus on reforms for a safe Ottoman future that included the Armenians. During his visit to Istanbul in 1898, Wilhelm II was given the provisional concession for the continuation of the railway project, which had started ten years before, extending as far as Baghdad. Although the Young Turks in opposition criticized German support for Abdulhamid, the Young Turk Revolution of 1908 only temporarily put into question the Ottoman-German friendship. The American railway project (the Chester Project) for the eastern provinces failed because the Ottoman government wanted to prevent trouble with the Germans. Under attack from Italy in 1911 and affected by war in the Balkans in 1912–13, Ottoman diplomacy realized that European assurances of the territorial status quo according to the Treaty of Berlin proved futile in the event of war. In order to bolster its imperial security, it sought a formal alliance with a European great power without focusing exclusively on Germany. Britain, for many the preferred partner, remained unreachable however—not least because it was doubtful whether the CUP would take Britain's side in the rivalry with Germany over the *Bagdadbahn*.[11]

The German politics of the *Bagdadbahn* reached their peak at the beginning of 1914. On February 8, 1914, the Ottoman government signed a new reform plan for the eastern provinces initially drafted by the jurist André Mandelstam, chief dragoman at the Russian embassy. Importantly, this draft was thoroughly revised with German participation according to Ottoman wishes, after Germany had done some soul-searching regarding the massacres and abandoned its hitherto sweeping anti-Armenian stance in 1913. In its final version, the "Armenian Reforms," as the Reform Agreement was often called, divided seven eastern provinces into a northern and a southern part, and placed them under the control of two powerful European inspectors, to be selected from neutral countries. It provided for a fair proportion of Muslims and Christians in the councils and the police. It prescribed the use of the local languages including for publishing laws and official pronouncements. Finally, it demobilized the *Hamidiye*, an irregular Kurdish cavalry that since its creation in 1891 had threatened the non-Sunni groups of the eastern provinces and had been involved in the anti-Armenian massacres.

As we have seen (Chapter 4), close Russian-German collaboration was key to this great moment of Belle Époque diplomacy. It promised to solve the so-called Armenian Question, which by then had become the core issue of the Eastern Question. Lepsius himself had contributed to the negotiations as an expert for Berlin's diplomacy and an advocate for the threatened Armenian people. He now stood side by side with a German *Orientpolitik* (Orient policy) that he hoped would incorporate both economic penetration and the evangelical aims of his Deutsche Orient-Mission. In a similar vein, Paul Rohrbach, a member of the executive board of the Deutsche Orient-Mission, propagated German "ethical imperialism." In those months, two German-Ottoman friendship associations were founded, the *Deutsch-Türkische Vereinigung* by Ernst Jäckh and the *Deutsch-Armenische Gesellschaft* by Lepsius, both sponsored by the German Foreign Office.[12] The Ottoman government—by 1913 a dictatorial regime controlled by the CUP—signed the Reform Agreement under pressure and began to implement a diametrically opposed ethnonationalist agenda of demographic engineering in Anatolia from early 1914 onward. Squads of its newly founded Special Organization terrorized and expelled some 200,000 Rûm from the Aegean littoral. When, on July 6, the Ottoman parliament discussed the expulsions, Talaat, interior minister and member of the CUP's Central Committee, using evasive language, emphasized the need to settle the Muslim refugees of the Balkans in those emptied villages.

The international crisis of July 1914 that had ensued after the assassination of Archduke Franz Ferdinand of Austria in Sarajevo, saved the regime from a diplomatic backlash against the expulsion and from precocious war with Greece. Since 1913, Talaat's circle wanted a war of revenge and intended to reconquer the Aegean islands and Thrace.[13] The July 1914 crisis gave Istanbul the opportunity to win a formal European ally. Even though a German military mission, led by Liman von Sanders, had been there since 1913, German diplomats did not seriously consider an official alliance with Turkey until mid-July 1914. This then changed, however, after incisive meetings of Enver Pasha, Talaat, and Grand Vizier Said Halim with the German and Austrian ambassadors. Fears of an Ottoman alignment with the Entente were conjured up, and Emperor Wilhelm strongly stressed reasons of opportunity.[14] The secret alliance was concluded on August 2, 1914. Under its shield, the CUP party-state began to implement its own domestic agenda and, despite being the junior allied partner, it improved its bargaining position vis-à-vis a senior partner eagerly anticipating Ottoman action against Russia. The Young Turks were proud of and energized by their alliance with an admired great power. Yet they also felt under pressure to show themselves to be a valuable military ally and to obey the compelling geodynamics as seen by strategists focused on the Istanbul-Berlin axis.[15]

Germany and the Armenian Genocide in 1915

What was the impact of war exigencies upon the CUP's interior agenda and the implementation of this agenda? For General Joseph Pomiankowski, the Austrian military attaché in Istanbul and frequent companion of Enver Pasha, the regime's intention to eliminate the Armenian Question and the Armenians themselves had "an important influence" upon its decision for war on the side of the Triple Alliance. At the same time, the Armenian issue was made a matter of internal politics into which the CUP rejected any immixture.[16]

The Germans, who had been involved in the reform negotiations, did not anticipate, let alone actively prevent, the worst case of physical extermination. Right from the start, Ambassador Wangenheim anxiously focused on the common war effort. On August 6, he accepted six proposals, among them "help for the abrogation of the capitulations," the recovery of the Aegean islands in the case of successful war with Greece, a German guarantee for Ottoman territorial integrity, and "a small correction" of Turkey's "eastern border, which shall place Turkey into direct contact with the Muslims of Russia." As we have seen in Chapter 4, the last item was highly sensitive with regard to the Armenians living in the region.[17]

In early August, strong pan-Turkist and pan-Islamist propaganda, soon to be coupled with jihadist propaganda made in Germany, began to appear in the Ottoman press. "The lands of the enemy will be ruined! / Turkey will grow and become Turan!" Ziya Gökalp wrote in a poem in *Tanin* on August 8. And slightly varied: "Russia will collapse and be ruined / Turkey will expand and be Turan!"[18] All this, together with the suspension of the reform plan and the recall of both inspectors mid-August, alienated and intimidated the Ottoman non-Muslims right from the beginning of the war. After Enver had started deceitful talks with Russian representatives on an alliance with the Entente on August 5, Russia, in contrast to Germany, insisted on the continuation of the Armenian Reforms in the case of an alliance.[19]

Bahaeddin Şhakir, a senior CUP member and chief of the Special Organization, invited the leaders of the Armenian Revolutionary Federation (ARF), who had been meeting in Erzurum since late July, to lead an anti-Russian guerrilla war in the Caucasus, aimed at preparing the Ottoman conquest. The ARF stated, however, that all Armenians had to remain loyal to the country in which they lived. Despite the ARF's refusal, attempts at revolutionizing the Caucasus began in early August. In September, the regime announced the abrogation of the capitulations, closed down numerous foreign post offices in the empire, and succeeded in obtaining large sums of money from Germany in order to prepare for attack. In early August 1914, the Ottoman army began to mobilize and requisition to a degree it had never done before, even though the empire only officially entered the war in November. The requisitions hit the non-Muslims in the eastern provinces in particular.[20]

On October 2, Enver stated to his confidant Captain Hans Humann (an insider and naval attaché at the German embassy) that the great mobilization "had to advance the people's *völkisch* [ethnonationalist Turkish] education." Part of this was a paramilitary education of the youth that had already begun in early 1914. On November 11, when the Ottoman Empire officially entered the war, a CUP circular declared that the Muslims had to be liberated from the infidels and that the national ideal was driving the Turks to destroy the Russian enemy in order to obtain a natural frontier that would include all branches of the Turkish race. The ruling single-party of a huge empire used both Islamist and radical pan-Turkish language: a striking foretaste of something more extreme than the policies of Wilhelminian Germany. Orientalists in the service of the German Foreign Office contributed to the ideological polarization by fabricating holy war propaganda. As already mentioned (Chapter 11), Max von Oppenheim, the author of a memorandum entitled *Revolutionizing the Islamic Possessions of Our Enemies*, used highly derogatory language when speaking of Oriental Christians.[21]

In September, units of the Special Organization began to terrorize Armenian villages this side and beyond the eastern frontier of Russia. On September 6, Interior Minister Talaat for the first time ordered comprehensive measures against the Armenian leadership in large parts of the country: "The local leaders and instigators of the Armenian political parties pursue ever increasing political aims and do not abstain from spreading evil and abominable deeds against the Ottomans and Ottomanity [*Osmanlılık*]. They must be surveilled and, as soon as required and ordered, be arrested."[22] *Osmanlılık* no longer referred to suprareligious Ottoman communality, as it had done in 1908, but to Ottoman Muslims only. Thus, the first organizational step toward a comprehensive attack against the Ottoman Armenians was already taken two months before the official Ottoman entrance into war.

German-led Ottoman naval attacks against strongholds on the Black Sea initiated open anti-Russian aggression at the end of October. In reaction, Russia declared war and its Caucasus army crossed the frontier at Erzurum but stopped before Turkish defenses. Unsatisfied by his generals' defensive attitude, Enver Pasha himself, accompanied by his German chief of staff Bronsart von Schellendorf, took command for an offensive toward the Caucasus, against the advice of Sanders. At the end of 1914, however, his campaign failed catastrophically in the snowy mountains of Sarıkamış. Tens of thousands of soldiers perished, and epidemics began to spread.[23] In January and February 1915, campaigns involving irregular forces—paramilitary tribes and gangs—in Northern Persia failed in a similar fashion. As a consequence, the pan-Turkish dream, which had galvanized the mobilization in August 1914, turned to trauma in spring 1915. The long Eastern Front was brutalized; irregulars and regulars, militias and forces of self-defense spread violence. Most Christians had lost all their trust in the government, and the catastrophic, frustrating situation at the long Eastern Front infuriated CUP leaders. Armed Christian forces relied, where possible, on Russian help in those zones. Best known is the Russian relief of the Armenians in Van who, since April 20, 1915, had resisted Jevdet's efforts of repression. Once relieved, they themselves acted vengefully against Muslim civilians.[24]

In contrast to the east, the Ottoman army in the west, commanded by the German general Sanders, won a first decisive Ottoman victory against the Entente at the Dardanelles on March 18, 1915. It was only in this double strategic and psychological setting of spring 1915 that the regime definitively decided on a policy of complete Armenian removal, at least partly implemented by extermination. Exploiting a distorted version of the Van events and the situation on the Eastern Front, propaganda predicting a general Armenian uprising and depicting scorpion- and serpent-like Armenian neighbors, was spread throughout Anatolia.

The Ministry of the Interior under Talaat coordinated the removal in three main steps[25]: first, there was the arrest of Armenian political, religious, and intellectual leaders, beginning with those in Istanbul on April 24, 1915. Second, from late spring to autumn, the Armenian population of Anatolia and European Turkey was transferred to camps in the Syrian desert east of Aleppo. This excluded Armenian men in eastern Anatolia who were systematically massacred on the spot. Finally, there was the forced starvation to death of those in the camps and the final massacre of many tens of thousands of those who still survived. Excluded from this last death march to and beyond Der ez-Zor was a large group of Armenians whom Cemal Pasha, governor of Syria, had converted *pro forma* to Islam and resettled in Syria and Palestine. Among the points which distinguish the murder of the Armenians from that of the Jews in the Second World War is this exception, as well as the assimilatory absorption, of an unknown but considerable number of Armenian children and women into the "perpetrator nation."[26]

German Reactions to Mass Crime

Although the offensive had failed, the war on the Ottoman Eastern Front, from a German perspective, absorbed growing Russian forces and made the distressed regime even more dependent on German assistance. Berlin's anti-Russian and anti-British propaganda projected a German-led Europe extending its dominance up to Baghdad and beyond. A few so-called liberal, socialist, or "ethical" imperialists between Berlin and Istanbul such as Jäckh, Oppenheim, Erwin Nossig, Friedrich Naumann, Helphand Parvus, and Rohrbach, were the leading ideologues in this matter.

By summer 1915, Rohrbach understood, though hesitantly, that the extermination of the Armenians "broke the moral neck of the alliance with Turkey" once and for all. The others continued to do their business as if, in terms of political culture, Germany was not morally losing its war precisely because of the Armenians. The iron logics of geostrategy and georevolution left no consideration for victims and collateral damage, the propagandists argued. The German *Endsieg* (final victory) depended upon the alliance at all costs, and with it on the anti-British incitement of the Muslim world and Russia's defeat.[27] Although large-scale anti-Armenian massacres had taken place in peacetime in the 1890s, the centralist policy of 1915 and its extremist ideology would have been inconceivable without a general war that strengthened the radicals at the head of the party-state, paralyzed internal discussion, and disabled international diplomacy. Removal-cum-extermination in the shadow of war and of a war alliance was only possible thanks to a European senior ally that did not set critical political and ethical limits to its alliance right from the start.

For the German officers and leading diplomats, Armenian removal in the war zones, that is, the eastern provinces, was justified for military reasons. In this sense, both German officers on the ground and representatives in the capital communicated approvingly with the CUP officials. There was a similar logic of thinking with regard to the Rûm on the Aegean coast. Greece's geographical proximity and initial neutrality in the war, however, demanded a more careful policy of removal. The Rûm were therefore led not to Greece or to the desert, but to the interior of Anatolia. Again, Muslims were resettled in the evacuated Rûm villages. In the case of the Rûm, Germany pressured its ally several times to cease or attenuate the removals.[28]

The provisional law of May 31, 1915, often called the Law of Deportation, officially sanctioned removal and served as a legal cover for the beginning of the destruction of the Armenians. Although it did not limit removal to clearly defined zones near the military front, and although the Entente had publicly warned of crimes against humanity, the German officials did not anticipate the risk of massive abuse and therefore did not counter it. In the Foreign Office in Berlin, Lepsius was shown a telegram sent by Wangenheim on May 31 asking for their understanding with regard to the removals. Lepsius, however, was alarmed and thus decided to travel to Turkey himself.[29] After approving limited Armenian removal for military reasons, the German diplomats also began to back the public Ottoman denial of any wrongdoing.[30] They made efforts in order to appease friends of the Armenians and experts of the region. But they completely failed to stop the destruction.

The uncritical approval of removal in the eastern provinces was a decisive breakthrough for a regime which a few months previously had found itself strictly bound to implement, jointly backed by Germany, a monitored coexistence of Christians and Muslims, Armenians, Syriacs, Kurds, and Turks in eastern Asia Minor. The breakthrough was all the more poignant since German officers on the ground, in a few instances, signed or approved removals. The best-documented case is Lieutenant Colonel Böttrich, head of the railway department of the Ottoman general staff. In October 1915, he signed an order of deportation for Armenian employees of the *Bagdadbahn* against the will of its civil direction, although he was well aware that this would involve the death of most or all of them.[31]

As early as mid-June 1915, Captain Hans Humann qualified the extermination as "hard, but useful."[32] In the provinces, Ottoman officials succeeded in creating the impression that the removal was German doctrine, and its horrors the consequence of German agency. The lack of human and Christian solidarity struck many Ottomans. Europe's long-proclaimed ethics and protection of minority Christians appeared to have been entirely sacrificed. Officer Eberhard Wolffskeel, who contributed to the crushing of the desperate Armenian resistance in Urfa—like Van and the Musa Dagh an exceptional case—described his acts in cool and smug words to his fiancée.[33] Other officers such as Sanders in Izmir and Erwin von Scheubner-Richter in Erzurum locally prevented, or tried to prevent, the anti-Armenian policy.[34] "I often notice how embarrassed silence or a desperate attempt to change the subject took hold of their [the German officers'] circles when a German with deep feelings and an independent judgment came to speak of the dreadful misery of the Armenians," wrote Martin Niepage, a former teacher in Aleppo.[35]

As explained in Chapter 13, it was in mid-June 1915 that Ambassador Wangenheim began to understand that the so-called removal from the war zones was part of a full-fledged program of removal-cum-extinction throughout Asia Minor. "It has come to light that the banishment of the Armenians is not only motivated by military considerations," he wrote on June 17 to Bethmann Hollweg.

The Minister of the Interior, Talaat Bey, recently spoke about this without reservation to Dr. Mordtmann, who is currently employed by the Imperial Embassy. He said, "that the Porte is intent on taking advantage of the World War in order to make a clean sweep of internal enemies—the indigenous Christians—without being hindered in doing so by diplomatic intervention from other countries."[36]

Wangenheim felt exploited and tricked. Worried about the loss of his own prestige as well as that of Germany, he began to send clear-cut reports to Berlin. "The expulsion and relocation of the Armenian people was limited until 14 days ago to the provinces nearest to the eastern theatre of war," he wrote to Chancellor Bethmann Hollweg on July 7,

since then the Porte has resolved to extend these measures also to the provinces [. . .] even though these parts of the country are not threatened by any enemy invasion for the time being. This situation and the way in which the relocation is being carried out shows that the government is indeed pursuing its purpose of eradicating the Armenian race from the Turkish Empire.[. . .] I have considered it my duty to point out to the Porte that we can only approve of the deportation of the Armenian people if it is carried out as a result of military considerations and serves as a security against revolts, but that in carrying out these measures one should provide protection for the deportees against plundering and butchery.[37]

The last sentences were wishful thinking.

Later on, during talks with Ambassador Wolff-Metternich, who had succeeded Wangenheim after his death in autumn 1915, the regime argued that military interests had justified the comprehensive removal.[38] Wolff-Metternich intervened more energetically than his predecessor and wanted public condemnation of the horrors. However, he was not backed by Berlin. The governmental attitude was summed up in Chancellor Bethmann Hollweg's fatal note of December 17, 1915, which reacted against a proposal by Wolff-Metternich. The Chancellor stated:

The proposed public reprimand of an ally in the course of a war would be an act which is unprecedented in history. Our only aim is to keep Turkey on our side until the end of the war, no matter whether as a result Armenians do perish or not. If the war continues much longer, we will need the Turks even more. I cannot understand how Metternich can make such a suggestion.[39]

In Germany, a few public voices, in particular Lepsius and the socialist deputy Karl Liebknecht, spoke for loyalty to truth, humanity, and appropriate actions. In lectures and in his report on the situation of the Armenians in Turkey, Lepsius gave the German intelligentsia the means to understand what was happening. His report was a brilliant piece of investigative journalism that exploited sources collected during his trip to Istanbul in July–August 1915.[40] In a lecture to German journalists in Berlin in October 1915, he complained that the extermination of the Armenians was having a disastrous impact on Turkey's economy. The rejoinder by Julius Kaliski, a pro-war socialist, was that the Ottoman Armenians would easily be replaced by Jews. This idea of Jewish settlement replacing the Armenians in Eastern Asia Minor was also adopted by Armando Moses, the Istanbul representative of the Bureau for German-Turkish Economic Questions.[41]

The German press and high state officials were full of praise for the CUP regime and its outstanding leader Talaat, "the embodiment of all that is powerful and forward-looking in Turkey."[42] Although this and similar glorifications smacked of crude wartime propaganda and falsehood, they were effective. They formed a particularly nasty component of the reality-distorting war propaganda that poisoned public political discourse in Germany and Europe. In favor of the German war effort, Socialist Parvus proclaimed in his freshly launched journal *Die Glocke* in the late summer of 1915: "We do not want to be influenced in our judgment by considerations for friends or comrades, not even by the pity for poor and persecuted people." The German war machine alone, in his perspective, had to bring about Russia's defeat and a socialist world revolution (see Chapter 11).

Alfred Nossig, a maverick Zionist, prolific propagandist, and collaborator of the Foreign Office, agreed with Moses's view of replacing the extinct Armenians by Jewish immigrants. He published a panegyric of the main CUP leaders after having interviewed them during the high noon of the extermination in late summer 1915 in Istanbul. Strauss, another Foreign Office collaborator, wrote from Istanbul that "this extermination of a rebellious Turkophobe and Anglophile human race, which had been stirred up by foreign money, could be the first step towards the amelioration of the economic situation" in Turkey—that is, in CUP vocabulary, toward the "national economy" (*millî iktisad*). Their extermination eliminated exploitation by the indigenous Christians' alleged "compradore bourgeoisie," Strauss and his ilk deliberated.[43]

Could Germany Have Prevented the Genocide?

General Pomiankowksi answered no to this question because of the constraints of the alliance, including the CUP's strict separation—asserted vis-à-vis Germany—between military matters and untouchable internal politics. He argued that only a timely declaration of war by the United States, which possessed important missionary institutions throughout Anatolia, could have prevented the extinction of the Anatolian Armenians. Given the context of early 1915, an Entente strategy that seriously considered a landing at the poorly defended coast of Adana or Iskenderun, instead of stubbornly trying and failing to break through at the well-defended Dardanelles, would have been more realistic. An invasion from that coast would at least have stopped the second phase of the genocide: the death camps and final extermination in Syria.

The political and military authorities of Germany could indeed have prevented the Armenian catastrophe right from the start if they had possessed the audacity to radically reassess their political self-understanding and abandon their vague, but overambitious, overstretched war policy. For the sake of a more modest, but politically sustainable future, it would have required the audacity to break in time the ill-conceived alliance with the genocidal CUP party-state. It is improbable that any European power would have decided on steps that would have amounted to political self-denial in times of national-imperial competition and total war. In the long run, a sober political analysis can but favor functioning democracies that treat others as equals. But the assertion of democratic values, including human, social, and minority rights, counted little in comparison to the attraction and promises of imperial power. This hard fact lies at the core of wider Europe's cataclysm that started in 1914. Europe's seminal catastrophe testified to a global powerhouse that not only lost its moral compass but already lacked a just and egalitarian project for the world it desired to dominate.

One might argue that, in the summer of 1915, the German authorities could have bargained much more effectively in order to exclude certain groups and regions from removal. However, since Germany did not possess the means to control the whole interior, the CUP regime would nonetheless, if undefeated, have found ways to implement its policy of de-Armenization in the long run. Germany's last viable chance to prevent for good the Armenian genocide would have been in late March and early April 1915. After the first victory at the Dardanelles, the depression of the Turkish elite then turned into chauvinistic exuberance; anti-Armenian statements were rampant, triggered by conflicts with Armenians in Zeytun, Dörtyol, and Van. German diplomacy was informed in good time.

But no consideration was even given to threatening the dictators in Istanbul with a withdrawal from the war alliance. On the contrary, Berlin anxiously prioritized the alliance with them. "After my return [from Zeytun], Celal Bey, the vali of Aleppo, let me know that a current which is inclined to consider all Armenians as suspicious or even hostile, is apparently gaining the upper hand in the Turkish government," the German consul in Aleppo Walter Roessler wrote to both Wangenheim and the chancellor on April 12, 1915. "He thinks of this development as a misfortune for his fatherland and begged me to persuade His Excellency the Imperial Ambassador to counteract this trend."[44] Celal was one of those few high officials who courageously defended a sense of public honor and humanity.

Emphasizing its leading role in the first Ottoman victory at the Dardanelles and the further defense of the Ottoman capital, Germany could then have made clear, once and for all, that it remained committed to the Armenian reforms of 1914 and would henceforth veto any anti-Armenian steps without fear of a break in the alliance. But there was no will and no preparedness to act in this way. In late April 1915, Wangenheim assured US Ambassador Morgenthau that "he would help Zionists but not Armenians."[45] By June, having grasped the reality of extinction, he and German diplomacy remained egocentric and self-pitying, fearing repercussions also for Germany due to the crimes against humanity. Germany's reactions were by and large limited to damage control on the level of public relations: rejecting accusations of guilt and, in the same instance, to facilitate some humanitarian assistance. In telegrams to the embassy in late May and early June 1915, Consul Roessler insisted that Wangenheim intervene with the CUP leader in favor of the first deportees arriving in Aleppo. He informed him that Celal was being sacked and that a special CUP envoy had taken power in Aleppo. Outraged vis-à-vis extinction in action and a passive German embassy, Roessler also directly informed the chancellor.[46]

The CUP leaders did not take soft verbal interventions by Germans seriously. They did, however, take seriously the Germans' expectation that Armenians, that is, survivors, should return to their homes after the war. "There has not been, until now, objection by the Germans against our Armenian policy and its consequences," Talaat wrote to Enver on February 16, 1916, shortly after a visit by German deputy Matthias Erzberger. "And we understand that they consent. [. . .] Yet I felt, during recent interviews with German deputies, that they were committed to the return of the removed Armenians to their homes." To prevent any such unacceptable perspective, Talaat therefore proposed, in a telegram to Enver Pasha, to "profit from the present situation and [. . .] bring the undertaken policy to an irreversible end."[47] Minister of the Interior Talaat started active extermination, beyond deliberate starvation, in Northern Syria in March 1916. Any Armenian counted for him as potentially guilty. "We have been reproached for making no distinction between the innocent Armenians and the guilty: but that was utterly impossible in view of the fact that those who are innocent today might be guilty tomorrow," he explained to a devoutly listening German journalist.[48]

Talaat and his circle, in particular the well-connected Minister of Finances Cavid Bey, were aware of German diplomacy's repeated signals, since summer 1915, that it would not be able to defend Turkey during postwar peace talks in matters regarding the Armenians. This, along with the statements on Armenian return, were in fact the only consistent points that Germany stated against the CUP's policy of destruction. The CUP hardliners feared Armenian survival in Syria and the Caucasus, regarding it as a possible starting point for a reversal of what genocide had achieved in Asia Minor. They expected that a future democratic Germany, as represented by Erzberger, would promote such reversal. After the February 1917 Revolution, they additionally feared that "a democratic Russia will not conclude peace without having addressed the Armenian issue."[49] Years later, however, at the Conference of Lausanne (see Chapter 5), the successors of Talaat's party-state succeeded in suppressing the Armenian Question from the agenda of international diplomacy.

Apart from some early aid by local agents, German diplomacy did not begin to facilitate humanitarian help until autumn 1915. The Swiss teacher Beatrice Rohner, a member of a German missionary organization, was called to Istanbul for secret talks with missionary leaders and diplomats in November. She then traveled to Aleppo where, assisted by local Armenians and backed by German and American diplomacy, she set up a legal orphanage in early 1916. At the same time, she communicated illegally with the deportees in the camps via disguised couriers. Her work was sponsored mainly by American and Swiss sources. The money collected by Lepsius went to his collaborators in Urfa, namely to Jakob and Elisabeth Künzler, whose humanitarian work included Kurdish deportees in 1916–17. The Künzlers were co-sponsored by the American Near East Relief that had begun in autumn 1915. They remained supported by American and German diplomacy even after the United States entered the war in Europe in spring 1917.[50]

The Pervasive Impact of the Armenian Genocide on Interwar Germany

How to explain the almost complete absence of any effective German resistance against, and response to, the unexpected yet predictable mass crime next door? Its victims were humans for whom European diplomacy had guaranteed security and a future in 1878, and again in 1913–14, this time with central German involvement. Liebknecht, Lepsius, Rohrbach, and others felt in 1915 that something had gone wrong in German political and ethical culture, that Germany missed the poignant challenge the Armenians had set them. The Armenians could have been a tremendous and timely lesson for Germany. To point at the main Turkish culprit alone, as Lepsius did after the end of the Great War, could not suffice however.

Evil—in the sense of a hushed up, but afterward increasingly accepted and internalized genocide—entered Germany's political realm through a backdoor. One can consider this a consequence of an ill-begun war and an ill-conceived war alliance, and thus part of the *Schuldfrage*. After 1918, most political and intellectual actors, including Lepsius, blended the questions of guilt (or shared guilt) for war and of co-responsibility for the murder of the Armenians together, and answered them in the negative. In a Weimar Republic that broadly cultivated the myth of German innocence, the decisive damage of 1914 and 1915 could therefore not be recognized and repaired. Even worse, several actors began to rationalize and endorse extermination, referring implicitly or explicitly to an unavoidable, even necessary brutality against Armenians for the sake of Turkey's national rebirth. In this sense, the under-discussed or wrongly discussed German experience of the Armenian genocide contributed to the acceptance and adoption of exterminatory schemes in the interwar period.

In February 1918, Emperor Wilhelm had approvingly endorsed paramilitary action against the "Jew-Bolsheviks" in the Baltic, referring to the forces as "analogy Turks in Armenia," in other words comparing the attack in the Baltic to how the Turks had had to deal with Armenian agitation. He saw the people in revolutionary Russia as being "at the mercy of the revenge of the Jews." As many Germans did in the Wilhelmine era and again in Nazi-occupied France vis-à-vis members of the *Résistance*, he equated the Jews with the Armenians.[51] Max von Scheubner-Richter, German officer and vice-consul in Erzerum, had, in May and June 1915, tried to help the victims and to use German diplomacy in order to intervene in their favor. However, within a few years, this seemingly upright German patriot became a fanatic, possessed by fear of internal enemies that would annihilate Germany.

Like in the case of Rıza Nur and other Turkish ultranationalists, anti-Jewish and anti-Armenian attitudes went hand in hand. What most haunted Scheubner-Richter and the early Nazis, however, was not the Armenian *qua* Levantine Jew, but the humiliating Armenian victim experience itself. In Adolf Hitler's imagination, the Armenians remained the paragon of a "miserable existence" that Germany was determined to avert by violent means.[52] Scheubner-Richter's home town of Riga had been occupied by the Red Army and he himself had narrowly escaped execution. After this traumatic experience, in the context of German defeat, the Versailles Treaty, and hyperinflation, his ethical references completely broke down.

> All illusions of the solidarity of the international proletariat, all illusions that it suffices to be peace-loving in order to lead the neighbor to peace, all illusions that a nation is justly dealt with if it is righteous, all illusions that foreign nations will not permit the destruction of the German nation [. . .] all these stupid dreams and illusions must die.[53]

Introduced to Hitler by Alfred Rosenberg, himself a native of the Baltics, Scheubner-Richter was one of the first National Socialists in Munich. There, he and Hitler together internalized the fear of "becoming like the Armenians," and the conclusive idea of preventive annihilation. Their fear and hatred of Bolshevik Russia began to echo the Turkish resentments against tsarist Russia before and during the First World War.

"A solution of the Jewish question has to be found," Hitler said to a Munich newspaper at the end of 1922, probably inspired by talks with Scheubner-Richter. "If no solution is achieved, there will be two possibilities, either the German people will be a people like the Armenians or the Levantines, or a bloody clash will follow."[54] In early 1923 Scheubner-Richter stated that the "rise of Germany and the German nation from today's shame and defenselessness" could only take place, "if first of all we remove ruthlessly and completely from Germany and the German lines all those that carry guilt for the destruction of the German national body and for the failure of resistance of the German nation." Like the radical Turkists after the Balkan Wars, Scheubner-Richter now pleaded for "ruthless cleansing from Germany of all elements that are intentionally hostile and that work against the völkisch union of all German tribes."[55] As a German officer who had moved among Turanist officers and the perpetrators of the CUP Special Organization in Erzurum next to the Russian front in 1915, Scheubner-Richter was well aware of what these words meant.

Like many other Germans, the military engineer and interwar author Karl Klinghardt, who had been in the service of Cemal Pasha, bore witness to death caravans, massacres, and starvation camps. Consequently, he suffered from a memory filled with traumatic images. "But I have not spoken about these experiences. Nothing to help. With the brutality of natural events a stroke of human history produced itself. [. . .] These experiences should forever be silenced." In a text for *Der Orient*, he nevertheless wanted to prove that he knew what the "true misery of the Armenians" had been. Arguing against a "propaganda of outrage," Klinghardt revealed a fascination with cold-blooded, rational, functional mass killings. "The mass killing was executed almost every time in a quick and functional manner, without any fear of blood [*Blutscheu*], but also without any particular cruelty." Turkey would have been "damned to a *völkisch* and national death," had it not annihilated the Armenians, he concluded in 1928.[56]

"If we abstract from the human aspect," Dagobert von Mikusch, an early successful biographer of Mustafa Kemal, wrote with similar logic and a sweeping comparison in 1929, "the exclusion of the Armenians from the body of their state was no less a constraining necessity than [. . .] was the extermination of the Indians for the new state of the white people in America."[57] Many German patriots of those years admired the Turkish nationalists, their successful revision of the Paris-Sèvres Treaty in Lausanne in 1923, and their rapid construction of a nation-state based on Turkism. Dazzled by this success, they went on to accept the whole process of nation building in Asia Minor, including previous demographic engineering and extermination. In an article of 1929, the renowned orientalist Richard Hartmann saw the killing of the Armenians as part of a racial war and described Turkey "after the racial wars" as a nation free from "notable *völkisch* minorities."[58] A healthy homogeneous nation-state, many—including prominent jurist Carl Schmitt—came to believe, was incompatible with egalitarian plurality. Though they admired the Turkish success and tried to rationalize what had happened to the Armenians, many did so with hesitation, marking their distance by referring to "true Asiatic ruthlessness."[59] They were both confused and fascinated by the eliminatory logics. They wondered about the general approval of mass killing among Turkish nationalists and their rejection of any criminality. "In the Armenian question they [the Kemalists] have covered up for the Young Turks and not explicitly, but tacitly, approved their policy of extermination," Mikusch stated.[60]

The trial against Talaat Pasha's killer Soghomon Tehlirian in Berlin in 1921 created a division between right-wing patriots and voices such as Lepsius and his circle. It divided the early Nazis from humanitarians, lawyers, and the left-wing newspaper *Vorwärts*. The young student of law Robert M. W. Kempner welcomed the trial and Tehlirian's acquittal as a step toward international justice for unpunished mass crimes. The context of this trial in Germany and the release "of all Turkish war criminals" in 1922 made another law student, Raphael Lemkin, aware of the need for a new concept in international law, which finally led to the term "genocide" being coined. Rosenberg, in contrast, praised Talaat and condemned the "Jewish press of all colors" who had welcomed the outcome of the trial.[61] When Rosenberg's party was in power, it burned Franz Werfel's 1933 *The Forty Days of Musa Dagh*, the story of a successful Armenian resistance in 1915. As a symbol of hope, Werfel's novel was widely read among eastern European Jews; it represented an important link between the Armenian and the Jewish experience of genocide. State authorities and the press in Germany and Turkey led vicious campaigns against "the Jew" Werfel.[62]

From the Armenian Genocide to the Holocaust

Though comparison is not its main topic, differences, analogies, and links between the Armenian genocide and the Shoah have been touched upon in this chapter. In both cases, young national-imperial elites had traumatically witnessed the loss of power, prestige, territory, and homes. Would-be saviors of what they claimed to be a superior cultural-racial identity, they feared imperial and personal ruin in the cataclysmic era of Greater Europe. A new kind of revolutionists from the right, they succeeded in establishing a single-party regime that allowed them to implement policies of expulsion and extinction based on dizzying yet well-calculated social Darwinist engineering.

The extermination of the Armenians was part of a comprehensive act of demographic engineering, which considered Anatolian Christians to be non-assimilable. It turned out to be a brutal but successful model for eliminating the issue of minorities, which, due to its ethnonationalistic rationale, was condoned by Western diplomacy at the Near East Conference of Lausanne in 1922–3. With a fatal attraction for German revisionists and many other nationalists, the revisionist Treaty of Lausanne tacitly endorsed comprehensive policies of expulsion and extermination of hetero-ethnic and hetero-religious groups. The reception of this paradigm is the politico-diplomatic bridge between Wilhelminian Germany, that was, on the whole, deeply embarrassed by the genocide perpetrated by its junior partner, and Nazi Germany, which approved of and adopted it.

During the twentieth century, convenience in both Western diplomacy and academia had not allowed for the exploration of German paths that had led from the Armenian to the Jewish Genocide. Germany's heated *Historikerstreit* of the 1980s made its critical points against moral and cognitive relativism, but certainly did not promote a contextualized understanding of Nazi extermination, nor did it help in overcoming convenient Armenian genocide denial. This deficit had, among several other reasons, to do with a politically induced scarcity of academic research into the late Ottoman Armenians. Contemporary observers, however, had linked both experiences. Lemkin, the pioneer of the Genocide Convention, specifically thought of the death camps in the Syrian desert, the final phase of the Armenian genocide, when he evoked the "heat of the ovens of Auschwitz and Dachau" and the "murderous heat in the desert of Aleppo which burnt to death the bodies of thousands of Christian Armenian victims of genocide in 1915." For him, a road, crooked though it may be, led from Der ez-Zor to Auschwitz, and from both those places to the Genocide Convention.[63]

Among some German officers and civilians serving in Turkey during the First World War, willingness to exterminate a scapegoated group of citizens was no exception, as the example of Enver Pasha's bosom friend Hans Humann shows. Among contemporary Germans in general, however, including in Ottoman Turkey, this attitude was far from a majority. Within two decades, this was to change. Extreme violence in word and deed against the outlawed minority of Armenians was a fact of everyday life in Ottoman Turkey during the First World War. This ongoing experience in dealing with Turkey, combined with years of laudatory press about virtuous allies and their energetic new leaders, left its pernicious mark on Germany.

The effect was all the more drastic because many Germans in the interwar period looked with envy at the political successes Ankara had achieved under the ex-CUP Kemalists despite defeat in the World War. Thus, for many Germans, "aggressive nationalism" (Adorno) was apparently crowned with success and therefore became socially acceptable. For good reason, Theodor W. Adorno, at the beginning of his 1966 essay "Education after Auschwitz," spoke of genocide as an "expression of an extremely powerful social tendency" and German ignorance. He pointed "to a fact which very characteristically seems to be hardly known in Germany [. . .]. Already in World War I, the Turks—the so-called Young Turk movement under the leadership of Enver Pasha and Talaat Pasha—had murdered well over a million Armenians."[64] Although it was rather well known in interwar Germany, it was misunderstood by many at the time as a prerequisite for enviable political success. If the use of force was violent enough, so the new-found opinion then went, international diplomacy would swallow the deed, as it had done in Lausanne.

Epilogue

This book has focused on extreme violence and ultranationalism in the final years of the Ottoman Empire and its aftermath. But its overarching question and concept has been that of functioning social contracts based on democratic principles. It thus has provided a tentative answer to the notorious question of peace in the modern Middle East, albeit often only in the negative, that is, by referring to factors of anti-democracy. It has also emphasized the entangled history of Turkey and Germany, in politics and political thinking, at the end of the Wilhelmine and Ottoman Empires.

The book's case studies and biographical essays gave insight into imperial bias and nationalist maximalism, of which defining elements survived in Europe until 1945 and, until today, in the post-Ottoman Middle East. However, the inquiry also revealed constructive dissent and constitutional windows of opportunity, even if these democratic ferments have never gained the upper hand in post-Ottoman politics. Thus, in today's Turkey and its neighborhood, the search for new social contracts beyond imperial and religious hierarchies has not yet resulted in a situation that we may call peace within societies and between states. A hundred years after the Near East Peace of Lausanne, the picture is, on the contrary, bleak.

This study has especially concentrated on, and contextualized, what has been least explored in the scholarship of the era and area, although their impact has endured: antidemocratic ideas of Islamist (pan-Islamic) or ultranationalist, namely Turkist, futures as conceived at the end of the Ottoman Empire and espoused by predominant politicians and ideologues of the last Ottoman generation. The men at the center of late Ottoman power, the capital Istanbul, which was moved to Ankara, are a case in point. Most of these cadres of the CUP party-state were able to continue their political career in Ankara. Other radical Muslim nationalists, like Dr. Rıza Nur, joined them. Therefore, anti-democratic power relations, politics of identitarian supremacy, and pan-Turkish historical projections heavily impacted the new state founded in Ankara in 1923, after the Lausanne Conference had endorsed and recognized the new government in Ankara. Eager to strike a deal after a decade of war and diplomatic collapse, the Conference passed almost silently over their dark side: ultranationalism and extreme violence including genocide.

The "Lausanne moment" thus set a fatal precedent and also changed the status of the League of Nations. Becoming the final helper of ethnic cleansing by co-organizing the "Greek-Turkish population exchange," the League was no longer able to pursue the early post–Great War objective of law-based democratic peace. It could no longer remain a beacon of hope for small nations who turned to it in their struggle for protected self-determination against overbearing hegemons. Iroquois representatives, for example, pilgrimaged to Geneva in summer 1923, desirous of being recognized as a sovereign nation in America and given League membership.[1] These Native

Americans were still hoping for a fair and just internationalism at this point, as were the indigenous Armenians, Kurds, and Assyrians from Anatolia and Mesopotamia. The latter were let down at Lausanne's negotiating table but could hardly resign to a reality in contradiction to principles globally preached a few years earlier by the promotors of the League of Nations.

Among the most prominent right-wing thinkers of anti-democracy in the context of Lausanne and the First World War were the Turkish ideologist Ziya Gökalp, the spiritual father of Turkish nationalism, and the German lawyer Carl Schmitt, an eminent, never repented Nazi and anti-semite, who was twelve years younger than Gökalp. Both mirror the tension and turbulences of the era of extremes starting in the early 1910s, which informs their conclusions. Both welcomed the revolutionary power of the right and behaved submissively toward their leaders. For them, the individual must disappear as the instrument of an admirable state whose outstanding leader is given sovereignty to decide beyond law and separation of powers the fate of the nation. The highest religion is therefore a "political religion," that is, a credo and commitment to serve the "total state" that rules over a forcibly homogenized society.[2]

This political thought has nothing to do with democratic social contracts, consensually concluded by humans living together as equals who have thrown off the shackles of despotism. It gives no or only a subordinate value to the individual, the small people and the weak. After the Conference of Lausanne, the League of Nations was the instrument of an internationalism that had lost its initially intended democratic orientation. In critical situations like the ultimate dispossession of Anatolia's Armenians or the destruction of Dersim, the League took the side of the perpetrators in power, not of the victims who would most have needed rightful backing. This was a bad omen for interwar Europe—which however was given a new chance of democratic reconstruction after total destruction in the Second World War—and for the post-Lausanne Middle East. Here, people still keep on grappling with anti-democracy and trying to emerge from under it in the twenty-first century.

After the Lausanne Conference, revisionist nationalists referred to Ankara's success. They combined the postulate of violent national homogenization with dire ideas of illiberal mass democracy (C. Schmitt) or of authoritarian democracy in which the sublime chief takes his authority from the subservient people (M. E. Bozkurt). Both doctors of law thus perverted democracy to basically a *Führerstaat* (see Chapter 10). For both of them, democracy necessarily involved, as Schmitt wrote shortly after Lausanne, "first homogeneity and secondly—if necessary—the elimination or annihilation of the heterogeneous." This later star jurist of the Nazis described the new Republic of Turkey as a "modern democracy" that it had been able to become thanks to "its radical expulsion of the Greeks and its ruthless Turkification of the country." Turkey was a decade ahead of Germany in methodically implementing antidemocratic thought.

Schmitt was not willing or capable of grasping the power generated by alterity in a heterogeneous community held together by the empowering rules of a democratic social contract. Schmitt insisted that the "political power of a democracy [. . .] proved itself in the fact that it knows how to eliminate or keep away that which is foreign and unequal, that which threatens homogeneity."[3] For Schmitt's compatriot Tröbst, "The Turks have given proof that the purification of a people from its foreign elements is possible on a grand scale."[4]

Two examples served as references for Schmitt on his path to National Socialism and his desire for a cleansed homogeneous nation: the Republic of Turkey and, significantly, Australia. This new state established by predominantly Anglo-Saxon settlers "kept out undesirable immigration by immigration legislation and, like other Dominions, admitted only those immigrants who corresponded to the *right type of settler*," that is, who were whites preferably from Europe or North America.[5] Only whites enjoyed full access to these types of polities existing at that time. These sorts of polities excluded from full participation longtime natives and indigenous people, such as the Aborigines in Australia or Native and African Americans in the United States. In terms of democracy, their social contract was heavily deficient. But the inbuilt democratic principle of human equality opened the door for amelioration in the future, that is, the recognition and integration of otherized individuals and groups.

The Lausanne Treaty enabled the founding fathers of Republican Turkey in Anatolia—many of them, like Ataturk, immigrants from the Balkans—to suppress the identity, rights, history, and victimhood of the non-Turkish indigenous peoples for good. As a result, the latter and their history were by and large silenced or distorted in Turkey and internationally. Schmitt's and the Kemalist notion of democracy invalidated the very concept of law- and social contract–based democracy. They excluded the right to be different from their understanding of a successful polity. True democratic polities, however, set out the principles of living together in otherness and diversity, according to agreed constitutional rules. By affirming and defending common humanity, they unite their forces and thrive on the recognition of the other within. If unavoidable friction arises, democracy knows means and mechanisms to ensure that diversity does not become disruptive and destructive.

The most salient finding of Alexis de Tocqueville's masterpiece *De la démocratie en Amérique* (1835) was the place left to, and the role played by a diversity of religious communities in the United States. This was striking, at least for French readers accustomed to the idea of a clash between religion and modern political thought. Religious communities played a vital role in the non-religious functioning of modern America's democratic grassroot polities. Societal peace has indeed to benefit from existing sources of togetherness, public confidence, and hope. Peace in the violence-prone Middle East is a question of new social contracts beyond, yet appreciative of, religious, ethnic, and tribal bonds and sources. It must overcome ethnoreligious prejudices and claims of supremacy. At the same time, it has to do justice to the elements of eschatological hopes contained in the three Levant-born monotheisms. But it must translate them into a democratic language, so that they do not—as they actually do—clash with but rather inspire and enrich the polities of tomorrow.

"Parousia," "millennium," "mahdi," "coming of the messiah, son of humankind"—these and similar eschatological notions all carry the expectation of a more just and fully humane future. They condense millennia of human longing, especially by the downtrodden. These legacies need to be appreciated, included, and dealt with. A modern democracy values all relevant and constructive resources. But it knows how to screen, name, and reject antidemocratic elements and traditions of all kinds.

*   *   *

At the beginning of the twentieth century, Anatolia was still a polyethnic, pluri-religious region where native Christians and Jews enjoyed considerable economic and cultural power. Refraining from grand ideology and healthily downsized, Anatolia could have become a rich and modern, resilient and peaceful constitutional polity. The squandered attempts toward, and opportunities for, new social contracts and constitutional rule deserve their own scholarship. Its findings and thus the legacy of best but crushed or sidelined minds must historically inform tomorrow's relevant political thought in Turkey and its neighborhood.

The Young Turk Revolution of 1908 did not lead to a constitutional country with rule of law and domestic peace. On the contrary, a partly arbitrary cataclysm violently transformed the Ottoman world from the 1910s to the 1920s. New nation-states in the Balkans, centrifugal forces in the late Ottoman Empire, and Europe's national empires in the era of high imperialism had challenged the premodern foundations of the sultan-caliph's realm. By 1912, when the empire's end loomed, a feverish projection of national-imperial futures by endangered state-affiliated elites emerged, drawing on new Turkist inspiration and currents. The losses in the Balkan War of 1912–13 and the mood of war and anti-European cum anti-Christian resentment influenced an increasingly radical Turkist-Islamist ideology. The effects of this explosive mixture culminated in the First World War. Overlapping with Europe's "Great War," an even worse "Ottoman Great War"—in terms of domestic toll—took place from late 1912 to 1922.

Contemporaries in the Levant experienced this war decade as an unheard-of and never-before-seen crystallization of violence, coercion, and misery. As for the years 1914–18, it was accompanied by a party-state's prolific production of ideals that sounded utopian and desirable for the circles they addressed, but dystopian and exterminatory to those they excluded. They scapegoated Anatolia's small Christian nations and other non-Turkish groups who were now targeted not only by state coercion, societal violence, and exterminatory social engineering, but also by plunder by locals to which the state gave license to do so. The leaders of the CUP party-state homed in on a reinvigorated Anatolian core of empire and therefore sought to make Anatolia an exclusively Turkish-Muslim home. After defeat in the World War, their successors, the Kemalists, had to settle for the Anatolian home as a unitary nation-state instead of the cleansed core of a renewed empire. However, this important change could not eradicate the deeply rooted imperial prejudices ("imperial bias") of the ruling elites and their habitus of domination.

The First World War in the Ottoman world was a total war and jihad, directed both outwards and inwards. It was total in a more comprehensive sense than in Europe, as it carried extreme violence into an Ottoman society whose fabric, as a consequence, was destroyed and transformed. The centrally planned erasure of Anatolia's non-Turkish nations went along with religiously fueled domestic jihad in the provinces, thus contributing to mass violence far from military frontlines. Genocide underpinned a self-declared "social revolution" that expelled, dispossessed, and often exterminated indigenous Christians while attempting to assimilate non-Turkish Muslims. A comparably violent social-revolutionary dimension entered continental Europe only in late 1917 with the Bolshevik revolution.

Due to Russia's imperial collapse in the Caucasus in 1917, the imagination of new grand futures had proliferated in Istanbul more than ever. Earlier visions of a new era of Turkish awakening now turned unambiguously social Darwinist and proto-fascist. Gökalp's catchwords related to "new Turkey" aimed to serve a party-state in the Anatolian core of a tricontinental Turkish-led sultanate-caliphate. From his ideological angle, nature gave the stronger players, that is, the Muslim Turks, the right to suppress the ideals and the life of weaker nations. It allowed them to enrich themselves with the spoils taken from those they had subdued and exterminated. In this process, the Turks would be enabled to build a productive national economy. "The whole campaign for Turkification [of Anatolia], as it was called, was a thinly veiled explanation for theft and murder, primitive accumulation, that would transform the Turks overnight into a bourgeoisie," ninety-two-year-old historian Harry Harootunian concluded in his recent book *The Unspoken as Heritage*.[6]

After defeat in the World War, Gökalp adapted his doctrine without revising his main tenets. Exalted Turkishness and Islamic-Turkish corporatism continued to inspire the same cadres who reorganized state power in Ankara under the leadership of Mustafa Kemal (Atatürk). The compromise with the Western powers at the Lausanne Conference allowed Kemalism to establish a powerful paradigm of a finally West-turned but illiberal and partisan state. What the Kemalists rejected or downplayed as pan-Turkish and pan-Islamic wartime illusions were never fully exorcised from post-Ottoman Turkish political thought. If we take this into account, we are not surprised by the return of pre-Lausanne Turkish Islamism and by the surge of Lausanne Treaty revisionism under President Erdogan. He promotes reexpanded boundaries and a more Eurasian orientation of a Turkey made great again.

This book has time and again emphasized that there is a Janus face of Turkish nationalism. Although antidemocratic forces have always had the upper hand in its various crises since the early twentieth century, a deep longing for democratic life persisted. There was no pride with being recognized as repressive, despotic, or fascist by impartial observers. Hitler, Stalin, and Mussolini, by contrast, were proud dictators. Both Kemalism and the current AKP rule have failed democracy in drastic ways. But the memory of genuine constitutional efforts in the late Ottoman period and of various moments of democratic opening since then has never disappeared. Nothing short of a fair, just, and plural polity beyond racial, religious, and imperial myths will satisfy the longing for *huzur*, for true societal peace.

Notes

Introduction

1 See also the Acknowledgments.
2 See Chapter 5. For in-depth explorations of the Lausanne Conference and Treaty see now: Jay Winter, *The Day When the Great War Ended: 24 July 1923* (Oxford: Oxford University Press, 2023); Hans-Lukas Kieser, *When Democracy Died: The Middle East's Enduring Peace of Lausanne* (Cambridge: Cambridge University Press, 2023); Michelle Tusan, *The Last Treaty: Middle Eastern Front and the End of World War I* (Cambridge: Cambridge University Press, 2023).
3 Cavid Bey, *Meşrutiyet Rûznamesi* (Ankara: TTK, 2014–15), 3:174–5, February 23 and March 2, 1916; 3:304–7, December 15–16, 1916; 3:355, February 4, 1917.
4 For the term "anti-democracy," see notably Hamit Bozarslan, *L'anti-démocratie au XXIe siècle: Iran, Russie, Turquie* (Paris: CNRS éditions, 2021).
5 See Chapter 9.
6 For new approaches in this sense, see Barlow Der Mugrdechian, Ümit Kurt, and Ara Sarafian, eds., *The State of the Art of the Early Turkish Republic Period: Historiography, Sources and Future Directions* (Fresno: The Press, 2022).
7 The in-depth exploration of the Ottoman 1910s is recent. It includes topics like imperial nationalism, genocide, and subsequent post-genocide societies. For this terminology, see Talin Suciyan, *The Armenians in Modern Turkey: Post-Genocide Society, Politics and History* (London: I.B. Tauris, 2016). Recent research focusing on the 1910s is referenced in *World War I and the End of the Ottomans: From the Balkan Wars to the Armenian Genocide*, ed. Hans-Lukas Kieser, Kerem Öktem, and Maurus Reinkowski (London: I.B. Tauris, 2015); and *The End of the Ottomans: The Genocide of 1915 and the Politics of Turkish Nationalism*, ed. Hans-Lukas Kieser, Margaret Lavinia Anderson, Seyhan Bayraktar, and Thomas Schmutz (London: I.B. Tauris, 2019).
8 See Hans-Lukas Kieser, *Talaat Pasha: Father of Modern Turkey, Architect of Genocide* (Princeton, NJ: Princeton University Press, 2018).
9 M. Şükrü Hanioğlu, *Atatürk: An Intellectual Biography* (Princeton, NJ: Princeton University Press, 2011), 192.
10 See notably Christopher Clark's *The Sleepwalkers: How Europe Went to War in 1914* (London: Penguin, 2012).
11 The hitherto most important studies on this theme are by Stefan Ihrig, notably his *Atatürk in the Nazi Imagination* (Cambridge, MA: Harvard University Press, 2014). See also H. Kieser and D. J. Schaller, eds., *Der Völkermord an den Armeniern und die Shoah / The Armenian Genocide and the Shoah* (Zurich: Chronos, 2002).
12 The American Board of Commissioners for Foreign Missions (ABCFM), founded in Boston in 1811.
13 For the history of the manuscript of this book, see Acknowledgments.

Chapter 1

1 See UN Treaty Series on the UN website: https://treaties.un.org/doc/publication/unts/volume%2078/volume-78-i-1021-english.pdf.

2 See footnote 59 in Karl Barth, *Der Römerbrief—Zweite Fassung 1922* (Zurich: TVZ, 2010), 630–1.

3 Art. 1: "The Contracting Parties confirm that genocide, whether committed in time of peace or in time of war, is a crime under international law which they undertake to prevent and to punish."

4 https://www.congress.gov/congressional-record/volume-165/house-section/page/H8559-8568. A reflection on this is Hans-Lukas Kieser, "Gedenken an den Armeniermord und den Holocaust: Öffentliche Wahrheit als Kern historischer Gerechtigkeit," in *Holocaust-Gedenken und -Erinnern in schweizerischer und transnationaler Perspektive*, ed. Fabienne Meyer and Jacques Picard (Vienna: Böhlau, 2021), 373–86.

5 Ana Filipa Vrdoljak, "Human Rights and Genocide: The Work of Lauterpacht and Lemkin in Modern International Law," *The European Journal of International Law* 20, no. 4 (2010): 1181; Dominik J. Schaller and Jürgen Zimmerer, eds., *The Origins of Genocide: Raphael Lemkin as a Historian of Mass Violence* (London: Routledge, 2009).

6 See UN website: https://legal.un.org/icc/statute/romefra.htm. Crimes against humanity thus clearly include attacks against non-ethnoreligious—e.g., politically, socially, or economically defined—groups of civilians. These groups are, however, not included in the UN definition of genocide.

7 Daniel M. Segesser, "Die historischen Wurzel des Begriffs 'Verbrechen gegen die Menschlichkeit," *Jahrbuch der Juristischen Zeitgeschichte* 8 (2006–7): 75–101; Pierre Serna, "Que s'est-il dit à la Convention les 15, 16 et 17 pluviôse an II ? Ou lorsque la naissance de la citoyenneté universelle provoque l'invention du 'crime de lèse-humanité," *La Révolution française* 7 (2014), https://journals.openedition.org/lrf/1208; Antaki Mark, "Esquisse d'une généalogie des crimes contre l'humanité," *Revue Québécoise de droit international*, hors-série avril (2007): 63–80, https://www.persee.fr/doc/rqdi_0828-9999_2007_hos_1_1_1393; Michael J. Perry, *The Idea of Human Rights: Four Inquiries* (New York: Oxford University Press, 1994).

8 Karl Barth, *Kirchliche Dogmatik*, Vol. I, Part 2 (Zollikon: Evangelischer Verlag, 1948), 443–504; Zygmunt Bauman, *Modernity and the Holocaust* (Ithaca, NY: Cornell University Press, 1989).

9 Raphaël Lemkin, *Axis Rule in Occupied Europe: Laws of Occupation, Analysis of Government, Proposals for Redress* (Washington: Carnegie Endowment for International Peace, 1944). Arnold J. Toynbee, *Armenian Atrocities: The Murder of a Nation* (London: n.p., 1915). The already existing term "Völkermord" is the official German translation of genocide since 1948, see Lepsius, *Der Todesgang des armenischen Volkes: Bericht über das Schicksal des armenischen Volkes in der Türkei während des Weltkrieges* (Potsdam: Tempelverlag, 1919), xxviii. Wangenheim to Reichskanzler, June 17, 1915, PA-AA/R (Archives of the German Foreign Office) 14086, no. 372; July 7, 1915, PA-AA/R 14086, no. 433.

10 Raphael Lemkin, *Totally Unofficial: The Autobiography of Raphael Lemkin*, ed. Donna-Lee Frieze (New Haven, CT: Yale University Press, 2013), 20.

11 "Book Review: Harry Harootunian, The Unspoken Heritage," *New Perspectives on Turkey* (2021): 5, doi:10.1017/npt.2021.8.

12 See Taha Parla and Ziya Gökalp, *Kemalizm ve Türkiye'de Korporatizm* (Istanbul: Metis, 2018). First published in 1986, this study rightly emphasizes Gökalp's corporatism; it lacks, however, new scholarly insights into genocidal rule and Gökalp's role in the 1910s, and for this reason Gökalp's formative proto-fascist tendencies. See also Chapter 8.

13 Ergun Özbudun, "Constitution Writing and Religious Divisions in Turkey," in *Constitution Writing, Religion and Democracy*, ed. Aslı Ü. Bâli and Hanna Lerner (Cambridge: Cambridge University Press, 2018), 168.

14 Umut Özsu, *Formalizing Displacement. International Law and Population Transfers* (New York: Oxford University Press, 2015); Hans-Lukas Kieser, "Minorities (Ottoman Empire/Middle East)," in *1914-1918-online. International Encyclopedia of the First World War* (Berlin, 2014), doi:10.15463/ie1418.10512/1.12014.

15 *Conférence de Lausanne sur les affaires du Proche-Orient (1922-1923). Recueil des actes de la conférence* (Paris: Imprimerie Nationale, 1923), first series, vol. 1, 163 (Ismet İnönü); 473-4, 577, 604, 607 (Rıza Nur).

16 "Dokumentation: Die Rede Himmlers vor den Gauleitern am 3. August 1944," *Vierteljahreshefte für Zeitgeschichte* 1, no. 4 (1953): 357-94. There are comparably explicit statements also by perpetrators of the Armenian genocide, see, e.g., Hans-Lukas Kieser, "Dr Mehmed Reşid (1873-1919): A Political Doctor," in Kieser and Schaller, *Der Völkermord an den Armeniern und die Shoah*, 245-79.

17 Hans van Wees, "Genocide in the Ancient World," in *The Oxford Handbook of Genocide Studies*, ed. D. Bloxham and D. Moses (Oxford: Oxford University Press, 2012), 239-58.

18 See also Jan Assmann, *Totale Religion. Ursprünge und Formen puritanischer Verschärfung* (Wien: Picus, 2018), 144.

19 1 Samuel 8. See also Mark G. Brett, "Narrative Deliberation in Biblical Politics," in *The Oxford Handbook of Biblical Narrative*, ed. Danna Nolen Fewell (New York: Oxford University Press, 2016), 540-9, and idem, *Political Trauma and Healing: Biblical Ethics for a Postcolonial World* (Grand Rapids, MI: W.B. Eerdmans Publishing Co., 2016).

20 Yehuda Bauer in his *Rethinking the Holocaust* (New Haven, CT: Yale University Press, 2002), 19-20.

21 "Whoever offends the god Asshur will be turned into a ruin," reads a more than 3000-year-old Assyrian poem. "He slits the wombs of pregnant women; he blinds the infants. He cuts the throats of their strong ones." Quoted in Wees, "Genocide in the Ancient World," 241.

22 As in passages by Plutarch (regarding the sacrifice of three young Persian men, see Plutarch, *The Parallel Lives: The Life of Themistocles* [Cambridge, MA: Harvard University Press, 1914], 13,1); and Aischylos (*Agamemnon*, regarding Iphigenia, www.projekt-gutenberg.org/aischylo/agamemno/agamemn1.html).

23 For the biblical story of Jephthah who sacrifices his daughter to Yahweh, see Judg. 11:29-40.

24 See René Girard's anthropological theory on violence, the scapegoat, and the sacred in his *La Violence et le Sacré* (Paris: Grasset, 1972), notably 429-46, and *Des choses cachées depuis la fondation du monde* (Paris: Grasset, 1978); *Le Bouc émissaire* (Paris: Grasset, 1982). Though a different approach and vocabulary, there is an analogy between Girard's understanding of archaic polities and Walter Benjamin's notion of "rechtsetzende mythische Gewalt" (law-stablishing mythical violence/might) and their circular reproduction that, for Benjamin, still vastly shapes the modern world. See

Walter Benjamin, "Zur Kritik der Gewalt," in idem, *Gesammelte Schriften* (Frankfurt: Surkamp, 1999), vol. 2.1, 200–4.

25 Girard, *Bouc émissaire*, 222.

26 As historian and legal scholar Samuel Moyn has argued, Karl Barth's concept became for Emmanuel Levinas (via Franz Rosenzweig) the horizon for his concept of intersubjectivity. See Samuel Moyn, *The Origins of the Other* (Ithaca, NY: Cornell University Press, 2005), 113–63; Liisi Keedus, "'The New World' of Karl Barth: Rethinking the Philosophical and Political Legacies of a Theologian," *The European Legacy* 25, no. 2 (2020): 167–85.

27 Carmen A. Lau, *Stories from Rwandan Churches Prior to the Genocide* (MA thesis, The University of Alabama at Birmingham, 2019), 49–62. See also Assmann, *Totale Religion*, 55.

28 For a collection of, and reflection on, relevant passages see Armina Omerika, "Gewalt im Koran. Zur Bedeutung des Kontextes in der islamischen Theologie," *Forschung Frankfurt* 1 (2016): 62–7.

29 Cf. Leon Ostrorog, "Les droits de l'homme et l'Islam," *Revue de droit international* 5, no. 1 (1930): 100–5.

30 Caroline Schneider, "The Yazidis: Resilience in Times of Violence," in *Collective and State Violence in Turkey: The Construction of a National Identity from Empire to Nation-State*, ed. Stephan Astourian and Raymond Kévorkian (New York: Berghahn, 2020), 400–25.

31 For an English translation of the Hamas Covenant see https://avalon.law.yale.edu/20th_century/hamas.asp.

32 A few references are listed in Omer Bartov, "The Hamas Attack and Israel's War in Gaza," Council for Global Cooperation, November 24, 2023, https://cgcinternational.co.in.

33 Zana Zangana, *Where Was God Hijacked?* (n.p., Lulu.com, 2018), 28–30; Human Rights Watch Middle East, *Iraq's Crime of Genocide: The Anfal Campaign Against the Kurds* (New Haven: HRW, 1995), https://www.hrw.org/reports/1993/iraqanfal.

34 Alex J. Kay, *Empire of Destruction: A History of Nazi Mass Killing* (New Haven, CT: Yale University Press, 2021), 19–40.

35 A paradoxical notion such as "autogenocide" might apply here. Used by several authors in the third quarter of the twentieth century, notably for modern mankind's capacity for self-destruction, "autogenocide" has, since the mass deaths under the Khmer Rouge in Cambodia, mostly been used to name this crime. See David Chandler, *Voices from S-21: Terror and History in Pol Pot's Secret Prison* (Berkeley: University of California Press, 2000), vii. For a sarcastic use—autogenocide as self-inflicted mass suicide by allegedly disloyal Armenians, Biafrans, or Jews—see Richard Marienstras, "Un genocide contrariant," in *Les nouveaux cahiers* 15 (Paris: Alliance israélite universelle, 1968), 6–10: "D'abord, les Arméniens sont surtout morts de soif, et ensuite, ils n'avaient qu'à être loyaux. Leur mort retombe sur eux, on ne peut parler de génocide mais seulement d'auto-génocide. Et s'il y a auto-génocide, on ne peut blâmer les Turcs."

36 This is in principal agreement with political thinkers from Jean-Jacques Rousseau to John Rawls. See notably the latter's "Justice as Fairness: Political Not Metaphysical," *Philosophy & Public Affairs* 14, no. 3 (1985): 223–51, and *Justice as Fairness: A Restatement* (Cambridge, MA: Harvard University Press, 2001).

37 https://www.tbmm.gov.tr/anayasa/anayasa_2018.pdf.

38 For a fine-grained recent study of "Indian Removals," see Eric Weitz, *A World Divided: The Global Struggle for Human Rights in the Age of Nation-States* (Princeton, NJ: Princeton University Press, 2019), 83–121.

39 This is the prevailing argument in Melvin L. Rogers, *The Darkened Light of Faith: Race, Democracy, and Freedom in African American Political Thought* (Princeton, NJ: Princeton University Press, 2023).

40 William E. Rappard, *The Geneva Experiment* (Oxford: Oxford University Press, 1931); idem, *The Crisis of Democracy* (Chicago, IL: University of Chicago Press, 1938). From 1920 to 1925, Rappard led the Mandates Division of the League of Nations, often trying to resist dominant French and British influence. See notably Susan Pedersen, *The Guardians: The League of Nations and the Crisis of Empire* (Oxford: Oxford University Press, 2017).

41 Given their global power and impact in the twenty-first century, the necessity of including and binding companies has become particularly urgent. For a recent reflection on the search for a social contract-based world peace, see Philippe M. Defarges, *Une histoire mondiale de la paix* (Paris: Odile Jacob, 2020), 99–132. See also the analogous goals of the World Federalist Movement (https://www.wfm-igp.org) and of Democracy Without Borders (https://www.democracywithoutborders.org).

42 See Chapter 5 and Kieser, *When Democracy Died.*

43 Hans-Lukas Kieser, *Nearest East: American Millennialism and Mission to the Middle East* (Philadelphia: Temple University Press, 2010), 15–33.

44 The League's successor, the United Nations Organization (UNO), continued the anti-Axis war alliance, so that it counted autocracies among its members right from the start. The UNO rested much less than the post-1918 League on a covenant among—as had been hoped for in the late 1910s—growing constitutional and democratic members, but it built directly on the power relations resulting from the Second World War, thus on very weak democratic credentials. The first conference of the World Movement for World Federal Government in Montreux in 1947 reacted against this unsatisfying peace perspective. See Montreux Declaration, https://www.wfm-igp.org/about-us/montreux-declaration.

Chapter 2

1 Dagobert von Mikusch, *Gasi Mustafa Kemal zwischen Europa und Asien. Eine Lebensgeschichte* (Leipzig: Paul List, 1929), 83.

2 Walter N. Wyeth, *Poor Lo! Early Indian Missions. A Memorial* (Philadelphia, PA: W. N. Wyeth, 1896), frontispiece.

3 See Joseph L. Grabill, *Protestant Diplomacy and the Near East: Missionary Influence on American Policy, 1810-1927* (Minnesota: University of Minnesota Press, 1971); Kieser, *Nearest East.* Cf. the Calvinist background: Calvinism's place of origin in the Swiss Confederation, and Calvinism's implantation in the bourgeoning United States.

4 Wyeth, *Poor Lo!,* 168.

5 Russell Thornton, *The Cherokees: A Population History* (Lincoln: University of Nebraska Press, 1990), 63–77.

6 Kieser, *Talaat,* 258–77.

7 Harold Bradley, "Jackson, Andrew," *Encyclopædia Britannica Online,* January 2008.

8 David S. Heidler and Jeanne T. Heidler, *Indian Removal* (New York: W. W. Norton, 2007), 30.

9 Sarah H. Hill, *Cherokee Removal: Forts Along the Georgia Trail of Tears*, 61, https://www.murraycountymuseum.com/adobe/Cherokee_Removal_02nov2011.pdf.

10 David M. Wishart, "Evidence of Surplus Production in the Cherokee Nation Prior to Removal," *The Journal of Economic History* 55, no. 1 (March 1995): 134.

11 John A. Andrew III, *From Revival to Removal. Jeremiah Evarts, the Cherokee Nation, and the Search for the Soul of America* (Athens: University of Georgia Press, 1992), 153.

12 Sean Wilentz, *Andrew Jackson* (New York: Times Books, 2005), 68–9.

13 James Mooney, *Myths of the Cherokee* (Mineola, NY: Dover, 1996 [first ed., 1897–8]), 118.

14 Clifton J. Phillips, *Protestant America and the Pagan World: The First Half Century of the American Board of Commissioners for Foreign Missions, 1810-1860* (Boston: Harvard University Press, 1969), 61.

15 Levi Parsons, *Memoir of Levi Parsons, First Missionary to Palestine from the United States* (Hartford, CT: Cook & Co. and Packard & Butler, [1824] 1830), 42.

16 Phillips, *Protestant America*, 70.

17 Evarts, *Cherokee Removal*, 3–40.

18 Evarts, *Cherokee Removal*, 282.

19 Andrew, *From Revival to Removal*, 262.

20 Phillips, *Protestant America*, 72.

21 Phillips, *Protestant America*, 74.

22 Hill, *Cherokee Removal: Forts*, 27.

23 Wishart, "Evidence of Surplus Production," 124–7; Kent Carter, "Wantabes and Outalucks: Searching for Indian Ancestors in Federal Records" (n.d.), https://warriornation.ning.com/forum/topics/wantabes-and-outalucks-searching-for-indian-ancestors-in-federal-.

24 Evarts, *Cherokee Removal*, 40.

25 Hill, *Cherokee Removal: Forts*, 43.

26 Phillips, *Protestant America*, 72–3.

27 For the current standard in scholarship, see notably Ronald Grigor Suny, *"They Can Live in the Desert but Nowhere Else": A History of the Armenian Genocide* (Princeton, NJ: Princeton University Press, 2015); Taner Akçam, *The Young Turks' Crime against Humanity: The Armenian Genocide and Ethnic Cleansing in the Ottoman Empire* (Princeton, NJ: Princeton University Press, 2012); Raymond Kévorkian, *The Armenian Genocide: A Complete History* (London: I.B. Tauris, 2011); Kieser, Anderson, Bayraktar, and Schmutz, *End of the Ottomans*.

28 See Kieser, "Minorities (Ottoman Empire/Middle East)."

29 M. Şükrü Hanioğlu, *A Brief History of the Late Ottoman Empire* (Princeton, NJ: Princeton University Press, 2008), 106.

30 *The Orient* (Istanbul: Bible House, January 22, 1913), vol. 4, no. 4, 5.

31 *The Orient*, January 22, 1913, 5.

32 "To Whom it May Concern," December 24, 1904, and "Paper on Some Phases of the Armenian Question," December 29, 1904, ABCFM archives 16.9.7, Houghton Library in Harvard, Massachusetts.

33 Hans-Lukas Kieser, *Der verpasste Friede. Mission, Ethnie und Staat in den Ostprovinzen der Türkei 1839-1938* (Zurich: Chronos, 2021 [first ed., 2000]), 193–243; Jelle Verheij, "Die armenischen Massaker von 1894-1896. Anatomie und

Hintergründe einer Krise," in *Die armenische Frage und die Schweiz (1896-1923)*, ed. H. Kieser (Zürich: Chronos, 1999), 69–129; Gunnar Wiessner, *Hayoths Dzor— Xavasor. Ethnische, ökonomische und kulturelle Transformation eines ländlichen Siedlungsgebietes in der östlichen Türkei seit dem 19. Jahrhundert* (Wiesbaden: Dr. Ludwig Reichert Verlag, 1997).

34 Hamit Bozarslan, "Histoire des relations arméno-kurdes," in *Kurdistan und Europa*, ed. H. Kieser (Zürich: Chronos, 1997), 161–3; Dikran Kaligian, *Armenian Organization and Ideology under Ottoman Rule, 1908-1914* (New Brunswick: Transaction, 2012), 53–65; Mehmet Polatel, "Armenians and the Land Question in the Ottoman Empire, 1870-1914" (Ph.D thesis, Istanbul: Boğaziçi University, 2017).

35 Kieser, *Der verpasste Friede*, 123.

36 See Talin Suciyan, *Outcasting Armenians: Tanzimat of the Provinces* (Syracuse, NY: Syracuse University Press, 2023).

37 Kieser, *Talaat*, 173–258; Fuat Dündar, *L'ingénierie ethnique du Comité Union et Progrès et la Turcisation de l'Anatolie* (Ph.D thesis, Paris, EHESS, 2006), 63–167; see also idem, *İttihat ve Terakki Müslümanları iskân politikası (1913-1918)* (Istanbul: İletişim, 2001); idem, *Modern Türkiye'nin Şifresi. İttihat ve Terakkki'nin etnisite ve mühendisliği 1913-1918* (Istanbul: İletişim, 2008).

38 ABCFM doctor Daniel Thom in Mardin, in a letter of August 16, 1914, quoted in Kieser, *Der verpasste Friede*, 336.

39 Joseph Pomiankowski, *Der Zusammenbruch des Ottomanischen Reiches. Erinnerungen an die Türkei aus der Zeit des Weltkrieges* (Zurich: Amalthea-Verlag, 1927), 154.

40 On this aspect, the most recent research is Oktay Özel, "The Role of Teşkilat-ı Mahsusa (Special Organization) in the Armenian Genocide," in *The First World War as a Caesura? Demographic Concepts, Population Policy, and Genocide in the Late Ottoman, Russian, and Habsburg Spheres*, ed. Christine Pschichholz (Berlin: Duncker & Humblot, 2020), 81–108.

41 *The Orient*, January 29, 1913, 5.

42 Reproduced in Kieser, *Der verpasste Friede*, 434–5.

43 Henry H. Riggs, *Days of Tragedy in Armenia. Personal Experiences in Harpoot, 1915-1917* (Michigan: Gomidas Institute, 1997), 140.

44 On this civil servant of integrity, see Chapter 4 and Kieser, *Talaat*.

45 Letter of Dr. Floyd Smith to James Barton, September 18, 1915, ABCFM archives 16.9.7.

46 Mehmet Polatel and Uğur Üngör, *Confiscation and Destruction. The Young Turk Seizure of Armenian Property* (London: Bloomsbury, 2013); Kieser, *Talaat*, 268–74.

47 On May 26, 1915, when Armenian removal began, Peet, for example, wrote to US Ambassador Henry Morgenthau in the same city:

> I also enclose the document which you kindly handed me yesterday in regard to refugee Armenians who have been expelled from the Zeitoun region. I had a call this morning from Consul Mordtmann from the German Embassy, who came to deliver a message received through the German Consul at Erzroom from our missionaries at Erzroom asking for relief funds to aid the [Armenian] Christians who are now being expelled from Erzroom in pursuance of orders lately given. I am today telegraphing Lt.150.00 for this purpose. (quoted in Kieser, *Der verpasste Friede*, 339)

48 For Urfa, see notably Jakob Künzler, *In the Land of Blood and Tears: Experiences in Mesopotamia during the World War, 1914–1918* (Arlington, VA: Armenian Cultural Foundation, 2007). The couple Jakob and Elisabeth Künzler were members of Johannes Lepsius's Potsdam-based *Deutsche Orient-Mission*.

49 On this topic, see recent research: Khatchig Mouradian, *The Resistance Network: The Armenian Genocide and Humanitarianism in Ottoman Syria, 1915-1918* (East Lansing: Michigan State University Press, 2021).

50 H. Kieser, "Beatrice Rohner's Work in the Death Camps of Armenians in 1916," in *Resisting Genocide: The Multiple Forms of Rescue*, ed. J. Sémelin, C. Andrieu, and S. Gensburger (London: C. Hurst, 2010), 367–82.

51 Susan B. Harper, "Mary Louise Graffam: Witness to Genocide," in *America and the Armenian Genocide of 1915*, ed. Jay Winter (Cambridge: Cambridge University Press, 2003), 214–39.

52 Mikusch, *Gasi Mustafa Kemal*, 83.

53 Guenter Lewy, "Were American Indians the Victims of Genocide?," *History News Network*, originally published in *Commentary*, 2004, http://hnn.us/articles/7302 .html, accessed March 5, 2021; idem, *The Armenian Massacres in the Ottoman Turkey. A Disputed Genocide* (Salt Lake City: University of Utah Press, 2005). For a review of this book, see Hans-Lukas Kieser, "Der Völkermord an den Armeniern 1915/16: neueste Publikationen (Rezension)," *sehepunkte* 7 (2007): 3.

54 Protestant American millennialism, a main motor of the mission, believed that with the American Revolution "modern times" had begun and the "kingdom of God on Earth" could and must be realized in a modern synergy of Bible belief, human benevolence, enlightened democracy, and technological progress. See Kieser, *Nearest East*; Helmut R. Niebuhr, *The Kingdom of God in America* (Middletown, CT: Wesleyan University Press, 1988 [first ed. 1938]).

55 Kieser, *Nearest East*, 21–8.

56 Kieser, *Der verpasste Friede*, 545–6.

57 Quoted in Richard E. Ellis, *Andrew Jackson* (Washington, DC: CQ Press, 2003), 246–7, http://www.twofrog.com/gover.html.

58 Heidler and Heidler, *Indian Removal*, 1.

Chapter 3

1 On "tragic mind" and suicidal readiness to kill in the contemporary Middle East, see Hamit Bozarslan, *Violence in the Middle East: From Political Struggle to Self-Sacrifice* (Princeton, NJ: Markus Wiener, 2004); and more generally: idem, *Une histoire de la violence au Moyen-Orient: de la fin de l'Empire ottoman à Al-Qaida* (Paris: La Découverte, 2008). On politics of violence, including genocide, see Jacques Sémelin, *Purify and Destroy: The Political Uses of Massacre and Genocide* (London: Hurst, 2013).

2 The term "Levant" in this chapter encompasses the core lands of the late Ottoman Empire: modern-day Turkey, Iraq, Syria, Lebanon, Palestine, and Israel.

3 On modern Muslim eschatology, see David Cook, *Contemporary Muslim Apocalyptic Literature* (Syracuse, NY: Syracuse University Press, 2005); Jean-Pierre Filiu, *Apocalypse in Islam* (Berkeley: University of California Press, 2011). On modern Levant-centered Christian eschatology, see Kieser, *Nearest East*. On Ben-Gurion's use of the Hebrew Bible, see Anita Shapira, "Ben-Gurion and the Bible: The Forging of an Historical Narrative?," *Middle Eastern Studies* 33, no. 4 (1997): 645–74.

4 Studies on the 1894–6 and 1909 massacres are Jelle Verheij, "Diyarbekir and the Armenian Crisis of 1895," in *Social Relations in Ottoman Diyarbekir 1870–1915*,

ed. Joost Jongerden and Jelle Verheij (Leiden: Brill, 2012), 85–146; Owen Robert Miller, "Sasun 1894: Mountains, Missionaries and Massacres at the End of the Ottoman Empire" (Ph.D thesis, Columbia University, 2015); and *Etudes arméniennes contemporaines* 2017, a thematic issue on "The Massacres of the Hamidian Period." On forced conversion, see Selim Deringil, *Conversion and Apostasy in the Late Ottoman Empire* (Cambridge: Cambridge University Press, 2012).

5 According to the sharia, *zimmi* (*dhimmi*) refers to protected or tolerated but politically and legally subordinated Christian and Jewish communities living within the Islamic state. However, the term "unbeliever" (*gavur, kafir*) is largely, but theologically wrongly, applied also to *zimmis* by Muslims of the modern era.

6 Celâl Bayar, *Ben de yazdım: Millî mücadeleye giriş* (Istanbul: Sabah kıtapları, 1997), 8:119–20; Kévorkian, *The Armenian Genocide*, 71–96.

7 This direct connection to the Islamic empire distinguishes the late Ottoman pogroms from other religiously motivated atrocities, such as the 1965 massacres in Indonesia, where local Muslim perpetrators—condoned by the Cold War–affected United States—acted as instruments of the army, killing around a million supposed communists, many of them ethnic Chinese. See on the whole Cold War period, Paul T. Chamberlin, *The Cold War's Killing Fields: Rethinking the Long Peace* (New York: HarperCollins, 2018).

8 The large minority of Anatolian Alevis, which today constitutes about a fifth of the population, rejects—or only partially accepts—the pillars of Sunni Islam, and have organized themselves outside the state-controlled mosques. Since the sixteenth century, Alevis have traditionally been considered infidels or heretics by conservative Sunnis.

9 For the 1937–8 massacre in Dersim, see below and Chapter 6.

10 Wahhabism is a radical Sunni movement that emerged in the eighteenth century, aimed at restoring "original Islam"; it became Saudi Arabia's state ideology and has largely determined the IS's religious tenets.

11 Feras Krimsti, "The 1850 Uprising in Aleppo. Reconsidering the Explanatory Power of Sectarian Argumentations," in *Urban Violence in the Middle East: Changing Cityscapes in the Transition from Empire to Nation-State*, ed. Ulrike Freitag et al. (New York: Berghahn, 2015), 145; Nora Lafi, "The 1800 Insurrection in Cairo," idem, 40–5.

12 On the Great War as part of a larger cataclysm (1912–22) see Kieser et al., *World War I and the End of the Ottomans*, 1–18.

13 See Chapter 4. On the Balkan Wars as a matrix of fear, revenge, and violence, see Eyal Ginio, *The Ottoman Culture of Defeat: The Balkan Wars and Their Aftermath* (London: Hurst, 2016). An analysis of denial and justification of violence by Turkish leaders is Fatma M. Göçek, *Denial of Violence: Ottoman Past, Turkish Present, and Collective Violence against the Armenians, 1789-2009* (Oxford: Oxford University Press, 2015).

14 Mustafa Aksakal, "The Ottoman Proclamation of Jihad," in *Jihad and Islam in World War I: Studies on the Ottoman Jihad on the Centenary of Snouck Hurgronje's "Holy War Made in Germany"*, ed. Erik-Jan Zürcher (Leiden: Leiden University Press, 2016), 53–69. This volume offers new and hitherto neglected insights into jihad in the First World War.

15 Marc Neuwirth, *Historische Argumente bei der Debatte um die Annäherung der Türkei an die Europäische Union in den Institutionen der EU* (Ph.D thesis, University of Zurich, 2015).

Chapter 4

1 For the full text of the Reform Agreement as well as the preceding Mandelstam draft, both in French, see André N. Mandelstam, *Le sort de l'empire ottoman* (Lausanne: Payot, 1917), 218–22 and 236–8.

2 Roderic H. Davison, "The Armenian Crisis, 1912–1914," in idem, *Essays in Ottoman and Turkish History, 1774–1923: The Impact of the West* (Austin: University of Texas Press, 1990), 183–6.

3 Hans-Lukas Kieser, Mehmet Polatel, and Thomas Schmutz, "Reform or Cataclysm? The Agreement of 8 February 1914 regarding the Ottoman Eastern Provinces," *Journal of Genocide Research* 17, no. 3 (2015): 290.

4 Rober Koptaş, "Zohrab, Papazyan ve Pastırmacıyan'ın kalemlerinden 1914 Ermeni reformu ve İttihatçı-Taşnak müzakeleri," *Tarih ve Toplum Yeni Yaklaşımlar* 5 (Spring 2007): 164–7; Zaven Der Yeghiayan, *My Patriarchal Memoirs* (Barrington: Mayreni, 2002), 22–4.

5 Kapancızâde Hamit, *Bir Milli Mücadele valisi ve anıları: Kapancızâde Hamit Bey*, ed. Halit Eken (Istanbul: Yeditepe, 2008), 465–6.

6 Hans-Lukas Kieser, *Türklüğe İhtida. 1870-1939 İsvicre'sinde Yeni Türkiye'nin Oncüleri* (Istanbul: İletisim, 2008), 109–14; Doğan Çetinkaya, "'Revenge! Revenge! Revenge!': 'Awakening a Nation' through Propaganda in the Ottoman Empire during the Balkan Wars (1912–13)," in Kieser et al., *World War I and the End of the Ottomans*, 77–102.

7 Doğan Çetinkaya, *The Young Turks and the Boycott Movement* (London: I.B. Tauris, 2014), 39–159.

8 Kieser et al., "Reform or Cataclysm?," 292–3. See also Michael Reynolds, *Shattering Empires: The Clash and Collapse of the Ottoman and Russian Empires, 1908–1918* (Cambridge: Cambridge University Press, 2011), 58–70.

9 Mustafa Hayri, *Şeyhülislam Ürgüplü Mustafa Hayri Efendi'nin Mesrutiyet, Büyük Harp ve Mütareke günlükleri (1909–1922)*, ed. Ali Suat Ürgüplü (Istanbul: Türkiye İş Bankası, 2015), 281–2, April 1, 1913.

10 Hayri, *Şeyhülislam Ürgüplü Mustafa Hayri Efendi'nin Mesrutiyet*, 286, April 6, 290–1; April 14–15, 1913; 295, April 27.

11 Zekeriya Türkmen, *Vilayât-ı Şarkiye Islahat Müfettişliği* (Ankara: Türk Tarih Kurumu, 2006), 33; Hayri, *Günlükleri*, 299–300, May 13, 1913.

12 Mandelstam, *Empire ottoman*, 224.

13 Austrian ambassador Pallavicini, Istanbul, to Foreign Minister Berchtold, June 28, 1913, in: *The Armenian Genocide* [in Austrian State Archives] (Munich: Institut für armenische Fragen, 1988), 104–5.

14 Mehmed Cavid, *Meşrutiyet Ruznâmesi* (Ankara: TTK, 2015), 2:170, October 22, 1913, henceforth quoted as CD (= Cavid Diary); Pomiankowski, *Zusammenbruch*, 163. See also Chapter 13 on Wangenheim.

15 Wangenheim and Bethmann Hollweg, November 19, 1913, PA-AA/R 14082.

16 Thomas Schmutz, "The German Role in the Reform Discussion of 1913-14," in Kieser et al., *World War I and the End of the Ottomans*, 195–6.

17 Robert Graves, *Storm Centers of the Near East: Personal Memories, 1879–1929* (London: Hutchison, 1933), 287.

18 CD, 2:250–1, November 13, 1913; cf. 2:280–2, November 20, 1913; 2:366–7, December 4, 1913.

19   Muhittin Birgen, *İttihat ve Terakki'de on sene. İttihat ve Terakki neydi?* (Istanbul: Kitap, 2006), 172.

20   CD, 2:340, November 30, 1913.

21   CD 2:420, December 26, 1913.

22   CD, 2:426, December 28, 1913.

23   Krikor Zohrap, *Collected Works* (in Armenian), ed. Albert Charourian (Erivan, 2003), 4:356–7 and 363.

24   Schmutz, "The German Role," 93.

25   CD, 1:770, July 12, 1913; 2:341, November 30, 1913.

26   Kieser, *Talaat*, 63–6.

27   "One lives with a little, nearly nothing, but the experience shows that one lives nevertheless. No functionary has left his post. One expects better days, and the payment of even the most miserable salaries is welcomed like a feast." Diary of Louis Rambert, vol. 47, April 5 and April 14, 1914 (Museum of the Vieux Montreux, Montreux); henceforth: Rambert diary.

28   Mustafa Aksakal, *The Ottoman Road to War in 1914: The Ottoman Empire and the First World War* (Cambridge: Cambridge University Press, 2008), 48.

29   Halil Menteşe, *Osmanlı Mebusan Meclisi Reisi Halil Menteşe'nin anıları* (Istanbul: Hürriyet Vakfı, 1986), 165–6; similar figure (119, 938) given by the Rûm Patriarchate. The figure for all Rûm expelled in the first half of 1914 is ca. 250,000, see Emmanuil Emmanuilidis, *Osmanlı İmparatorluğu'nun son yılları* (Istanbul: Belge, 2014), 51 and 152.

30   Menteşe, *Anıları*, 166. Talaat's telegram from contemporary Greek sources, quoted in Fuat Dündar, *Modern Türkiye'nin şifresi. İttihat ve Terakki'nin etnisite mühendisliği (1913-1918)* (Istanbul: Iletisim, 2008), 211. As Dündar notes, the Ottoman authorities denied the originality of the telegram, chillingly arguing that they would give such an order orally, not in written form.

31   Félix Sartiaux, "Le sac de Phocée et l'expulsion des Grecs ottomans d'Asie Mineure en juillet 1914," *Revue des deux mondes* 84 (November–December 1914): 656; Emre Erol, "Macedonian Question, in Western Anatolia: The Ousting of the Ottoman Greeks before World War I," in Kieser et al., *World War I and the End*, 110.

32   Andrew D. Kalmykow, *Memoirs of a Russian Diplomat: Outposts of the Empire, 1893-1917* (New Haven, CT: Yale University Press, 1971), 258.

33   Rambert diary, vol. 48, June 12, 16, 18, and 19, 1914; Emmanuilidis, *Osmanlı İmparatorluğu'nun son yılları*, 266. See also Ahmet Efiloğlu, *İttihat ve Terakki azınlıklar politikası* (Ph.D thesis, University of Istanbul, 2007), 281.

34   Rambert diary, vol. 48, June 12, 1914; Hasan Babacan, *Mehmed Talât Paşa, 1874–1921. Siyasi hayatı ve icraatı* (Ankara: TTK, 2005), 93.

35   Armen Garo (alias Karekin Pastermadjian): "My Last Encounter with Talaat Pasha," *Hayrenik* 1, no. 2 (1922): 39–45.

36   Meclis-i Mebusan Zabıt Ceridesi (MMCZ), İçtima-ı Fevkalâde, period 2 (Ankara, 1991), 2:606–14, meeting of July 6, 1914 (23 Haziran 1330).

37   "Les déclarations de Talaat bey," *Le Jeune-Turc: Journal ottoman quotidien*, July 8, 1914, 1.

38   BOA DH. ŞFR 43/71. See also Dr. Mehmed Reşid, *Mehmed Reşid [Şahingiray]: Hayatı ve Hâtıraları*, ed. N. Bilgi (İzmir: Akademi Kitabevi, 1997), 22.

39   Wangenheim to Auswärtiges Amt, August 6, 1914, PA-AA/R 1913.

40   The Ottoman government declared the Reform Agreement invalid on December 31, 1914. See BOA.DH.ID 186/72, quoted in Türkmen, *Vilayât-ı şarkiye*, 84.

41 Yektan Turkyılmaz, *Rethinking Genocide: Violence and Victimhood in Eastern Anatolia, 1913–1915* (Ph.D thesis, Duke University, Durham, NC, 2011), 217–19.
42 PA-AA/R 14085.
43 Note quoted in Akçam, *The Young Turks' Crime against Humanity*, 133.
44 PA-AA/R 14085.
45 As he writes in a report of May 31, 1915, PA-AA/R 14086.
46 PA-AA Kon. 169.
47 These Kurmanj Kurdish verses are quoted in Nuri Dersimi, *Hatıratım* (Stockholm: Roja Nû, 1986), 75.
48 Quoted in Hans-Lukas Kieser, "Réformes ottomanes et cohabitation entre chrétiens et Kurdes," *Etudes rurales* 186 (2010): 53.

Chapter 5

1 For a comprehensive new study of the Lausanne Conference, see Kieser, *When Democracy Died*.
2 Zara Steiner, *The Lights that Failed: European International History 1919–1933* (Oxford: Oxford University Press, 2007), 123–5.
3 Matthew S. Anderson, *The Eastern Question, 1774–1923* (New York: St. Martin's Press, 1966); Steiner, *Lights that Failed*, 123–5.
4 *Huzursuz* used here in the sense of "deprived of societal peace" (*huzur*).
5 Kieser, *Talaat*, 395–403.
6 Kieser and Schaller, *Der Völkermord an den Armeniern und die Shoah*, 5 and 34–9.
7 Lewis V. Thomas and Richard N. Frye, *The United States and Turkey and Iran* (Cambridge, MA: Harvard University Press, 1951), 61–2.
8 Gazi Mustafa Kemal (Atatürk), *Nutuk* (Istanbul: Kaynak, 2015), 582.
9 Mandelstam, *Empire ottoman*, 406 and 414. See also his *La Société des Nations et les puissances devant le problème arménien* (Paris: A. Pedone, 1925). See also Hülya Adak, "The Legacy of André Nikolaievitch Mandelstam (1869–1949) and the Early History of Human Rights," *Zeitschrift Für Religions- und Geistesgeschichte* 70, no. 2 (2018): 117–30.
10 See the files in the League of Nations archives related to Mandelstam's fight for the rights of stateless Armenians (https://libraryresources.unog.ch/lontad), and also Varoujan Attarian, *Le génocide des Arméniens devant l'ONU* (Bruxelles: Complexe, 1997), 49.
11 Bilal Şimşir, ed., *Lozan Telgrafları* (Ankara: TTK 1990), vol. 1, xiv. See also Chapter 6 on Nur.
12 Harold G. Nicolson, *Curzon: The Last Phase, 1919–1925: A Study in Post-War Diplomacy* (London: Constable, 1934), 314–50.
13 Kemal, *Nutuk*, with dozens of pages on the Conference of Lausanne. For an elaborate example from the press by then-journalist and later minister Necmeddin Sadık Sadak, see *Necmeddin Sadık (Sadak) Bey'in Lozan Mektupları*, ed. Mustafa Özyürek (Ankara: Gece, 2019).
14 "İkinci dönemi açarken," August 13, 1923, in: Mustafa Kemal Atatürk, *Atatürk'ün Söylev ve Demeçleri* (Ankara: Atatürk Kültür Dil ve Tarih Yüksek Kurumu, 1997), vol. 1, 336.
15 Kieser, *Talaat*, 257–8 and 319–20.

16 Rıza Nur, *Hayat ve Hatıratım* (Istanbul: İsaret, 1992), vol. 3, 163–4.

17 Kemal, *Nutuk*, 534.

18 Sara-Marie Demiriz, *Vom Osmanen zum Türken: Nationale und staatsbürgerliche Erziehung durch Feier- und Gedenktage in der Türkischen Republik 1923–1938* (Baden-Baden: Ergon, 2018), 73–98; Hans Kieser, "Die Herausbildung des türkisch-nationalen Geschichtsdiskurses (spätes 19.–Mitte 20. Jahrhundert)," in *Vom Beruf zur Berufung. Geschichtswissenschaft und Nationsbildung in Ostmittel- und Südosteuropa im 19. und 20. Jahrhundert*, ed. Markus Krzoska and Christian Maner (Munster: Lit, 2005), 59–98.

19 *Lausanne Conference on Near Eastern Affairs (1922-1923): Records of Proceedings and Draft Terms of Peace* (London: His Majesty's Stationery Office, 1923—from now *LCNE*), 1–5.

20 Necmeddin Sadık, "Lozan Mektupları: 26-27 Kanûn-i Evvel 1922," in Özyürek, *Lozan Mektupları*, 193–8.

21 Norman M. Naimark, *Fires of Hatred: Ethnic Cleansing in Twentieth-Century Europe* (Cambridge, MA: Harvard University Press, 2002), 54.

22 "Report by Dr. Nansen," *League of Nations Official Journal*, January 1923, 127.

23 Mehmed Şükrü (Koçoğlu), quoted in Lerna Ekmekcioglu, "Republic of Paradox: The League of Nations Minority Protection Regime and the New Turkey's Step-Citizens," *International Journal of Middle East Studies* 46, no. 4 (2014): 657–8.

24 *LCNE*, 53.

25 *Conférence de Lausanne sur les affaires du Proche-Orient (1922-1923). Recueil des actes de la conférence* (Paris: Imprimerie Nationale, 1923), first series, vol. 1, 182, 244.

26 Nicolson, *Curzon*, 79.

27 Noradunghian Papers and Actes de la délégation nationale, Bibliothèque Nubar, Paris.

28 For this Convention, see *LCNE*, 817–27.

29 Rıza Nur, *Ermeni Tarihi*, manuscript (Staatsbibliothek zu Berlin, Ms. Orient Quart 1394), 473.

30 Alexandre Khatissian, *Eclosion et développement de la République arménienne* (Athens: Editions Arméniennes, 1989, in Armenian 1930), 317–428.

31 *LCNE*, 342, 374, 390, 404.

32 Notably *LCNE*, 211–12.

33 Özbudun, "Constitution Writing," 168.

34 Mahmut Bozkurt, "Türk Medenî Kanunu nasıl hazırlandı?," in *Medenî kanunun XV. Yıl Dönümü İçin* (Istanbul: Kenan Matbaası, 1944), 8.

35 Ismet İnönü, *İsmet İnönü'nün hatıraları: Büyük zaferden sonra Mudanya Mütarekesi ve Lozan Antlaşması* (Istanbul: Yenigün, 1998), 54–5.

36 C. J. Burckhardt and H. von Hofmannsthal, *Briefwechsel* (Frankfurt, 1991), 119–20, letter of August 4, 1923.

37 Burckhardt and Hofmannsthal, *Briefwechsel*, 120.

38 Karl Helfferich, *Die deutsche Türkenpolitik* (Berlin: Vossische Buchhandlung, 1921), 3 and 31.

39 Hitler's secretary Fritz Lauböck to Hans Tröbst, a German officer fighting for Ankara during the Anatolia wars; quoted in Thomas Weber, *Becoming Hitler: The Making of a Nazi* (Oxford: Oxford University Press, 2017), 275.

40 Hans Tröbst, *Soldatenblut: Vom Baltikum zu Kemal Pascha* (Leipzig: Koehler, 1925), 329.

41 Schmitt, *Die geistesgeschichtliche Lage des heutigen Parlamentarismus* (Berlin: Duncker & Humblot 1926), 14. Hauptmann [Hans] Tröbst, "Mustafa Kemal Pascha und sein

Werk (VI)," *Heimatland*, Oktober 15, 1923, quoted in Ihrig, *Atatürk in the Nazi Imagination*, 85–6.

42 Mandelstam, *Société des Nations*, 340.

43 Leonhard Ragaz, *Mein Weg* (Zürich: Diana, 1952), vol. 1, 182.

44 See Kieser, "Gedenken an den Armeniermord und den Holocaust," as well as idem, "Die Schweiz des Fin de siècle und 'Armenien,'" in idem, *Die armenische Frage und die Schweiz*, 133–58.

45 Karl Meyer, *Armenien und die Schweiz* (Bern: Blaukreuz-Verlag, 1974), 142–3.

46 He established an "Armenian home" for orphans in Begnins, between Lausanne and Geneva. See Antony Kraft-Bonnard, *L'Arménie à la Conférence de Lausanne* (Alençon: Foi et vie, 1923) and also the recent homage, including by descendants of Begnins' orphans: Sisvan Nigolian and Pascal Roman, eds., *Sauver les enfants, sauver l'Arménie: la contribution du pasteur Antony Kraft-Bonnard (1919–1945)* (Lausanne: Antipodes, 2020).

47 Archives Cantonal Vaudoises, ATS: A. Fonjallaz, "Ismet Pacha et le colonel Fonjallaz," *Journal de Genève*, November 15, 1922, 10; Claude Cantini, *Le colonel fasciste suisse, Arthur Fonjallaz* (Lausanne: Pierre-Marcel Favre, 1983). For the comparable turn to Kemalism, Fascism, and Nazism of the Vaudois Paul Gentizon, see Olivier Decottignies, "Un correspondant de presse en Turquie: Paul Gentizon ou l'Orient en marche," in *Turcs et Français: Une histoire culturelle, 1860–1960*, ed. G. Işıksel and E. Szurek (Rennes: Presses universitaires de Rennes, 2014), 195–211.

48 Mahmut Esat Bozkurt, *Atatürk ihtilali* (Istanbul: Kaynak, 1995; first ed., 1940), 73. See also Chapter 10.

49 Major du Bois, "Eine Unterredung mit Ismet Pascha," *Neue Zürcher Zeitung*, no. 1016, July 25, 1923.

Chapter 6

1 A framed photograph of the Treaty's signing was presented to then-Turkish Prime Minister Erdogan at a memorial ceremony in Moscow in 2011. "Meeting of High-Level Russian-Turkish Cooperation Council," March 16, 2011, http://en.kremlin.ru/events/president/news/10657.

2 Nur, *Hayat*, vol. 3, 167.

3 Nur, *Ermeni Tarihi*, 477.

4 See Introduction and Chapter 9.

5 See Tanıl Bora, *Cereyanlar—Türkiye'de siyasi ideolojiler* (Istanbul: Iletisim, 2016), 271.

6 See several related articles in the Turkish press in 1963–4, reproduced in Nur, *Hayat ve Hatıratım*, vol. 1, 31–68. See notably Cavit O. Tütengil, "Gizli kalmış önemli bir belge," *Cumhuriyet*, March 9, 1964, 2, reproduced in ibid., 36–40. The party program is partly reproduced in the 1967 edition of *Hayat ve Hatıratım*, 9–17, and in full extent in vol. 2, 463–532, of the 1992 edition.

7 *Ziya Gökalp'ın neşredilmemiş yedi eseri ve aile mektupları*, ed. Ali Nüzhet Göksel (Istanbul: Işıl, 1956), 8–9.

8 Rıza Nur, *Türk Tarihi* (Istanbul: Toker, 1994, first published 1924), vol. 1, 11.

9 Köprülüzade (Mehmet Fuat Köprülü), *Türkiya Tarihi: Anadolu istilasina kadar Türkler* (Istanbul: Kanaat Kütüphanesi, 1923), 4–6.

10 Nur, *Türk Tarihi*, 19.

11 Nur, *Türk Tarihi*, 19.

12 Nur, *Türk Tarihi*, 20. For an analogous view by Atatürk of foreign invasion in Anatolia, see *Atatürk'ün Söylev ve Demeçleri*, vol. 2, 130–2.

13 Nur, *Ermeni Tarihi*, 226, see also 462.

14 Nur, *Hayat*, vol. 2, 260.

15 Nur, *Türk Tarihi*, vol. 1, 12.

16 Nur, *Hayat*, vol. 2, 411.

17 Nur, *Ermeni Tarihi*, 482.

18 Nur, *Ermeni Tarihi*, 426–8.

19 Nur, *Ermeni Tarihi*, 239 and 268, see also 439 and 476–9.

20 Nur, *Ermeni Tarihi*, 474.

21 Nur, *Ermeni Tarihi*, 473 and 487.

22 Nur, *Ermeni Tarihi*, 7.

23 Nur, *Ermeni Tarihi*, 473.

24 Nur, *Ermeni Tarihi*, 490.

25 Nur, *Hayat*, vol. 2, 347–8.

26 *LCNE*, 303–8.

27 *İnönü'nün Hatıraları*, 120.

28 Khatissian, *Eclosion*, 413.

29 *LCNE* 322, 333, 335, and 348.

30 "Conférence de Lausanne: Quelques minutes avec Riza Nour," *Gazette de Lausanne*, July 20, 1923, 4.

31 Nur, *Hayat*, vol. 2, 247.

32 Andrew Mango, *Atatürk* (London: John Murray, 1999), 381–4.

33 CD vol. 4, 522–3, April 8, 1923.

34 See special issue on Rıza Nur of the *Wiener Zeitschrift für die Kunde des Morgenlandes*, in preparation for 2024.

35 Until 1935 under a different name. See Etienne Copeaux, *Espaces et temps de la nation turque: analyse d'une historiographie nationaliste, 1931–1993* (Paris: CNRS Editions, 1997), 60–1.

36 Murat Gencoğlu, "Atsız, Dr Rıza Nur'u Anlatıyor," *Millî Yol Dergisi*, September 7, 1962.

37 Nihal Atsız, "Kürdler ve Komünistler," *Ötüken*, April 30, 1966, online at https://huseyinnihalatsiz.com/makale/kurdler-ve-komunistler.

Chapter 7

1 Reşat Halli, *Türkiye Cumhuriyetinde ayaklanmalar (1924–1938)*, ed. Directorate of the General Staff for Military History (Ankara: Genelkurmay Basımevi, 1972).

2 Naşit H. Uluğ, *Tunceli Medeniyete açılıyor* (Istanbul: Kaynak, 2007 [first ed. 1939]).

3 From cirrhosis due to chronic heavy alcohol consumption, see Mango, *Atatürk*, 518.

4 See Hans-Lukas Kieser, "Return of the Suppressed: Atatürk's History Doctrine, Islam, and the Armenian Genocide," in *After the Ottomans: Genocide's Long Shadow and Armenian Resilience*, ed. Hans-Lukas Kieser, Seyhan Bayraktar, and Khatchig Mouradian (London: I.B. Tauris, 2023), 33–54.

5 Halli, *Ayaklanmalar*, 375.

6 Naşit H. Uluğ, *Derebeyi ve Dersim* (Istanbul: Kaynak, 2009 [first ed. 1932]).

7   M. Kalman, *Belge ve Tanıklarıyla Dersim Direnişleri* (Istanbul: Nujen, 1995), 135–68; Hüseyin Aygün, *Dersim 1938 ve zorunlu iskân, Telgraflar, dilekçeler, mektuplar* (Ankara: Dipnot, 2009), 57–89.

8   Elazığ was renamed from Elaziz in 1937; Turkification of local names began during the First World War.

9   Jandarma Umum Kumandanlığı Raporu, *Dersim. Jandarma Umum Kumandanlığı raporu* (Istanbul: Kaynak, 2010 [first ed. 1932]), 59.

10 Hans-Lukas Kieser, "The Anatolian Alevis' Ambivalent Encounter with Modernity in Late Ottoman and Early Republican Turkey," in *The Other Shiites. From the Mediterranean to Central Asia*, ed. A. Monsutti, S. Naef, and F. Sabahi (Bern: Peter Lang, 2007), 41–58.

11 Halli, *Ayaklanmalar*, 351–2.

12 Gezik, *Alevi Kürtler: Dinsel, etnik ve politik sorunlar bağlamında* (Ankara: Kalan, 2004), 141–76; Kieser, "The Anatolian Alevis," 142–3.

13 Nuri Dersimi, *Hatıratım* (Stockholm: Roja Nû, 1986 [first ed. 1952]), 100–3; Halli, *Ayaklanmalar*, 373–4; Kieser, *Der verpasste Friede*, 396; Hülya Küçük, *The Role of the Bektashis in Turkey's National Struggle* (Leiden: Brill, 2001), 212–23.

14 Bozarslan, "Histoire des relations arméno-kurdes," 170–1.

15 Erol Ülker, "Assimilation, Security and Geographical Nationalization in Interwar Turkey: The Settlement Law of 1934," *European Journal of Turkish Studies* 7 (2008), https://doi.org/10.4000/ejts.2123.

16 Nur, *Hayat*, vol. 2, 260; idem, *Türk Tarihi*, vol. 11–12, 433.

17 *Son Posta*, September 20, 1930, cited in Şaduman Halıcı, *Yeni Türkiye'de devletinin yapılanmasında Mahmut Esat Bozkurt (1892–1943)* (Ankara: Atatürk Araştırma Merkezi, 2004), 348. For a similar statement of the Prime Minister at the time, Ismet İnönü, on the Turks' exclusive "ethnic and racial rights" in Asia Minor, see *Milliyet*, August 31, 1930. The vision of Kurds as assimilable inferior people is built in Gökalp's definition of Turkish nationalism, see Chapter 8.

18 Ülker, "Assimilation, Security and Geographical Nationalization," 8; İsmail Beşikçi, *Tunceli kanunu (1935) ve Dersim jenosidi* (Ankara: Yurt Kitap-Yayın, 1992, first ed. 1990), 17.

19 Aslan Şükrü, ed., *Herkesin bildiği sır: Dersim* (Istanbul: İletişim, 2010), 411.

20 Suat Akgül, *Yakın tarihimizde Dersim isyanları ve gerçekler* (Istanbul: Boğaziçi Yay., 1992), 37–40, 63–8.

21 Halli, *Ayaklanmalar*, 375.

22 Akgül, *Yakın tarihimizde*, 124–5; Dersimi, *Hatıratım*, 237–9; report of Vali Tevfik Sırrı of November 28, 1933, BCA Yer No: 30 10 00. 110.741.21, Başbakanlık Cumhuriyet Arşivi, Ankara.

23 Halli, *Ayaklanmalar*, 390–1 and 491.

24 İhsan Sabri Çağlayangil, "Kader bizi una değil, üne itti," in *Çağlayangil'in anıları*, ed. Tanju Cilizoğlu (Istanbul: Bilgi Yayınevi, 2007), 69–73; Kieser, *Quest*, 249–51.

25 Halli, *Ayaklanmalar*, 412.

26 Akgül, *Yakın tarihimizde*, 155.

27 Aygün, *Dersim 1938 ve zorunlu iskân*, 72.

28 Halli, *Ayaklanmalar*, 463.

29 Halli, *Ayaklanmalar*, 465. See also Özel, "The Role of Teşkilat-ı Mahsusa."

30 Halli, *Ayaklanmalar*, 463.

31 Aslan, *Herkesin*, 411.

32 David McDowall, *A Modern History of the Kurds* (London: I.B. Tauris, 2000), 209.

33 Dersimi, *Hatıratım*, 318–20.

34 İlhami Algör, *Ma sekerdo kardaş? Dersim Tanıklıkları* (Istanbul: Doğan, 2010), 159; Faik Bulut, *Belgerle Dersim raporları* (Istanbul: YÖN, 1991), 299–301. "Giavour" (*gavur*) means "unbeliever," that is, non-Muslim, in the popular language of Turkey.

35 For further information and a rich collection of interviews with Armenian survivors, or descendants of survivors, of 1938, see Kâzım Gündoğan, *Alevileş(tiril)miş Ermeniler* (Istanbul: Ayrıntı, 2022).

36 Quoted in MacDowall, *Modern History*, 209.

37 Bulut, *Belgerle*, 183–206 and 299–304; see "Dersim Katliamı'ndaki askerler konuştu," *CNN Turk*, May 3, 2011.

38 Soldier Halil Çolak, in Bulut, *Belgerle*, 300–1.

39 Notably Aygün, *Dersim 1938 ve zorunlu iskân*, and idem, *Dersim 1938: Resmiyete karşı hakikat* (Istanbul: Dipnot, 2010); Cemal Taş, *Dağların kayıp anahtarı. Dersim 1938 anlatıları* (Istanbul: İletisim, 2010).

40 Wolf-Gero Westhoff, "1937–38 Dersim Oral History Project," in *2012–13 Year End Report* (Worcester: Strassler Center for Holocaust and Genocide Studies, 2013), 10.

41 Namely Kâzım and Nezahat Gündoğan, *İki tutam saç—Dersim'in kayıp kızları* (2010) and *Hay Way Zaman: Dersim'in Kayıp Kızları* (2014), both films on the destiny of girls targeted by violence, intimidation, and a systematic child transfer that served the destruction of Dersim's autonomous culture. Both films are based on documentation collected in the same book, *Dersim'in kayıp kızları: "Tertelê Çêneku" (Kızların kıyımı)* (Istanbul: İletisim, 2012). Nezahat Gündoğan's third related documentary *Vank'ın çocukları* (2015) focuses on Armenians who survived in Dersim; it includes the massacres of 1895–6 and the genocide of 1915. Kâzım Gündoğan has published the relevant research in *Keşiş'in Torunları: Dersimli Ermeniler* (Istanbul: Ayrıntı, 2016).

42 Şükrü Laçin, *Dersim isyanından Diyarbakır'a bir Kürt işçisinin siyasal anıları* (Istanbul: Sun, 1992), 26–9 and 41–2.

43 Uluğ, *Tunceli Medeniyete.*

44 Esra Sarıkoyuncu, "Amerikan basınında doğu isyanları 1925-1938," *Akademik Bakış 3* (Summer 2010): 97–121.

45 Dersimi, *Hatıratım*, 333–8; Kieser, *Quest*, 245–55; Taş, *Dağların kayıp anahtarı*, 36–7; BCA 030.10 0 0.111.745.11.

46 Abdülkadir Badıllı, *Bediüzzaman Said Nursi, Mufassal Tarihçe-i Hayatı* (İstanbul: Timaş, 1990), 1134 (as according to *Zaman*, December 4, 2008).

47 Laçin, *Dersim isyanından*, 37; cf. Beşikçi, *Tunceli*, 256–64.

48 Particularly poignant is Haydar Karataş's novel *Gece Kelebeği/Perperık-a Söe*, which is based on the first-hand account of the author's mother (Istanbul: İletişim, 2010); now also in English, translated by Caroline Stockford, *Butterfly of the Night* (London: Palewell Press, 2021).

49 Hıdır Göktas, *Kürtler: İsyan—tenkil* (Istanbul: Alan, 1991), 5.

50 Bilgin Ayata and Serra Hakyemez, "The AKP's Engagement with Turkey's Past Crimes: An Analysis of PM Erdoğan's 'Dersim Apology'," *Dialect Anthropology* 37 (2013): 131–43.

51 Ali Civi in *Zaman İsviçre*, November 27, 2009.

52 *Hürriyet Daily News*, April 27, 2010.

53 Beşikçi, *Tunceli kanunu (1935) ve Dersim jenosidi.*

54 Martin van Bruinessen, "Genocide in Kurdistan? The Suppression of the Dersim Rebellion in Turkey (1937-1938) and the Chemical War against the Iraqi Kurds

(1988)," in *Genocide—Conceptual and Historical Dimensions*, ed. G. Andreopoulos (Philadelphia: University of Pennsylvania Press, 1994), 143.

55 Nicole Watts, "Relocating Dersim: Turkish State-Building and Kurdish Resistance, 1931-1938," *New Perspectives on Turkey* 23 (Fall 2000): 5–30; Van Bruinessen, "Genocide in Kurdistan?"

56 See now notably Ahmet K. Gültekin and Erdal Gezik, *Kurdish Alevis and the Case of Dersim: Historical and Contemporary Insights* (Lanham, MD: Lexington Books, 2019); Annika Törne, *Dersim—Geographie der Erinnerungen: Eine Untersuchung von Narrativen über Verfolgung und Gewalt* (Berlin: De Gruyter, 2019); Ozlem Goner, *Turkish National Identity and Its Outsiders: Memories of State Violence in Dersim* (Routledge: Taylor & Francis), 2018.

57 Erik Jan Zürcher, *Turkey, a Modern History* (London: I.B. Tauris, 2004), 176.

58 See Kieser, "Return of the Suppressed."

Chapter 8

1 "Kızılelma," *Türk Yurdu*, January 23, 1913, transcribed edition: Ankara: Tutibay, 1998, vol. 2, 118. Quotations below from this edition.

2 Alp (alias Moïz Kohen Tekinalp), *Le Kemalisme* (Paris: Librairie Félix Alcan, 1937), 24.

3 Yahya Kemal, "Şahsî hatıralar," *Türk Yurdu*, December 1924, 8: 104.

4 Richard Hartmann, "Ziya Gökalp's Grundlagen des türkischen Nationalismus," *Orientalistische Literaturzeitung* 28 (1925): 579; August Fischer, *Aus der religiösen Reformbewegung in der Türkei: Türkische Stimmen verdeutscht* (Leipzig: Harrassowitz, 1922), 5–7.

5 Birgen, *İttihat ve Terakki'de on sene*, 382.

6 Although Gökalp often modified poems, the verses in question appear to be a later addition, though well in line with Gökalp's rhetoric. Erdoğan, "Asker Duası şiirini yeniden okudu: Minareler süngü, kubbeler miğfer," *Karar*, March 7, 2019; Murat Bardakçı, "Şiiri böyle montajlamışlar," *Hürriyet*, September 22, 2002.

7 Falih R. Atay, *Çankaya* (Istanbul: Pozitif, n.d.), 429.

8 Alparslan Türkeş, "Türk milliyetçiliğinin dayanması gereken temeller," *Devlet*, October 4, 1974, 6–7, quoted in Mehmet Günal, "Alparslan Türkeş'in ekonomi anlayışı ve dokuz ışık doktrininde ekonomi," in: Y. Sarıkaya and İ.F. Aksu (eds.), *Doğumun 100. Dönümünde lider Türkiye için Alparslan Türkeş vizyonu* (Ankara: TASAV, 2018), 247–8.

9 Niyazi Berkes, "Ziya Gökalp: His Contribution to Turkish Nationalism," *The Middle East Journal* 8, no. 4 (Autumn 1954): 375. Nevertheless, the most recent attempt at a biography of Gökalp in a Western language dates from 1950. See also idem, *Turkish Nationalism and Western Civilization: Selected Essays of Ziya Gökalp* (New York: Columbia University Press, 1959); Uriel Heyd, *Foundations of Turkish Nationalism: The Life and Teachings of Ziya Gökalp* (London: Harvill, 1950); Taha Parla, *The Social and Political Thought of Ziya Gökalp 1876-1924* (Leiden: Brill, 1985), and Enver B. Şapolyo, *Ziya Gökalp: İttihat ve Terakki ve Meşrutiyet tarihi* (Istanbul: Güven, 1943). For a recent critical analysis of Gökalp: Hamit Bozarslan, "M. Ziya Gökalp," in *Modern Türkiye'de siyasi düşünce: Tanzimat ve Meşrutiyet'in birikimi* (Istanbul: Iletisim, 2001), 314–19; and idem, *Histoire de la Turquie: De l'Empire à nos jours* (Paris: Tallandier,

2013), 454–63. For a recent analysis emphasizing the intra-Ottoman and intra-Islamic sources of Gökalp's thought: Alp Eren Topal, "Against Influence: Ziya Gökalp in Context and Tradition," *Journal of Islamic Studies* 28, no. 3 (2017): 283–310 (including a review of literature).

10 Tanıl Bora, *Türk sağının üç hâli* (Istanbul: Birikim, 2003), 115–16.

11 There are many more examples by contemporaries for the use of "race" alongside a Muslim supremacist tone in nationalist poetry, not least in Mehmet Akif Ersoy's *İstiklal Marşı*, the Turkish National Anthem (1921).

12 Poem "Bana Türke değil diyene," quoted in Jean Deny, "Zia Goek Alp," *Revue du monde musulman* 61 (1925): 3.

13 Deny, "Zia Goek Alp," 1.

14 See Kieser, *Talaat*.

15 Ziya Gökalp, "Türklük," journal *Genç Kalemler*, August 9, 1911; poem in Turkish and French in Deny, "Zia Goek Alp," 25–6. Eren, "Against Influence," 302–7, explores Gökalp's connection with Ibn Khaldun's Ottoman reception.

16 Pertinent in this respect is Masami Arai's analysis of the CUP's *İslâm Memuası* in his book *Turkish Nationalism in the Young Turk Era* (Leiden: E.J. Brill, 1992).

17 See, in this vein, Parla, *Political Thought*. Influenced by Parla, dismissing poetry: Andrew Davison, "Secularization and Modernization in Turkey: The Ideas of Ziya Gökalp," *International Journal of Human Resource Management*, 24:2 (1995), 189–224.

18 A triumvirate of Talaat, Enver, and Cemal, with Talaat already being the *primus inter pares*, is true only for the eve of the First World War. See Kieser, *Talaat Pasha*, 163.

19 Taking up a thesis put forward in "'Révolution de droite' à partir des marges de l'Empire ottoman tardif: Le maître à penser Ziya Gökalp et le *comitadji* Mehmed Talat," in Hamit Bozarslan (ed.), *Marges et pouvoir dans l'espace (post)ottoman XIXe-XXe siècles* (Paris: Karthala, 2018), 98–100.

20 Ryan Gingeras, *Eternal Dawn: Turkey in the Age of Atatürk* (Oxford: Oxford University Press, 2019) 158–9; Christian J. Neddens, "'Politische Religion': Zur Herkunft eines Interpretationsmodells totalitärer Ideologien," *Zeitschrift für Theologie und Kirche*, 109–13 (September 2012), 307–36.

21 Birgen, *İttihat ve Terakki'de on sene*, 500.

22 M. Şükrü Hanioğlu, *The Young Turks in Opposition* (New York: Oxford University Press, 1995), 121.

23 Gökalp, "Felsefi vasiyetler (3): Pirimin vasiyeti" (October 23, 1922), in the new edition of *Küçük Mecmua* (Antalya: Müdafaa-I Hukuk Yay., 2009), vol. 2, 123.

24 Masami Arai, "Between State and Nation: A New Light on the Journal *Türk Yurdu*," *Turcica* 24 (1992): 289; Sabine Adatepe, "'Das osmanische Muster': Das frühe Ideal des M. Ziya (Gökalp) anhand ausgewählter Artikel in der Wochenschrift Peyman," in *Strukturelle Zwänge—persönliche Freiheiten: Osmanen, Türken, Muslime; Reflexionen zu gesellschaftlichen Umbrüchen: Gedenkband zu Ehren Petra Kapperts*, ed. Hendrik Fenz (Berlin: Walter de Gruyter, 2009), 31–45.

25 In his prose, Gökalp did not adhere to biological racialism, even if in many places, especially in his poems, he is ambivalent. "I am racially a Turk [. . .]. However, I would not hesitate to believe that I am a Turk even if I had discovered that my grandfathers came from the Kurdish or Arab areas; because I learned through my sociological studies that nationality is based solely on upbringing," he wrote autobiographically in 1923 in *Küçük Mecmua* (English translation in Berkes, *Essays*, 44). See also Umut Uzer, "The Kurdish Identity of Turkish Nationalist Thinkers: Ziya Gökalp and Ahmet

Arvasi between Turkish Identity and Kurdish Ethnicity," *Turkish Studies* 14, no. 2 (2013): 399–400; Heyd, *Gökalp*, 38.

26 *Peyman*, July 19, 1909, transcribed in Ziya Gökalp, *Kürt Aşiretler hakkında sosyolojik tetkikler* (Istanbul: Kaynak, 2011), 115.

27 *Peyman*, August 30, 1909, transcribed in Gökalp, *Kürt Aşiretler*, 118.

28 Ziya Gökalp, *Türkçülüğün esasları*, ed. Salim Çonoğlu (Istanbul: Ötüken, 2014; 1st ed. Ankara, 1339 [1923]), 28.

29 As Said Halim, a CUP grand vizier, put it a few years later, he otherwise critiqued Gökalp for maintaining, as he saw it, a stance that was too revolutionary. Ahmet Şeyhun, *Islamist Thinkers in the Late Ottoman Empire and Early Turkish Republic* (Leiden: Brill, 2015), 164. German translation of Said Halim's 1921 booklet *İslamlaşmak* in Fischer, *Aus der religiösen Reformbewegung*, 15–39.

30 Ziya Gökalp, "İçtimaî Neviler," *İslâm Mecmuası*, January 28, 1915, 517–23, transcribed in *İslâm ve Muallim Mecmuası Yazıları*, ed. Salim Çonoğlu (Istanbul: Ötüken, 2019), 51–9.

31 Birgen, *İttihat ve Terakki'de on sene*, 363–4; Uzer, "Gökalp," 398.

32 Gökalp, *Türkçülüğün esasları*, 28–9.

33 *Yurdcular Yasası. İsviçre'de Cenevre şehrine yakın Petit-Lancy Köyünde Pension Racine'de kurulan İkinci Yurdcular Derneği'nin muzakerat ve mukerreratı* (Istanbul: Yeni Turan Matbaası, 1914), transcribed in Kieser, *Türklüğe İhtida*, 247–50.

34 "Millet ve Vatan," published in *Türk Yurdu*, May 28, 1914, as well as "Dinin İçtimaî Vazifeleri," *İslâm Mecmuası*, 1915, both referenced and translated in Berkes, *Essays*, 78 and 192.

35 Ziya Gökalp, "Mefkure," first published in *Türk Yurdu*, January 10, 1913, translated in Berkes, *Essays*, 69.

36 Elton L. Daniel, "Theology and Mysticism in the Writings of Ziya Gökalp," *MW* 67, no. 3 (1977): 179. Eren draws attention to an early article (1909) in which Gökalp "celebrated the dervish lodges (tekke) as an improved version of military barracks and points out the fact that Sufi terms such as *ribât, murâbıt, tarîk, cihâd* and *mücâhid* all have two denotations, one military and one spiritual." Eren, "Against Influence," 298, referring to Ziya Gökalp, *Makaleler I* (Ankara: Kültür Bakanlığı, 1976), 856.

37 Şapolyo, *Ziya Gökalp*, 7–8, 135.

38 Quoted in Şapolyo, *Ziya Gökalp*, 169.

39 Hayri *Günlükleri*, 372, April 29, 1917.

40 Daniel, "Theology and Mysticism," 180–1; Eren, "Against Influence," 297–8.

41 Ziya Gökalp, "Türkün tekbiri," August 9, 1914, quoted in Erol Köroğlu, "Propaganda or Culture War: Jihad, Islam, and Nationalism in Turkish Literature during World War I," in *Jihad and Islam in World War I*, ed. Erik-Jan Zürcher (Leiden: Leiden University Press, 2016), 147; Rauf Yekta, "Millî tekbir hakkında," *Yeni Mecmua: Çanakkale özel sayısı 18 Mart 1918*, transcribed edition (Istanbul: Yeditepe, 2006), 175–6.

42 "Ehl-i İslâm Kızılelma'ya değin fethedecektir," quoted in Halil Ibrahim, "'Kızılelma' üzerine" (introduction) in: Ziya Gökalp, *Kızılelma* (Istanbul: Ötüken, 2015), 12. See also Hans-Lukas Kieser, "Djihad, Weltordnung, 'Goldener Apfel': Die osmanische Reichsideologie im Kontext west-östlicher Geschichte," in *Imperialismus in Geschichte und Gegenwart*, ed. Richard Faber (Würzburg: Königshausen & Neumann, 2004), 183–203.

43 "Kızılelma," *Türk Yurdu*, 2:31 (January 23, 1913), 2:115–20.

44 Poem "Turan," *Altın Armağan*, supplement of *Türk Yurdu*, 1:24, October 17, 1912; transcribed edition, 1: 418.

45 A term used by Gökalp disciple and theorist of Kemalism Moïz Kohen Tekinalp, see
    Alp, *Kemalisme*, 24. See also Kieser, *İhtida*, 200–13.
46 See Zürcher, Jihad, and Josef van Ess, *Dschihad gestern und heute* (Berlin, Boston: de
    Gruyter, 2012), 26–47.
47 Quoted in Köroğlu, "Islam, and Nationalism," 137 and 147; Emmanuilidis, *Osmanlı
    İmparatorluğu'nun son yılları*, 93.
48 Rahmi Apak, a young officer in the campaign: "We went to Turan. We were to
    enter Iranian Azerbaijan to arm the Azeri Turks, then to proceed to Turkestan [vast
    territory east of the Caspian Sea], to arm the Turks there. Thus we wanted to work for
    the great cause of Turan." Rahmi Apak, *Yetmişlik bir subayın hatıraları* (Ankara: TTK,
    1988), 95. The circular is quoted in Tekin Alp, *Türkismus und Pantürkismus* (Weimar:
    Kicpenheuer, 1915), 53.
49 Telegram of Halil Edib, quoted in Reşid, *Hayatı*, 29.
50 "Tal'at Bey," *Tanin*, September 1, 1915, 2.
51 Hüseyin Cahid Yalçın, *Siyasal anılar* (Istanbul: Türkiye İş Bankası, 2000), 316; Fuad
    Köprülü, "Ziya Gökalp'e âit bâzı hâtıralar," in *Ziya Gökalp, Limni ve Malta mektupları*,
    ed. Fevziye A. Tansel (Türk Tarih Kurumu, Ankara, 1989), xxiv.
52 CD, 3:135 and 375–6, August 16 to September 11, 1915 and April 10, 1917.
53 Berkes, "Contribution," 376–7.
54 Belatedly published: Baha Said, "Türkiye'de Alevî zümreleri: Teke Alevîliği-içtimaî
    Alevîlik," *Türk Yurdu*, September 1926, 11: 105–12. Gökalp's report on the Kurds is in
    Gökalp, *Kürt Aşiretler*, 15–110.
55 Zekeriya Sertel, *Hatırladıklarım* (Istanbul: Gözlem, 1977); Yıldız Sertel, *Annem:
    Sabiha Sertel kimdi ve neler yazdı* (Istanbul: Yapı Kredi, 1994), 88–91.
56 Quoted in Nejat Birdoğan, *İttihat-Terakki'nin Alevilik Bektaşilik araştırması* (İstanbul:
    Berfin, 1994), 7–8. See also Markus Dressler, *Writing Religion: The Making of Turkish
    Alevi Islam* (New York: Oxford University Press, 2013), 124–33.
57 Birgen, *İttihat ve Terakki'de on sene*, 370.
58 As Birgen reports from meetings with Talaat, Gökalp, and other CUP luminaries in
    ca. September 1917, Birgen, *İttihat ve Terakki'de on sene*, 401.
59 Otto von Lossow, military attaché at the embassy in Istanbul, in Bernstorff to Foreign
    Office, May 23, 1918, PA-AA/R 14100, English translation from www.armenocide.de.
60 Cavid, *Rûznamesi*, vol. 3.
61 Enver to the commander of the Third Army, Vehib Pasha, June 9, 1918, facsimile in
    Reynolds, *Shattering Empires*, between 166 and 167.
62 Gökalp in *Yeni Mecmua*, July 4, 1918, referred to in Deny, "Zia Goek Alp," 14.
63 Yahya Kemal, "Şahsî hatıralar," 103.
64 Gökalp kept on insisting on the speech of Istanbul as the basis for the new, purified
    "national language," see his 1923 summa *Türkçülüğün esasları*, 125–6.
65 Ziya Gökalp, *Rusya'daki Türkler ne yapmalı?* (Istanbul: Tanin Matbaası, 1918)
    and idem, "İçtimaiyat 'Turan' Nedir?," *Yeni Mecmua* 31 (February 8, 1918): 82–4;
    Necmettin Sadık, "İrtica aleyine . . .," *Yeni Mecmua* 34 (March 7, 1918): 141; Reşid
    Safvet, "Kafkas etekleri Türk ticaret yolları," *Yeni Mecmua* 43 (May 9, 1918): 325.
66 Köprülü, "Ziya Gökalp'e âit," xxiii–xxiv.
67 Talaat to Cavid, December 21, 1919 and January 6, 1920, in Hüseyin C. Yalçın,
    İttihatçı liderlerin gizli mektupları (Istanbul: Temel, 2002 [1944]), 145–7.
68 Before moving to Ankara, he was asked by health and social minister Rıza Nur to
    prepare a report on Kurdish tribes to facilitate their Turkification. Based on Gökalp's
    former studies, posthumously published: Gökalp, *Kürt Aşiretler*, 15–110. See also

Ercan Çağlayan, *Cumhuriyet'in Diyarbakır'da kimlik inşası* (Istanbul: Iletisim, 2014), 17–18; introduction to *Ziya Gökalp'ın neşredilmemiş yedi eseri ve aile mektupları*, ed. Ali Nüzhet Göksel (Istanbul: Işıl, 1956), 8–9. On Nur see Chapter 6.

69 Gökalp, *Türkçülüğün esasları*, 32.

70 Gökalp, *Türkçülüğün esasları*, 30–1.

71 Gökalp, *Türkçülüğün esasları*, 40–5.

72 Gökalp, *Türkçülüğün esasları*, chapter 10 "Hars ve tehzîb," 116–23.

73 "Millet, dilce, dince, zevkçe ve ahlâkça bir olan, yani aynı şartlar altında yetişmiş fertlerden mürekkep bir topluluktur. Şu hâlde Türküm diyen her ferdi Türk tanımaktan başka çare yoktur." Gökalp, *Türkçülüğün esasları*, 13. See also Eric-Jan Zürcher, "The Core Terminology of Kemalism: *Mefkûre, millî, muasır, medenî*," in *Aspects of the Political Language in Turkey*, ed. Hans-Lukas Kieser (Istanbul: Isis, 2002), 104–16.

74 Yusuf Mazhar, *Turkish daily Cumhuriyet*, August 22, 1925, quoted in Deny, "Zia Goek Alp," 3.

75 Making Gökalp a mentor of "solidaristic democracy," as does Parla, *Thought of Ziya Gökalp*, 79, mocks the anti-racist struggle by social democrats for democratic solidarity beyond ethnoreligious boundaries.

76 Berkes, "Contribution," 376.

77 Gökalp, *Türkçülüğün esasları*, 117–21.

78 Ziya Gökalp, *Yeni hayat* (Istanbul: Yeni Mecmua, 1918), transcribed in idem, *Yeni hayat ve doğru yol* (Ankara: Kültür Bakanlığı, 1976), 14.

79 Berkes, "Contribution," 376.

80 Max Weber, "Die protestantische Ethik und der 'Geist' des Kapitalismus," *Archiv für Sozialwissenschaft und Sozialpolitik* 20 (1904): 1–54, and 21 (1905), 1–110.

81 Gökalp, "İttihat ve Terakki Kongresi 6," *İslâm Mecmuası* 3–48, November 9, 1916, and "İttihat ve Terakki Kongresi 6 (Devam)," *İslâm Mecmuası* 4–49, November 30, 1916, reproduced in Gökalp, *İslâm ve Muallim Mecmuası Yazıları*, 98–9 and 104.

82 Ziya Gökalp, "İslamiyet ve asrî medeniyet," *İslâm Mecmuası* 4–52, March 1, 1917, transcribed in Gökalp, *İslâm ve Muallim Mecmuası Yazıları*, 134–5.

83 Gingeras, *Dawn*, 156–9; Markus Dressler, "Rereading Ziya Gökalp: Secularism and Reform of the Islamic State in the Late Young Turk Period," *IJMES* 47 (2015): 517.

84 Kemal Kirisci, "National Identity, Asylum and Immigration: The EU as a Vehicle of Post-National Transformation in Turkey," in *Turkey Beyond Nationalism*, ed. Hans-Lukas Kieser (London: I.B. Tauris, 2006), 188–90.

85 Yahya Kemal, "Şahsî hatıralar," 8: 102.

86 Hans-Lukas Kieser, "Türkische Nationalrevolution, anthropologisch gekrönt. Kemal Atatürk und Eugène Pittard," *Historische Anthropologie* 1 (2006): 111–14.

87 Gökalp, *Türkçülüğün esasları*, 45.

88 Atatürk, "Bakanlar kurulunun görev ve yetkisini belirten kanun teklifi münasebetiyle," December 1, 1921, *Atatürk'ün Söylev ve Demeçleri*, vol. 1, 211. During the Lausanne Conference, the representatives of the Ankara government started to claim the notion of democracy for their regime. The Kemalists continued to do so.

89 Birgen, *İttihat ve Terakki'de on sene*, 697–8.

90 Hanioğlu, *Atatürk*, 191–2.

91 There is novel scholarly literature that takes into account the last Ottoman decade, for too long under-researched, and multiple impacts on interwar Germany. Notably: Ihrig, *Atatürk in the Nazi Imagination*; idem, *Justifying Genocide: Germany and the Armenians from Bismarck to Hitler* (Cambridge, MA: Cambridge University Press,

2016); and Kieser, *Talaat.* Halil Karaveli, *Why Turkey Is Authoritarian: From Atatürk to Erdoğan* (London: Pluto, 2018), underlines the intrinsic fascist traits of Kemalist Turkey and puts sharp distinctions between Kemalism and European fascisms into question. See also for recent comparative fascism studies: Reto Hofmann, *The Fascist Effect: Japan and Italy 1915-1952* (Ithaca, NY: Cornell University Press, 2020), and David D. Roberts, *Fascist Interpretations: Proposals for a New Approach to Fascism and Its Era, 1919-1945* (New York: Berghahn, 2018), 167–74.

Chapter 9

1   See now also Ozan Ozavci, "Honour and Shame: The Diaries of a Unionist and the 'Armenian Question,'" in Kieser et al., *End of the Ottomans*, 193–220; Ayşe Köse Badur, "A Portrait of a Unionist in the Early Republican Era: Mehmed Cavid (1876–1926)," in *The State of the Art in the Early Turkish Republic Period*, ed. B. Der Migrdechian, Ü. Kurt, and A. Sarafian (Fresno: The Press, California State University, 2022), 135–76.
2   Ali Çankaya, *Yeni Mülkiye Tarihi* (Ankara: Mars Matbaası, 1968-9), 711.
3   Cavid, *Meşrutiyet Ruznâmesi*, vol. 4, 425–6, December 26, 1922. Henceforth quoted as CD (= Cavid Diary).
4   CD 1: 19–20, March 8, 1909.
5   CD 4: 374–5, June 29, 1922.
6   CD 3: 135.
7   Cavid Bey, *Şiar'ın Defteri* (Istanbul: Iletisim, 1995). Important are also Cavid's letters to his wife from prison in 1916, the minutes of his interrogation, and his personal defense, in: Çankaya, *Mülkiye*, vol. 3, 693–716.
8   Çankaya, *Mülkiye*, 678–9; *Ali Münif Bey'in hâtıraları*, ed. Tahat Toros (Istanbul: Isis, 1996), 91.
9   Graves, *Storm Centers*, 200–1.
10 CD 1:34, April 12, 1909.
11 CD 1:44, and 47–8, April 30, 1909, April 30 and May 5–7, 1909.
12 Diary of Louis Rambert, vol. 38, November 6, 1910 (Museum of the Vieux Montreux, Montreux).
13 CD 1:62, February 7, 1911.
14 CD 1:107 and 113, April 20, 1911.
15 CD 1:156–7, September 12, 1911; Rambert diary, vol. 39, September 11, 1911.
16 CD 1:186–7, October 29, 1911.
17 CD 1:168–9 and 174, October 16 and 18, 1911.
18 CD 1:442–3, July 22–23, 1912.
19 CD 1:463, October 4, 1912.
20 CD 1:463, October 3–4, 1912.
21 CD 1:537–46, December 23, 1912–February 1, 1913.
22 *Şeyhülislam Ürgüplü Mustafa Hayri Efendi'nin Mesrutiyet*, 257, February 9, 1913; 273–4, March 6, 1913; 284–5, April 1, 1913.
23 CD 1:554, February 6, 1913.
24 CD 2:250–1, November 13, 1913; 2:280–2, November 20, 1913; 2:366–7, December 4, 1913.
25 CD 2:426, December 28, 1913.

26 CD 3:136.
27 On June 13, 1914. Sartiaux, "Le sac de Phocée et l'expulsion des Grecs ottomans," 656.
28 CD 1:512, November 10, 1912.
29 Rambert diary, vol. 47, 5 1914.
30 CD 2:613–16, August 2, 1914.
31 CD 2:616–20, 4, August 10 and 14, 1914.
32 CD 2:642–5, September 5 and 6, 1914.
33 CD 2:675 and 684, October 30 and November 3, 1914.
34 Zohrap, *Collected Works*, 4:401–2.
35 CD 2:682–4, November 3, 1914.
36 See CD 3:21–2, November 30 and December 1, 1914; and 3:141–2,3:141–142, September 22, 1915.
37 CD 3:15, November 23, 1913.
38 CD 3:37, February 19–21, 1915.
39 CD 3:47–51, March 18–30, 1915.
40 CD 3:128, August 19, 1915.
41 CD 3:136–7, n.d. (early September 1915).
42 CD 3:194, June 13, 1916.
43 CD 3:203–6 and 211–12, July 4 and 12, 1916; 3:353, February 3, 1917.
44 CD 3:360, February 14, 1917.
45 "Hayât-ı Teşriyye Meclis-i Mebûsan'da," *Tanin*, February 16, 1917.
46 CD 3:350, February 3, 1917.
47 CD 3:352, February 3, 1917.
48 CD 3:375–6, April 10, 1917. See also 3:562, September 27, 1918.
49 CD 3:449, December 5, 1917. See also 3:377–89, April 11–May 6, 1917; and 3:416, September 5, 1917. For the German position, see also CD 3:147 (Wangenheim); and 3:169, January 5, 1916 (Wolff-Metternich).
50 CD 3:581–2, October 16, 1918.
51 CD 3:407, August 25, 1917; 3:559, September 21, 1918.
52 CD 3:524, July 31, 1918.
53 CD 4:246–7, March 16, 1921.
54 Çankaya, *Mülkiye*, vol. 3, 684, 701–2.
55 CD 4:186–8, December 4 and 7, 1920.
56 CD 4:243–4, March 13, 1921.
57 Ozavci, "Honour and Shame," 219.
58 CD 4:262, April 9, 1921.
59 CD 4:326.
60 CD 4:392, October 5, 1922.
61 CD 4:334.
62 CD 4: 373, June 29, 1922.
63 CD 4:389–90.
64 See Kieser, *Talaat*, 214–15. Nur, *Hayat*, vol. 2, 332.
65 CD, vol. 4, 493; Nur, *Hayat*, vol. 2, 334.
66 CD, vol. 4, 487–8.
67 Bey, *Şiar'ın defteri*, 28–30, November 22, 1924.
68 CD, vol. 4, 326, 336.
69 Ahmet Emin (Yalman), "Mustafa Kemal'in Ahmet Emin'e Verdiği Mülâkat," *Vakit*, January 10, 1922, 1, transliterated version in Mustafa Kemal Atatürk, *Atatürk'ün Söylev ve Demeçleri*, vol. iii, 39–50.

70 CD 4:580, September 10, 1923.

71 CD, vol. 4, 578, September 6, 1923.

72 See Kieser, *Democracy Died*, 224–32.

73 CD, vol. 4, 513, March 17, 1923.

74 CD, vol. 4, 522–3, April 8, 1923.

75 Mango, *Atatürk*, 447.

76 Bey, *Şiar'in Defteri*, 86, April 16, 1925.

77 Bey, *Şiar'in Defteri*, 74–5, March 8, 1925.

78 Bey, *Şiar'in Defteri*, 75–6, March 9, 1925.

79 Erik J. Zürcher, *The Unionist Factor. The Rôle of the Committee of Union and Progress in the Turkish National Movement 1905-1926* (Leiden: Brill, 1984), 155. See also Mango, *Atatürk*, 447–53.

80 Mango, *Atatürk*, 453.

81 Quoted in Mango, *Atatürk*, 452.

82 E.g., Yahya Kemal Beyatlı, quoted in Çankaya, *Mülkiye*, vol. 3, 684–9.

83 Çankaya, *Mülkiye*, vol. 3, 716.

84 Atay, *Çankaya*, 470–1.

Chapter 10

1 *Açık Söz*, June 26, 1928, 1, quoted in Şaduman Halıcı, *Yeni Türkiye devleti'nin yapılanmasında Mahmut Esat Bozkurt (1892-1943)* (Ankara: Atatürk Araştırma Merkezi, 2004), 538.

2 Mahmut Esat Bozkurt, "Esbabı mucibe lâyihası," in *Yargıtay içtihadı birleştirme kararları ve İsviçre Federal Mahkemesi kararları ile notlu Medenî Kanun, Borçlar Kanunu tatbikat kanunu ve ilgili kanunlar-tüzükler yönetmelikler* (Istanbul: Fakülteler Matbaası, 1984, first ed. 1926), XXIX, XXX, and XXXII.

3 For the use of the term "assertive secularism" and the issue of "total state monopoly," see Özbudun, "Constitution Writing and Religious Divisions in Turkey," 159 and 166.

4 Like all other Muslim Turkish nationals, Mahmut E. Bozkurt took a family name only in the early 1930s. Following the Surname Law of 1934, Mahmut Esat adopted the surname "Bozkurt," the name of the emblematic animal (gray wolf) that for the Turkists symbolizes Turkdom. The name had already been given to him informally by Atatürk in 1927 in response to his legal success, in the Bozkurt-Lotus lawsuit in The Hague. Regarding the collision of the ships "Bozkurt" and "Lotus," see Hakkı Uyar, *"Sol milliyetçi" bir Türk aydını Mahmut Esat Bozkurt (1892-1943)* (Ankara: Büke, 2000), 76; Halıcı, *Yeni Türkiye*, 365.

5 Tarık Ziya Işıtman, *Mahmut Esat Bozkurt, Hayatı ve Hatıraları, 1892–1943* (Izmir: Güneş Basım ve yayınevi, 1944), 9–10.

6 Işıtman, *Bozkurt*, 9 and 84.

7 *Ceride-i Adliye* 4-101 (1330/1912), S. 5662–75, quoted in Gülnihal Bozkurt, *Batı hukukunun Türkiye'de benimsenmesi. Osmanlı Devleti'nden Türkiye Cumhuriyeti'ne resepsiyon süreci (1839-1939)* (Ankara: Türk Tarih Kurumu, 1996), 163. See also Halıcı, *Yeni Türkiye*, 278.

8 Quoted in Bozkurt, *Batı hukukunun Türkiye'de benimsenme*, 165.

9 Halıcı, *Yeni Türkiye*, 25.

10 The *Türk Ocağı* were ideologically identical with the *Foyers Turcs* or *Türk Yurdu*;
    Foyers Turcs is used in this chapter as a generic term for both. The proceedings of this
    Geneva congress were published in 1913 in Istanbul in *Yurdcular Yasası*.
11 For a detailed study of this diaspora, see my book *Vorkämpfer der "Neuen Türkei."*
    Revolutionäre Bildungseliten am Genfersee (1868-1939) (Zurich: Chronos, 2005,
    revised Turkish translation: *Türklüğe İhtida*).
12 *Yurdcular Yasası*, 48–50, see also 37.
13 *Yurdcular Yasası*, 64–5.
14 *Lozan Türk Yurdu Cemiyeti'nin Muharrerat ve Zabt-ı Sabık Defteri*, Library of the
    Turkish Historical Association (TTK) in Ankara.
15 *Yurdcular Yasası*, 24.
16 *Yurdcular Yasası*, 29.
17 *Yurdcular Yasası*, 61.
18 *Yurdcular Yasası*, 69–70.
19 Much later Şükrü became the Turkish Prime Minister in 1942–6.
20 Bayar became the President of the Republic of Turkey in 1950–60.
21 *Lozan Türk Yurdu Cemiyeti'nin*, minutes of the undated 68th session.
22 See Orhan Koloğlu, *Aydınlarımızın bunalım yılı 1918. Zafer nihai'den tam teslimiyete*
    (Istanbul: Boyut Kitabları, 2000).
23 *Lozan Türk Yurdu Cemiyeti'nin*, 97th, 98th, and 102nd session (May 4 and 11 and June
    22, 1919).
24 "About the 'Mohammedan Greeks'!," *Turkey*, no. 2, March 1921, 6.
25 Halıcı, *Yeni Türkiye*, 580. The thesis was published a few years later: Mahmoud Essad,
    *Du régime des capitulations ottomanes: leur caractère juridique d'après l'histoire et les
    textes* (Stamboul: S.A. de Papeterie et d'Imprimerie Fratelli Haim, 1928).
26 *TBMM Gizli Celse Zabıtları* (Ankara: Türkiye İş Bankası Kültür Yayınları, 1985), vol.
    2, 143.
27 Uyar, *Mahmut Esat Bozkurt*, 72.
28 The whole speech is reproduced in Uyar, *Mahmut Esat Bozkurt*, 206–12, here 207.
29 Article reproduced in Uyar, "*Sol milliyetçi*," 162–91.
30 Uyar, "*Sol milliyetçi*," 35.
31 Uyar, "*Sol milliyetçi*," 39 and 42; *Gazi Mustafa Kemal Atatürk, Atatürk'ün söylev
    ve demeçleri* (Ankara: Atatürk Kültür Dil ve Tarih Yüksek Kurumu, 1997), Vol. II,
    129–32.
32 Bozkurt, "Türk Medenî Kanunu nasıl hazırlandı?," 11.
33 *Son Posta*, September 20, 1930. Cited in Halıcı, *Yeni Türkiye*, 348. For a similar
    statement of the Prime Minister at the time, Ismet İnönü, on the Turks' exclusive
    "ethnic and racial rights" in Asia Minor, see *Milliyet*, August 31, 1930.
34 Bozkurt, "Esbabı mucibe," XXX–XXXI.
35 For Bozkurt's own, posthumously published retrospective on the introduction, see his
    article "Türk Medenî Kanunu nasıl hazırlandı?," in *Medenî kanunun XV. yıl dönümü
    için* (İstanbul: Kenan Matbaası, 1944), 7–20 (quotations on pp. 9 and 12). See also
    Halıcı, *Yeni Türkiye*, S. 289–92. For an exploration of differences in the translation, see
    Ruth A. Miller, "The Ottoman and Islamic Substratum of Turkey's Swiss Civil Code,"
    Journal of Islamic Studies 11, no. 3 (2000): 335–61.
36 "Türk Medenî Kanunu nasıl hazırlandı?," 19–20.
37 Halıcı, *Yeni Türkiye*, 289–92.
38 "Türk Medenî Kanunu nasıl hazırlandı?," 13.
39 Yusuf Kemal Tengirşek, *Vatan Hizmetinde* (Istanbul: Bahar Matbaası, 1967), 124.

40 See "Türk Medenî Kanunu nasıl hazırlandı?," 14–17.
41 A position he held until his death.
42 Uyar, *Sol milliyetçi*, 101.
43 See his book *Le Kémalisme* (Paris: Félix Alcan, 1937). Tekinalp (sometimes Tekin Alp), a Turkish Jew who was nine years older than Bozkurt, was no less of a Turkist. He published not only in Turkish, but also in French; in contrast to Bozkurt, he abstained from outspokenly racist pronouncements.
44 Uyar, *Sol milliyetçi*, 101–2.
45 Bozkurt, *Atatürk ihtilali*, 164.
46 Bozkurt, *Atatürk ihtilali*, 107.
47 Bozkurt, *Atatürk ihtilali*, 106–7, see also 287. Falih Rıfkı Atay also believed that Hitler saw himself as Atatürk's disciple, see Atay's *Mustafa Kemal Mütareke Defteri* (Istanbul: Sel yay, 1955), 67, quoted in Halil Gülbeyaz, *Mustafa Kemal Atatürk: vom Staatsgründer zum Mythos* (Berlin: Parthas, 2003), 228.
48 Bozkurt, *Atatürk*, 287.
49 Tarık Ziya Işıtman, *Mahmut Esat Bozkurt. Hayatı ve hatıraları 1892–1943* (İzmir: Güneş, 1944), 63–4.
50 "Masonluk meselesi, sabık Adliye Vekili Mahmut Esat Beyin Masonlara cevabı I," *Anadolu*, October 18, 1931, cited in Uyar, *Bozkurt*, 65.
51 Bozkurt, *Atatürk*, 73.
52 "Türkiye Medenî Kanunu nasıl hazırlandı?," 11. Also quoted in Ernst E. Hirsch, "Vom schweizerischen Gesetz zum türkischen Recht," *Zeitschrift für schweizerisches Recht* 95, no. 3 (1976): 223–48.
53 "Türkiye Medenî Kanunu nasıl hazırlandı?," 17.
54 Compare Özbudun, "Constitution," 160.

Chapter 11

1 A scholarly biography of Parvus dates from the 1960s: Winfried B. Scharlau and Zbyněk A. Zeman, *Freibeuter der Revolution: Parvus-Helphand: Eine politische Biographie* (Cologne: Verlag Wissenschaft und Politik, 1964), published in English as *The Merchant of Revolution: The Life of Alexander Israil Helphand (Parvus), 1867-1924* (London: Oxford University Press, 1965). Because at the time of its writing the Ottoman world of the 1910s was utterly under-researched, this biography could not sufficiently reflect on Parvus's impact in and from Istanbul.
2 "Rightist revolution" is a term elaborated in the edited volume, Kieser and Schaller, *Der Völkermord an den Armeniern und die Shoah*, 11–80.
3 *Die Glocke* no. 1, September 1, 1915.
4 M. Asım Karaömerlioğlu, "Helphand-Parvus and His Impact on Turkish Intellectual Life," *Middle Eastern Studies* 40, no. 6 (2004): 145–65, quotation 159. The same fascination characterizes Paul Dumont, "Un économiste social-démocrate au service de la Jeune Turquie," in *Mémorial Ömer Lütfi Barkan* (Paris: Maisonneuve, 1980), 75–86.
5 Scharlau and Zeman, *Freibeuter der Revolution*, 138.
6 See also Houri Berberian, *Roving Revolutionaries: Armenians and the Connected Revolutions in the Russian, Iranian, and Ottoman Worlds* (Berkeley: University of California Press, 2019).

7   Heinz Schurer, "Alexander Helphand-Parvus: Russian Revolutionary and German Patriot," *Russian Review* 18 (October 1959): 313–31.

8   Monika Bankowski-Züllig, "Zürich—das russische Mekka," in *Ebenso neu als kühn: 120 Jahre Frauenstudium an der Universität Zürich*, ed. Katharina Belser et al. (Zurich: eFeF-Verlag, 1988), 127–39.

9   Israil Helphand, *Adresse an Professor Carl Bücher bei seinem Weggang von Basel*, Autumn 1890 (Basel: M. Schwenck, n.d. [1890]), copy held at the Universitätsbibliothek Basel. The faculty was not enthusiastic about his dissertation, which Bücher had directed, so that he passed only *de rite* (the lowest accepted degree). Israil Helphand, "Technische Organisation der Arbeit: 'Cooperation und Arbeitstheilung,'" (Ph.D diss., University of Basel, 1891).

10 Eduard Bernstein, *Die Leiden des armenischen Volkes und die Pflichten Europas: Rede gehalten in einer Berliner Volksversammlung (26. Juni 1902)* (Berlin: n.p., 1902).

11 Axel Meissner, *Martin Rades "Christliche Welt" und Armenien. Bausteine für eine internationale Ethik des Protestantismus* (Berlin: Lit, 2010), 51–157, and Margaret Anderson, "'Down in Turkey, Far Away': Human Rights, the Armenian Massacres, and Orientalism in Wilhelmine Germany," *The Journal of Modern History* 79, no. 1 (March 2007): 80–111.

12 Among many works: Ladislas Mysyrowicz, "Université et revolution: Les étudiants d'Europe orientale à Genève au temps de Plekhanov et de Lénine," *Schweizerische Zeitschrift für Geschichte* 25, no. 4 (1975): 514–62.

13 See Kieser, *Vorkämpfer.*

14 One of these students, Ali Kemal, described this in his memoirs: *Ömrüm* (Istanbul: Isis, 1985, first ed. 1913), 90–1.

15 Anahide Ter Minassian, "Elites arméniennes en Suisse. Le rôle de Genève dans la formation des élites arméniennes au début du XXe siècle," in Kieser, *Die armenische Frage und die Schweiz*, 29–52; Ronald G. Suny, *Looking toward Ararat: Armenia in Modern History* (Bloomington: Indiana University Press, 1993), 63–93; Taline Ter Minassian, "Genève: 'capitale' de l'édition arménienne? La presse et les éditions arméniennes en Suisse avant la première guerre mondiale," in Kieser, *Die armenische Frage und die Schweiz*, 53–65.

16 Berberian, *Roving Revolutionaries*; Alain Brossat and Sylvie Klingberg, *Revolutionary Yiddishland. A History of Jewish Radicalism* (New York: Verso, 2017).

17 Quoted in Mehmed Ş. Hanioğlu, *Preparation for a Revolution: The Young Turks, 1902-1908* (New York: Oxford University Press, 2001), 182.

18 Christian Rakovsky, *Selected Writings on Opposition in the USSR 1923-30*, ed. Gus Fagan (London: Allison & Busby, 1980), quoted from Marxists' Internet Archive, http://www.marxists.org.

19 Kaligian, *Armenian Organization*, 137–8.

20 *Lozan Türk Yurdu Cemiyeti'nin Muharrerat ve Zabt-ı Sabık Defteri.*

21 *Türk Yurdu* and *Türk Ocağı* were both translated into French as *Foyers Turcs.*

22 *Yurdcular Yasası* (Istanbul: Yeni Turan Matbaası, n. d. [1913]), 69–70.

23 Parvus, *Im Kampf um die Wahrheit* (Berlin: Verlag für Sozialwissenschaft, 1918), 7.

24 Scharlau and Zeman, *Freibeuter der Revolution*, 35.

25 Scharlau and Zeman, *Freibeuter der Revolution*, 43–59.

26 Scharlau and Zeman, *Freibeuter der Revolution*, 70–2 and 101–9, quotation 71.

27 Parvus, "Philister über mich. Meine Antwort an K. Kautsky," *Die Glocke* 5, no. 42 (January 17, 1920), 1331–9.

28 Published in Parvus, *In der russischen Bastille während der Revolution: Eindrücke, Stimmungen und Betrachtungen* (Dresden: Kaden, 1907).

29 Karl Heinrich Pohl, *Adolf Müller, Geheimagent und Gesandter in Kaiserreich und Weimarer Republik* (Cologne: Bund Verlag, 1995), 124–5.

30 "Parvus—Reden bei der Trauerfeier am 17. Dezember 1924," *Die Glocke* 10, no. 38 (December 20, 1924): 1231–2. Parvus himself used similar words in *Im Kampf um die Wahrheit*, 24.

31 Parvus, *Der Klassenkampf des Proletariats* (Berlin: Buchhandlung Vorwärts, 1911), 147 (first ed. of this chapter in 1910).

32 Parvus, *Klassenkampf*, 136–47.

33 Except for his publications, there is a paucity of sources and exact data as far as Parvus's stay in Istanbul is concerned. An undated note in Parvus's notebook suggests direct contacts with Talaat ("Adressez-vous directement à Falih Rifky bey au bureau du ministre de l'intérieur"). Falih Rıfkı Atay, a young journalist, later Kemal Atatürk's intimate, was a private secretary of Minister of the Interior Talaat (Geheimes Staatsarchiv Preussischer Kulturbesitz Berlin, VI. HA NI Max Stein no. 139, page 42).

34 See his article "La révolution turque," *Le Socialisme* no. 37 (August 1, 1908): 1–2.

35 Letter to Kautsky of April 3, 1911, Kautsky Papers, D XVII, International Institute of Social History, Amsterdam.

36 As Stepan Sapah-Gulian remarked. Quoted in Kévorkian, *The Armenian Genocide*, 132–3.

37 Parvus, "Philister über mich," 1331–9, here 1334. Cf. Scharlau and Zeman, *Freibeuter der Revolution*, 137 f.; Parvus, *Im Kampf um die Wahrheit*, 24; Parvus, "Ein Verleumdungswerk," *Die Glocke* 1, no. 3 (October 1, 1915): 123–30.

38 For a study of the late Ottoman economic situation that relies on Parvus's concepts, see Muammer Sencer, *Türkiye'nin malî tutsaklığı. Parvus efendi* (Istanbul, May 1977). In the annex, some of Parvus's Istanbul writings are reproduced in transliteration.

39 "İktisat," *Türk Yurdu*, 9 Mart 1327 [March 22, 1912], 1: 145–6.

40 Nobody else could have dared to use the term [Anatolian] Armenia in *Türk Yurdu*. "Iktisat - Köylüler," *Türk Yurdu*, 9 Mart 1327 [March 22, 1912], 1: 145–8, quotation 148.

41 Ironically, the article was written by the Ottoman Jew Moïz Kohen Tekinalp, an ideologue of Turkism, under the pseudonym of Monsieur Risal: "Türkler bir rûh-i millî arıyorlar," *Türk Yurdu*, 23 Ağustos 1328 [September 5, 1912], 1: 350–3. Parvus must have known Tekinalp.

42 Parvus, *Klassenkampf*, 148–9; "Türk gençlerine mektub," *Türk Yurdu*, 30 Mayıs 1329 [June 12, 1913], 2: 40–1. For a rhetorically significant address turned to Russia see Parvus, *Meine Antwort an Kerenski & Co.* (Berlin: Verlag für Sozialwissenschaft, 1917).

43 Monsieur Risal: "Türkler bir rûh-i millî arıyorlar," *Türk Yurdu*, 6 Eylül 1328 [September 19, 1912], 1: 365.

44 "İş işten geçmeden gözlerinizi açınız," *Türk Yurdu*, 23 Mart 1329 [April 3, 1913], 2: 200–3, quotation 200–1.

45 Halidé Edib, *Memoirs* (New York: The Century Co., 1926), 333.

46 Parvus, "Iktisat—Köylüler," 147.

47 See again, e.g., "Türk gençlerine mektub," 40 f.

48 Quoted in Alp, *Türkismus und Pantürkismus*, 53.

49 Erol Köroğlu, *Ottoman Propaganda and Turkish Identity: Literature in Turkey during World War I* (London: I.B. Tauris, 2007) and M. Şükrü Hanioğlu, *A Brief History*

of the Late Ottoman Empire (Princeton, NJ: Princeton University Press, 2008), 179. Interestingly, however, in 1912–14 more positive impressions of economic and cultural achievements in Russia prevailed in the Ottoman press. An Ottoman-Russian war alliance would therefore also have found propagandists in 1914, Volker Adam has argued. See Adam, *Russlandmuslime*, 219–305 and 455. For Talaat's thoughts on an alliance with Russia in 1914, see Kieser, *Talaat*, 170–2.

50 Parvus, *İngiltere galib gelirse... İtilaf-ı müselles'in zafer ve galibiyetinde husula gelecek tebedüllat-ı araziye* (Istanbul: Kader Maatbası, 1330 [March 1914–March 1915]), 12–31, quoted in Aksakal, *The Ottoman Road to War*, 54–5.

51 "Devlet ve millet," *Türk Yurdu*, 15 Teşrînisâni 1328 [November 28, 1912], 2: 56–7.

52 Raymond Kévorkian, *Le génocide des Arméniens* (Paris: Odile Jacob, 2006), 175.

53 Parvus, "Armenische Wirren" (name of the newspaper not mentioned), January 8, 1913, Eduard Bernstein Papers, G 354, International Institute of Social History, Amsterdam.

54 The German documentation on the reform issue, mainly letters by Ambassador Wangenheim, is in PA-AA/R14077–14084 (PA-AA meaning Politisches Archiv des Auswärtigen Amtes = Political Archive of the Foreign Ministry). Quotation from PA-AA/R14078 (according to the internet edition on www.armenocide.de, established by Wolfgang and Sigrid Gust, which includes the English translation for this piece).

55 E.g., Paul Rohrbach, "Basra—Kuwait," *Frankfurter Zeitung*, May 27, 1913, in Rohrbach to Zimmermann, June 22, 1913, PA-AA/R14079/MF7093/65-75.

56 Wangenheim's report of January 8, 1915, to the GFO on his meeting with Parvus, facsimile in Ladislaus Singer, *Raubt das Geraubte: Tagebuch der Weltrevolution: 1917* (Stuttgart: Seewald Verlag, 1967), 153–4; Wolff (no first name), "La Bulgarie germanophile," *Gazette de Lausanne*, January 26, 1915.

57 Kévorkian, *Génocide*, 175; report of the Russian Ministry of the Interior, dated December 15, 1915, quoted in Elisabeth Heresch, *Geheimakte Parvus: Die gekaufte Revolution: Biographie* (Munich: Langen Müller, 2000), 225.

58 Gottfried Hagen, "German Heralds of Holy War: Orientalists and Applied Oriental Studies," *Comparative Studies of South Asia, Africa and the Middle East* 24, no. 2 (2004): 149–50.

59 Memorandum by Dr. Helphand, without date, but dated by the GFO March 9, 1915, published in Scharlau and Zeman, *Freibeuter der Revolution*, 361–74.

60 Lepsius to GFO, December 22, 1914, PA-AA/R14085.

61 Wangenheim's report of January 8, 1915 in Singer, *Raubt das Geraubte*, 153–4.

62 *Almanya galib gelirse*, reproduced in Sencer, *Türkiye'nin malî tutsaklığı*, 277–9.

63 "Meine Stellungnahme zum Krieg," *Die Glocke* 1, no. 3 (October 1, 1915): 148–62.

64 Scharlau and Zeman, *Freibeuter der Revolution*, 9–11 and 175–6.

65 Memorandum, dated by the GFO March 9, 1915, published in Scharlau and Zeman, *Freibeuter der Revolution*, 361–74.

66 Scharlau and Zeman, *Freibeuter der Revolution*, 248–66; Gautschi, *Lenin*, 164–76 and 249–71. Besides the considerable sums of German money he received, he financed Dr. Victor Naumann, who had direct contacts with the Imperial Chancellery, out of his own pocket for his services as a special emissary for himself and Adolf Müller in those years. Pohl, *Adolf Müller*, 182–3.

67 Mete Tunçay, *Türkiye'de sol akımlar 1908–1925* (Istanbul: Iletisim, 2009), 65–6; documentation on the Stockholm congress on https://socialhistoryportal .org/stockholm1917; Johann H. Bernstorff, *Erinnerungen und Briefe* (Zurich: Polygraphischer Verlag, 1936), 127; Scharlau and Zeman, *Freibeuter der Revolution*, 11.

68 Alexander Helphand, *Der Arbeitersozialismus und die Weltrevolution: Briefe an die deutschen Arbeiter* (Olten [Switzerland]: Kommissionsverlag W. Trösch, 1919), 13 and 16–17.

69 Parvus, *Meine Antwort an Kerenski*.

70 Parvus, *Aufbau und Wiedergutmachung* (Berlin: Verlag für Sozialwissenschaft, 1921), especially 233 and 252; Parvus, *Die soziale Bilanz des Krieges* (Berlin: Verlag für Sozialwissenschaften, 1917), in particular 16.

71 Parvus, *Aufbau und Wiedergutmachung*, 195–8, 241.

72 Kieser, *Talaat*, 395–9.

73 Scharlau and Zeman, *Freibeuter der Revolution*, 229 f.

74 Scharlau and Zeman, *Freibeuter der Revolution*, 319–43.

75 Parvus, *Aufbau und Wiedergutmachung*, 91–162.

Part IV

1 CD, 3:174–5, February 23 and March 2, 1916; 3:304–7, December 15–16, 1916; 3:355, February 4, 1917.

2 Ernst Jäckh, *Das grössere Mitteleuropa: ein Werkbund-Vortrag* (Weimar: Kiepenheuer, 1916); idem, *Weltsaat. Erlebtes und Erstrebtes* (Stuttgart: Deutsche Verlagsanstalt, 1960), on Parvus 59; for radical militarist statements by Parvus in favor of German domination during a visit to the GFO in December 1917, see Scharlau and Zeman, *Freibeuter der Revolution*, 301.

Chapter 12

1 Hans-Lukas Kieser, "Johannes Lepsius: Theologian, Humanitarian Activist and Historian of Genocide. An Approach to a German Biography (1858-1926)," in *Logos im Dialogos: In Search of Orthodoxy. Gedenkschrift für Hermann Goltz*, ed. A. Briskina-Müller, A. Drost-Abgarjan, and A. Meißner (Berlin: Lit, 2011), 209–29. See also Kieser, *Nearest East*.

2 Kieser, *Nearest East*, 15–62.

3 *Ex Oriente lux. Jahrbuch der deutschen Orient-Mission*, ed. Johannes Lepsius (Berlin: Verl. der Deutschen Orient-Mission, 1903).

4 Hilton Obenzinger, *American Palestine: Melville, Twain, and the Holy Land Mania* (Princeton, NJ: Princeton University Press, 1999).

5 Helmut R. Niebuhr, *The Kingdom of God in America* (Middletown, CT: Wesleyan University Press, 1988, first ed. 1938), XX.

6 Carl F. Ehle, *Prolegomena to Christian Zionism in America* (New York: New York University, 1977), 331, quoted in Mehmet A. Doğan, "From New England into New Lands: The Beginning of a Long Story," in *American Missionaries in the Middle East: Foundational Encounters*, ed. Mehmet A. Doğan and Heather J. Sharkey (Salt Lake City: University of Utah Press, 2011), 11.

7 "The Kingdom of Christ," *The Kingdom of Christ* 3, no. 9 (1900): 260; "The Revelation of John," *The Kingdom of Christ* 7 (1901): 372.

8 Quoted in Pierre Heumann, *Israel Originated in Basel* (Zurich: Weltwoche ABC Verlag, 1997), 97.

9 Jakob Eisler, ed., *Deutsche Kolonisten im Heiligen Land. Die Familie John Steinbeck in Briefen aus Palästina und USA* (Stuttgart: Verlag S. Hirzel, 2001), 32 f.

10 *Die Nachfolge Christi: Vortrag von Johannes Lepsius gehalten auf der sechsten Eisenacher Konferenz in Potsdam, 27-29. Mai 1907* (Potsdam: Tempel-Verlag, 1909), 14.

11 Joseph K. Greene, *Leavening the Levant* (Boston: The Pilgrim Press, 1916).

12 For detailed insights into this wide-ranging missionary work, including Lepsius's Deutsche Orient-Mission, see Kieser, *Der verpasste Friede*.

13 Kieser, *Der verpasste Friede*, 309–13.

14 See, among other things, Wangenheim's report of February 24, 1913, to the Reich Chancellor: PA-AA/R14078, online at www.armenocide.de.

15 See Kieser, "Johannes Lepsius," 216–18. The rich literature on the Baghdad railway hardly addresses this aspect.

16 Kieser, "Johannes Lepsius," 220.

17 *Armenien und Europa: eine Anklageschrift wider die christlichen Grossmächte und ein Aufruf an das christliche Deutschland* (Berlin: W. Faber, 1896) and *Bericht über die Lage des armenischen Volkes in der Türkei* (Potsdam: Tempelverlag, 1916).

18 See also Manfred Gailus, "Deutsche Protestanten im Ersten Weltkrieg," in *Johannes Lepsius—eine deutsche Ausnahme*, ed. Rolf Hosfeld (Göttingen: Wallstein Verlag, 2013), 95–109.

19 See also Kieser, *Nearest East*, 130–6.

20 Johannes Lepsius, *Jesus at the Peace Conference* (The Hague: n.p., 1919), 16.

21 In a text with reference to Kurt Eisner (Lepsius Archive Halle, LAH 14568).

22 Johannes Lepsius, *Macht und Sittlichkeit im nationalen Leben. Reden und Abhandlungen Teil 3*, Lecture delivered at the 7th Hauptversammlung der freien kirchlich-sozialen Konferenz in Düsseldorf, April 30, 1902 (Berlin: Reich Christi-Verlag, 1902), 36–7, quoted from Andreas Baumann, *Johannes Lepsius' Missiology* (Theological Dissertation of the University of South Africa, October 2005), 136–7.

23 Barth's more serene later critique is most comprehensive in *Die protestantische Theologie im 19. Jahrhundert* (Zollikon: Evangelischer Verlag, 1946).

24 Johannes Lepsius, *Die Wurzeln des Weltkrieges: auf Grund der neuen Bismarck-Akten dargestellt* (Munich: Süddeutsche Monatshefte, 1922), 136.

25 In the context of the Munich tribunal on behalf of "Eisnersche Aktenfälschung," LAH 14568, vgl. LAH 14390.

26 Birgen, *İttihat ve Terakki'de on sene*, 395.

27 His friends in Basel sharply criticized his panegyric of Bismarck; otherwise, they continued supporting him. Albert Oeri to Lepsius on July 8, 1922, LAH 13522. Cf. Lepsius, *Die Wurzeln des Weltkrieges*, 130.

28 Lepsius, *Todesgang des armenischen Volkes*, XXVIII.

29 To his theological study friend Albert Weckesser, Lepsius wrote on December 2, 1922 (LAH 1555): "[Johann F.] Heman himself was of the opinion that all nations would fail in the Gospel and that finally the Reich [Kingdom of God] would return to the Jews. Until now, Zionism does not allow itself to do this."

Chapter 13

1 On the Young Turk committee during the 1910s, see Şükrü Hanioğlu, "The Second Constitutional Period, 1908-1918," in *The Cambridge History of Turkey*, IV, ed. Reşat Kasaba (Cambridge: Cambridge University Press, 2008), 62–111; on Kieser, *Talaat*.

2 Birgen, *İttihat ver Terakki'de on sene*, 358–90; Enver B. Şapolyo, *Ziya Gökalp. İttihat ve Terakki ve Meşrutiyet tarihi* (Istanbul, 1943); Kieser, *Talaat*, chapters 3 and 5.

3 Letter of September 21, 1915 to Ernst Jäckh (Jäckh Papers, Yale University Library). The project of German world dominance based on Central European and Middle Eastern supremacy is described in a propagandist article by Rohrbach published in the New York *Evening Mail* in August 1915 (copy in the archive of the Deutsche Bank, Frankfurt/M., OR 1388).

4 Stefan Ihrig, *Justifying Genocide*; idem, *Atatürk in the Nazi Imagination*.

5 For more detailed information on Humann, see Jürgen Gottschlich, *Beihilfe zum Völkermord. Deutschlands Rolle bei der Vernichtung der Armenier* (Berlin: Ch. Links, 2015).

6 On Jäckh, see Margaret L. Anderson, "Helden in Zeiten eines Völkermords?," in Hosfeld, *Johannes Lepsius. Eine deutsche Ausnahme*, 138–47.

7 Undersecretary of State in the Foreign Office Zimmermann to Wangenheim, January 10, 1913, PA-AA, R14077, No. 34.

8 "Zum Tod von Baron Wangenheim," Pallavicini to foreign secretary Baron Burian, October 29, 1915, Austrian State Archives, K. and K. Ministry of Foreign Affairs, Carton 209, 00126984-87.

9 Wangenheim to Jagow, AA, August 8, 1913, in: *Die Grosse Politik der europäischen Kabinette 1871-1914. Sammlung der Diplomatischen Akten des Auswärtigen Amtes* (Berlin: Deutsche Verlagsgesellschaft für Politik und Geschichte, 1926), vol. 38, 128.

10 Wangenheim to Chancellor Bethmann Hollweg, June 10, 1913, *Die Grosse Politik der europäischen Kabinette 1871-1914*, 75.

11 Private letter of August 8, 1913 from Wangenheim to Jagow, in: *Die Grosse Politik der europäischen Kabinette 1871-1914*, 131.

12 CD 2: 103.

13 Wangenheim to Secretary of State in the Foreign Office Gottlieb von Jagow, in: *Die Grosse Politik der europäischen Kabinette 1871-1914*, vol. 38, 142.

14 Private letter of August 8, 1913, from Wangenheim to Jagow, in: *Die Grosse Politik der europäischen Kabinette 1871-1914*, 127. Sigurd Stangeland and others have drawn attention to this culturalist aspect of German Oriental policy for good reason (Sigurd S. Stangeland, *Die Rolle Deutschlands im Völkermord an den Armeniern 1915-1916* (Ph.D thesis, University of Trondheim, 2013), 344–8).

15 Private letter from Wangenheim to Jagow, August 28, 1914, PA-AA, R22402.

16 CD, 1:554, February 6, 1914.

17 CD, 2:170, October 22, 1913; Pomiankowski, *Zusammenbruch*, 163.

18 Wangenheim to Auswärtiges Amt, July 31, 1914, PA-AA, R 1913, Nos. 391 and 395.

19 Wangenheim to Auswärtiges Amt, October 23, 1913, in: *Die Grosse Politik der europäischen Kabinette 1871-1914*, vol. 38, 153.

20 Kieser, *Talaat*, 187–7. Yusuf H. Bayur (1891–1980), a Kemalist historian critical of the CUP, already pointed out with regard to the formation of the alliance how the committee seized the opportunity presented by the Sarajevo assassination: Yusuf H. Bayur, *Türk İnkılâbı tarihi* (Ankara: TTK, 1991), vol. 3, part 4, 776. The relevant documents from the Foreign Office are published on: www.armenocide.de.

21 CD, 2:647–9, September 9, 1914.

22 Birgen, *İttihat ve Terakki'de on sene*, 184.

23 Wangenheim to Auswärtiges Amt, August 6, 1914, PA-AA, R1913, no. 438.

24 Diary entry for October 29, 1914, Henry Morgenthau, *United States Diplomacy on the Bosphorus: The Diaries of Ambassador Morgenthau 1913-1916*, ed. Ara Sarafian (Princeton, NJ: Princeton University Press, 2004), 116.

25 Published in: Tim Epkenhans, "Geld darf keine Rolle spielen," Teil II, Dokument, *Archivum* Ottomanicum 19 (2001): 121–63. See also Wolfgang G. Schwanitz, "Max von Oppenheim und der heilige Krieg. Zwei Denkschriften zur Revolutionierung islamischer Gebiete 1914 und 1940," *Sozial.Geschichte* 19, no. 3 (2004): 28–59.

26 On Lehmann-Haupt, see Sebastian Fink et al., eds., *Carl Friedrich Lehmann-Haupt. Ein Forscherleben zwischen Orient und Okzident* (Wiesbaden: Harrassowitz, 2015).

27 İrâde-i Seniyye of December 29, 1914 (copy of December 30, 1914, BOA DH. İD. 186–72).

28 Der Yeghiayan, *My Patriarchal Memoirs*, 56–7.

29 Entry for January 19, 1915, in Morgenthau, *Diaries*, 168.

30 Hans-Lukas Kieser, "The Ottoman Road to Total War," in Kieser et al., *World War I and the End of the Ottomans*, 29–53.

31 See Erol, "Ousting of the Ottoman Greeks," 103–30.

32 Wangenheim to Auswärtiges Amt, March 27, 1915, PA-AA, R14085, BoKon 168.

33 Enclosure in Wangenheim to Chancellor Bethmann Hollweg, April 16, 1915, PA-AA, R14085.

34 Wangenheim to the chancellor, April 15, 1915, PA-AA, R14085.

35 Wangenheim to Auswärtiges Amt, May 31, 1915, PA-AA, R14086.

36 Wangenheim to the chancellor, June 5, 1915, PA-AA, R14086.

37 Wangenheim to the chancellor, July 7, 1915, PA-AA, R14086.

38 Entries for June 12 and 27 and July 3 and 8, in: Morgenthau, *Diaries*, 252–71.

39 Consul Walter Rössler, for example, supported internationally organized aid efforts in Aleppo, see Kai Seyffarth, *Entscheidung in Aleppo—Walter Rössler (1871-1929): Helfer der verfolgten Armenier* (Bremen: Donat, 2015).

40 Undersecretary of State Zimmermann to the embassy in Constantinople, August 4, 1915, PA-AA, R14086.

41 Armando Moses from the German-Turkish Society's Istanbul information center for German-Turkish economic questions continued proposing to settle Eastern European Jews in Eastern Anatolia well into the summer of 1916; see Isaiah Friedman, *Germany, Turkey, Zionism 1897-1918* (New Brunswick: Transcation, 1998), 268–9; entries for September 17 and October 7, 12, and 28, 1915, in Morgenthau, *Diaries*, 332, 351, 355, and 368.

42 Entries for October 23 and 25, 1915, in Morgenthau, *Diaries*, 363–6.

43 On the progressive expansion of the treaty of alliance during the World War, see Carl Mühlmann, *Deutschland und die Türkei 1913-1914* (Berlin: Walther Rothschild, 1929).

44 Zimmermann to the embassy in Constantinople, August 4, 1915, PA-AA, R14086.

45 Birgen, *İttihat ve Terakki'de on sene*, 395–435; Talaat to Enver, February 16, 1916 *Arşiv belgeleriyle Ermeni faaliyetleri 1914-1918* (Ankara: Genelkurmay Basım Evi, 2008), 8:104 and 253; CD, 3:581–2, October 16, 1918.

Chapter 14

1 Birgen, *İttihat ve Terakki'de on sene*, 449.

2 See also Birgen, *İttihat ve Terakki'de on sene*, 448–69.

3 Birgen, *İttihat ve Terakki'de on sene*, 449.

4 Erzberger was assassinated in 1920 by a far-right militant when he was serving as minister of finance in the Weimar government. Among recent literature on Erzberger, see notably Christopher Dowe, ed., *Matthias Erzberger. Ein Demokrat in Zeiten des Hasses* (Karlsruhe: G. Braun, 2013).

5 Ibid., 449.

6 Klaus Epstein, *Matthias Erzberger und das Dilemma der deutschen Demokratie* (Berlin: Leber, 1962), 129–37.

7 *Allgemeine Rundschau*, October 21, 1911, quoted in Christian Leitzbach, *Matthias Erzberger: ein kritischer Beobachter des Wilhelminischen Reiches 1895-1914* (Bern: Peter Lang, 1998), 470.

8 *Allgemeine Rundschau*, October 21, 1911, quoted in Leitzbach, *Erzberger*, 472.

9 Epstein, *Erzberger*, 94.

10 Leitzbach, *Erzberger*, 464–5.

11 See Marion Dönhoff, *Preussen, Mass und Masslosigkeit* (München: Siedler, 1991).

12 Manfred Gailus, *Protestantismus und Nationalsozialismus: Studien zur nationalsozialistischen Durchdringung des protestantischen Sozialmilieus in Berlin* (Köln: Böhlau, 2001), 637–66.

13 Reproduced in Alfred von Tirpitz, *Deutsche Ohnmachtspolitik im Weltkriege* (Hamburg: Hanseatische Verlagsanstalt 1926), 69–72.

14 Wolfdieter Bihl, *Die Kaukasus-Politik der Mittelmächte. Ihre Basis in der Orient-Politik und ihre Aktionen 1914-1917* (Vienna: Böhlau, 1975), 66, including quote "lobby the Armenians."

15 Winfried Becker, ed., *Frederic von Rosenberg. Korrespondenzen und Akten des deutschen Diplomaten und Außenministers 1913-1937* (München: Oldenbourg, 2011), 7.

16 Federal Archives Koblenz, Nachlass Erzberger, N 1097/3: Volume on the Armenian Question.

17 The relevant documents from the Foreign Office have been published online by Wolfgang Gust on www.armenocide.org. The above-mentioned is a report by Rössler to the Foreign Office dated April 12, 1915, Political Archive of the Foreign Office, PA-AA, R14085.

18 Ambassador Wangenheim to Auswärtiges Amt, May 31, 1915, PA-AA, R1408.

19 Federal Archives Koblenz, Nachlass Erzberger, N 1097/3.

20 See John Horne and Alan Kramer's analysis of German Catholic voices concerning French accusations of German war atrocities in Belgium and France: John Horne and Alan Kramer, *Deutsche Kriegsgreuel 1914. Die umstrittene Wahrheit* (Hamburg: Hamburger Edition, 2004), 406–8.

21 The difference in attitude can also be gleaned from the decision by the above-mentioned assembly in comparison with that of German Catholic representatives of November 12, 1915, which Erzberger forwarded to the chancellor. See the latter's letter of November 12, 1915, to Erzberger, PA/AA, R14088.

22 Michael Hesemann, *Völkermord an den Armeniern. Mit unveröffentlichten Dokumenten aus dem Geheimarchiv des Vatikans* (Munich: Herbig, 2015), 209–10.

23 Ambassador Wolff-Metternich concluded in his report to the chancellor of December 27, 1915:

> Monsignore Dolci confirms that Halil Bey, the Foreign Minister, had promised him at the time that the persecution of the Catholic Armenians would be stopped and the deportees would be allowed to return to their homes; but this assurance, which incidentally was not given in any binding way, was not fulfilled, at least in so far as

the return of the deportees is concerned. If there has been no further mention of persecutions since, the reason is that the expulsion of the Armenians has been largely concluded. A further step by the apostolic delegate to obtain the reopening of the closed Catholic churches and the return of the banished clerics to their dioceses was interpreted by the Porte as "an interference in Turkey's domestic affairs" and remained unsuccessful, except maybe for the fact that the Bishop of Kaisseri (Caesarea) was subsequently deported to Aleppo. (PA/AA, R14089)

24 "Whatever blame the Armenians may bear, the precepts of humanity, which the Turkish government must not turn a deaf ear to either, demand that the impending eradication of the entire Armenian people be opposed." PA/AA, BoKon/171, appendix 2.

25 Deputy Erzberger to Frederic Rosenberg, secretary for Oriental Affairs in the Foreign Office, December 10, 1915, PA-AA, R14089 (including passages from Straubinger's letter, November 25, 1915); Ambassador Wolff-Metternich to the chancellor, January 27, 1916, R14090 (including Straubinger's memorandum, January 18, 1916).

26 Wolff-Metternich to the chancellor, February 11, 1916, PA-AA, R14090, appendix 2.

27 See also Hilmar Kaiser, *At the Crossroads of Der Zor. Death, Survival and Humanitarian Resistance* (Princeton, NJ: Gomidas, 2001).

28 Reinhard Schiffers and Manfred Koch (eds.), *Der Hauptausschuss des Deutschen Reichstags, 1915-1918* (Düsseldorf: Droste, 1981), vol. 2, 429.

29 See Kieser, "Johannes Lepsius: Theologian, Humanitarian Activist," 220–2.

30 Federal Archives Koblenz, Nachlass Erzberger, N 1097/3: Letter of August 1, 1916.

31 Yusuf H. Bayur, *Türk inkılâbı tarihi* (Ankara: TTK, 1991) vol. 3, part 3, 206–11.

32 Ulrich Trumpener, *Germany and the Ottoman Empire, 1914-1918* (Princeton, NJ: Princeton University Press, 1968), 122–39; Manfred Nebelin, *Ludendorff. Diktator im Ersten Weltkrieg* (Munich: Siedler, 2011), 287.

33 Quoted in Thomas Schnabel, "Matthias Erzberger als Realpolitiker," in *Matthias Erzberger 1875-1921. Patriot und Visionär*, ed. Christoph E. Palmer and Thomas Schnabel (Stuttgart: Hohenheim, 2007), 170.

34 Register entries of the stenographic Reichstags-reports (Bavarian State Library, online-version, www.reichstagsprotokolle.de): Entries of March 19, 1918, cols. 4483 f.; of March 22, 1918, cols. 4545, 4553 f.; of June 24, 1918, col. 5607; of June 25, 1918, cols. 5655–64. See also Schiffers and Koch, *Hauptausschuss*, vol. 4, 2070–1.

35 Schiffers and Koch, *Hauptausschuss*, vol. 4, 2066.

36 Erich Matthias, ed., *Der interfraktionelle Ausschuss 1917/18* (Düsseldorf: Droste, 1959), vol. 2, 410; the relevant minutes are also to be found among Erzberger's papers in the Federal Archives, Nachlass Erzberger, N 1097/26. I would like to thank Guido Thiers for the hint and the quotes.

37 Matthias Erzberger, *Erlebnisse im Weltkrieg* (Stuttgart: Deutsche Verlags-Anstalt, 1920), 82.

38 Wolfdieter Bihl, *Die Kaukasus-Politik der Mittelmächte. Die Zeit der versuchten kaukasischen Staatlichkeit (1917-1918)* (Vienna: Böhlau, 1992), 69.

39 Bigen, *İttihat ve Terakki'de*, 449; words of the chancellor related by Finance Minister Mehmed Cavid from his visit in Berlin: CD, 3:524, July 31, 1918.

40 Matthias Erzberger, *Der Völkerbund: der weg zum Weltfrieden* (Berlin: Reimar Hobbing, 1918), 10–13.

41 Erzberger, *Erlebnisse*, 74.

42 See also Chapter 12 and Kieser, "Johannes Lepsius: Theologian, Humanitarian Activist," 226–9.

Chapter 15

1   Donald Bloxham, *Genocide, the World Wars and the Unweaving of Europe* (London: Vallentine Mitchell, 2008), 87; Vahakn N. Dadrian, *German Responsibility in the Armenian Genocide: A Review of the Historical Evidence of German Complicity* (Watertown, MA: Blue Crane Books), 1996, 186; Christoph Dinkel, "German Officers and the Armenian Genocide," *The Armenian Review* 44 (1991): 77–130; *Der Völkermord an den Armeniern 1915/16: Dokumente aus dem Politischen Archiv des deutschen Auswärtigen Amts*, ed. Wolfgang Gust (Springe: Zu Klampen, 2005), 76–108; and Eberhard Graf Wolffskeel von Reichenberg, *Zeitoun, Mousa Dagh, Ourfa: Letters on the Armenian Genocide*, ed. Hilmar Kaiser (Princeton, NJ: Gomidas Institute Books, 2001), x–xvi.

2   Remember the Fritz Fischer debate in the 1960s on the origins of the First World War.

3   Internet edition on www.armenocide.de, of which a selection is printed and introduced in Gust, *Völkermord an den Armeniern*. Where not mentioned otherwise, the PA-AA documents quoted in this chapter have been accessed on this site.

4   Colmar von der Goltz, *Millet-i müsellaha: asrımızın usul ve ahvali askeriyyesi* (Istanbul: Matbaa-ı Abüzziya, 1305).

5   Dönhoff, *Preussen, Mass und Masslosigkeit.*

6   Quoted in Norbert Saupp, *Das Deutsche Reich und die armenische Frage* (Cologne: n.p., 1990), 30.

7   Verheij, "Die armenischen Massaker von 1894-1896," 69–129; Verhej, "Diyarbekir and the Armenian Crisis of 1895," 85–145.

8   Describing persecutions of the Jews, René de Weck, Swiss legate in Bucarest during the Second World War, refered to the Armenian massacres of the 1890s which were more present to his mind than the genocide of 1915; letter of November 28, 1941, quoted in Gaston Haas, *"Wenn man gewusst hätte, was sich drüben im Reich abspielte...": 1941-1943: was man in der Schweiz von der Judenvernichtung wusste* (Basel: Helbing und Lichtenhahn, 1994), 82.

9   Kieser, *Nearest East*, 60–1.

10 Lepsius, *Armenien und Europa.*

11 See John A. Denovo, *American Interests and Policies in the Middle East: 1900–1939* (Minneapolis, MN: University of Minnesota Press, 1963), 58–87, and Joseph Heller, *British Policy towards the Ottoman Empire: 1908-1914* (London: Frank Cass, 1983), 62–4.

12 Davison, *Essays in Ottoman and Turkish History, 1774–1923*, 180–205, and *Deutschland, Armenien und die Türkei 1895-1925. Thematisches Lexikon*, ed. Hermann Goltz and Axel Meissner (Munich: Saur, 2004), 35–6, 122–3, 246. According to Joseph Pomiankowski, the German commitment to reform was insincere since the leading representative, Ambassador Hans von Wangenheim, did not believe in the pluralistic, egalitarian order being aimed for. Pomiankowski, *Zusammenbruch*, 163; for the German documentation on the reforms see PA-AA/R14077–14084.

13 See Kieser, *Talaat*, 141–80.

14 See Kieser, *Talaat*, 186–8; Aksakal, *The Ottoman Road to War*, 93–118; and Trumpener, *Germany and the Ottoman Empire*, 21–61.

15 Djemal, *Erinnerungen eines türkischen Staatsmannes* (Munich: Drei Masken Verlag, 1922), 119.

16 Pomiankowski, *Zusammenbruch*, 162–3.
17 CD, 2:613–17, August 4, 1914; Mühlmann, *Deutschland und die Türkei*, 44–5; Wangenheim to Auswärtiges Amt, August 6, 1914, PA-AA/R 1913; Aksakal, *Ottoman Road to War*, 127. See also Trumpener, *Germany and the Ottoman Empire*, 28, and Chapter 4.
18 Quoted in Birgen, *İttihat ve Terakki'de on sene*, 382; Köroğlu, "Propaganda or Culture War: Jihad, Islam, and Nationalism in Turkish Literature during World War I," 137–47.
19 Aksakal, *Ottoman Road to War*, 107–8 and 127–30.
20 Kaligian, *Armenian Organization*, 219–22; Kévorkian, *Le génocide des Arméniens*, 221 and 275; Bihl, *Die Kaukasus-Politik der Mittelmächte*, 1: 230–45; Taner Akçam, *A Shameful Act: The Armenian Genocide and the Question of Turkish Responsibility* (New York: Metropolitan Books, 2006), 136–8; and Kieser, *Der verpasste Friede*, 331, 335–6, 445.
21 Aksakal, *Ottoman Road to War*, 169; Handan N. Akmeşe, *The Birth of Modern Turkey: The Ottoman Military and the March to World War I* (London: I.B. Tauris, 2005), 163–76; Köroğlu, *Ottoman Propaganda*; CUP circular quoted in Tekin Alp, *Türkismus und Pantürkismus*, 53; and Hagen, "German Heralds of Holy War," 149–50; report of Wangenheim to Chancellor Bethmann Hollweg of February 24, 1913, PA-AA/ R14078.
22 BOA DH. ŞFR. 44-200, to the provinces of Edirne, Erzurum, Adana, Bitlis, Van, Hüdâvendigâr, Haleb, Sivas, Mamuretülaziz, Diyarbekir, and the sanjaks of İzmit, Canik.
23 Maurice Larcher, *La Guerre Turque dans la Guerre Mondiale* (Paris: Chiron & Berger-Levrault, 1926), 367–436, and Pomiankowski, *Zusammenbruch*, 98–105.
24 Kieser, *Der verpasste Friede*, 448–53, and Bihl, *Kaukasus-Politik*, 233.
25 The most systematic, detailed, and up-to-date account based on primary sources is Kévorkian, *Génocide*. For the most recent research, see *End of the Ottomans*.
26 For comparative and contextualizing approaches see Kieser and Schaller, *Der Völkermord an den Armeniern und die Shoah*; Bloxham, *Genocide, The World Wars and the Unweaving of Europe*; and Ihrig, *Justifying Genocide*.
27 Hans-Walter Schmuhl, "Friedrich Naumann und die 'armenische Frage,'" in Kieser and Schaller, *Der Völkermord an den Armeniern und die Shoah*, 503–16, and Jäckh, *Das grössere Mitteleuropa*; Rohrbach's remark is in a letter on September 21, 1915, to Ernst Jäckh (Jäckh Papers, Yale University Library). The project of Central European- and Near East-based German world power is described, for example, in Rohrbach's propagandistic article in the New York *Evening Mail* in August 1915 (copy in the Archive of the Deutsche Bank, OR 1388).
28 Dündar, *Modern Türkiye'nin şifresi*, 230–6.
29 Lepsius, *Todesgang des armenischen Volkes*, v–vii.
30 Trumpener, *Germany and the Ottoman Empire*, 209–10.
31 PA-AA/BoKon/171, November 18, 1915.
32 Humann quoted in Hilmar Kaiser, "Die deutsche Diplomatie und der armenische Völkermord," in *Osmanismus, Nationalismus und der Kaukasus. Muslime und Christen, Türken und Armenier im 19. und 20. Jahrhundert*, ed. Fikret Adanır and Bernd Bonwetsch (Wiesbaden: Reichert, 2005), 213–14.
33 Wolffskeel, *Zeitoun, Mousa Dagh, Ourfa*.
34 Gust, *Völkermord an den Armeniern*, 87–91.
35 PA-AA/R14093, report to the chancellor of September 10, 1916.

36 PA-AA/R14086, June 17, 1915, English translation on the site (www. armenocide.de).

37 PA-AA/R14086.

38 "Die Türkische Regierung vertritt den Standpunkt, daß die Umsiedelungsmassnahme nicht nur, wie wir zugegeben haben, in den Ostprovinzen, sondern im ganzen Reichsgebiet durch militärische Gründe gerechtfertigt war." Ambassador Wolff-Metternich to Bethmann Hollweg, April 3, 1916, PA-AA/R14091.

39 Note on an embassy report of December 7, 1915, PA-AA/R1408.

40 Lepsius, *Bericht über die Lage des Armenischen Volkes*. Published only in July 1916 and soon (not strictly) confiscated, parts of the *Bericht* circulated since autumn 1915. See Goltz and Meissner, *Thematisches Lexikon*, 72–4.

41 In a memorandum, on August 1, 1916, of the Auskunftstelle für Deutsch-Türkische Wirtschaftsfragen, an office established by the Turkish-German Society (Türkisch-Deutsche Vereinigung). See Friedman, *Germany, Turkey, Zionism*, 268–9. See also Chapter 13.

42 *Deutsche Levante-Zeitung*, no. 9 (May 1, 1917), 1–2.

43 Ernst Jäckh-Papers, Yale University Library, 461-2-52, Christian Gerlach, "Nationsbildung im Krieg: Wirtschaftliche Faktoren bei der Vernichtung der Armenier und beim Mord an den ungarischen Juden," in Kieser and Schaller, *Der Völkermord an den Armeniern und die Shoah*, 382–3; Alfred Nossig, *Die neue Türkei und ihre Führer* (Halle, Saale: Otto Hendel, 1916); and Parvus, *Die Glocke* no. 1 (September 1, 1915): 2.

44 Roessler to Bethmann Hollweg, April 12, 1915, DE/PA-AA/R14085, translation on the site.

45 Morgenthau, *Diaries*, 217–18, April 26–27, 1915; cf. 393, November 23, 1915.

46 Roessler to Wangenheim, reports of June 3 and 6, 1915, PA-AA/BoKon/169. Roessler, report of June 5 to Chancellor Bethmann Hollweg, PA-AA/R 19992; Wangenheim to Bethmann Hollweg, including Rössler's reports, May 27, 1915, PA-AA/R14086. See also Seyffarth, *Entscheidung in Aleppo—Walter Rössler*.

47 Talaat to Enver, February 16, 1916, published in *Arşiv belgeleriyle Ermeni faaliyetleri*, 8:104 and 8:253; Matthias, *Der interfraktionelle Ausschuss*, 2:410.

48 Wilhelm Feldmann, "Unterredung mit Talaat Bei," *Berliner Tageblatt*, May 4, 1916, 4.

49 CD, 3:377–89, April 11–May 6, 1917; 3:416, September 5, 1917; 3:449, December 5, 1917. Besides the record in the German archives, the German position on Armenian return is present in Ottoman documents, because it was voiced to Ottoman interlocutors. Wangenheim, for example, did so again to Cavid shortly before his death (3:147, September 26–October 18, 1915, no precise date); Metternich did so in İzzet Pasha's house on January 5, 1916 (3:169).

50 Kaiser, *At the Crossroads of Der Zor*, 33–8; Kieser, "Beatrice Rohner's Work in the Death Camps of Armenians"; and Kieser, *Der verpasste Friede*, 348–55 and 482–7.

51 Quoted in Donald Bloxham, *The Final Solution: A Genocide* (New York: Oxford University Press, 2009), 80–1. Brossat and Klingberg, *Revolutionary Yiddishland*, 97.

52 Max Domarus, *Hitler: Speeches and Proclamations 1932–1945* (Wauconda, IL: Bolchazy-Carducci Publishers, 1990), 2779.

53 Scheubner-Richter quoted in Paul Leverkühn, *Posten auf ewiger Wache. Aus dem abenteuerreichen Leben des Max von Scheubner-Richter* (Essen: Essener Verlagsanstalt, 1938), 192.

54 Adolf Hitler, *Sämtliche Aufzeichnungen: 1905–1924*, ed. Eberhard Jäckel and Axel Kuhn (Stuttgart: Deutsche Verlags-Anstalt), 1980, 775, English translation in Mike Joseph, "Max Erwin von Scheubner-Richter: The Personal Link from Genocide to

Hitler," in *The Armenian Genocide, Turkey and Europe*, ed. Hans-Lukas Kieser and Elmar Plozza (Zurich: Chronos, 2006), 165.

55 Leverkühn, *Posten*, 190.

56 Karl Klinghardt, "Als Augenzeuge der armenischen Katastrophe," *Der Orient* no. 5* (finally suppressed proof) (1928): 160–5, copy of the University Library Basel.

57 von Mikusch, *Gasi Mustafa Kemal*, 83. See also Chapter 2.

58 Richard Hartmann, "Die neue Türkei," *Der vordere Orient* 4 (1929): 105, quoted in Dominik J. Schaller, "Die Rezeption des Völkermords an den Armeniern in Deutschland, 1915-1945," in Kieser and Schaller, *Der Völkermord an den Armeniern und die Shoah*, 539–40.

59 E.g., Klinghardt, "Augenzeuge," 159.

60 Mikusch, *Gasi*, 83.

61 Kempner and Rosenberg quoted in Schaller, "Rezeption des Völkermords an den Armeniern," 537–8, and Raphael Lemkin, "Totally Unofficial Man," in *Pionieers of Genocide Studies*, ed. Samuel Totten and Steven L. Jacobs (New Brunswick, NJ: Transaction Publisher, 2002), 371.

62 Emmanuel Szurek, "Auto-da-fe in Istanbul: Nationalist Turkey's First Denialist Crisis (1935)," in Kieser et al., *After the Ottomans*, 155–94. Yair Auron, *Banality of Indifference: Zionism and the Armenian Genocide* (New York: Transaction Publishers), 293–311.

63 Letter of July 1950 quoted in *The Encyclopedia of Genocide* (Santa Barbara, CA: ABC-Clio, 1999), 79, and Dr. Lemkin, "Father of Genocide Convention, Reviews Work Relating to Turkish Massacres," *The Hairenik Weekly*, January 1, 1959, 1.

64 Theodor W. Adorno, "Erziehung nach Auschwitz," in idem, *Erziehung zur Mündigkeit, Vorträge und Gespräche mit Hellmut Becker 1959-1969* (Frankfurt am Main: Suhrkamp, 1970), 92–3.

Epilogue

1 Aram Mattioli, *Zeiten der Auflehnung: Geschichte des indigenen Widerstands in den USA* (Stuttgart: Klett-Cotta, 2023), 45–67.

2 For Gökalp's political thought, see Chapter 8 and "Europe's Seminal Proto-Fascism? Historically Approaching Ziya Gökalp, Mentor of Turkish Nationalism," published in *Die Welt des Islams* 61 (2021), 411-47. For Schmitt, notably on the relation of state and individuals, see Carl Schmitt, *Der Wert des Staates und die Bedeutung des Einzelnen* (Tübingen: J.C.B. Mohr, 1914.); idem, *Politische Theologie: vier Kapitel zur Lehre von der Souveränität* (München: Duncker & Humblot, 1922); notably on the total state: idem, *Der Begriff des Politischen: Text von 1932 mit einem Vorwort und drei Corollarien* (Berlin: Duncker und Humblot, 1963).

3 Schmitt, *Geistesgeschichtliche Lage*, 13–14.

4 Tröbst, "Mustafa Kemal Pascha," quoted in Ihrig, *Atatürk in the Nazi Imagination*, 86.

5 Schmitt, *Geistesgeschichtliche Lage*, 14, see also 15–16. Passage in italic in the original German text.

6 Harry Harootunian, *The Unspoken Heritage: The Armenian Genocide and Its Unaccounted Lives* (Durham, NC and London: Duke University Press, 2019), 145. In this partly autobiographical account, the author finally decided to look back into the long-suppressed life story of his parents, survivors of the Armenian genocide.

Index

Note: Page locators followed by 'n' refer to notes.
Muslim Ottomans, in general, did not have family names. They are in this index alphabetized by personal name: "Talaat," "Enver," "Cavid"; and, where more than one personal name was usual: "Ali Rıza," "Ziya Gökalp" (not "Rıza, Ali," "Gökalp, Ziya"). Little-used first personal names are given together with the frequent one in brackets, and generally used titles are added: "Talaat (Mehmed Talaat) Pasha." Those Muslim Ottomans who survived into the Republic of Turkey and adopted a family name by the mid-1930s, as required by the newly intro- duced Swiss Civil Code, are alphabetized by family name: "Atatürk, Mustafa Kemal," "Uzer, Hasan Tahsin." To facilitate identification, at times the index makes cross-references, mentions alternative spellings, and includes titles or functions.

Abalıoğlu, Yunus Nadi   130
ABCFM; see American Board of
        Commissioners for Foreign
        Missions (ABCFM)
Abdülhamid II (r. 1876–1909)   3, 34, 49,
        53, 126
Abraham   16–17, 146
Açıkalın, Ahmed Cevad   104
Adalet ve Kalkınma Partisi (AKP)
        party   45, 58, 100, 116,
        122, 232
Adıvar, Halide Edib   140
Aegean Rûm   72
Ağaoğlu (=Agayef), Ahmed   132, 174
agrarian question   35
Ahmed İzzet Pasha   70
Akçura, Yusuf   132, 172, 174
Aleppo   54, 75, 206–7, 216, 221–2, 226
        Armenians in   39
        Swiss connections in   39
Alevis   5, 7, 36, 49, 52, 54–5, 57, 63, 66,
        108–9, 130, 241 n.8
"Allahu Akbar" (God is the greatest)   128
Alpdoğan, Abdullah   110–12
Amalekites   18, 20
American Africans   23
        lynching violence against   47
American Board of Commissioners for
        Foreign Missions (ABCFM)   6,
        27–8, 31–40, 43–4, 184, 233 n.12

archives   43
Cherokee, vision for   42
churches and schools   31
in education and health care   186
fervor for Indians   31–3
imperial Muslim resentment,
        contributed to   34
members   38
missionaries   31–2, 37–40, 43
to Oriental Christians   186
in Ottoman Anatolia   33
policy for assimilation   31
teaching English   31
visions for Ottoman   42
as witness   37–40
American Christianity   184
American Indians   23
        marriages between Whites and   31
        as "other"   31
        removal   28–33
American millenarianism   184
American missionaries   23, 31, 34, 40,
        50, 184, 186–7, 207–8
Anatolia   84–5
Anatolian Alevis   241 n.8
Anatolian Christians   94–5
Anatolian wars (1919–22)   4, 14–15,
        23–4, 88
Ancient Israel   17–18
Anglo-Saxon empire   23

Ankara   1–5, 7, 14, 15, 23–4, 51, 57–8,
        83–110, 113, 121, 123–4, 132,
        134–5
    Bolshevism and   84
    demands in Lausanne   51
    League of Nations and   97
    National Assembly   2, 7, 89, 96–7, 99,
        101, 105–6, 108, 156
    new secularism   92
    political Islam and   84
    scapegoating Cavid   148–50
    success in Lausanne   97
anti-Armenian massacres   54, 76,
        213–14, 217
anti-Christian violence   57, 207
anti-democracy   3–5, 9, 20–2, 25
    aggression   10
    democracy *versus*   20
    and genocide   10–11
    violent   20–2
anti-egalitarian policy of Islamic
        unity   34
anti-Hamidian revolution in
        Turkey   174
anti-imperialism   163, 179
anti-Rûm exploits   71–3
anti-Rûm policy   71–2
anti-Russian guerrilla war   176
Apak, Rahmi   253 n.48
aphorism   166
apocalypticism   59–61, 178–80
appeasement   5, 24, 72, 81, 147
Arab Alawis   52
"archaic" polities   19
Armenian Question   31, 34–5, 48, 63–6,
        68, 90, 96, 118, 176, 190, 193–4,
        198, 202–3, 205–10, 214–15,
        222, 225
Armenian Reforms; *see* Reform
        Agreement of 1914
Armenian Revolutionary Federation
        (ARF)   35, 63, 167, 176
Armenians   4
    autonomy/independence   34
    destruction of Ottoman   33–7
    in eastern Anatolia   34–5, 37
    emigration   34–5
    in the First World War   15
    genocide   5, 36

and Germany   211–27
in *Katolik millet*   36
millet-i sadike   34
in *Protestant milleti*   36
records of church administrations   15
religious categorization   15
removal from Asia Minor   27, 33–7
versus Rûm *versus* Jews   33
from Zeytun   37
Art. 61 of Berlin Treaty   35, 65, 76, 186
Asia Minor   13–14, 160
    collapse of constructive reform for   64
    demographic de-Christianization
        of   15
    genocide of Armenian community
        in   164
    multiethnic eastern   35
    post-Great War wars in   56
    Reform Agreement of 1914 and   35,
        62–4
    Turkish sovereignty over   157
    into *Türk Yurdu*   74
assertive secularism   152
Asshur   18
Assyrian Christians (*Süryani*)   66
Assyrians   4–5, 39, 50–1, 64, 66, 84, 86,
        104, 229
Atabinen, Reşid Saffet (Safvet)   106,
        132, 156
Atatürk, Mustafa Kemal   1, 15, 40, 87
Atatürk İhtilali (The Revolution of
        Atatürk; Bozkurt)   159–60
Atatürk Revolution   97
Atay, Falih Rıfkı   122
autogenocide   236 n.35
Aygün, Hüseyin   116

Bagdadbahn   189
Baha Said   130
Bahaeddin Şakir; *see* Shakir
Balkans   5, 34, 48, 55, 65, 102, 108,
        128, 146
    in Asia Minor   66
    Christians of   34
    muhacir from   66, 71, 73–4, 197
    Muslim migrants from   34
    socialism in   171
    territorial losses in   34, 212–13
Balkan Wars   40, 45, 56, 71–3

bandits 111–13
Barth, Karl 20, 188
Barton, James 40
Basel Mission 183–4
Bauer, Yehuda 37
Bauman, Zygmunt 102
Bayar, Celal 155
Baykara, Barbaros 115
Baykut, Câmi Abdülkadir 147
Bedirhan, Abdurrezzak 67
Beirut 54
Bektashiye 109
Belle Époque diplomacy 64–6
Berkes, Niyazi 130, 133
Berlin Congress 35
Berlin Treaty (1878) 34–5, 56, 59, 64–5,
    76, 186–7, 202–3, 212–13
Beşikçi, Ismail 116
Beyatlı, Yahya Kemal 135
Bible Lands 2, 28, 31–3, 42, 184
biblical eschatology 48
biblical genocide commands 20
Bieberstein, Marschall von 140
Bilen, Ismail 115
biographies 119
Birgen, Muhittin 124, 202
Bitler, Elizur 32
Bleda, Midhat Şükrü 69
bloody sacrifices 19
Bolshevism 23–4, 84, 124, 181
Books of Moses, Joshua, and
    Samuel 18
Bosnia-Herzegovina 67
Bozkurt, Mahmut E. 92, 97, 110,
    152–62, 257 n.4
    adolescence 152–3
    Atatürk İhtilali (The Revolution of
        Atatürk) 159–60
    childhood 152–3
    democracy, conception of 159–60
    early influences 152–3
    ethnonationalism 161
    on fascism 161–2
    Foyer Turc movement of (pan-)
        Turkism and 154–5
    Janus face 160–2
    Nazism, views on 160
    post-religious modernity, commitment
        to 158
    president of *Foyer Turc* in
        Lausanne 155–6
    "Principles of the Turkish Revolution,
        The" 157
    rightist revolution 152
    as right-wing revolutionist 152
    sovereignty, conception of 160
    Swiss Civil Code and 152, 157–9
    theorist and propagandist of
        Kemalism 159–60
    on ultranationalism 161–2
Britain 4, 29, 68, 83, 85–7, 91, 136, 150,
    168, 175, 194, 212–13
Bruinessen, Martin van 116–17
Bücher, Carl 166
Bulgaria 48, 67, 102, 104, 141–2, 168
Burckhardt, Carl J. 94, 166

Çağlayangil, Ihsan Sabri 111–12
Cahit (Hüseyin); *see* Yalçın, Hüseyin Cahit
Cairo 53–4
Çakmak, Marshal Fevzi 108, 111
Caliphate abolition (1924) 107
Canaan 18
Canaanites 18
cariye 54
Cavid Bey (1877–1926) 2–3, 68–9, 100,
    119, 137–51
    Ankara's scapegoat and 148–50
    cohort 138
    constitutionalist Turkish
        patriot 137–9
    CUP's central figure 138–40
    diaries 137–9
    ego-writing 138–9
    in Lausanne 146–8
    letter to Churchill 140
    member of dictatorial and genocidal
        war regime 142–6
    murder 150–1
    Notebook for Şiar 138, 149
    overview 137
    post-great war diplomacy and 146–8
    relation with Talaat 142–8
    revolutionary young Turk 139–42
    in Switzerland 147
    Talaat and 139–41
    Zohrab and 140–1
Celâl Bey 66, 75–6

Cemal (Ahmed Cemal Pasha)   37
Cevad, Ahmed; *see* Açıkalın, Ahmed
       Cevad
Cevdet, Ahmed; *see* Oran, Ahmed Cevdet
Chamberlain, Houston Steward   188
Château d'Ouchy   104
chauvinism (*şovinizm*)   2–3, 37, 133,
       141, 181
Cherokee nation   28–32
Christianity   50, 54, 134, 184, 188
Christians   50
   Anatolian   94–5
   Assyrian (*Süryani*)   66
   of Balkans   34
   ethics and protection of
       minority   218
   Hutu   20
   Levantine   54
   Ottoman   3–4, 6, 15, 20, 25, 46, 51,
       53–5, 64, 67–71, 73–4, 76, 79,
       89, 155–6, 172, 174, 190
   Rwandan genocide against   20
Churchill, Winston   140
Civil Law (1926)   152
civil liberties   2, 11, 126
class enemy   154
coercion   1, 6, 29, 42, 52, 58, 71–4, 86, 94,
       149–51, 171, 231
Cold War   51–2, 58–60, 115
colonial violence   53
Committee of Union and Progress
       (CUP)   2–3, 13, 51, 55–8,
       62–4, 81
   ally with Germany   64
   anti-Armenian stance   67
   and Armenian Dashnaktsutiun
       alliance   35
   Central Committee members   100
   coup d'état in January 1913   38
   dictatorship   65–6
   extermination of Armenians   86
   Greek-Orthodox Rûm, campaigns
       against   36
   millet system, demographic
       classification of   36
   missionaries with   38
   Ottoman nation   3
   radicalization of   77–9
   revival (*ihya*)   148

revolutionist right-wing policy   36
   terror squads   72
   violence as self-defense, use of   57
Comte, Auguste   127
common good   9–11, 13, 31–2
constitutional law   11
constitutional Ottomanism   47–8
constitutional patriotism
       (*Verfassungspatriotismus*)   137–9
covenant-based peace   16–20
"Covenant of the Islamic Resistance
       Movement" of Hamas
       (1988)   20
Crawford, David   69
Crete   67
crime de lèse-humanité   86
crimen magnum   12
Crime of Genocide   9–10, 117
crimes   12; *see also* violence
   against *citoyenneté universelle*   12
   against humanity   12, 22, 41, 202
crucifixion of innocent individual   19
CUP; *see* Committee of Union and
       Progress (CUP)

Daniel, Elton   127
Dashnaktsutiun   167
Das Reich Christi   185
death, management of   52
Decalogue   17
de-Christianization   15, 64
deity   18
democracy   11–12, 84, 157
   anti-democracy *versus*   20
   dialectical historical progress and   16
   to eastern Anatolia   35
   law-based   11
   Russian   177
democratic social contract   11–12
Deny, Jean   123
Der christliche Orient   185
Dersim
   Alevi population   108
   for Armenian refugees   109
   genocide/campaign   5, 7, 57, 78, 81,
       107–18
       actors   110–11
       context   107–9
       decision-makers   110–11

facts, legal and historical
   interpretation of 116–18
  memories 114–16
  organizers 110–11
  victims 111–13
  witnesses 113–14
 history of banditry 109
 Kurds 108
 pacification of 110
 population 108
 region 108
 topography 108
Dersimi, Nuri 111, 115
despotism 48, 149, 229
destruction of Izmir (1922) 110
dhimmis 20
dialectical historical progress 16
diplomatic expediency 12
disciplinary campaign; *see* Dersim
discrimination against women 54
divine commands 18
"divide and rule" practices 51
Diyarbekir 38–9, 54, 65–7, 124–6, 132
domestic jihad 20, 47, 49, 52–5
 and expansion of modern Europe's
   imperial nation-states 52–3
 against Ottoman non-Muslims 52–3
Dreyfus, Alfred 19
Durkheim, Émile 127
"Duty" (*Vazife;* Gökalp) 133

eastern Anatolia
 Armenians in 34–5, 37
 democracy to 35
 reforms in 34
Eastern Question 46, 48, 52–3, 64–5, 83,
   168, 176, 184, 214
Ehle, Carl F. 184
Elazığ 110
Emmanuilidis, Emmanuil 73
empathy 18, 86, 189
Emrullah Efendi 140
"Enlightenment" thinking 13
Enver (İsmail Enver Pasha) 36, 100
equal human rights 32
equality 35, 47
equity 2
Erdoğan, Tayip 45, 107, 116,
   122, 232

*Ermeni Gregoryen milleti (millet-i
   Ermeniyan)* 33, 36
Ermeni Tarihi (History of the
   Armenians) 103
Erzberger, Matthias (1875–1921) 8, 181,
   200, 202–10, 267 n.4
 First World War and 204–6
 on massive evil 206–8
 perceptive democrat 210
 repositioning 208–10
 soul-searching 208–10
 young politician 203–4
Esbabı mucibe layihası 158
eschatology 50–2
 into Levant from West 50
 myths 51–2
 and reign of God 50
 Shiism and 60–1
Ethiopia 110
ethnocide 116, 118
ethnonationalism 161
Europe 22–3, 231
 cataclysm 221
 diplomatic collapse 64
 Eastern Question 52–3, 83
 ethics and protection of minority
   Christians 218
 Great War 4
 imperial nation-states 52–3, 71
 internal problems 85
 post-Ottoman region 59
 progressive civilization 169
 prophets of Great War 121–2
 universal civilization (*medeniyet*) 169
 Western 96
 Zeitgeist in 71
Evarts, Jeremiah 31–2, 40
evangelical modernity 40
exclusion 6, 12, 14–15, 18–19, 21–2, 28,
   36, 40, 56, 86, 124, 148, 181, 225
expulsion 11, 15, 20, 22, 29, 36, 72–3, 79,
   86, 94, 214, 219, 226, 229
extermination 16, 18, 20, 207, 217–18
 in Ancient Testament 18
 exercise of "barbaric" collective 12
 of Indians 40
 of Kurdish Alevis in Dersim 5
 in modern Europe 11
 of other tribes and peoples 18

of Ottoman Armenians   12–13,
    41, 86, 131, 203, 207–11,
    217–18, 220
of Ottoman Christians   51
physical   215
for social Darwinist minds   40
state's policy of   103
Turkish fears of   173
of twentieth century   117
victims of   188
Young Turks' Armenian
    policy   199
extreme ideology   2; *see also*
    anti-democracy; proto-fascism;
    ultranationalism
extreme violence   4, 50; *see also*
    genocide; violence
    biblical utopia and   18–19
    social contract and   22

fascism   20, 161–2
favoritism   53
Feudal Lords and Dersim, The   108
First Balkan War   77–9
First World War   5–7, 13, 15, 27, 33, 36,
    43, 45, 48, 50–2, 56–9, 62, 74,
    76, 103, 108–9, 112, 121, 132,
    144, 153–6, 160, 164–5, 168,
    170, 179, 181, 184, 188, 202–6
Fischer, August   121
"Five Civilized Tribes"   30, 41
Fonjallaz, Arthur   96
fortiori non-Muslims   58
foundational violence   1, 19
Foyers Turcs   153–6, 168–9
    in Geneva   155–6
    in Lausanne   155–6
Foyer Turc movement of (pan-)
    Turkism   154–6
France   1, 4, 19, 83, 85–6, 91, 106–7, 111,
    168, 178, 212
freedom (*hürriyet*)   2, 11, 23, 53, 76, 94,
    97, 105, 126, 149, 158, 162, 175
free society   19
Fuad, Ali   37

Gandauer, Georg   170
gardener state   102
Garo, Armen   73

Gasprinski, Ismail   174
Gazi Kemal; *see* Atatürk
Genesis (14:18-20)   17
Genghis Khan   128, 154
génocidaires   10
génocidaire statesman   21
genocide
    anti-democracy-cum-genocide
        10–11
    as crime   9
    de-Christianization from   15
    definition   9
    legacy of Republican Turkey   1–3
    polities based on   22
    Turkey case   1–3, 13–16
    in twentieth-century revolutions
        10–11
    against Yazidis   20
genocide commands   17–18, 20
George, Lloyd   156
German National Socialism   15
German Orient Mission   185–7
German-Ottoman war alliance
    (1914)   191–2, 211–27
Germany   4–5, 21, 38, 40–1, 163–80
    and Armenian Genocide
        (1915)   215–17
    and Armenians   211–27
    CUP ally with   64
    foreign policy   189
    and genocide   74–6
    and holocaust *versus* Armenian
        genocide   225–7
    metanoia   189
    pervasive impact of Armenian
        genocide on interwar   223–5
    reactions to mass crime   217–23
    reform-adverse destruction and   74–6
    Reform Agreement of 1914 and   64–5
    war and   74–6
Girard, René   19, 21
Gobat, Samuel   184
God   16–18
    eschatological reign of   50
    kingdom of   184–5
Gök-Alp of 1910s   126–9
Gospel narrative   19, 31–2, 43
Graves, Robert   65, 69, 139
Great War   3–5, 7–8, 13–14, 175–8

Greco-Turkish War   4, 83
Greece   4, 15, 17–18, 36, 67, 71–3, 89–90,
        102, 214–15, 218
greed   41
Greeks   15, 18, 72–3, 89, 94, 105, 156,
        194, 229
Gulkevich, Konstantin   62, 70

Haab, Rudolf   88
Hadiths   20
Halajian, Bedros   69, 140
Halide Edib; *see* Adıvar
Halil; *see* Menteşe
Halim; *see* Said Halim
Halli, Reşat   107, 112–13
Hamdi Bey   108, 110
Hamid Kapancızâde   38, 65
Hamidiye   70
Hartmann, Richard   121
Harun Aliçe   156
Haso (Seyit)   111
Hayri (Mustafa Hayri), Efendi
        67–8, 127
Hebrew Bible   17–18, 48
Helphand, Israil; *see* Parvus
Herzen, Alexander   166
*Hilfsbund für christliches Liebeswerk im
        Orient*   39
Himmler, Heinrich   16
history of salvation   17, 101
Holocaust (1941-5)   15, 21
holy scriptures   20, 52
Huber, Eugen   153
human dignity   11, 12, 16–17
human equality   12, 16–17
Humann, Hans   178
human rights   16, 21–2, 29, 53, 84, 126
human sacrifices   18
human self-organization   19
Hüseyinzâde Ali   132, 174, 177–8
Hussein, Saddam   21
Hutu Christians   20

Iliad, The   18
imperial bias   13
imperial Islam   59–61
Indian Removal Act (May 28, 1830)   29
*Indictment against the Christian Great
        Powers* (Lepsius)   187

"infidel's" (*gavur, kafir's*) blood   48–9
Inönü, Ismet (Pasha)   15, 92, 98
invalids   20
Iranian Islamic revolution (1979)   60
Islam   20–1, 48
Islamic State (IS)   20, 45, 50
Islamic State of Iraq and Syria (ISIS)   61
Islamic Turkification   13–14
Islamic Turkism   127–8
Islamic *ummah*   47, 50–2, 57
Islamic unity, anti-egalitarian policy
        of   34
Islamism (Hamidism)   14, 46, 49, 51,
        55–60, 67, 135, 191, 213, 232
Islamist throat-cutting of civilians   49
Ismet Pasha; *see* Inönü
Israel   42, 46, 185
    ancient   17–18
    Ben-Gurion, David and   48
    restoration   50
    violent deaths in   59
    wars   59
Istanbul   2, 54, 71, 170
Italian fascism   15, 96
Italy   4, 85–6, 110, 213
    Ethiopia, invasion of   110
    foreign policies   110
    Libya, invasion of   56, 140,
        203–4
Izmir   54, 72
İzzet Pasha; *see* Ahmed İzzet Pasha

Jäckh, Ernst   178, 180, 192
Jackson, Andrew   23, 29–32, 42
Japan   4
Jenkins, Paul   183–4
Jenni-Hoppeler, Emma   153
Jesus   61
    on Earth   28
    role in Gospels   19
Jews   15, 21, 33
    monotheism   17
    restoration of   50
jihad   20, 45, 47, 51–5; *see also*
        domestic jihad
Judaism   19
Jura, Bernese   184
justice   2, 19, 23, 43–4, 51, 65, 90, 92,
        147, 149–52

Kalmykow, Andrew 72
Kapancızâde Hamid; *see* Hamid
        Kapancızâde 38, 65
Kautsky, Karl 171
Kaya, Şükrü 104, 108, 110–11
Kemal (Yusuf); *see* Tengirşek, Yusuf
        Kemal
Kemalism 1, 14, 48, 57–9, 110, 159
Kemalist Revolution 84
Kemalist Turkism 107–8, 132–4
Kevork V 65
Khatissian, Alexandre 90
kingdom of God 184–6
King Saul 18
"Kızıl Destan" (Red Epic) 129
"Kızılelma" (Red Apple;
        Gökalp) 121, 128
Koçgiri uprising (1921) 107–8, 110
Komiteci (1913-14) 193–4
Köprülü, Mehmed Fuad 132
Koranic eschatology 48
Koranic tradition 47
Korkmaz, Ahmed 114
Krafft-Bonnard, Antony 95–6
Kriegsunschuldlegende 189
Kurdish Alevis in Dersim 5
Kurdish-Armenian question 63
Kurdishness 133
Kurdish tribe of Zaza 133

Laçin, Şükrü 114
land question 63, 65
Latin alphabet 107
Lausanne conference 5, 7, 83–93, 97, 99,
        102–7, 149
    Ankara's delegation in 86–8
    defining contexts 83–8
    exclusion 86
    fallout 85
    home for native Armenians issues
        and 88–9
    humanitarian issues and 88–9
    milestones of 88–93
    minority rights issues and 88–9
    Nur, Rıza and 104–6
    paradigm of 94–6
    population exchange 86
    post-Ottoman mandate 85
    social Darwinist rationale 84–5
        successes 87
        ultranationalism domination 85–6
Lausanne Treaty (1923) 1, 5, 10, 15,
        22–4, 40, 46, 48, 51, 83–98
    collective and individual rights
        and 86
    Lausanne conference 83–93
    paradigm of 94–6
    positive outlook on 84
    post-Lausanne century 96–8
Lauterpacht, Hersch 12
law-based polities 16–20
Law of Settlement (1934) 109,
        111–12, 116
Law Revolution (*Hukuk Devrimi*) of
        1920s 92
League of Nations 4, 22–4, 85–7, 89,
        91, 97, 104, 107, 111, 187, 210,
        228–9
Legal Revolution (*Huku Devrimi*) 157
Lemkin, Raphael 12–13, 37, 225–6
Lepsius, Johannes 13, 176, 183–9
    cataclysm 187–8
    Christliche Orient-Mission of 186
    Das Reich Christi 185
    Der christliche Orient 185
    goals 183
    *Hülfsbund für christliches Liebeswerk
        im Orient* 186
    *Indictment against the Christian Great
        Powers* 187
    in informal movement 183
    with informal Protestant
        International 183–5
    millenarianism and German Orient
        Mission 185–7
    near East millenarianism 183–5
    as Protestant in Second German
        Empire 187
    *Report on the Situation of the Armenian
        People, The* 187
    World War and 188–9
lèse-humanité 12
lèse-majesté 12
lèse-nation 12
Levant 240 n.2
Levantine Christians 54
Levantine Jews 54
Lewy, Guenter 41

liberty 11
Libya 77–9
Liebknecht, Karl 170
Luther, Martin 183
Luxemburg, Rosa 164, 166
lynching 47, 53

Mamuretülaziz 38–9
Mandelstam, André N. 68, 86, 95
Marchelewski (Karski), Julian 166
Marshall, John 32
Marx, Karl 165
Masliyah, Nesim (=Mazliyah,
        Nissim) 177–8
massacres of Armenians in Adana
        (1909) 55
mass crimes 12, 81, 88, 225; *see also*
        genocide
mass murder; *see* genocide
Mehmed Sadık 140
Mehmed Shahingiray; *see* Reşid
        (Mehmed Dr.)
Melchizedek 17
Menteşe, Halil 69
Metzger, Max J. 11
Meyer, Karl 95
Middle Eastern violence 55
Midhat (Bleda); *see* Bleda, Midhat Şükrü
Mikusch, Dagobert von 40–1
millet-i sadike 34
millets 15, 32–3
millet system, demographic classification
        of 36, 47
mimetic theory 19
minorities 20
minority rights 40
missionaries 50
monotheism 16, 47
Montaigne, Michel de 143
Mooney, James 30–1
Mosaic Covenant 13
Mosaic Law 11, 17
Moslemization 84–5
municipal polity 17
Münir, Mehmed 104
murder 10, 12
murder of nation 13
Muslims 63
    eschatologies 50

Greeks 156
    nationalism 49
    unity, politics of 76
Mussolini, Benito 85

Nadi (Yunus); *see* Abalıoğlu,
        Yunus Nadi
Nansen, Fridtjof 89
National Assembly, Ankara 2, 7, 89,
        96–7, 99, 101, 105–6, 108, 156
national defense 87
national identity 25
national-imperial self-assertion 76–9
nationalist modernity 40–2
"National Pact" (Misaki-i Millî) 14, 87
national renaissance 33
nation by will (*Willensnation*) 137
Nazım (Dr.) 101
Nazis
    antisemitism 21
    demographic engineering 21
    euthanasia program 21
Near Eastern millenarianism 183–5
Near Eastern Relief (NER) 39–40
Near East Peace Treaty of Lausanne
        (1923) 1, 5, 10, 15, 22–4,
        83–98
Necmettin Molla 68
New Echota Treaty of 1835 32
Nicolson, Harold 90
Niebuhr, Helmut 184
Nietzsche, Friedrich 166
nonconformists 20
non-Muslim minorities 49
non-Muslims 6, 49–51, 71, 86, 89,
        117, 215
    ABCFM and 34
    claims of equality by 25
    domestic jihad against 52
    equality of 35
    ethnoreligious onslaught against 3
    intra-societal violence against 45
    othering of 14
non-violence 12
Noradunghian, Gabriel 64, 90
North Atlantic Treaty Organization
        (NATO) 45
Nubar, Bogos (Pasha) 65
Nur, Rıza 86–7, 95, 99–106

Ankara's diplomatic success in
    Lausanne and   105–6
Conference of Lausanne and   104–6
on democracy   105
Ermeni Tarihi (History of the
    Armenians)   103
Greater Turkey   102
History of the Armenians versus *History
    of the Turks*   101–3
on Islamization   103
memoirs   103
müfrit nasiyonalism   100
overview   99–100
pan-Turkish ideologue   100–1
political peak   104–6
political surgeon   100–1
on state's policy of extermination   103
Turanism   101
Turkist anti-democracy triumphing
    and   106
Türk Tarihi (History of the
    Turks)   101–3
turning point   104–6
writings   100
Nuremberg Charter (1945)   12

Obenzinger, Hilton   184
Oghuz Khan   123, 128
Oghuz union (*Oğuz birliği*)   132–3
Oppenheim, Max von   176, 178
Oran, Ahmed Cevdet   156
Oriental Christians   34
Orthodox Ottomans (Rûm)   34
Osmanlıcı   154
"otherizing" humans   10
others/otherness   15, 20–2, 41, 50–1
Ottoman capitulations   74
Ottoman Christians   3–4, 15, 25, 67,
    155–6
  mob violence against   53–4
  removal and extermination of   51
Ottoman constitutionalism   137–9
Ottoman Deportation Act (May
    1915)   35–6
Ottoman Empire   1–4, 8, 13, 23, 28, 31, 34,
    37–8, 45–54, 57, 74, 76–7, 184–6
  American missionary to   31
  as community of Turkish-speaking
    Muslims   3

crisis of   185
diversity in   53
in "European concert" of monarchical
    powers   52–3
extreme violence   4
legal and actual equality   53
Near East Peace Treaty of Lausanne
    and   83–98
plurality-cum-equality   28
research on   3
single-party regime   4
transformation of   4
versus Western Europe   53
Ottoman Islamism   49
Ottomanism   34
Ottoman massacres   55
Ottoman *millet* system   36, 47
Ottoman Muslim refugees (*muhacir*)   55,
    71–4
Ottoman Muslims   15, 25
Ottoman nation   3–4, 66, 71, 154
Ottoman politics   51
Ottoman Reform Edict (*Hatt-ı Hümayun*)
    of 1856   33, 53–4
Ottoman Rûm   71–2
Ottoman sovereignty   63
Ottoman Tanzimat   47
Ottoman total war   76–8, 81
Ottoman Turkey   25
Özbudun, Ergun   14

Palestine   50
pan-Islamism   49
pan-Turkism   48, 100–1, 154–6
paradox   18–19
Paris Peace Conference   4
Paris peace treaties (1919-20)   23, 40, 83
Parsons, Levi   31
Parvus, Alexander Israil Helphand   8,
    163–80
  activism in Switzerland   165–9
  articles   172
  belated conversion from
    warmongering
    apocalypticism   178–80
  collaboration with CUP   163, 167–80
  education   165–9
  Great War and   175–8
  intellectual activity   164–5

Index

283

from leftist to rightist revolution-and
to World War   171–5
and link between revolution   164–5
political and intellectual
biography   165
prolific socialist writer and activist,
career as   164–5
from Russia via Switzerland to
Germany and Turkey   169–70
success in Istanbul   172–4
to Turkish fears of extermination   173
Pax Ottomanica   33
peace   1–2
Peet, William   39
Penn, William   32
Persian Gulf war (1991)   59
Phillips, Clifton J.   31
Pirinççizâde, Feyzi   132
Pittard, Eugène   135
Plekhanov, Georgii   166–7
Poland   4
political pluralism   158
political religion   124
political violence   10, 21
polity of humble humans   17
Pomiankowski, Joseph   37
Pontic Rûm   4
population exchange   15
Posen Speeches   16
post-Lausanne century   96–8
post-Ottoman world   96–7
primitive tribes   12
"Principles of the Turkish Revolution,
The" (Bozkurt)   157
prolegomena   5, 9
prophetic monotheism   46–50
Prophet Samuel   18
Protestant American
millennialism   240 n.54
"Protestant Ethic and the Spirit of
Capitalism, The" (Weber)   134
Protestant International   183–6
Protestant milleti   33
proto-fascism   3–5
Prucha, Francis P.   33
pseudo-socialist cynicism   177–8
public violence   46–50; *see also* lynching
along politico-religious lines   47
decade (1912–22)   55–9

during the First World War   52
versus genocide of 1915   49–50
Islamist throat-cutting of civilians   49
Ottoman   54–5
Sunni   55
urban mob violence   49
of women   54

quasi-religious ideologies   10
Quran   20
Qutb, Sayyid   50

racism   21, 41
Radek, Karl   164
radical ethnic nationalism   4
radicalization *versus* reform efforts   66–71
Ragaz, Leonhard   95
Rahmi, Vali   72
Rakovsky, Christian   168
Rambert, Louis   71–3, 140
rape   49
Reform Agreement of 1914   35,
62–4, 190
Reform Edict of 1856   33, 53–4
reform efforts *versus*
radicalization   66–71
refugee crisis   71
refugees   89
Reich Gottes (Kingdom of God)   184–6
Reichskanzler   75
religion   16
categorization   15
violence and   45
religious Turkism   124
renewed Turkey mantra   193–4
*Report on the Situation of the Armenian
People, The* (Lepsius)   187
Republican Turkey   107
anti-Hamidian revolution in   174
CUP and   3
dynamic human landscape   2
eschatological expectations   48
extreme violence in   1–4
formation of   3–4
genocide   1–3, 13–16
German ally   5, 64
history   1–3
humanity and human rights issues,
crimes against   5

interaction with European
   Union   58–9
nationhood   66
policy (1915–18)   199–200
political fabric   4
post-genocidal conditions of
   minorities in   5
Swiss Civil Code to   157–9
ultranationalist refoundation   81
Reşid (Mehmed Dr.)   38–9, 73, 101,
   129, 174
Resik Hüseyin   111
revolutionary socialism   4
Riggs, Henry   38
Rıza (Seyyid)   110–11, 114
robbing   49
Rohner, Beatrice   39
Rohrbach, Paul   192
Rome Statute of the International
   Criminal Court (1998)   12
Rössler, Walter   75
Rûm   4, 33
Rumbold, Horace   91–2, 95
Russian Bolsheviks   4
Russian Revolution of 1917   166
Russian socialism   166
Rwandan genocide, Christians against
   Christians (1995)   20

Sadak, Necmettin Sadık   132
Safvet, Reşid; see Atabinen, Reşid Saffet
   (Safvet)
Said Halim   62, 70, 72, 75, 130, 142–3,
   195, 214
Salem   17
Salih Zeki   37
salvation   19
Şapolyo, E. B.   127
Saraçoğlu, Şükrü   154–6
Sazonov, Sergej   65
scandal   18–19
scandal of cross   19–20
scapegoats/scapegoating   10, 19–21
Schmitt, Carl   29, 94
Schurer, Heinz   165
Second World War   15
(self-)censure rule   53
Senn, Alfred   166
Sermon on Mount   11, 20

Sertel, Zekeriya   130
settler violence   53
Şevket, Mahmud   67
Seyyid Rıza; see Rıza
Shahingiray, Mehmed Reşid; see Reşid
   (Mehmed Dr.)
Shakir (Bahaeddin Dr.)   37, 101, 140,
   145, 168
Shiism   60
Shiite apocalypticisms   60–1
Shoah (1933-45)   15, 21
Şiar'ın Defteri   138, 149
slavery   53
Smith, Floyd   38
social contracts   10–13, 16, 17–20,
   46–50
   anti-democratic   21
   democratic   11–12
   extreme violence and   22
   modern   21
   Muslim faithful and their caliph   20
   US Constitution and   22
social democracy   166
social peace   48
social revolution (*içtimâî inkılâb*)   126
sociopolitical violence   25
"Soldier's Prayer" poem (Gökalp)   122
Soviet Union   24
spoliation   49
state-led violence   51
state-organized removal of entire groups
   ABCFM and   37–40
   American Indian removal   28–33
   Jackson's removal policy   29–30
   Ottoman Armenians, destruction
      of   33–7
   overview   25–6
strong leader (*reis*)   50
Şükrü Kaya; see Kaya
Sun Language theory   159
Sunni   25
   apocalypticisms   60–1
   empowerment   76
   Kurds   158
   Muslims   48
   public violence   55
Sunni-Orthodox social order   48
Sunni-Shiite divide   45
Suny, Ronald G.   13

Suphi, Hamdullah; *see* Tanrıöver, Hamdullah Suphi
Swiss Civil Code   107, 152–3, 157–9
Switzerland   47
   Cavid (1877–1926) in   147
   Civil Code   107, 152–3, 157–9
   ethnic and linguistic pluralism in   158
   Parvus activism in   165–9
   political pluralism   158
Syria
   Arab Alawis in   52
   war in   45
systematic plunder   22
systemic corruption   53

Talaat, Mehmed   4, 13, 14, 20–1, 57, 65–72, 104, 129–30
Tali, Ibrahim   108
Tanrıöver, Hamdullah Suphi   132, 153
Tanzimat   28, 33–6, 38, 47, 53–4, 108, 134, 137, 186, 212
Taray, Cemal Hüsnü   154
tarikat (religious order)   128
tekbîr/takbîr   49
Tekinalp, Moïz Kohen   159
Tengirşek, Yusuf Kemal   99, 101, 158–9
terror   71–4
Third Zimmerwald Conference   177
topoi   172
Tower of Babel   157
Toynbee, Arnold   13
Trail of Tears   29–33, 37
Treaty of Brest-Litovsk   131
Treaty of Lausanne; *see* Lausanne Treaty (1923)
Treaty of Sèvres   83, 89–90, 94
Treaty of Versailles   94
Tröbst, Hans   94–5
Trotsky, Leon   164, 170–1
Tucholsky, Kurt   11
Tunceli   107–18; *see also* Dersim
Tunceli Is Made Accessible to Civilization   114
Tunceli Law   110, 116
Tunceli Law and the Dersim Genocide, The   116
Turan   13–14, 56, 128–9, 191
"Turan" campaign   37
"Turanian" (proto-Turkish) race   100

Turanism (mix of pan-Turkism and pan-Islamism)   51
Türkçülüğün Esasları (Principles of Turkism)   102, 128, 132
Turkey policy (1915–18)   199–200
Turkification   84–5
Turkish-Armenian accord   63
Turkish Civil Code   158
Turkish History Thesis   159
Turkish nation   160–1
Turkish nationalism   59–61
Turkishness   57–8, 133
Turkish Revolution   157–9
Turkism   5, 15, 48, 96, 100–1, 168
   Islamic   127–8
   Kemalist   107–8, 132–4
   religious   124
Türklük   122–3
Türk Ocağı organization   153, 159
Turks (Muslims in Greece)   15
Türk Tarihi (History of the Turks)   101–3
Türk Yurdu organization   13, 74, 153, 159, 168

ultranationalism (*müfrit nasyonalizm*)   2–5, 14–15, 100, 160–2
   appeasement of   81
   of hitherto Bolshevik-backed elite in Ankara   83–4
   imperial   14–15, 63, 200, 202, 228
   in Lausanne   81, 85–6
   mentor of   121–3
   Nur's   100–1, 103
   pan-Turkism   48, 100–1
   revolutionist   151–2
Uluğ, Naşit   108, 114
UN Convention on the Prevention and Punishment of the Crime of Genocide   10
UN Declaration of Human Rights   10
unitary   28
United Kingdom   53
United Nations Organization (UNO)   237 n.44
United States   38
   Constitution   22
   invasion of Iraq   45
   lynching violence in   47

urban mob violence 49
Urfa 39

Vartkes 69
victimhood 95
  instrument of propaganda 71
  Muslim 55
  of non-Turkish indigenous
      peoples 230
  Ottoman 88
victimization 19, 21
violence 45
  as act of self-affirmation 45
  apocalypticism and 59–61
  decade (1912–22) 55–9
  domestic jihad 20, 47
  eschatology and 50–2
  foundational 1, 19
  imperial Islam and 59–61
  and Kemalism 55–9
  management of 52
  Middle Eastern 55
  patterns of 51
  public 46–50
  religion and 45
  Turkish nationalism and 59–61
  urban mob 49
  western aggression 52–5
Vlachow, D. 171
voice of Yahweh 18

Wahhabism 52, 60, 241 n.10
Wangenheim, Hans von 13, 75, 141,
      190–201
  as ambassador 195–6
  biographical information on 191
  and German-Ottoman war alliance
      (1914) 191–2
  politically/morally/personally 196–8
  and renewed Turkey mantra 193–4
  on Turkey policy 1915–18 199–200
  weakness for *Komiteci* (1913–
      14) 193–4
War of Liberation 14
Weber, Max 134
western aggression 52–5
Wilentz, Sean 30
Wilson, Woodrow 108
Worcester, Samuel 32

world conqueror (*sahib-kırân*) 50
World Wars 5–7, 10–11, 13, 15, 27,
      33, 36, 40–6, 48, 50–3, 56–9,
      62, 64, 74, 76, 79, 83, 96, 103,
      108–9, 112, 121, 132, 135–6,
      142, 148, 152–6, 160, 163–5,
      168, 171–80
Wyeth, Walter N. 29

Yahya Kemal; *see* Beyatlı, Yahya Kemal
Yalçın, Hüseyin Cahit 138, 140–1
Yeni Mecmua 131–2
Yezidis 49–51, 54
  coercive conversion of 76
  genocide against 20, 55
Young Turk
  cohort 14
  genocides 1–3
  ideologue 14
  and Nazi rule 15
  regime 24
Young Turk Revolution (1908) 2–3, 34,
      36, 63, 96, 126, 170

Zeller, Margarethe 184
Zimmer, Max 176
Zimmermann, Arthur 69
zimmi 54
Zionism 46, 48, 58, 140, 183–5
Ziya Gökalp 4, 14, 48, 54, 56, 100, 119,
      121–36, 191
  and Atatürk 124
  contribution to secularism in
      Turkey 123
  CUP and 122–9
  doctrine of racial and national
      greatness 102
  "Duty" (*Vazife*) 133
  essays 122
  father of Turkish nationalism 121
  founders of Turkish sociology 127
  Gök-Alp of 1910s 126–9
  from Hamidian Diyarbekir 124–6
  intellectual germination 124
  interpretations of 123
  Kemalist principles of Turkism 132–4
  "Kızıl Destan" (Red Epic) 129
  "Kızılelma" (Red Apple) 121
  mefkûre 128–9

member of Turkey's new constitution
    committee 133–4
Oghuz union (*Oğuz birliği*)
    132–3
poetry 101, 121–2
prophet of war and military
    spirit 129–32
proto-fascism 134–6
in Salonica 125–6
"Soldier's Prayer" poem 122
"Talaat Bey" 129–30

topical ideologist 121–4
Turan 128–9
Türkçülüğün Esasları (Principles of
    Turkism) 128, 132
Turkish *millet* for 133–4
Türklük 122–3
ultranationalism 122
at University of Istanbul 127
utopia 121
vision of leader-led corporatism 128
Zohrab, Krikor 65, 70, 140–1, 143